FIGHTING BACK
IN APPALACHIA

FIGHTING BACK
IN APPALACHIA

Traditions of Resistance and Change

Edited by
Stephen L. Fisher

Temple University Press
Philadelphia

Temple University Press, Philadelphia 19122
Copyright © 1993 by Temple University. All rights reserved
Published 1993
Printed in the United States of America

Chapter 7 copyright © 1993 by Hal Hamilton and Ellen Ryan
Chapter 12 copyright © 1993 by Guy and Candie Carawan

♾ The paper used in this publication meets the minimum requirements of
American National Standard for Information Sciences—Permanence of Paper for
Printed Library Materials, ANSI Z39.48-1984

Library of Congress Cataloging-in-Publication Data
Fighting back in Appalachia : traditions of resistance and change /
    edited by Stephen L. Fisher.
        p.   cm.
    Includes bibliographical references.
    ISBN 0-87722-976-7 (cloth : alk. paper). — ISBN 0-87722-977-5
(paper : alk. paper)
      1. Community organization—Appalachian Region.   2. Dissenters—
Appalachian Region.   3. Appalachian Region—Rural conditions.
I. Fisher, Stephen L., 1944–
HN79.A127F54   1993
307.72'0974—dc20   92-17683

ISBN 13: 978-0-87722-977-3 (paper : alk. paper)

021108P

Contents

Acknowledgments

This book has its origins in my experience as activist, teacher, researcher, and witness in the Appalachian region. It is a direct response to my frustration over the portrayal of Appalachians as passive victims, the dearth of material documenting the extent and nature of dissent in the Appalachian mountains, and the lack of Appalachian voices and examples in national discussions of community organizing strategies.

Many people helped make this book a reality. First, and foremost, I want to thank the contributors for their cooperation, responsiveness, and belief in the importance of this project. In many ways this was a collective endeavor. Mary Anglin suggested the title. Some of the contributors attended a meeting, organized by Jim Sessions, where they discussed each other's essays and made suggestions for the overall project. A number of the contributors critiqued the Introduction and Conclusion. Candie Carawan helped select and locate photographs for several of the essays. Throughout the process Mary Anglin, Beth Bingman, Dick Couto, and Joe Szakos offered advice and encouragement that kept me grounded and focused.

Mike Yarrow read the entire manuscript, and this is a much better book because of his insightful suggestions. Harry Boyte, Nina Gregg, Bill Horton, and Herb Reid offered valuable comments on particular essays or the manuscript as a whole. Michael Ames of Temple University Press understood and supported the political and intellectual motives behind the project and gave gentle but firm direction throughout the editing process. Emory & Henry College provided generous financial support for my work on this book through the Mellon Challenge Fund for Faculty Development and the Reverend E. L. McConnell Scholarship. Finally, I most gratefully acknowledge the love, support, and good company of family and friends. I am indebted, in this venture as in so many others, to my wife, Nancy Garretson, for her companionship, her unyielding support of my work, and her empowering optimism.

This book owes its existence and is dedicated to the countless individuals who have fought over the years for social and economic justice in Appalachia.

The Appalachian Community Fund, an activist-controlled foundation committed to supporting progressive social change in central Appalachia, will receive the royalties from the sales of the paperback edition of this book.

FIGHTING BACK
IN APPALACHIA

Introduction

Stephen L. Fisher

In the midst of the long and bitter United Mine Workers of America (UMWA) national strike in 1977–78, angry miners, feeling that the news coverage of the strike had been unfair, confronted a CBS camera crew at a union meeting near Phelps, Kentucky. "It makes us out to be the troublemakers," said one miner. "Why aren't you telling our side of it?"

This question has been raised time and again throughout the Appalachian mountains and reflects a long history of media bias and neglect that has firmly implanted in the national consciousness two conflicting images of the people who live in Appalachia. Appalachians are generally viewed as backward, unintelligent, fatalistic, and quiescent people who are complicit in their own oppression. But, at the same time, these "submissive" mountaineers are seen as among the most vicious and violent people in the United States.[1] The many bloody mine wars and skirmishes between miners and the coal industry throughout this century are responsible, in large part, for this latter image. As contradictory as these stereotypes may appear at first glance, they are related. For most of the nation, the coal miners are uninformed workers blindly following corrupt and manipulative union leaders. In the end the verdict is the same—they are gun-happy, illiterate bumpkins who are culturally incapable of rational resistance to unjust conditions.

The media are not alone in developing and perpetuating this portrait of Appalachians. Novelists, missionaries, social workers, industrialists, folklorists, politicians, and academicians have in their own ways and for their own reasons portrayed Appalachia as an isolated, underdeveloped area of inferior and dependent people.[2] During the 1960s and 1970s, some in Appalachia sought to counter this image, either by painting highly romanticized pictures of traditional Appalachian culture and then lamenting its destruction by outside forces or by describing the many ways in which the region had been economically exploited by the rest of the country. But far too often these efforts unwittingly reinforced the notion of Appalachians as victims, as non-actors in determining their fate.

In the 1980s and 1990s, an impressive array of scholarly studies have laid the groundwork for transforming the way we understand and think about the Appalachian region. They explain how, why, and for whose benefit the damaging and misleading stereotypes of Appalachians were developed. They document how the economic problems faced by many in Appalachia are a result not of isolation and a lack of economic development, but of the type of modernization that has occurred there. They describe the nature and extent of the region's many problems and make clear that the traditional solutions to these problems—changing people's cultural values and trickle-down economics—are misguided and have done more harm than good. These works often acknowledge the diversity that exists in the Appalachian mountains and stress the importance of making connections between events in Appalachia and national and global trends.[3]

Much of this important recent work on Appalachia recognizes that the region has never lacked a politics of resistance and alternative development. But, with the exception of works on the UMWA, there has been little systematic study of dissent in Appalachia. Information on citizen resistance there has come primarily from brief reports on specific events or groups in alternative publications and church and organizational newsletters and from articles and testimony by organizers of and participants in citizen groups that describe and celebrate a particular victory.[4]

While these sources have often romanticized the resistance efforts and glossed over problems and shortcomings, they have been an important chronicle of dissent in Appalachia. But their focus has been on practice, not theory. Recently, however, a number of scholars and activists have begun to examine change-oriented movements in Appalachia in some detail and to relate these movements to broader theoretical discussions within academic and community organizing circles. This book, a collection of sixteen original essays, highlights and integrates some of this work. It seeks to document the extent and variety of resistance and struggle in the Appalachian region since 1960, to enhance understanding of how and why particular resistance efforts and strategies have arisen and have succeeded or failed, and to relate the study of Appalachian dissent to the issues and debates that inform scholarly and progressive discussions of dissent nationally.

This collection weaves together personal narratives and formal analysis. This diversity of approaches and styles reflects the many different voices and experiences present in the region today and is part of what Alan Banks, Dwight Billings, and Karen Tice describe in Chapter 14 as the ongoing regional dialogue between activists and scholars concerning social and economic justice issues and strategies in the mountains.

Certainly one of the goals of this volume is to dispel mainstream notions of Appalachians as passive victims by allowing people in the region to tell their side of the story. But the intent is to do more than illustrate the courage, determination, and wisdom of Appalachian people. The essays are more than case studies that simply describe a particular victory or a successful organizing strategy. The authors consciously strive to draw conclusions related to one or more of the book's major questions—questions that are drawn from the broader activist literature on community organizing and change. What factors have led to the success or failure of particular change efforts? How have issues of race, class, gender, and culture shaped resistance efforts? What impact have national and global structures and events had on local movements for change? What is legitimate about the notion of regional identity, and what role, if any, has it played in progressive efforts? What organizing strategies make sense for the future?

Studying Resistance in Appalachia

"Appalachian history," says one observer, "is full of rebellions and rebels."[5] That may well be true, but, if so, much of that history has yet to be written. A number of studies describe how and why Appalachian coal miners emerged in the 1920s and 1930s as one of the most militant and class-conscious workforces in the United States. But except for this long and bitter union campaign, we know little about collective resistance efforts in the Appalachian region prior to 1960. Discussions of such efforts frequently note the challenge by western Pennsylvania farmers to the tax on liquor production imposed by President George Washington's administration, which culminated in the Whiskey Rebellion of 1794; the Cherokee battle to preserve their culture and land in the Carolina mountains; the strength of the pre–Civil War abolitionist movement in some Appalachian counties; how the coal miners of east Tennessee rid themselves of the competition of convict labor in the 1890s; and the work of the Council of the Southern Mountains, an organization of religious workers, academicians, professionals, and social workers that began its outreach work early in this century.

What stands out in the literature describing life in Appalachia before 1960 is not the extent of resistance, but rather the obstacles to dissent, the conditions leading to quiescence.[6] The industrialization of Appalachia was characterized by single-industry economies; the control of land and resources by large absentee companies; high levels of poverty and unemployment; the frequent use of red baiting, intimidation, and physical force to squelch dissent; political corruption; and a highly stratified and oppressive class system. Collective resistance was further undermined by cultural traditions that stressed individualism, nurtured racial prejudice, and dictated passivity and acquiescence for women, and by the strength of capitalist ideology, the absence of a grassroots regional identity and strong local organizations, illiteracy, and poor transportation and communication systems. During this period one could find throughout Appalachia examples of the starkest deprivation and most blatant political and economic oppression in American society.

In recent years anthropologists and social and feminist historians have taught us that when faced with such repressive conditions, people still find ways to resist. However, these ways often assume forms far less visible than picket lines and mass movements and include such behavior as gossip, backtalk, holding on to one's dialect, moonshining, open violation of game and fencing laws, and migration. Such protest is part of what James Scott refers to as the "hidden transcript" of the oppressed, and what Sherry Cable in Chapter 4 describes as "periodic fussin'."[7]

Increasingly, Appalachian scholars are coming to recognize the existence and importance of such resistance in Appalachia's history and to understand that it has most frequently occurred in struggles to preserve traditional values and ways of life against the forces of modernization. For example, Helen Lewis, Sue Kobak, and Linda Johnson describe the various ways in which mountain families and churches became defensive and turned inward to protect members from some of the harmful impacts of industrialization.[8] Kathleen Blee and Dwight Billings reinterpret early ethnographic studies of the region to show that work attitudes and other practices previously attributed to a culture of poverty could be better understood as forms of resistance to the capitalist separation of work and control.[9] Altina Waller argues that the legendary Hatfield-McCoy feud can be seen as a battle between local defenders of community autonomy and outside industrial interests.[10] While much remains to be done, these and similar studies broaden our understanding of the nature and extent of resistance by rural working-class people in Appalachia in the 1800s and the first half of this century.

As the chapters in this book make clear, many of the factors that hampered collective resistance throughout Appalachia's history are still present today. But changing conditions after 1960 paved the way for organized resistance in a wide variety of forms and settings. The contributors describe the impact of many of these changes. The civil rights movement helped legitimize dissent in general and the strategy of nonviolent civil disobedience in particular throughout the region and the nation. The environmental and women's movements offered models and resources for local groups in the mountains. Moreover, these movements provided the impetus for national legislation that created opportunities for local organizations fighting to save their land and communities from environmental destruction or working to create alternative economic opportunities for women. The anti-war and student movements called into question the notions of "progress," "modernization," and "national interest" that had been used for so long to justify the destruction of traditional ways of life in Appalachia. The War on Poverty spawned the Appalachian Volunteers and community action agencies throughout the mountains. Despite their weaknesses, these programs brought young organizers into the region and provided opportunities for local leaders to develop. Mainstream churches, reflecting a new social consciousness, sent to Appalachia clergy and other church workers committed to social and economic justice. The construction of more and better roads, the availability of video recording equipment, open meeting and record laws, and increased church and foundation funding of Appalachian citizen groups also contributed to local organizing efforts.

These and other factors led to an outburst of grassroots community organizing across Appalachia in the late 1960s and early 1970s that continues today.[11] Local residents fought to prevent the destruction of their land and homes by strip miners, dam and highway builders, the U.S. Forest Service, toxic waste dumpers, and recreation and second-home developers. People organized to secure welfare benefits, to enact tax reform, to build rural community centers and health clinics, to fight for better schools for their children, and to establish literacy and child care programs. Renewed militancy among coal miners led to black lung and UMWA reform movements and a number of long and combative strikes. Community groups pursued a wide variety of alternative economic development strategies that resulted in agricultural and craft cooperatives, worker-owned factories, and new job opportunities for women. Efforts to preserve and celebrate local culture flourished in the mountains, and Appalachian Studies courses appeared as people began to develop a consciousness of and pride in being Appalachian. Most of the organizing arose in response to single issues, but there were also attempts to build region-wide coalitions, and some of the single-issue groups provided the impetus for the development of multi-issue, grassroots citizen organizations committed to the long haul.

This book is not a comprehensive account of these efforts in Appalachia during this period. The chapters offer a broad overview of key events, organizations, strategies, and trends, but they tell only a small piece of the story. The Ivanhoe Civic League, the Mountain Women's Exchange, and the Western North Carolina Alliance are just a few of the many organizations currently working for change in Appalachia whose stories are not told here.[12] While some chapters mention the contributions of particular African Americans or critique a group's anti-racism work, none describe organizing efforts by African American citizen groups in Appalachian communities.[13] The voices of Appalachian migrants fighting for cultural and economic survival in large urban centers are also missing. This book is only a first step toward reconstructing the story of resistance in Appalachia. But while its chapters leave many stories untold, they serve to dispel the notion of Appalachian people as passive victims and demonstrate that the study of resistance and reform in Appalachia has much to contribute to national debates and discussions about community organizing and change.

Rethinking Resistance in Appalachia

This volume is organized into three parts. The chapters in Part I discuss and evaluate obstacles to community organizing in the Appalachian region, conditions that helped transform individual protest into collective resistance after 1960, strengths and weaknesses of single-issue organizing, efforts to build a regionwide social movement, and strategies that led to the creation of multi-issue, democratic citizen organizations in the mountains.

The grassroots anti–strip mining movement was at the heart of the initial outburst of community organizing in Appalachia in the latter half of the 1960s and the early 1970s. Local activists organized sit-ins on strip mine sites, destroyed mining equipment, challenged coal operators in court, and lobbied to change state laws. There was substantial opposition to strip mining throughout the coal mining counties of central Appalachia, but the most vigorous and determined resistance occurred in eastern Kentucky. Drawing upon recent interviews with some of the protesters, Mary Beth Bingman, herself a participant in the protest, describes in Chapter 1 how a group of women shut down a strip mine operation in Knott County, Kentucky, in January 1972. Bingman uses this episode to reflect upon the history of the early anti–strip mining movement, its legacy, and the reasons for its failure to stop strip mining in the mountains.

The struggle against strip mining was built on people's deep connection to and love for their land. But confronted with the economic realities of the region, local residents in loosely organized, reactive, single-issue groups could only resist; they could not abolish strip mining. Bingman concludes that single-issue work, which has characterized much of the organizing in Appalachia, can win occasional victories but cannot by itself lead to fundamental change. By demonstrating that tackling issues as complex as strip mining requires ongoing, multi-issue, reflective, democratic organizations, Bingman provides a rationale for the type of organizing described in the chapters by Bill Allen, Joe Szakos, and Hal Hamilton and Ellen Ryan.

Since the 1960s activists have attempted to organize anti–strip mining and other single-issue groups in the Appalachian mountains into a regionwide grassroots movement that could ultimately become part of a national, multiracial coalition for social and economic justice.[14] These efforts have failed for a variety of reasons, but primarily because, unlike class, race, and gender, region does not provide an adequate political and economic focus for social movements. What has occurred in Appalachia has been a series of skirmishes—a form of guerrilla warfare.[15] As Bill Horton points out, most of these struggles have been local, but they have often been assisted by and associated with other groups and individuals within a network of Appalachian organizations. At times that network has had a name (Council of the Southern Mountains, Appalachian Alliance); at other times it has been little more than an informal chain of individuals. But it persists, says Horton, and there may be no other network like it in the United States.[16]

The Highlander Research and Education Center in eastern Tennessee has played a central role in encouraging these networks and in various efforts to create a social movement in Appalachia. In the three decades after its founding in 1932, Highlander served as an educational center for southern labor and farmers' unions, civil rights groups, and dozens of other social justice organizations. Beginning in the mid-1960s, the Center's staff turned its attention to Appalachia. While much has been written on Highlander's early history, the story of its attempt to nurture an Appalachian movement has never been told. John Glen's account of Highlander's efforts in Appalachia since 1965 (Chapter 2) reveals much about the strengths and weaknesses of Highlander's philosophy and approach and examines Highlander's relationship to various resistance organizations in the region. In addition, his explanation of the Center's failure to promote a campaign in Appalachia that resembled earlier struggles by labor unions and civil rights organizations in the South offers important insights into the character of dissent in Appalachia and expands our traditional concept of social movements.

Racism is a major barrier to grassroots organizing and coalition building in Appalachia, as it is throughout the nation. Don Manning-Miller charges in Chapter 3 that many of Appalachia's community organizations, while committed either explicitly or implicitly to combating racism and to building a multiracial coalition for progressive social change, in practice fail to challenge the cultural conservatism and racism of their constituency. In explaining how and why this occurs and then offering tactical measures and suggestions for developing a systematic program to confront racism in Appalachia, Manning-Miller provides a framework for assessing the anti-racism work of citizen organizations and labor unions across the region.

Sherry Cable (Chapter 4) describes the formation and activities of the Yellow Creek Concerned Citizens (YCCC) in eastern Kentucky. Cable is less concerned with documenting the accomplishments of YCCC, one of the region's best-known single-issue groups, than she is with examining the conditions that transform individual dissent into collective resistance. Cable explains how a long history of economic oppression limited resistance to the contamination of Yellow Creek to individual acts of protest and then identifies the social and structural changes at the national and local level that facilitated and shaped the formation of YCCC. She concludes by examining the impact of these changes on gender relationships and describing the similarities between the pattern of resistance in Yellow Creek and that of other oppressed groups.

Since the 1960s hundreds of new citizen groups have been organized throughout Appalachia to tackle local issues. Most have proved unable to establish continuity or to see beyond the immediate crisis. These single-issue groups have worked together from time to time, have helped create local leadership, and have won important victories; but most have been short-lived, disappearing quickly once their issue was resolved. One of the most exciting and hopeful developments in community organizing in Appalachia in recent years is the establishment and success of thriving and influential multi-issue, membership-driven organizations such as Save Our Cumberland Mountains (SOCM), Kentuckians For The Commonwealth (KFTC), and the Community Farm Alliance (CFA).

Bill Allen describes in Chapter 5 how and why SOCM, organized in 1972 to fight strip mining in a five-county area in the northern coalfields of Tennessee, changed from a single-issue, staff-run group to a multi-issue, grassroots organization able to exercise power and influence at the state and national levels. Joe Szakos, one of the initial organizers and the current coordinator of KFTC, examines in Chapter 6 how and why this organization, started in mid-1981 by a small group of eastern Kentucky residents who wanted to address community problems that crossed county lines, has grown into a statewide, multi-issue, social justice organization of more than twenty-three hundred members in ninety counties. In Chapter 7 Hal Hamilton and Ellen Ryan describe the CFA's transformation from a handful of people who were replicating the mistakes of the national farm movement of the 1980s to a growing and successful membership-based organization with over a dozen chapters across Kentucky.

These three essays provide a virtual handbook of the hows and whys of rural organizing. The authors stress the importance of local indigenous leadership recruitment and training, shared and long-term consciousness raising, the development of internal democratic social relations, ideological patience, and the willingness to connect with people as they are.[17] They point out the necessity of building statewide organizations and of connecting local issues to state, national, and global patterns and concerns. The authors not only discuss the strengths and successes of these groups but candidly assess their weaknesses and problems. These chapters offer valuable lessons for organizers and citizen groups across the region and the nation.

Since a number of insightful works address labor struggles and union reform movements in Appalachia,[18] the chapters selected for this volume emphasize recent events and trends leading to workplace strategies different from those of the past. The essays in Part II examine how changing political and economic conditions led to new organizing strategies by women to gain access to and equality in the labor market and by coal miners to increase their bargaining power.

The late 1970s, for a variety of reasons, offered a "window of opportunity" for women who wanted to break out of stereotypical occupations and get "men's" jobs that paid more and provided greater benefits. Three very different organizations took advantage of this window: the Coal Employment Project, which targeted the coal industry; the Southeast Women's Employment Coalition, which focused on highway jobs; and Women and Employment, which took on the building trades in West Virginia. In Chapter 8 Chris Weiss takes a retrospective look at these organizations, examining their successes and failures, how they chose to confront the issue of race, recent changes in leadership and structure, and their regional and national impact.

Richard Couto presents the UMWA's strikes against the A. T. Massey Coal Group in 1984–85 and the Pittston Coal Company in 1989–90 as the union's response to company efforts to undermine the industrywide standard on labor terms that has worked in the past to protect both the industry and miners from the consequences of debilitating competition. In Chapter 9 he reviews changes in coal production methods and management structure that have dulled the memory and conscience of the industry's managers and explains how miners' historical memory of mining conditions before the adoption of an industrywide standard was in large part responsible for the unity and determination shown by miners and their supporters during these strikes. He shows how changing conditions required new strategies and tactics by miners and evaluates the ways in which the union and workers adapted.

Perhaps the signal event of the Pittston strike was the September 1989 occupation by union miners of Pittston's mammoth coal preparation plant near St. Paul, Virginia. Jim Sessions, the executive director of the Commission on Religion in Appalachia, was invited to join this action as a sympathetic witness to the nonviolent character of the takeover. Sessions offers an insider's view of the occupation, while his wife, Fran Ansley, describes the remarkable scene that developed among union members and supporters who massed outside the plant. Their moving and insightful account (Chapter 10) illuminates the combination of factors—historical memory, class solidarity, kinship and community ties, cultural tradition, strong leadership, and brilliant tactical planning—that contributed to this significant labor victory.

The current struggle for occupational health in America owes a great deal to the efforts of retired and disabled Appalachian coal miners in the Black Lung Association and southern textile workers in the Brown Lung Association. In the early 1980s these two organizations, along with the White Lung Association (which addresses asbestos exposure), formed the Breath of Life Coalition (BLOC). Over the past several years, the BLOC has concentrated on a federal program that challenges many of the prevailing conceptions and practices regarding compensation and occupational issues in general. In his examination of the recent struggle for compensation by coal, textile, and asbestos workers and the reasons for the formation of the BLOC (Chapter 11), Bennett Judkins points to the significance of coalition building across industries as a future organizing strategy. He also suggests that "community," which often provides the glue for collective action, is not necessarily bound by geographic terrain. Workers' common experience in the fight for their own health, as well as their cooperative struggle against the institutions that control them, can be an important component of a broader effort for social change.

Many activists and scholars have shied away from discussions of "culture" in Appalachia because of previous pejorative, romanticized, or contrived notions of cultural forces and values in the Appalachian mountains. But the authors who have contributed to Part III, although pursuing different agendas and approaches, argue that the study of resistance in Appalachia should involve an examination of regional culture as a force that informs the construction of class consciousness, gender relations, regional identity, and community life.

Guy and Candie Carawan contend in Chapter 12 that regional identity and cultural pride are not naturally part of community life. Drawing upon their many years of cultural field work in grassroots communities and social movements, the Carawans describe the careful educational work involved in establishing and maintaining links between community struggles and local cultural resources—music, songwriting, storytelling, and dancing. They explore concrete examples of cultural expression as a central part of community organizing: a community improvement campaign in Pike County, Kentucky, in the late 1960s; a series of cultural workshops at the Highlander Center between 1972 and 1982; and the 1976–79 UMWA strike against Blue Diamond in Stearns, Kentucky.

In Chapter 13 Mary Anglin examines the activities of working-class Appalachian women in the mica industry in western North Carolina as a way of illustrating the importance of analyses of gender to the study of waged labor. Her study is an effort to find a middle ground from which we can study the ways in which women and men, individuals and communities, remake tradition in the wake of deindustrialization. Her analysis extends and complicates the arguments advanced by the other authors in this section concerning culture and the creation of regional identity.

Alan Banks, Dwight Billings, and Karen Tice begin Chapter 14 by considering the emergence and significance of Appalachian Studies as a form of resistance, and the political implications of a new direction in Appalachian Studies in the late 1980s—postmodernism. Drawing upon the work of postmodern feminist scholars, the authors critique the universalism and essentialism that have characterized much of the writing on Appalachia and argue that opposition to such thinking provides avenues to transform the knowledge base in Appalachian Studies and inform the practice of regional politics and dissent. They then discuss and evaluate recent contributions to the Appalachian literature that advance a postmodern sensibility. Their chapter provides a context in which to discuss and appreciate the importance of the arguments advanced by the Carawans and Anglin and sets the stage for Stephen Foster's case study of the politics of culture (Chapter 15).

Foster, like the Carawans, insists that regional identity is not a geographic or cultural given in Appalachia but must be understood as an outgrowth of political dynamics and social change. He focuses on the construction of culture and identity in Ashe County, North Carolina, in reference to a drama presented during a rally held to promote county solidarity and resistance to a proposed hydroelectric dam project. He reveals the strategic use of expressive form as a cultural resource and political weapon that local people in Appalachia have developed in their struggles with the national economy and the modern world system.

The essays in Part III illustrate how cultural traditions are "historically formed, situated, and altered by people interacting with each other and with social and economic forces."[19] They describe how community networks sustain people during protracted struggles and enable them to foster protest on their own terms. They reinforce David Whisnant's insistence that Appalachian culture is "a web of both resistance and complicity."[20] The authors respond creatively to Whisnant's challenge that those engaged in cultural work should search through the regional culture to locate its most humane, progressive, and transformative elements and then look for ways to link these transformative elements to a larger human agenda for change. This means, says Whisnant, that we in Appalachia must examine and relate ourselves to other cultures, thereby ending our cultural isolationism and reaching toward some kind of global solidarity.[21]

Whisnant's call for an end to isolationism and parochialism is echoed throughout this collection. The contributors demonstrate how changing national and global political and economic conditions have facilitated or undermined local change efforts. They point to the need for new organizing strategies that build bridges across county, state, and national lines. Linking local fights to national and global struggles is a difficult and slow process, but it is the only approach that has a chance of bringing about fundamental change in Appalachia.[22]

This book does not attempt to develop an "Appalachian" theory of resistance; rather, it is the beginning of an effort to rethink and reconstruct the nature of resistance in the region and to understand the ways in which this resistance is similar to or different from dissent in other parts of the nation. The Conclusion (Chapter 16) uses the lessons set forth in the preceding chapters to discuss which organizational instruments and strategies are best suited for building progressive movements. This discussion underscores the relevance of these analyses of resistance in Appalachia to questions about dissent and change in this postsocialist and postmodern era.

Notes

1. James G. Branscome and James Y. Holloway, "Non-Violence and Violence in Appalachia," *Katallagete* 5 (Winter 1974): 33.
2. Because of the region's geographic, geologic, and historical diversity and the fact that the notion of Appalachia has been largely shaped by people and institutions outside the mountains, there is no single definition of Appalachia that will satisfy everyone. As David Whisnant has observed, "Appalachia's boundaries have been drawn so many times by so many different hands that it is futile to look for a 'correct' definition of the region." See *Modernizing the Mountaineer: People, Power, and Planning in Appalachia* (Boone, N.C.: Appalachian Consortium Press, 1981), 134. For a sampling of various efforts to define Appalachia, see part I of Bruce Ergood and Bruce E. Kuhre, eds., *Appalachia: Social Context Past and Present*, 3rd ed. (Dubuque, Iowa: Kendall-Hunt, 1991).

3. See "The Appalachian Region" in the Bibliography.
4. See "Community Organizing in Appalachia" in the Bibliography.
5. Thomas S. Plaut, "Extending the Internal Periphery Model: The Impact of Culture and Consequent Strategy," in *Colonialism in Modern America: The Appalachian Case*, ed. Helen M. Lewis, Linda Johnson, and Donald Askins (Boone, N.C.: Appalachian Consortium Press, 1978), 358.
6. Ronald D. Eller, *Miners, Millhands, and Mountaineers: Industrialization of the Appalachian South, 1880–1930* (Knoxville: University of Tennessee Press, 1982); and John Gaventa, *Power and Powerlessness: Quiescence and Rebellion in an Appalachian Valley* (Urbana: University of Illinois Press, 1980).
7. James C. Scott, *Domination and the Arts of Resistance: Hidden Transcripts* (New Haven: Yale University Press, 1990).
8. Helen M. Lewis, Sue E. Kobak, and Linda Johnson, "Family, Religion, and Colonialism in Central Appalachia, or Bury My Rifle at Big Stone Gap," in Lewis, Johnson, and Askins, eds., *Colonialism in Modern America*, pp. 113–39.
9. Kathleen Blee and Dwight Billings, "Reconstructing Daily Life in the Past: An Hermeneutical Approach to Ethnographic Data," *Sociological Quarterly* 27 (1986): 443–62.
10. Altina L. Waller, *Feud: Hatfields, McCoys, and Social Change in Appalachia, 1860–1900* (Chapel Hill: University of North Carolina Press, 1988).
11. Graham Day reports that in 1983 there were sixty-two local citizen groups active in eastern Kentucky alone. "The Reconstruction of Wales and Appalachia: Development and Regional Identity," in *Contemporary Wales: An Annual Review of Economic and Social Research*, vol. 1 (Cardiff: University of Wales Press, 1987), 83.
12. These groups are singled out because of their recent accomplishments, staying power, and creative strategies. See the pertinent articles and listings in "Community Organizing in Appalachia" in the Bibliography and in the Directory of Organizations.
13. Despite the widely held notion of Appalachia as a white, Anglo-Saxon, Protestant enclave, African Americans have played a crucial role in the region's social and economic history, and they fought side by side with European immigrants and native mountaineers in the UMWA's battles to unionize the coalfields. See Ronald L. Lewis, *Black Coal Miners in America: Race, Class, and Community Conflict, 1780–1980* (Lexington: University Press of Kentucky, 1987); and William H. Turner and Edward J. Cabbell, eds., *Blacks in Appalachia* (Lexington: University Press of Kentucky, 1985).
14. The most important attempts to foster a regionwide opposition movement were made by the Council of the Southern Mountains, the Peoples Appalachia Research Collective, the Congress for Appalachian Development, the Highlander Research and Education Center, and the Appalachian Alliance. See Whisnant, *Modernizing the Mountaineer*; Pierre Clavel, *Opposition Planning in Wales and Appalachia* (Philadelphia: Temple University Press, 1983); and John M. Glen, "Like a Flower Slowly Blooming: Highlander and the Nurturing of an Appalachian Movement," in this volume.

15. I thank Sue Ella Kobak for this description of the nature of resistance in Appalachia.
16. It is worth quoting Horton further on the nature and significance of this network. Perhaps, says Horton, this network "is the form that the Appalachian social movement has taken—slowly winning victories, working together, laying the groundwork, building or trying to build democratic organizations. Perhaps this is the way the movement will be built, piece by piece like a patchwork quilt until it comes together to rid the region of oppressive structures and practices, in turn becoming a piece of a much larger quilt that must be created to rid the nation of those same structures and practices." Bill Horton, review of John Glen's *Highlander: No Ordinary School, 1932–1962* (Lexington: University Press of Kentucky, 1988) in the *Appalachian Journal* 16 (1989): 370.
17. See Lawrence Goodwyn's more general treatment of these organizing tactics in "Organizing Democracy: The Limits of Theory and Practice," *democracy* 1 (January 1981): 41–60.
18. See "Labor Issues and Struggles" in the Bibliography.
19. Laura A. Schwartz, "Immigrant Voices from Home, Work, and Community: Women and Family in the Migration Process, 1890–1938" (Ph.D. diss., State University of New York at Stony Brook, 1983), 78.
20. David E. Whisnant, "Brief Notes Toward a Reconsideration of Appalachian Values," *Appalachian Journal* 4 (1976): 46.
21. David E. Whisnant, "Farther Along: The Next Phase of Cultural Work in the South," *Southern Changes* 13 (May 1991): 7–8.
22. Larry Wilson, "Moving Toward a Movement," *Social Policy* 20 (Summer 1989): 53–57.

PART I

BUILDING GRASSROOTS CITIZEN ORGANIZATIONS

Top: The women walked over two miles in the mud to reach the strip mine site.

Bottom: The women stop the bulldozers. (*Both photos © Robert Cooper, 1972*)

1

Stopping the Bulldozers
What Difference Did It Make?

Mary Beth Bingman

Getting up in the dark, rattling around, a few of us trying to eat. We dress, pile into cars, and drive to the mouth of Clear Creek to meet the others. Several carloads, twenty women and a dozen or so men, including newsmen. We drive up Trace Fork and through an open gate. Not feeling much, neither fear nor excitement. A jeep speeds by us. We meet it at the second gate, the gate to the mine, the chain locked across the road. Two men, one with an automatic rifle, stand guard. We get out, stand around in the rain for a while. The guard is uncertain how to react, and some people start to move. Then Helen is on the other side of the gate calling to us. A few of us, then all the women cross over or under the chain. Two newsmen join us.

We walk down the road, sloshing through mud, some in boots, others with only flats, bareheaded or carrying umbrellas. We're excited and cheerful. We walk maybe a mile, see the other women who had hesitated at the gate following us, wait for them to catch up. We join forces and move on down the road. Women, young and old, feeling strong together.

A jeep passes us, the men inside laughing. We keep walking. The road is now on top of a spoil bank, water and the highwall on one side, a long mud and rock slope on the other. It's like being on a curving bridge. Women joke, ridiculing the men and their operation.

We come up a steep muddy slope and onto the bench, the site where the men are working. There's a truck loaded with powder, men in the cab. There's some kind of big drill, a bulldozer and a front-end loader. The operators sit on their equipment, shut off now. We see another, bigger bench around the ridge— huge highwalls, slopes, and dozers. We spread our tarp in front of the dozer blade and have coffee and bread. "You're not all from Knott County. I don't know you. Bet none of them go to church or worked a day in their lives." Most of the men's hostility is hidden behind jokes.

The mine is shut down. We stay all day in the mud and rain, gathering wood and coal and building a fire, eating some sandwiches, happily greeting three more women who join us. The workmen come and go, and the women joke and banter with them. They never fail to put down what the men say. A few women go back to the gate and return with rope and a few clothes. We hear that the state police have been there, but no action.

Towards late afternoon we realize that we may not be arrested that day. We take our tarp and rig up a tent, build another fire and collect wood and coal for the night. Most of the women have to leave, to get home to their families, and about 4 p.m. they set off. Sally and Helen come back from the gate—the guards wouldn't allow food or blankets to be passed to them. Things were tense. Bessie's daughters come up, having run by the guards. Her boys had been stopped. Some of us want to leave for the night. Most want to stay, so we do. Don, one of the newsmen, and Doris leave to walk part way back with her sisters. They plan to be back in half an hour.

Dark comes. We have a tent, two fires, some food, no drinking water but what we catch. A new shift has come on. The bulldozer operator is ordered to shove our tent over the hill. He refuses to take sides and is fired. He's a preacher, tries to convince us to leave, but when we won't, he stays with us.

Dark brings more men, younger, tough, lewd. We all get under our tent, only eight of us now. We sing, scared. It keeps on raining, and we're all wet. There's no place to sit, we're standing in water, it's getting colder. We wait, listening, watching trucks come and go, watching a huge fire on the other bench. Rocks fall from the highwalls and crash into the water. Sounds like thunder or blasting. We talk to the men standing with us about stripping. They don't much like it, but they need the jobs. They keep offering to accompany us off. We become more tempted, some of us, but we'll stick together.

Around ten o'clock more men start coming toward us with flashlights. Two state police offer to escort us off, but aren't willing to arrest us. Earlier, when the company offered us a ride down, we said we'd go if we were arrested or if one of our people came and got us. We ask for time to decide what to do.

This is the hardest part, all of us torn between our determination to stay and not give up and our fear and discomfort. We don't have enough wood and coal to last all night. The men are getting drunker. Maxine is sick. We're all cold and wet. The police said someone had reported shooting and violence down below. Don and Doris have never come back. It is still ten hours till daylight.

But we'd said we'd stay. More women might join us in the morning. Our men might be in the hills behind us. The police might be trying to scare us off. They're tearing up the mountains.

When we find out that it had been Doris who had called the police, we decide to leave. At the bottom of the hill we discover that the cars have been shot up and wrecked, four men have been beaten, the roads are full of pick-ups. We probably had made the right choice. But we aren't sure.[1]

And eighteen years later we are still not sure. Not entirely clear about why we went, whether we should have stayed, what difference it all made. We only know that we would probably do it again. In the spring of 1990, seven of the women who were up on the strip mine that January day in 1972, and two of the men who waited down below, met in Whitesburg, Kentucky, to remember, reconstruct, reconsider, that time eighteen years before.

We had been part of a group of people fighting strip mining and had occupied a strip mine in Knott County, Kentucky. The occupation of the mine was part of an effort to mobilize opposition locally and statewide. Afterward, although we continued to work together on various things, we never talked through our experiences of that day. This book provided the impetus. We talked for most of a day. This chapter is drawn from that day's discussion about what we did, our reasons for doing it, and the impact of the action for ourselves and the region. Unless otherwise noted, all quotations are from those present that day: Bessie Smith Gayheart, Eula Hall, Maxine Kenny, Rich Kirby, Sally Maggard, Helen Rentch, Jim Rentch, Doris Shepherd, and me.

Why People Opposed Stripping

We talked about why we did it, why people cared about strip mining, why we cared.

> I didn't know much about strip mining. I don't guess that anybody did from the mountains until they got in there and started destroying. What I knew was deep mining. It wasn't so destructive. But then when we seen what strip mining could do, I think that's when people really got concerned and got afraid that they'd really just bury the mountain people alive. I know what inspired me was seeing the damage that they did to people that had to live around strip mining. You know, I was terrified of that huge equipment and the dirt they moved and the rock they piled behind people's houses. They cared so little and were so rude when they done it.

> Looking at those strip mining sites in the wintertime was a scar that you couldn't forget.

> In Lotts Creek, Kelly Fork was pathetic. You couldn't get in and out of it, that huge big slip [landslide] kept coming. We had to leave home before the baby was born because we couldn't get through. And then when I came down to stay with Mom, I waded through mud and rock up to my knees—in the main road. The school bus couldn't run; the kids didn't go to school unless they walked through the mud to get to the bus. It was

deep enough that a four-wheel drive couldn't even get through it; it took a dozer or a grader or something to get through it, really. You couldn't get the county to come out and clear the road, and the miners wouldn't clear it, they didn't give a damn.

In Knott County, on Clear Creek and Lotts Creek especially, there aren't bottom lands there. And the hills that they were stripping was people's livelihood. And you know Grandpa hoed and raised corn on those hillsides, and we helped; and after they got started, there was nothing there but gullies and mudslides. You couldn't raise a goat on it, let alone a garden. And all the gardens back up on top of the hill and the apple orchards . . . you know, we'd go back up there when I was a little girl and carry back big sackloads of apples. And the corn that he raised on those hillsides fed a couple of hogs, and his mule that he raised his garden with, and a cow and his chickens, and all of a sudden with just one swipe of that blade, it's gone. Gone.

You know, it destroyed the wildlife, too. You couldn't see a bird around those big strip operations, you could not see one speck of life. I've been there, and I'd set for hours, and there wouldn't be a bird ever fly by that place.

You know, if the strippers had come through and had shown any kind of compassion or just being half human and went around graveyards and things like that, I'm not sure that it would have ever come to the point that it did. People may have set back and let them railroad them more. But now people, you don't go out here and move one of these old-timer's graves, I mean, you just don't do it, not in eastern Kentucky, if you want to live. That was one of the things that really raged the warfare on strip mining. Because people understood at that point that there was no consideration for the people or the property or the future generations.

Reclamation isn't enforced, it's just a name. It's a pacifying name to the people. It's a, it's a—nothing.

"The People Was the Only Law"

Strip mining began in Appalachia in the early 1950s. Bulldozers and steam shovels cut benches around the mountains, taking out the exposed coal and augering what could not be uncovered. As the decade progressed, the twisted paths of strip mine benches wound around the sides of more and more mountains. Highwalls interrupted the already steep slopes, and the unwanted material, the spoil, cascaded down into the creeks.

The destruction increased dramatically in 1961 when the Tennessee Valley Authority signed contracts to buy 16.5 million tons of strip-mined coal. Tens of thousands of acres were stripped. Streams were polluted with sediment and acid runoff. Millions of dollars worth of timber was left to rot.[2]

Strip mining damaged all the Appalachian coalfield states and was resisted in all. But nowhere was it as devastating to people as in eastern Kentucky. And nowhere was it resisted as fiercely. In other states the land that was stripped was usually either owned outright by coal companies or was stripped only with the permission of the landowner. But in Kentucky land could be stripped without the surface owner's consent. The state courts interpreted the old broad form deeds that gave the mineral owner rights of access to the coal (deeds that had been signed decades before, when the only mining was deep mining) as granting the right to strip with or without the permission of the current surface owner. The mineral owner's right to mine superseded the surface owner's right to clean water, sacred graves, or a front yard.[3]

Thus eastern Kentucky was the site of intense resistance to strip mining. In Pike County in 1967, Jink Ray stood in the path of bulldozers about to strip his land, and his and his neighbors' actions persuaded the governor to revoke the company's permit to mine Ray's land.[4] Others used more direct action. Over $2 million worth of mining equipment was blown up in eastern Kentucky in 1967 and 1968.[5]

One of the major centers of resistance was on Clear Creek in Knott County, where in 1967 residents spent months holding off the strippers, trading shots in the hills. This valley was not mined until three years later, when one family sold out and went to Indiana—"which is a good thing because if they'd stayed they'd have got killed," as one neighbor later put it.

The Appalachian Group to Save the Land and People was formed in Knott County out of the struggle on Clear Creek and continued for several years to fight strip mining in the hills and in Frankfort, the state capital. Uncle Dan Gibson, at the time in his eighties, was the patriarch of the Group. The Group's members frequently blocked mining operations, sometimes armed, sometimes sitting unarmed in front of equipment.[6]

> They blocked coal trucks, they blocked dozers and loaders from pushing it [coal] over the hill and mining it. And at one time I thought there was going to be war. There was shooting going on from both sides. Nobody got killed . . .
>
> H. M., he's a man on Defeated Creek, and they were coming in on his property, and he called wanting some support. So we all went over there, and there was just huge big boulders and things all over his property, just

above his house in fact, and the trees and things were just splintered where the rocks had hit them. And they [the Kentucky reclamation agency] were not doing anything, they wouldn't help him at all. So we went down and picketed Reclamation because of that.

In addition to activities by a variety of groups throughout eastern Kentucky, unknown numbers of individuals tried to block mining on their land. Many were beaten up. Some were successful.

There were also attempts to challenge the broad form deed and strip mining in court. In 1955 a Knott County man challenged the deed's validity in the Circuit Court. The judge ruled against him and was upheld by the Kentucky Court of Appeals.[7] The same judge ruled in a 1967 Knott County case that while the coal company had the right to strip the coal, they did have to pay damages. The Court of Appeals reversed this decision, giving all rights to the company.[8] Kentucky courts held to this interpretation of the old deeds until the state constitution was amended in 1989.[9]

Legislation to regulate strip mining was passed in Kentucky in 1966. To receive a permit to strip, the operator had to submit a reclamation plan and put up a bond. No stripping was to be allowed on slopes over thirty-three degrees. The law had little effect: enforcement was lax, and on such steep terrain real reclamation was impossible. In June 1970 the county government banned strip mining in Knott County, but its decision was ignored by the state.

I remember that court house in Hindman, there were at least—in my mind there were at least ten thousand people. I can remember Uncle Dan Gibson coming in with a rifle and walking kind of down the middle of the courtroom to try to get a tie vote broken [in the county government]. It was tied, and he came in with that gun to get the tie vote broken. The state overturned that and said the county didn't have the right to interfere with contracts.

Legal battles were supported by demonstrations and hearings, demanding both tougher laws and enforcement of laws already passed. There were also regional efforts to publicize the devastation of strip mining. A press tour of eastern Kentucky was conducted by the Appalachian Volunteers in 1967. At a "People's Hearing" in Wise, Virginia, in December 1971, over two hundred people from Virginia, West Virginia, Tennessee, Kentucky, and Ohio testified about the damage to their land. Many expressed their hopes for a people's movement against strip mining.

> It is difficult for the people of Appalachia to speak collectively and to be heard; we have no advocates, no churchmen, no elected representative . . . to speak for us. As social units, these groups are more apt to speak against us, even to use their ability and positions against us; we must, therefore, understand that we will only be heard by American Society and even by our fellows in Appalachia as we find the means and, God willing, the courage to speak as a united people. It is now imperative that we be heard in defense of our land, and we should be the more encouraged in knowing that incidental to our own striving, we are striving against the national disease of technological pretense and technology's demand for worship.[10]

But while the Council of the Southern Mountains and other regional groups had visions of becoming a collective mountain voice, none was able to sustain itself as a broad-based regional organization.

How the Coal Industry Fought Back

The coal industry has been good at dealing with opposition. As strip mining expanded rapidly, so did the power of the operators. Many people were bought off. This was only too easy in an impoverished region.

> I think the thing really that let them get as far as they did, they would hire a person in a community to work for them, and survival means a lot to these people in the mountains. There's no jobs here now, just like there weren't then. It's poor; people have to live, and they know how to get to them.

Economic need made it easier to isolate protesters.

> One of their tactics was to turn people against other people. It got to the point that it was not Bessie and Madge fighting the strippers or the strip mining, it was Bessie and Madge fighting the people mining the coal, the neighbors. And that was a good tactic on their part, that worked real well. It kind of smoothed and glossed over the fact that it was strip mining destroying the land that they were fighting. It got to be a personal thing. And it shouldn't have been that way.

Red baiting was also used to isolate people. Attempts to blame unrest on "the communists" have occurred in Appalachian struggles since the twenties, and have often been used against opponents to strip mining. Organizers in Pike County were arrested and charged with sedition. [11] People in Knott County faced the same situation.

> Troublemakers and communists. They wanted to hang something on somebody, so they had to hang "communist" on us. That was also a scare tactic at that time, that was the ultimate sin. "Communist" was something people in Kentucky always feared, and the older people especially. And I guess that had a lot to do with our movement, you know; lots of them was convinced that we all turned communist.

If economic pressure and red baiting didn't stop the opposition, there was always intimidation and violence. People were followed. "There was a lot of unrest, a lot of threats, and a lot of people got harassed."

> S. H. was stripping [in Floyd County] and everything he stripped, every way he went, was illegal. He was one of the biggest outlaws in eastern Kentucky. [When he mined] he went right around the cemetery there, where my daddy and a lot of my brothers and sisters, the older ones, was buried. He blasted so hard he just flattened those graves. We got after him; I got some people from Reclamation to go out and take some pictures and kind of got to easing in on him. Maxine and Steve was involved, and he went in on them with his gun. He had some thugs with him, and he come back on me the same night, but he didn't get away with much with me because I knew the two boys he had with him. And he'd hired them to do this stuff. So Maxine called me when he left their house, and I said, "I'll be awaiting on him."
>
> So I was watching for S. He stopped and let those two young men out. They come up on the porch, and I was so mad that he'd go over on Steve and Maxine and then to think that he'd have the gall to come back and put these two out on me, I met them at the door. I thought about just doing them in good, then I thought, "Well, the poor little things, they took a hire to come here." So I took Nanetta's high heel that was laying there at the door, and I just let them have it. They run over to a neighbor's house. S. picked them up over on the main road; I guess he took them to the doctors. They never did come back around me no more.

"You Can't Dodge Bullets After Dark"

The women who occupied the strip mine in 1972 were associated with four organizations: the Floyd County chapter of the Eastern Kentucky Welfare Rights Organization (EKWRO), Mountain People's Rights (MPR), Save Our Kentucky (SOK), and the Appalachian Group to Save the Land and People from Knott County. By 1972 the Group's members (most prominently Bessie Smith and Madge Ashley) were using highly visible civil disobedience tactics to harass strip operators. MPR was an eastern Kentucky legal rights organization that had been working with local organizations since 1968. SOK was an activist lobbying group. EKWRO, a poor people's organization, had worked on health and education issues as well as welfare rights and had recently become involved in opposing strip mining. Representatives of these four groups secretly planned the strip mine action about two weeks before it happened. Frustration with the lack of enforcement of Kentucky's 1966 strip mine law and the hope of pressuring the recently elected governor, Wendell Ford, to support stricter enforcement and stricter laws led to the action. The plan was to go onto a strip mine, get arrested, and create media attention that we hoped would mobilize local opposition. We were aware of the industry's willingness to use violence, and that was a primary reason women were the ones most directly involved. We thought women could get away with more than men. We expected to go up on the mine, stop the operation, get arrested, and plan from there.

But someone, somewhere, decided not to arrest the women, but to leave us exposed on the mountainside. We were not prepared for this. We had not planned or expected to stay.

When we gathered to remember what had happened, we quickly reconstructed the events on the bench where we spent the day. We remembered the rain, the funny occurrences, the fear and indecision at the end. What we didn't remember was what most of us had never learned— what had happened to Doris when she went out to the gate the last time. We did remember her anguish the next day, when we met at the MPR office in Hazard and learned that she felt we had taken an unreasonable, unconscionable risk. In our 1990 reunion we heard why she felt we had been on the edge of tragedy.

Doris had gone back and forth from the mine to the gate several times. After she walked back with her younger sisters, she was unable to return. As she waited at the gate, she became aware of the ugliness of the mood and the potential for serious violence.

> Each time I went out I was passed by Blazers . . . a constant traffic going up that holler, and it was thugs and stuff that they brought in. Down at the first gate was . . . a big block building, and that was the congregation place for all kinds of people. The booze was there for the taking, it was a

big party going on down there. It was kind of like the things you see on westerns where you're inciting a group, you know—one of these lynching parties. That was the attitude that was there.

All those Blazers passing that day, they'd go by and yell. You could tell, some of them were not hillbillies—I mean, they didn't have no hillbilly accent. You could tell they were Yankees straight in and out. They was thugs brought in from Chicago.

Two of my little sisters had come back up and had come down with us the last trip. Me and Sary and Shirley were at the first gate, and both of them were little, one of them was nine and the other one was ten or eleven. And they [the men] were talking about which one of the little girls they were going to rape, which first. And one of the fellows that is still a trucker was there, a mean fellow, you know—a fellow that had given policemen more hell than you could even think about—he came over when that [talk] started, he just kind of walked over and stood with us across the road and he didn't say anything. I will love him till the day I die because I have no doubt that he saved my hide. He walked over there and stood there with us, and those guys, they didn't shut up, but they backed off a little.

It started getting much uglier around dark. I wanted to go back up and tell everybody, "Look, it's time to get out of here right now." And when I started back they had one of these big outdoor lights there, and this man just told me, "If you go out of this light, lady, you're dead." So I stayed there.

While she was waiting, two newsmen and a SOK staff member came down from the gate. They had been in a fight and were hurt. They got into their car and started off toward the hospital in Hazard. As the strip miners and truckers jumped into their vehicles to chase them, Doris and her sister blocked the one-lane road.

Shirley and I stood with our hands together across the road to keep them from going. We walked like that for I don't know how far. We walked in front of those [vehicles]. They'd beep and get real close to us like they were going to hit us and hit their gas real fast. We walked with our hands together across the road till we got probably halfway down Trace before we finally got scared that they were not going to just warn us, and we jumped over the hills. And they were out of there like—I mean, you should have seen, there was maybe twenty-five vehicles that followed them to the hospital.

Doris and Shirley went to a house and called the state police and eventually convinced them that the situation was serious. It was the next day before Doris found out that nothing had happened to the rest of us—that the police had come and we had left the mine.

As we listened to Doris' story, we realized that we had underestimated the coal operators' willingness to use violence. We expected to be roughed up. We knew that isolated individuals might be in danger. We did not expect what seems to have been an organized mob, possibly including outside thugs. Even today we wonder why the operators were so concerned.

Conclusion

In some ways our protest can be judged a success. We did shut down the mining operation. Our action received national publicity, including articles in the *Washington Post*[12] and the *New York Times*[13] and was widely covered in Kentucky papers and by journals of the women's movement. It helped increase state and national awareness about strip mining and probably contributed to the passage of reform legislation.

Our action, along with the many other early anti–strip mining protests, undoubtedly helped to lay the groundwork for later efforts. The movement continued through individual acts of resistance and through the work of organizations like Virginia Citizens for Better Reclamation (VCBR), Save Our Cumberland Mountains (SOCM), and, more recently, Kentuckians For The Commonwealth (KFTC). Members of these broad-based, multi-issue groups have worked to protect their land primarily by lobbying to change the law instead of directly confronting strip mine operations. But their legislative efforts are grounded in the memories and possibilities of direct action. The work of the opposition movement, both the direct action of the past and the more carefully constructed organizations of today, has led to better reclamation laws and enforcement, and the broad form deed—as noted above—was outlawed by a Kentucky constitutional amendment in 1989.

But in the late 1960s and early 1970s, we wanted to stop, not regulate, strip mining. This didn't happen. In fact, although no one realized it at the time, our action marked the end of the era in which Kentucky mountain people tried in an organized way to limit strip mining by direct action. The power of the industry swelled after the oil embargo of 1973 increased the demand for coal, and the strip mines offered jobs in an area with few other employment opportunities. And the anti–strip mine movement did not build organizations that could survive the long-term struggle involved in seriously challenging such a powerful and ruthless force.

In the early 1970s people opposed to strip mining had some awareness of the economic implications. For example, we talked about the fact that it took more deep miners than strip miners to dig the same amount of coal. But no one was opening these deep mines; people could get jobs on strip mines. And those jobs were important.

> I remember the contrast between us and the kids whose parents worked on a strip job. And I can remember thinking, "That's a good thing to do, look what they've got." A part of me could understand that those people wanted those jobs for good reasons. And I never felt like it should be us against them, and that always bothered me that that was the way that it seemed to be. But I know that the moving from here to where there was work and coming back was always traumatic, and I could see anybody wanting to avoid that, almost at any cost.

> Well, we didn't have anything to offer the local people except in our organization protecting their land. We didn't have anything to feed them with, we didn't have anything to work their sons with. We didn't have any jobs to offer their children or their husbands. Therefore we was outnumbered to begin with.

> I think it was at that point [after the violence] that I realized we were up against a real complicated and very powerful situation. I think I had not realized how complex it was because of not seeing how deeply the job situation was involved with the issue of strip mining.

Resistance to strip mining came from people's connection to and love for the land, for the mountains, for their communities. But the economic realities of the region meant that people in loosely organized groups could only resist. We could not win.

Confronting an issue as complex as strip mining in a region with a seriously depressed economy requires careful organization and a long-term strategy. Most early anti–strip mine organizations did not have either. Of the four organizations involved in this action, only EKWRO was a broad-based, multi-issue group, and it was active in only a small area. MPR and SOK were basically staff organizations. The Appalachian Group was a single-issue group without a strong organizational structure.

It is clear that we did not give enough thought to how direct action would translate into a movement capable of mobilizing a lot of people. While most of the people involved in this action dreamed of some kind of strong people's organization, that organization did not exist. Encouraging a people's movement had been an ongoing topic for discussion in MPR, but there was never an effective or even clearly defined strategy. We may have hoped our action would be a catalyst, but we had not laid the foundation. We didn't have the model of careful, multi-issue, member-based, democratic organization building, as practiced today by SOCM and KFTC. Some of us were influenced by romantic slogans and the notions of armed struggle which were part of the anti-war movement of the late 1960s. We did not appreciate the long, slow work that fundamental social change requires.

Reflecting on our action and its context, we can learn several "lessons." First, there is some value in the kind of direct confrontation we took. We helped publicize the issue of strip mining and may have served as an inspiration to other people in various struggles. Our action was a conscientizing experience for many of us, an important part of our political education. Most of us are still in the Appalachian region and still working for social change. While none of the organizations involved in the women's action survived more than a few years after 1972, new groups were organized, often with the same people: food co-ops, environmental groups, health clinics, peace organizations.

But we also learned lessons about movement. Some of us have worked around single issues and see value in this work: strip mining is somewhat regulated; the United States did not invade Nicaragua; Pittston was not able to defeat the United Mine Workers. But single-issue work, by itself, will not lead to fundamental social change.

> After this I felt more consciously that you can't try to fight on an issue like this without having to fight the whole system—and you can't successfully organize the community to fight such an issue without trying to change the whole system. The need to protect the environment is deeply intertwined with people's need for good jobs and means of protecting themselves and their family economically. Save the Land cannot be separated from Save the People.

The jobs-versus-environment issues are still real. Damage from strip mining continues. The energy industry is expanding oil and gas exploration. Appalachian communities are targeted as sites for landfills for out-of-state garbage. But today groups opposing environmental damage are usually aware of economic issues and work with multi-issue groups like SOCM, KFTC, or the recently formed Coalition for Jobs and the Environment in southwest Virginia. Connections are made regionally, nationally, and internationally.

The models we had in 1972—the civil rights movement, the anti-war movement, international revolutionary struggles—did not fit the Appalachian context historically, culturally, or ideologically. We believed in a people's movement for social change, but had no clear idea of what it might take to bring such a movement about. Activists in Appalachia probably still do not have *the* answer. There is still no model movement. But there is a lot going on, and much of the organizing is multi-issue, reflective, with a commitment to building broad-based democratic organizations. We keep on keeping on.

Notes

1. M. A. W., "Feeling Strong Together," in *Growin' Up Country*, ed. Jim Axelrod (Clintwood, Va.: Council of the Southern Mountains, 1973), 251–54.
2. Harry M. Caudill, *My Land Is Dying* (New York: Dutton, 1973).
3. For the history of the broad form deed, see Ronald D. Eller, *Miners, Millhands, and Mountaineers: Industrialization of the Appalachian South, 1880–1930* (Knoxville: University of Tennessee Press, 1982), 44–85.
4. Marc K. Landy, *The Politics of Environmental Reform: Controlling Kentucky Strip Mining* (Washington, D.C.: Resources for the Future, 1976), 200–201.
5. Tony Dunbar, *Our Land Too* (New York: Pantheon, 1971), 137.
6. James Branscome, "Paradise Lost," *Southern Exposure* 1 (Summer–Fall 1973): 29–41; Guy and Candie Carawan, *Voices from the Mountains* (Urbana: University of Illinois Press, 1982), 23–55; Caudill, *My Land Is Dying*; and Landy, *Politics of Environmental Reform*, 130–35.
7. Dunbar, *Our Land Too*, 134.
8. Ibid., 135.
9. The battle to amend the Kentucky constitution to abolish the broad form deed was led by Kentuckians For The Commonwealth. See the essay by Joe Szakos in this volume (Chapter 6).
10. Warren Wright quoted in *People Speak Out on Strip Mining* (Berea, Ky.: Council of the Southern Mountains, 1971), 1.
11. Paul Good, "Kentucky's Coal Beds of Sedition," *Nation* 205 (September 4, 1967): 166–69; and Bruce Jackson, "In the Valley of the Shadows: Kentucky," *Transaction* 8 (June 1971): 28–38.
12. Peter Mullins, "Kentuckians Risk Lives in War on Strip-Mining," *Washington Post*, January 31, 1972.
13. George Vecsey, "20 Women Occupy Strip Mining Site," *New York Times*, January 23, 1972.

2

Like a Flower Slowly Blooming

Highlander and the Nurturing of an Appalachian Movement

John M. Glen

In May 1990 more than one thousand people gathered at the Highlander Research and Education Center in east Tennessee for a memorial celebration honoring Myles Horton, co-founder of the school and its guiding spirit for nearly sixty years. Three generations of activists came to pay tribute to the past and plan for the future. The diverse backgrounds of the participants, the attention given to cultural expressions, the memories of earlier successes in the organized labor and civil rights movements, and the workshops covering topics from toxic waste to community economic development, racism, and women's struggles, were a striking reminder of the many roads Highlander has traveled since the mid-1960s in seeking to build a grassroots movement for opportunity and justice in Appalachia.

Indeed, over the past quarter-century Highlander has had to rethink its role in social movements, for what constitutes a movement in Appalachia does not fit easily into common definitions of the term. Activists and analysts alike tend to measure social movements by their level of organization, shared commitment to a system of beliefs, and articulation of goals by commanding figures.[1] The emphasis is on structure, definition, cohesion. In contrast, the "social movement" that has risen in Appalachia more closely resembles a coalition, a loose alliance, a network of disparate groups, leaders, followers, and tendencies—a movement of movements. It has focused on single issues and addressed complex, interlocking sets of issues; it has battled powerful and shifting targets; it has sought to relate short-term victories to long-term change; and it has uncovered connections between local problems and national and global crises. Organizations and activists have come and gone. Others have remained. Financial support has rarely been secure. Yet this Appalachian movement has also been persistent, and it has challenged Highlander to develop a new, integrative vision and educational strategy that would help end the exploitation of the region and its people and give individuals and communities control

Typical workshop circle at the Highlander Center. (*Highlander archives*)

over their lives, workplaces, and resources. The effect on the Center has been at least as great as its contributions to the contest over Appalachia's economic, political, and cultural future.

Certainly Highlander was historically prepared to promote a campaign resembling earlier struggles by labor unions and civil rights organizations in the South. Established in Monteagle, Tennessee, in 1932 and originally called the Highlander Folk School, its educational approach reflected Horton's conviction that a new social order could be created by bringing ordinary people together to share their experiences in addressing common problems. During the 1930s staff members achieved modest success in organizing and educating mine, mill, timber, and unemployed workers in east Tennessee. The school's reputation grew as it became directly involved in the southern organizing drives mounted by the Congress of Industrial Organizations in the late 1930s. For most of the next decade, Highlander hosted numerous training workshops for CIO and other union local officers. But postwar differences over the priorities of the labor movement broke up the Highlander-CIO relationship and prompted the staff to attempt a revival of the southern wing of the Farmers' Union and the formation of a regional farmer-labor coalition. Frustrated by the continued reluctance of existing organizations to overcome racial barriers to change, Highlander's teachers began holding workshops on public school desegregation in 1953, nearly a year before the momentous *Brown* v. *Board of Education* decision and the subsequent emergence of the civil rights movement in the South. Residential workshops attracted Rosa Parks, Martin Luther King, Jr., college student sit-in leaders, and hundreds of other black and white activists. Highlander-sponsored Citizenship Schools, first held on the South Carolina Sea Islands, taught thousands of southern blacks the literacy skills they needed to secure the right to vote. Outraged southern segregationists spearheaded a drive to close the Folk School in 1962. By then Horton had secured a charter for the Highlander Research and Education Center, and from a new Knoxville location the staff continued its civil rights programs.[2]

Beginning in 1964, however, Horton and his colleagues recognized that Highlander should consider a new direction. As a matter of policy, the school withdrew from social movements once they were underway in order to encourage independent action, and despite the steady demands for their services, staff members maintained that the black struggle for freedom should have black leadership. The growing number of black organizations and leaders indicated that Highlander was no longer a necessary element in the civil rights movement. So too did the militancy of young black activists, who asserted that whites could best aid their cause by organizing poor whites, the only group blacks could accept as allies. Highlander's approach also emphasized working with people in potential social movements. Horton noted that while black protest had spurred organizing among Chicanos, Puerto Ricans, and Native Americans, he doubted whether these groups could become a powerful force for change without white allies. Organizing poor, predominantly white Appalachians would therefore help create a genuinely multicolored coalition capable of affecting national economic and social policy.

Appalachia itself seemed ripe for change. President Lyndon B. Johnson had declared war on poverty in 1964, and the early wave of media attention toward the mountain poor was accompanied by the infusion of millions of dollars in federal aid, dozens of community action programs, and hundreds of anti-poverty warriors. The Highlander staff suspected that the campaign would ultimately disappoint large numbers of people in Appalachia. But there were signs, such as the roving picket movement of unemployed coal miners in Hazard County, Kentucky, that these same people could be aroused to challenge the external forces that exploited the region's economy, an effort that by necessity would link up with other poor and working-class groups across the country.[3]

Context, crises, and opportunity thus dovetailed nicely in Highlander's analysis. There was one additional benefit for the center. An Appalachian program would allow Highlander to come back to its home region, to address problems that had been subordinated to the larger labor and civil rights campaigns throughout the South, and perhaps to achieve a true balance between its original goals of developing a new social order and preserving the indigenous cultural values of the mountains.

Highlander's first steps in building an Appalachian movement were tentative and reminiscent of past approaches, but promising nonetheless. In March 1964 thirteen volunteers recruited by the white student project of the Student Nonviolent Coordinating Committee attended a three-day workshop to examine Appalachia's problems and plan a project that would contribute to the War on Poverty. The group quickly learned the dimensions of the challenge facing the poor and unemployed in areas like eastern Kentucky: a deteriorating coal industry, increasing mine mechanization, a quiescent United Mine Workers of America, a history of dissent and agitation undermined by self-serving outside crusaders, racial prejudice coexisting with a tradition of interracial union activism and common economic concerns, an unresponsive public welfare system, and a handful of protest groups. Workshop participants concluded that change in Appalachia would begin when its people became aware of the tremendous gap between the announced intent of federal anti-poverty programs and what they actually delivered. Student volunteers must "make the transition from thought to responsible action," Sam Shirah of SNCC declared. They should help indigenous leaders understand government procedures and how they and their neighbors could make them serve their needs, setting the stage not only for increased assistance but for further community organization as well. The emphasis had to be on education, Horton observed, if the young activists hoped to strengthen the independence rather than the dependence of the Appalachian people.[4]

Over the next three years, while most of Highlander's energies and funds went to the development of black political leadership in the Deep South, Horton and a few other staff members tried to assess the mood in Appalachia as they experimented with several education programs. They worked with established organizations like the Council of the Southern Mountains and a larger number of newer groups, such as the Southern Student Organizing Committee, the Appalachian Economic and Political Action Conference, the Federation of Communities in Service (FOCIS), the Marrowbone Folk School, and the Congress for Appalachian Development. During the summer of 1965, four young men, including Myles Horton's son Thorsten, attempted to replicate the beginnings of the Citizenship Schools through an exploratory project in the once flourishing coal mining town of Habersham, Tennessee. There they maintained a low profile, quietly encouraging local people to take the initiative in public affairs and showing them how their grievances were part of larger economic and political issues. Although the project workers resisted formal organizing, the temptation to manipulate activities often competed with the need for patient communication, especially when their contacts showed little inclination to organize or act upon their own ideas. These experiences led to a series of workshops at Highlander for community leaders and Appalachian Volunteers (AVs), a federally funded group radicalized by their involvement in the War on Poverty. As the workshops grew in size and scope, participants thought they saw the beginnings of an Appalachia-wide movement; some started their own educational programs in places like Wise County, Virginia, and Harlan County, Kentucky. Highlander staff members Guy and Candie Carawan showed workshop groups how music and singing could become tools for organizing, and staged Appalachian music projects and festivals at the center and in eastern Kentucky.[5]

A general strategy for Highlander's Appalachian program began to emerge out of this "action research," as Horton called it.[6] Staff members learned that the region's poor must first be activated to form their own organizations before there could be any serious steps toward a widespread social movement. Short-term projects like the one in Habersham could not arouse any sense of urgency among the poor to organize. The college student and summer volunteers who came to the mountains had neither the experience nor the patience to wait until the poor themselves were ready to act. The War on Poverty's Community Action Programs, even when not compromised by the interests of local elites, usually pursued limited goals. Organizing in Appalachia therefore should not become too broad, too sweeping, too hasty. Instead, Highlander should concentrate on the nurturing of indigenous leadership and, along with other activist groups in the region, continue to experiment with organizing models that were responsive to the diversity of Appalachian communities. Eventually a social movement would grow out of these grassroots efforts, and then a formal alliance could be created to reinforce and give breadth to the local actions.[7]

Highlander had chosen a familiar path, guided by the presumption that its historic "bottom-up" approach to community organizing would work in Appalachia. The situation may be less structured than the labor movement of the 1930s, staff members admitted, but there were appealing parallels between Appalachia in the 1960s and the early days of the civil rights movement. The region contained a cadre of young but experienced organizers. Several issues, most notably strip mining, were generating unrest in coal mining areas. Appalachians were increasingly disillusioned with top-down, Washington-controlled solutions to poverty. And the similarities between the plight of the Appalachian poor and that of southern blacks remained tantalizingly close. Enough was "stirring" in Appalachia to enable the center to move beyond the civil rights movement, Horton reassured board members in 1967; it was "just a matter of figuring out how much we're going to put into it."[8]

Events in 1968 seemed to confirm Highlander's analysis of the effort it would take to build a multiracial poor people's movement. Shortly before his death, Martin Luther King, Jr., announced a poor people's march on Washington, D.C., which he hoped would unite the dispossessed of all races, appeal to the nation's conscience, and compel the federal government to provide jobs and income to all who needed them. But government officials were unmoved by the sight of several thousand poor people living near the Lincoln Memorial, and chaotic administration, ineffective demonstrations, and conflicts among black, Latino, and Native American leaders plagued the eight-week campaign. A contingent from Highlander stayed in Resurrection City and conducted music and cultural workshops until police closed down the shantytown in June 1968. Horton and Mike Clark, a former Appalachian Volunteer who had recently joined the Highlander staff, were disappointed that the Poor People's Campaign had failed to promote a broadly based program for radical change. Yet the virtual absence of organizations representing Appalachians and poor whites generally underscored how Highlander could substantially contribute to the multiracial coalition, and the well-run alternate community created at the Hawthorne

School in Washington during the campaign by five distinct ethnic groups testified to the ability of poor people to work together as equals for a common cause.[9]

Other developments signaled the beginning of the end for the War on Poverty in Appalachia. Federal appropriations steadily declined, state officials closely monitored funding proposals and reports, Community Action Programs operated under tightening budgetary and administrative constraints, community centers closed, the number of anti-poverty warriors decreased, and signs of progress disappeared. The Appalachian Volunteers became a particular target of state and local officials wary of any grassroots ferment. In 1968 the governors of West Virginia and Virginia refused to approve an extension of federal anti-poverty grants to the AVs in their states, and the Kentucky Committee on Un-American Activities held hearings on alleged subversion in Pike County, effectively killing the possibility of further grants to the AVs in that state. This shift in government attitudes was significant. An Appalachian movement would now have to proceed largely without the direct aid of federal legislation, agencies, revenue, and intervention, support that had helped the labor and civil rights movements make important gains.[10]

Highlander thus entered a complex transition period, seeking some way to spread a new consciousness that Appalachians must control their own movement. Several more years of exploratory work with Hispanic and Indian groups in the Southwest and with Appalachian and Puerto Rican groups in Chicago made it clear to the staff that hopes for a multiracial poor people's alliance were premature and that the center's resources should go toward mobilizing Appalachian protest. Even this step would take time. In 1969 Myles Horton recalled that five years earlier he had projected the development of a program to the point where it could be passed on to others, much as the Citizenship School program had been transferred to the Southern Christian Leadership Conference. But it had been "very difficult to get the poor to assert their independence in the face of a horde of missionaries, primarily from the government, who are always master-minding them." Activists in Appalachia were suffering from a "poverty of ideas," pursuing old dead-end strategies and repeating previous mistakes.[11] Highlander had not sufficiently tested its own ideas. The Center's workshops, however, pointed to the need for an education program, run by poor people themselves, which would establish a regional identity for an Appalachian movement. Since no areawide organization or structure existed to provide a base for such an effort, this education program had to be flexible and inclusive, addressing a wide variety of local problems while highlighting the common experiences of people from different sections of the region.[12]

The Appalachian Self-Education Program (ASEP) was Highlander's attempt to meet those needs. Once again the Citizenship Schools provided the model, tempered by the experiences of several former Appalachian Volunteers who joined the staff in the late 1960s. Instead of offering the poor the illusion of power, as many Community Action Agencies had done, the ASEP sought to insure their empowerment. There was to be no formally recognized leader or group, no preestablished guidelines, no organizing around a particular issue, no organizer-centered or agency-generated change. The ASEP would consist of community workshops whose agenda and content would be entirely determined by poor people. Community leaders would learn to be educators rather than organizers. The workshops would build contacts within and between communities, inspire confidence among participants, acquire information as well as the tools for using it, and foster a collective identity. Cultural components would celebrate the value of local and traditional art and music. Research and other special services would furnish materials and new technology, such as videotape recorders, to accelerate the spread of knowledge. Highlander's Appalachian staff would be "field coordinators" for the ASEP. They would identify potential workshop leaders, help them set up their own workshops, supply information and consultants when requested, and serve as liaisons between local groups.[13]

As Mike Clark recognized at the start of the program, the decentralized, nondirective intent of the ASEP made it different from anything Highlander had tried before. Progress would therefore come slowly. Ending old habits of dependency on outside reformers and local elites would be hard. Community groups struggled with an enormous range of problems, and all of them had to overcome a legacy of powerlessness. The workshops themselves would require months of patient field work by the Highlander staff, searching for sparks of response to the self-education idea. Yet if small, democratically run, autonomous groups could begin to formulate programs and policies at the local level and then work together to pressure local agencies and institutions to deliver according to the wishes of the community, mountain society would be "turned inside out": poor people would gain a new image of themselves, look to one another for ideas and support, and secure political justice and economic independence.[14]

It was this vision of Appalachia finally breaking free from the forces oppressing it that would motivate a new generation of Highlander staff members. Animated by a variety of influences—the anti–Vietnam war movement, the War on Poverty, community struggles against strip mining, the effort to establish Appalachian Studies programs at colleges in the region—the staff pursued the ideal of democratizing economic and political power in Appalachia with a passion not easily expressed in reports to the Center's board of directors, grant proposals, and public presentations. There was constant experimentation, considerable creativity, and a determination to identify those institutions, laws, and practices that perpetuated the region's problems. There were also ongoing debates over the relative merits of specific issues; questions about the constituencies to be served by Highlander; disputes over theory, analysis, and pedagogy; and internal tensions over long-term strategy. The Appalachian program placed Highlander in a new context, without the frame of reference offered by an active, developed social movement. Over time the vision would become more complex—and more elusive.

The primary challenge of the ASEP was to build a movement without organization. It was true, as Highlander and War on Poverty veterans could testify, that organizations often set in motion forces that defeated the insurgency that gave rise to a social movement. The question was whether an Appalachian movement based on local initiative would benefit from a deliberately unstructured education program.

In the tumultuous years of the late 1960s and early 1970s, keeping the issues specific seemed to be the key. Highlander responded to a request by the Council of the Southern Mountains for assistance in establishing closer ties with the poor by holding workshops on both the Council and the ASEP for people from West Virginia, southeastern Ohio, eastern Kentucky, southwest Virginia, and east Tennessee. The staff went one step further at the Council's 1969 conference at Fontana Lake, North Carolina, and supported the efforts of a coalition led by blacks, poor people, and students mobilized by Sue Ella Easterling of the Council's Youth Commission to force a major reorganization of the group. Highlander staff member Almetor King, a founding member of new Council commissions on Black Appalachians and Poor People's Self-Help, won election to a reconstituted board of directors whose majority represented the poor.[15]

Following the Council "revolution," Highlander explored the possibilities of starting new poor people's organizations through workshops attended by disabled miners, welfare recipients, housewives, subsistence farmers, and individuals wanting to form tenants' rights groups and credit unions. Staff members found very specific problems blocking collective action by the poor: pride, fear, dependency on outside help, inadequate government programs, and racial, legal, and financial barriers. In response, the staff intensified its field work, seeking to fashion an indigenous model of democratic problem-solving. Assistance to groups like Pickett United for Self-Help and LBJ & C Development Corporation in east Tennessee and in various "hotspots" of discontent in eastern Kentucky coal counties resulted in marketing cooperatives, job training projects, community centers, fights against strip mining abuses, and demands for school and road improvements. Additional workshops at Highlander studied ways to revive welfare and tenants' rights organizations, to use music to promote regional pride and social awareness, to assess how lawyers could advise poor people's groups without controlling them, and to use newspapers and other media as organizing tools.[16]

Highlander's Appalachian program seemed to be gaining momentum. A regional network of activists who had first met at the Center was growing, as were requests for help from poor people's groups. Highlander was once again serving as both a meeting place and a vital source of information. At the same time, the focus of the program was shifting. Having seen too many groups falter or dissolve after reaching a certain goal, too many leaders quit because of physical exhaustion or political pressure, and too many artificially created leaders divorce themselves from the people they were ostensibly helping, staff members announced in 1971 that they would concentrate on educational methods that involved groups rather than individuals from groups. The staff would continue to avoid paternalistic or "power-broker" relationships with community organizations. But it would seek workshop participants more motivated to work on local problems and more willing to make connections with other organizations. Even more critical was Highlander's decision to hold workshops on specific issues rather than general subjects like community organizing. Staff members were taking a calculated risk in adopting this strategy, reckoning that although there were few signs of unity among the dozens of organizations struggling in the mountains, Appalachia faced crises of such proportions that its people, for all their diversity, would have to forge a regional movement for their own survival.[17]

If issue organizing held out the promise of broader, more durable, even bolder citizens' associations, which issues had sufficient galvanizing power, and how could Highlander turn them into effective action? The Center's staff, which now included a number of native Appalachians in addition to Clark, chose to address the question on three fronts. First, residential workshops examined local issues that would sustain grassroots organizations. For a time staff members thought that the regionwide controversy over Area Development Districts, multicounty planning units that wielded virtually complete control over federal expenditures within their boundaries, could lead to a program involving thousands of people in a fight against "the most important change in local government since the Revolutionary War." Although that campaign never materialized, other workshops sought to build upon community struggles over strip mining, welfare rights, school reform, and other issues.[18]

A second front, research and advocacy, was headed by James Branscome, a former Appalachian Regional Commission staff member who had challenged Kentucky coal operators through the anti–strip mining group Save Our Kentucky. Branscome forcefully asserted that institutions in Appalachia professing to serve the region's people were actually working for their "extinction." With a critical eye that spared no institution (including Highlander), he wrote hard-hitting articles on the ARC, Appalachia's public school systems, federal and state regulatory agencies, and especially the Tennessee Valley Authority, attacking the agency's coal policies and opening its decision-making structure to public scrutiny for the first time in its history.[19]

Long-term leadership development programs constituted the third part of Highlander's strategy. Former miner Charles "Buck" Maggard, the staff's connection to the coal fields and subsistence farms of southeastern Kentucky, asserted that the cutoff of federal anti-poverty funds would leave Appalachian people hungry, aware, and ready to develop their own independent leadership. He and Branscome spent weeks at a time traveling up mountain hollows, looking for and listening to people with a good sense of leadership, passing on their ideas to leaders elsewhere—allowing the process, as Maggard put it, "to spread like molasses."[20]

This reorientation was one of several signs in the early 1970s that Highlander was making a decisive break from an analysis dating from the civil rights movement to one rooted in Appalachia. The shift was also expressed physically, as the center moved to a farm twenty-five miles east of Knoxville near New Market, Tennessee. Administrative leadership passed from Myles Horton to Frank Adams and then to Mike Clark. For board members and supporters who understood the school in terms of earlier social movements, the implications of these changes were unclear. Staff members themselves raised questions about their educational roles. These concerns perhaps reflected a vague uneasiness over whether a broad-based movement was indeed emerging in Appalachia.[21]

Thus in the mid-1970s the Highlander staff took another hard look at the relationship of its education program to Appalachia. Many of the community organizations that had emerged during the War on Poverty or in response to issues like strip mining had become inactive. The energy crisis of 1973–74 brought rapid economic expansion to some parts of the region as coal, oil, and gas prices boomed, while other areas suffered severe declines as small factories closed and small farmers lost their land. In Highlander's view the one constant in this changing picture was the growing power of corporations and government agencies in the mountains and their increasing lack of accountability to the public. Clark believed that an Appalachian movement was still very much alive, but it was not the poor people's coalition Highlander had anticipated in the mid-1960s. The movement was taking "a new direction." Older activists and groups

were "weeding themselves out." Union members and middle-class professionals were asking critical questions about the future of the region. Single
issues were becoming part of larger, multifaceted issues. Local problems
had connections to national and international developments. Highlander's
uncertainty in this situation, Clark asserted, stemmed from an educational
base that had become "extremely nebulous," with a great deal of time,
money, and effort being spent in Appalachia and little to show for it. Staff
members agreed that the Center needed to leave behind what Clark called
"the myth of Highlander." They had to gain a new sense of purpose, widen
their constituency to include people in Appalachia and elsewhere who
shared common concerns, expand their activities to areas outside the region's coalfields, and develop programs around a nucleus of issues that
had broad, long-term significance.[22]

A new, intensive wave of institution-building programs followed.
Dozens of workshops during the late 1970s and early 1980s brought several thousand Appalachian people together on an extensive range of issues:
strip mining, land ownership, coal taxation, tax reform, toxic wastes,
industrial health and safety, housing, welfare rights, public school reform,
child development, elderly rights, and more. Coalfield clinics established
by the UMWA asked for help in extending primary health care to rural
communities, leading to the formation of the Appalachian Health Exchange Leadership Project, headed by Helen Lewis. To support community
control of the clinics, AHELP recruited physicians, educated clinic board
members and staffs on health care finance and delivery issues, organized
health forums in three states, and promoted a network of assistance among
the clinics that proved vital when the 1978 UMWA contract sharply cut
back benefits from its Welfare and Retirement Funds.[23]

Highlander also renewed its ties with organized labor when staff
members June Rostan and Bingham Graves set up a high school equiva-
lency degree program for Knoxville-area members of the Amalgamated
Clothing and Textile Workers Union. The program spread to ACTWU
locals elsewhere in Appalachia. Meanwhile, training in labor education
began at Highlander for union officers from across the South. These and
other workshops, such as sessions on the debilitating lung diseases suffered
by textile mill workers and coal miners, reflected Highlander's renewed
emphasis on the links between Appalachia's problems and those found in
the rest of the rural South.[24]

Research at Highlander moved away from the individualistic approach favored by James Branscome to become a more formal part of the
Center's work. Operating on the principle that information is power, a
resource center, directed by John Gaventa and Juliet Merrifield, not only
provided research assistance and data but also trained citizens to do their

own research and thus participate effectively in public policy decisions. Research projects documented the economic and environmental record of coal companies; occupational safety issues and legislation; and the interlocking relationships between corporations and public officials. In the late 1970s Merrifield and Helen Lewis worked with a citizens' group in Kingsport, Tennessee, to call attention to the possibility that chemicals made and used at the Tennessee Eastman Company were hazardous to the health of workers and city residents. Although the Kingsport Study Group may have been little more than a nuisance to local industrialists, its persistence compelled Tennessee Eastman to make further efforts to comply with environmental regulations. Moreover, the links forged by the Kingsport group with conservationists throughout the region indicated that any emerging Appalachian movement would likely have an environmental component. Highlander also participated in a major collaborative study of land ownership in Appalachia. About one hundred activists and academics associated with the Appalachian Alliance pored over tax rolls and deed books in eighty selected counties in six Appalachian states to determine the owners of some twenty million acres of land and mineral rights. The 1,800-page survey, completed in 1981, confirmed what Appalachian natives had known for decades: corporate and absentee ownership of land and minerals was responsible for inadequate tax revenues, public services, housing, and schools; shrinking farm lands; and environmental abuses.[25]

The Kingsport and land study projects reflect the close attention staff members gave to grassroots activities that might coalesce into some larger effort. Their experience with emerging indigenous leaders who needed technical assistance, organizing support, and sometimes a shot of self-confidence led to the creation of the Southern Appalachian Leadership Training (SALT) program. Selected local leaders engaged in a period of intensive, individualized study on a particular community problem, such as the construction of an unwanted dam or the lack of flood relief. In the process SALT trainees honed their leadership skills; learned to take maximum advantage of what government and other outside agencies had to offer; shared ideas with other community leaders, organizations, and responsive professionals; and deepened their commitment to their home communities. The Center's cultural program continued to encourage the sharing of folk traditions among mountain and Deep South communities through Guy and Candie Carawan's workshops and performances before black and white audiences in Tennessee, Kentucky, West Virginia, and Georgia. A coalition formed in 1977 that for a time possessed considerable potential as a vehicle for reform was the Appalachian Alliance, composed of over thirty community groups seeking to speak with a more unified

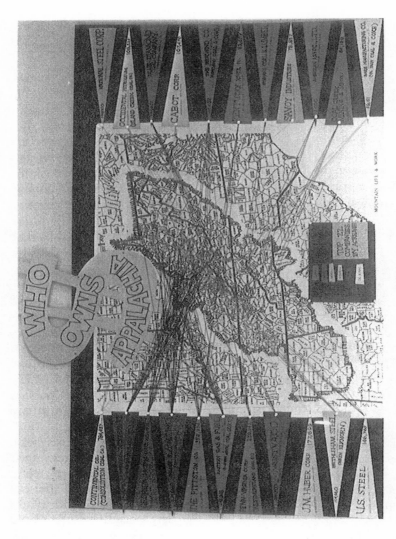

Graphic illustration of the Appalachian land study conducted by community groups throughout the region in 1980–81. Highlander assisted the Land Ownership Task Force of the Appalachian Alliance in coordinating this study. (*Highlander archives*)

voice on regional problems and public policies. Bill Horton, who coordinated the land ownership study with John Gaventa, became coordinator of the Alliance in 1981, and at various Highlander workshops Alliance representatives considered strategies addressing health, energy, education, economic, and gender issues.[26]

Highlander's leadership was comparatively slow to appreciate the growing prominence of gender as an analytical, organizing, and unifying concept. Women at the center had become increasingly conscious of the irony of working at an institution whose commitment to change had been historically carried out to a significant degree by women; whose workshops had inspired and empowered women for decades; whose efforts in Appalachia had brought it into contact with leaders like Eula Hall and Edith Easterling; yet whose policy decisions, administrative duties, and workshop agendas were determined by men. In the early 1970s Betty Liveright, Joyce Dukes, and other staff women made several proposals for workshops specifically designed for women at the Center and in Appalachia. Workshops composed entirely of women began in 1975, but it was the question of providing child care during workshops that enabled Highlander women to confront the "old boy network" and "blue jean machismo" of the male staff. For many years the Center had adhered to a "no kids or dogs" rule. Most staff men did not regard child care as important; after all, they asserted, Highlander was an adult education center. (There was an additional irony in this—Highlander had operated a fairly popular nursery school in the late 1930s and early 1940s.) Finally, after several years of lobbying by board member Sue Ella Kobak (née Easterling), staff members Helen Lewis and Candie Carawan, and other women, and after the number of staff members with children grew, Highlander established what proved to be an exemplary child care program in 1982. Thereafter the number of workshops devoted to women's issues increased rapidly, encouraging the formation of groups like the Southeast Women's Employment Coalition to support local efforts to achieve job equity and economic opportunities for women.[27]

In the course of all this activity, the lexicon of Highlander staff members and Appalachian activists in general underwent a subtle yet significant change. Talk of an Appalachian *movement* virtually disappeared. In its place came more carefully chosen words: "an ongoing mutual technical assistance and support system," "an emerging communications grid which may develop into a functioning network system," or, more simply and commonly, a *network*.[28] Granted the fundraising intent of such phrases, the words nevertheless connote a matured understanding of the breadth, depth, nuances, and occasionally contradictory characteristics of Appalachia's problems. Perhaps earlier efforts to create a social movement in

Appalachia had been naive or raised expectations too quickly. Perhaps groups like Highlander wanted to move faster and farther than other organizations were prepared to do. Perhaps the idea of a regionwide struggle drew too readily on the examples of the labor and civil rights movements when there were not enough points of cohesion among the many localized struggles in the mountains. Indeed, perhaps Highlander's focus on regional and local efforts overlooked the possibilities of achieving change at the state level. Whatever the reason, the new reality was that developing progressive leadership, sustaining grassroots organizing, and fashioning a regional campaign on the people's terms that was simultaneously tailored to varying community needs was, and would be in the foreseeable future, a long, laborious process.

Yet staff members were troubled by the impact this network was having on Highlander. In 1979 Clark observed that the most serious problem facing the Center was its lack of educational structure and the consequent inability of those who came there to identify with its ideas, or even understand them. Some board and staff members in the early 1980s saw Highlander as "perilously close to being all over the map," with program priorities that were vague, or too crisis-oriented, or reflecting personal commitments rather than Highlander's long-term interests. Still others asked questions about the relationship between program technique and content, the Center's diverse constituencies, the staff's work with grassroots leaders, the growing academic orientation of the staff, and the possibility that Highlander's major goal should not be coalition building but sowing the seeds for a coalition to be built by others. Hubert Sapp, a former SCLC assistant to Martin Luther King, Jr., who succeeded Clark as director in 1982, thought the essential issue was one Highlander had confronted throughout its history: "What balance do we strike between foresight and foreknowledge of [a] new movement, and the ability or the potential to respond to things as they emerge?"[29]

With the celebration of Highlander's fiftieth anniversary in 1982 came the third major refocusing of its educational program since Myles Horton and his colleagues turned their attention to Appalachia in the mid-1960s. Individual programs continued to be timely and informative. But they could not entirely escape the standards of the past, or significantly alter expectations of what the Center could feasibly accomplish, or provide satisfactory answers to ongoing questions about its overall mission. Juliet Merrifield suggested in 1983 that Highlander's contributions over the following decade would depend on the recognition of the underlying tensions in all of its work "between being sensitive and aggressive, between involvement in politics and entanglement in factionalism, between much traveling and the need for a clear focus, between regional focus and our world view."[30]

Recent years have seen the creation of a more structured curriculum under the leadership of Sapp and John Gaventa, who became the Center's director in 1989. A community empowerment project encouraged Appalachian and Deep South community groups to view their voter registration and education campaigns as part of a long-term struggle for community survival and development. Jane Sapp and the Carawans tied the cultural program into the community empowerment concept, creating the space for folk singers and other "culture bearers" to reclaim community traditions. Toxics issues mushroomed during the 1980s. The long-running battle between the Yellow Creek Concerned Citizens of Bell County, Kentucky, and a sewage treatment plant pumping chemicals into Yellow Creek renewed Highlander's efforts to promote ties among similar anti-pollution fights through its Community Environmental Health Program, Stop The Poisoning workshops, and Environmental/Economic Intern Program, co-ordinated by YCCC leader Larry Wilson. The Center's participatory research model assisted investigations of toxic hazards from North Carolina to Bhopal, India. Other research projects studied such issues as the commodification of water resources and the impact of military spending on the South. As the once-dominant coal, textile, and wood products industries in Appalachia gave way to low-wage employment in service and high-tech industries, the Highlander Economic Education Project, headed by Bill Horton, Helen Lewis, and Sue Thrasher, tried to demystify the change and introduce alternative development strategies. In addition, there were Summer Youth Workshops, a scaled-down SALT program, workshops on the uses of media and computer technologies, and exchanges with educators in Latin America, Africa, and elsewhere around the world.[31]

Questions about Highlander's Appalachian program and overall purpose persisted. Public statements consistently stressed the Center's responsiveness to the need for community empowerment, accessible information, and global links to local struggles. Privately, staff and board members were worried. To many of them the residential program lacked clarity, vision, coordination, or cohesion, even after the drafting of a new Statement of Mission in 1987. The staff's field work did not seem to weave back into an integrated set of workshops. Defining the Center's constituency had become very difficult. Some feared that Highlander was becoming less a center for education than a center for conferences. If it was not living up to the distinctive pedagogy of Myles Horton, it was burdened with the image of Horton as the patriarch of a tradition-bound institution. Horton himself suggested in 1986 a fresh evaluation of the history of the school and the South as a way to reenergize the "Highlander spirit" and adapt it to contemporary conditions.[32]

Some of this self-criticism was healthy. Part of Highlander's dilemma stemmed from problems in Appalachia that were all too familiar to its staff and other regional activists. By the end of the 1980s there still were few of the unifying elements that had undergirded the labor and civil rights movements, still an unnerving diversity of community organizations, still too much diffused regional dissent. New difficulties loomed ahead. Appalachia's economy was declining. Single-issue groups were discovering that their approach circumscribed their ability to inspire or achieve change, that the problem they confronted had many dimensions. At the same time, grassroots organizations were receiving diminishing support. A new wave of mountain leadership had not yet fully emerged. Highlander's quandary, however, was also the product of a generation-long adjustment by the staff, board, and supporters to the realization that in Appalachia, the character, methods, and problems of social change could not be the same as they once were. The Center therefore could not remain captive to what once was.

Highlander will continue to make its mark in Appalachia, but it will involve less a reaffirmation of its past work and more a reorientation of its vision. Staff members can build upon the intellectual impact they have had on the debate over Appalachia's identity and political economy and over how change should come to the mountains. Yet what may be needed most is patience, a renewed willingness to listen to the people of Appalachia, a deeper appreciation that the battle for the future of the region will remain an extended and sometimes confusing struggle, and a perspective that accepts the long view of social change while upholding Highlander's uniqueness as a resource and meeting place. The labor and civil rights movements that shaped so much of the school's past stand as singular instances in American history of major social movements that made dramatic advances in a relatively short time. Each sought to secure basic rights and enjoyed success as long as its efforts centered on those rights. Each had a centralizing organization and at least one charismatic national leader—John L. Lewis and Martin Luther King, Jr. And each demanded and eventually received a governmental commitment to its cause. The mobilization of a grassroots regional coalition to resist the exploitation of Appalachia and its people may well have to follow a different, more arduous route. The important question for Highlander and the Appalachian movement is not whether they will go on, but how they will choose to move ahead.

Notes

1. Three overviews of the literature on social movements are Rudolf Heberle and Joseph R. Gusfield, "Social Movements," in *International Encyclopedia of the Social Sciences*, ed. David L. Sills, vol. 14 (New York: Macmillan and Free Press, 1968), 438–52; Frances Fox Piven and Richard A. Cloward, *Poor People's Movements: Why They Succeed, How They Fail* (New York: Pantheon Books, 1977); David S. Meyer, "Peace Movements and National Security Policy: A Research Agenda," *Peace and Change* 16 (April 1991): 131–61.
2. John M. Glen, *Highlander: No Ordinary School, 1932–1962* (Lexington: University Press of Kentucky, 1988).
3. Myles Horton, "Civil Rights and Appalachia," c. 1968, Myles Horton Papers, Box 2, Highlander Research and Education Center, New Market, Tenn. (hereinafter cited as Horton Papers); Anne Braden to Bea Schneiderman, March 12, 1964, Highlander Research and Education Center Papers, Box 7, State Historical Society of Wisconsin, Madison (hereinafter cited as HREC Papers); author's interview with Michael Clark, August 10, 1978; Kate Black, "The Roving Picket Movement and the Appalachian Committee for Full Employment, 1959–1965: A Narrative," *Journal of the Appalachian Studies Association* 2 (1990): 110–27.
4. Quotation from report on Appalachia Workshop, March 12–14, 1964, Horton Papers, Box 8. See also *Highlander Reports: Three-Year Report*, August 21, 1961–December 31, 1964, HREC Papers, Box 1; memorandum, Myles Horton to Appalachian Provisional Organizing Committee, c. November 1964, HREC Papers, Box 32; Highlander press releases, March 2, 17, 1964; notes on Appalachia Workshop, c. March 12–14, 1964, HREC Papers, Box 80; transcript of audio recording of "Hazard Workshop," March 12–13, 1964, Highlander Research and Education Center Papers, Current Files, New Market, Tenn. (hereinafter cited as HC Papers). Highlander's most recent files, organized into Administrative, Current, Director's, Financial [and other] Reports, General Correspondence, and Research categories, have been transferred to the State Historical Society of Wisconsin, where they will be added to the Highlander Research and Education Center Papers. Some processed files will remain part of the Highlander Papers in New Market.
5. *Highlander Reports: Three-Year Report*, August 21, 1961–December 31, 1964, HREC Papers, Box 1; Carol Stevens, "A Proposal for Organizing Appalachia," c. November 7, 1964; memorandum, Highlander Center Appalachian Conference, November 7–8, 1964; Myles Horton to John Chater, January 20, 1965; memorandum, Horton to C. Conrad Browne, c. February 1965; memorandum, Horton to Appalachian Project Staff, April 22, 1965; Frank Adams, "Highlander Appalachian Project," summer 1965, HREC Papers, Box 32; Guy Carawan, report on East Kentucky Mountain Project, June 1–December 15, 1967, HREC Papers, Box 37; "Myles Horton's Report on

Field Trip to Development Residential Centers in Appalachia," July 2–7, 1967, HREC Papers, Box 100; Horton to Carl and Anne Braden, March 18, 1967, HREC Papers, Box 106; report on Appalachian Community Leaders Workshop, January 13–16, 1967; Jerry Knoll to Horton, March 17, 1967; announcement of public programs, "Appalachia: Its Human and Natural Resources," June 2–5, 1967; memorandum, Joe Mulloy to Community Leaders invited to attend the fifth Appalachian Community Leadership Workshop, November 17, 1967; "Appalachian Report: Five Highlander Community Leadership Workshops—Two Adult Education Centers in Appalachia Founded by Highlander Workshop Participants," March 1968, HREC Papers, Box 108; Karen Mulloy, report on Mountain Organizer Training Workshop, May 8, 1968, HREC Papers, Box 109; audio recording, Appalachian Project meeting, June 16, 1965, Highlander Research and Education Center Tape Collection, 515A/16, State Historical Society of Wisconsin. See also the chapter by the Carawans in this volume (Chapter 12).

6. Memorandum, Myles Horton to Appalachian Project Staff, April 22, 1965, HREC Papers, Box 32.

7. Memorandum, Myles Horton to Highlander Board of Directors, November 9, 1965, HREC Papers, Box 2; Appalachian Pilot Project meeting minutes, October 31, 1964, HREC Papers, Box 32; Horton to Wilfred J. Unruh, September 25, 1967, HREC Papers, Box 97; Horton to Anne Braden, May 16, 1967, HREC Papers, Box 106; Horton, "Introductory Remarks (Revised), Appalachian Community Leadership Workshop," October 6–9, 1967, HREC Papers, Box 108; Horton, "Rough Notes on Organizing in Appalachia," c. 1967, HC Papers, Ser. I, Box 4; Colin Greer, interview with Mike Clark, December 1990, copy in author's possession. An edited version of this interview appears in *Social Policy* 21 (Winter 1991): 53–57.

8. Quotation from Highlander Board of Directors meeting minutes, c. 1967, Horton Papers, Box 2. See also "Myles [Horton] Talking About Appalachia," May 1967, HREC Papers, Box 2; Proposed Highlander Center Project for Appalachian Poor, 1966, HREC Papers, Box 32; Horton to Abram Nightingale, October 2, 1966, HREC Papers, Box 97; Highlander Board of Directors meeting minutes, spring 1968, Horton Papers, Box 2; "Excerpts from an interview with Myles Horton, Director of Highlander Center, by James Coleman, a graduate student," February 1968, HC Papers, Ser. I, Box 4.

9. *Highlander Reports*, Fall 1968, HREC Papers, Box 1; C. Conrad Browne to Lucy Montgomery, August 9, 1968, HREC Papers, Box 97; Myles Horton, notes on southern mountain coalition, September 30, 1968, HREC Papers, Box 100; Horton, report on Poor People's Cultural Workshop, Resurrection City, Washington, D.C., May 20–June 29, 1968, HREC Papers, Box 109; transcript of meeting on Resurrection City and the Poor People's Campaign, June 6, 1968; Horton, notes on the Poor People's Campaign, June 23, 1968; Horton, report on Poor People's Coalition Convention, Washington, D.C., June 24–27, 1968; Horton, report on Highlander Center Poor People's Workshop, Hawthorne School, Washington, D.C., June 29–30, 1968; Joe

and Karen Mulloy, "Special Report on the Poor People's Campaign: The Appalachian Contingent," c. June 1968, HC Papers, Ser. III, Box 7; Michael Clark, critique of Charles Fager Ms. on Poor People's Campaign, December 13, 1968, Mike Clark Papers, Box 1, Highlander Research and Education Center, New Market, Tenn. (hereinafter cited as Clark Papers); Clark, personal notes on Resurrection City, c. 1968, Clark Papers, Box 2; Calvin Trillin, "Resurrection City: Metaphors," *New Yorker* 44 (June 15, 1968): 71–80; Charles Fager, *Uncertain Resurrection: The Poor People's Washington Campaign* (Grand Rapids, Mich.: Eerdmans, 1969); author's interview with Clark, August 10, 1978.

10. C. Conrad Browne to Norman Clement Stone, March 21, 1968, HREC Papers, Box 99; David E. Whisnant, *Modernizing the Mountaineer: People, Power, and Planning in Appalachia* (Boone, N.C.: Appalachian Consortium Press, 1980), 101–19, 191–208; John M. Glen, "The War on Poverty in Appalachia—A Preliminary Report," *Register of the Kentucky Historical Society* 87 (Winter 1989): 48–55.

11. Myles Horton to Cathy Male, September 3, 1969, HREC Papers, Box 97; "Transcript of Appalachian Staff Meeting," April 18, 1969, Horton Papers, Box 1.

12. C. Conrad Browne to Gerald Kreider, August 27, 1968, HREC Papers, Box 96; Browne to David L. Rothkop, November 26, 1968, HREC Papers, Box 98; Appalachian Program staff report, April 26, 1969, HC Papers, Ser. II, Box 1.

13. Proposal, Appalachian Self-Education Program, c. 1968; Myles Horton, "Suggestions for Appalachian Program," March 15–16, 1969, HREC Papers, Box 100; "The Highlander Center Program 1971," HREC Papers, Box 105; Horton to Dorothy Cotton, April 21, 1969, HREC Papers, Box 106; prospectus, Appalachian Education Program, c. 1968; Appalachian Program staff report, April 26, 1969; program proposal, Highlander Center, c. April 1970, HC Papers, Ser. II, Box 1; *Highlander Reports*, Summer 1969, Carl and Anne Braden Papers, Box 77, State Historical Society of Wisconsin, Madison; author's interview with Mike Clark, August 10, 1978; Clark to author, March 22, 1991.

14. Quotation from Almetor King, Mike Clark, and Michael Kline, "Report on the Appalachian Self-Education Program," April 1970, HC Papers, Ser. I, Box 1. See also Clark to "Herme," September 19, 1969, HC Papers, Ser. I, Box 1; "Text of a talk to VISTA workers by Mike Clark of the Highlander Center staff," October 1969, HC Papers, Ser. IV, Box 1; Clark, "Cult of the organizers" and other notes, c. 1969, Clark Papers, Box 2.

15. Appalachian Program staff report, April 26, 1969; King, Clark, and Kline, "Report on the Appalachian Self-Education Program," April 1970, HC Papers, Ser. I, Box 1; Clark, "Poor People Develop Poor People's Power," March 20, 1969; Clark and King, "The Appalachian Self-Education Staff Report to the Highlander Board, 1970–71"; "Highlander Center: The Appalachian Self-Education Program—A Two Year Report," October 1971, HC Pa-

pers, Ser. II, Box 1; Sue Easterling, "Greetings from the Youth Commission of the Council of the Southern Mountains," c. January 1969, Appalachian Volunteers Papers, Box 46, Southern Appalachian Archives, Berea College, Berea, Ky.; *Mountain Life & Work* 45 (May 1969): 3–9, 21–30; (June 1969): 3, 23; 46 (June 1970): 9–13, 22–23; Whisnant, *Modernizing the Mountaineer,* 26–28; John Glen, "The Council and the War," *Now and Then* 5 (Fall 1988): 4–12; Sue Ella Kobak to author, March 23, 1991.

16. King, Clark, and Kline, "Report on the Appalachian Self-Education Program," April 1970; Herman and Betty Liveright, report on Highlander activities, c. 1970, HC Papers, Ser. I, Box 1; Sam W. Howie, field report, July 8–12, 1969; Clark, field report, March 13, 1970; Clark, field trip report to Pickett Co. [Tenn.], March 12–13, 1971, HC Papers, Ser. I, Box 2; Charles Maggard, field reports, May 1971, October 4, 1971, HC Papers, Ser. I, Box 2A; Clark and King, "The Appalachian Self-Education Staff Report to the Highlander Board, 1970–71"; "Highlander Center: The Appalachian Self-Education Program—A Two Year Report," October 1971, HC Papers, Ser. II, Box 1; Howie, field report, July 18–24, 1969; Clark, field report, November 21, 1969, HREC Papers, Box 100.

17. Quotation from *Highlander Reports,* March 1971 (copies of this and all subsequent *Reports* are in the author's possession). See also Highlander staff meeting minutes, December 15, 1971, HC Papers, Ser. I, Box 2; Clark and King, "The Appalachian Self-Education Staff Report to the Highlander Board, 1970–71"; "Highlander Center: The Appalachian Self-Education Program—A Two Year Report," October 1971, HC Papers, Ser. II, Box 1; *Highlander Reports,* June 1974; George Vecsey, "Ideal of Unity Stirs Appalachian Poor," *New York Times,* April 23, 1972; author's interview with Clark, August 10, 1978; Clark to author, March 22, 1991.

18. Quotation from Highlander staff meeting minutes, November 7, 1972, HC Papers, Ser. I, Box 2. See also "Myles Horton's Field Trips," October 31–November 19, 1972; Mike Clark, report on Area Development District Meetings, Whitesburg, Ky., November 10–13, 1972, HC Papers, Ser. I, Box 2; *Highlander Reports,* June 1973, June 1974; Clark to author, March 22, 1991.

19. James Branscome, "Appalachia's People Begin to Unite," *South Today* 4 (December 1972): 3, 8.

20. "Jim Branscome's Staff Report," February 28–March 3, 1973, HC Papers, Ser. I, Box 2; Highlander staff meeting minutes, February 15–16, 1973, HC Papers, Ser. I, Box 2A; Charles Maggard, "Report to the Highlander Board of Directors," c. April 14–15, 1973, HC Papers, Current Files; author's interview with Mike Clark, August 10, 1978; author's interview with Maggard, April 1, 1991.

21. Highlander staff meeting minutes, December 15, 1971; November 7, 1972, HC Papers, Ser. I, Box 2; author's interview with Mike Clark, August 10, 1978; Clark to author, March 22, 1991.

22. Quotations from Highlander staff meeting minutes, December 13–14, 1974; April 11, 1975, HC Papers, Ser. I, Box 2A. See also Mike Clark, "Presi-

dent's Report to the Highlander Center Board of Directors," March 1974, HC Papers, Administrative Files; Clark, "President's Report to the Highlander Center Board of Directors," April 1974, HC Papers, Current Files; Highlander staff meeting minutes, October 18, 1976, Clark Papers, General Files; *Highlander Reports*, September 1978.

23. "Highlander Center in a Changing Appalachia: 1977–78 Program Report and Proposal for Further Activities," HC Papers, Administrative Files; Helen Lewis, "Health Program: Report 1977"; Proposal for Leadership Development Workshops for Emerging Leaders, July 1980; newsletter, *Appalachian Health Providers* 1 (October 1980); Highlander Center General Proposal, winter/spring 1982, HC Papers, Current Files; Highlander's 1976 Program Report; Ron Short, "Report to the Highlander Board: Appalachian Health Project," May 7, 1977; Lewis and Robin Gregg, "1979–80 Annual Report—Highlander Health Program," HC Papers, Financial [and other] Report Files; *Highlander Reports*, September 1978, July 1980.

24. "Highlander Center in a Changing Appalachia, 1977–78," HC Papers, Administrative Files; memorandum, Helen Lewis to Highlander Board of Directors, March 7, 1979; Proposal for Leadership Development Workshops for Emerging Leaders, July 1980; Highlander Center General Proposal, winter/spring 1982, HC Papers, Current Files; Highlander's 1976 Program Report; Bingham Graves, "Report to the Board: Labor Program," May 7–8, 1977; June Rostan, "Labor Education Program—Board Report," June 1980, HC Papers, Financial [and other] Report Files; *Highlander Reports*, September 1978; author's interview with Mike Clark, August 10, 1978.

25. "Highlander Center in a Changing Appalachia, 1977–78"; Helen M. Lewis, "Preparing Appalachian Communities for Changing Environmental and Occupational Health Needs: A Final Report," July 15, 1980, HC Papers, Administrative Files; John Gaventa, "Notes on Participatory Research at Highlander," c. 1981; Highlander Center General Proposal, winter/spring 1982; Final Report to the Ford Foundation from the Appalachian Public Policy Resources Program for Period of Four Years to April 19, 1982, HC Papers, Current Files; Highlander's 1976 Program Report; Gaventa, "Staff Report on Resource Center," April 19, 1977; "Resource Center Report to the Board," May 1980, HC Papers, Financial [and other] Report Files; *Highlander Reports*, September 1978; Patricia D. Beaver, "Participatory Research on Land Ownership in Rural Appalachia," in *Appalachia and America: Autonomy and Regional Dependence*, ed. Allen W. Batteau (Lexington: University Press of Kentucky, 1983), 252–66; Margaret Ripley Wolfe, *Kingsport, Tennessee: A Planned American City* (Lexington: University Press of Kentucky, 1987), 198–204; Mike Clark to author, March 22, 1991; author's interview with Lewis, March 23, 1991; author's interview with Joe Szakos, Kentuckians For The Commonwealth, April 10, 1991. Appalachian Land Ownership Task Force, *Who Owns Appalachia? Landownership and Its Impact* (Lexington: University Press of Kentucky, 1983), summarizes the findings of the land study project.

26. "Highlander Center in a Changing Appalachia, 1977–78"; Proposal for Funding of the Southern Appalachian Leadership Training Program (SALT), c. 1978–79, HC Papers, Administrative Files; Southern Appalachian Leadership Training Program, Final Narrative Report, October 1978; Highlander Center General Proposal, winter/spring 1982; workshop announcement, "'They'll Never Keep Us Down': The Role of the Cultural Worker in Our Changing South," May 28–31, 1982, HC Papers, Current Files; Guy and Candie Carawan, "Report to the Board: Music and Culture Program," May 7–8, 1977; Carawans, "Summary of Cultural Activities—1977"; Carawans, "Cultural Program: Report to the Board," May 1980, HC Papers, Financial [and other] Report Files; "Southern Appalachian Leadership Training Fellowship Program, Education Project," c. 1977–78; newsletter, *Alliance Advocate* 1 (February 1982), HC Papers, Research Files; Carawans, overview of Highlander cultural program, c. 1978, Clark Papers, General Files; *Appalachia in the Eighties: A Time for Action* (New Market, Tenn.: Appalachian Alliance, 1982).
27. Highlander Center General Proposal, winter/spring 1982, HC Papers, Current Files; Leslie Lilly, Southeast Women's Employment Coalition, to Mary Jane Harlan, National Organization for Women, July 25, 1979, HC Papers, Research Files; Bingham Graves, "Staff Report (June 1975 to March 1976)"; Highlander staff meeting minutes, August 17, 1977, Clark Papers, General Files; Leah Langworthy, "Struggles Within Struggles: Women's Experience at the Highlander Folk School" (thesis, Carleton College History Department, 1990); author's interview with Helen Lewis, March 23, 1991; Sue Ella Kobak to author, March 23, 1991; Joyce Dukes to author, April 16, 1991; Glen, *Highlander*, 52. See also Chris Weiss's discussion of the Southeast Women's Employment Coalition, Chapter 8 in this volume.
28. These examples are from Southern Appalachian Leadership Training Program, Final Narrative Report, October 1978; and Proposal for Funding of the Southern Appalachian Leadership Training Program (SALT), c. 1978–79, HC Papers, Current Files.
29. Quotations from Notes from the Highlander Board and Staff Workshop, January 7–9, 1983, HC Papers, General Correspondence Files. See also memorandum, Mike Clark to Highlander staff, November 30, 1979; Robin Gregg, "Setting the Context for Evaluation," January 27, 1981, HC Papers, Administrative Files; memorandum, Juliet Merrifield to Highlander staff, January 10, 1983, HC Papers, Current Files; memorandum, Doug Gamble to Highlander staff, January 2, 1980; memorandum, June Rostan to Highlander staff, January 10, 1980, HC Papers, Director's Files; Transition Discussion, March 16, 1983; notes on Staff Meeting Retreat, May 7, 1983, HC Papers, General Correspondence Files; *Highlander Reports*, March 1982; announcement, "Highlander Board Appoints New Director," c. June 19, 1982; Clark to author, March 22, 1991; author's interview with Charles Maggard, April 1, 1991.
30. Quotation from Notes from the Highlander Board and Staff Workshop, January 7–9, 1983, HC Papers, General Correspondence Files.

31. Highlander's Programmatic Work—1983, HC Papers, Administrative Files; Hubert E. Sapp to Richard Boone, Field Foundation, August 31, 1983; John Gaventa to Karen Menichell, Benton Foundation, December 16, 1983; Annual Report to Highlander's Board of Directors, April 9, 1985; Summary of Program Activities, FY86; Highlander Executive Committee meeting minutes, February 7–8, 1987; memorandum, Larry Wilson to Sapp, October 30, 1987; Highlander staff meeting minutes, March 7, 1988, HC Papers, Current Files; Highlander Executive Committee meeting minutes, January 14–15, 1984; Highlander proposal to the Fund for the Improvement of Postsecondary Education, April 10, 1984; Highlander Board of Directors meeting minutes, May 11–13, 1984; notes from Highlander Fall Retreat, September 17–18, 1984, HC Papers, Director's Files; Reports to the Highlander Board of Directors, April–May 1983; Highlander Board of Directors meeting minutes, May 20–22, 1983, HC Papers, General Correspondence Files; *Highlander Reports*, April 1983–Spring 1991; author's interview with Joe Szakos, April 10, 1991.

32. Quotation from Highlander Board of Directors meeting minutes, November 8–9, 1986, HC Papers, Current Files. See also memorandum, Jane Sapp to Program Staff, October 29, 1987; Statement of Highlander's Mission, November 1987; Highlander Program Staff meeting minutes, July 11, 1988, HC Papers, Current Files.

3

Racism and Organizing in Appalachia

Don Manning-Miller

Racism and the relationship of progressive movements to Black America have historically been central strategic issues for community organizers in the United States. Our history is cluttered with the cadavers of progressive coalitions undermined by white racism: the abolitionists, women's suffrage, the Reconstruction labor movement, the Populists, the Progressives, the Booker T. Washington entente, New Dealism, and the labor crusade of the thirties.[1]

For those of us who know this history and who were reborn, shaped, and educated in the fiery crucible of the civil rights and black liberation movements of the sixties and seventies, the current state of community organizing in Appalachia brings a depressing sense of déjà vu—a return in practice, if not in intent, to a period of naive, myopic whiteness which hopes that effective and progressive results will somehow mystically emerge from a process of organizing and struggle that fails to confront the cultural conservatism and the racism of its constituency.

After many decades of sometimes faddish, sometimes serious attention to the unique history and semi-colonial reality of Appalachia by politicians, scholars, activists, and organizers, the region has inherited a broad and impressive array of popular people's organizations of varying longevity. These include self-help, service-oriented organizations such as craft and credit cooperatives and child care centers, single-issue pressure groups, community economic development groups, and larger, multi-issue organizations with relatively sophisticated analytical, research, training, and political action components. As a result primarily of demographic dictates, particularly in the rural and highland areas, the constituencies that have been organized are predominantly or entirely white. Virtually all of the organizers, activists, and leaders are white as well.

Most of the organizations and the organizers and activists are committed either explicitly or implicitly to combating racism and to building a multiracial people's coalition for progressive social change. However, these generic commitments, often found in applications for funding and more rarely in organizational brochures and literature, tend to translate in practice into private expressions of deep-seated but perplexed and frustrated concern. The commitments remain for most organizations at an abstract and unattended level with little or no program for implementation. When the issue of combating racism is raised for discussion in organizer and activist peer groups, the response is often one of confused frustration or defensiveness and hostility. "Oh, our people are *so* racist!" confides an organization staffer in rural Kentucky in a fairly typical reaction. Or, as an experienced organizer in an urban Appalachian community plaintively expressed it, "I wish the issue of race would just go away and never be heard again, don't you?" In short, although racism is rampant and omnipresent in predominantly white Appalachia, it is not being addressed by progressive citizen organizations in any systematic or effective manner.

The almost universal "approach" of organizations in the region to racism is one of avoidance. The issue is submerged and evaded in the hope that it will simply not arise. There are both personal and theoretical reasons for this. On the personal level, organizers and activists avoid the issue because they lack the experience and knowledge to address the problem effectively. Furthermore, they recognize and fear the power of cultural racism and white supremacy among the people they are trying to organize.

On the theoretical level, conscious organizing decisions provide reassuring rationales for neglecting racism as an issue. There are at least two strands in this decision-making process. First, racism is assigned the status of a minor tactical problem, rather than a strategic issue central to organizing. This allows organizers and leaders to be satisfied with an *intent* to deal with the issue as an immediate tactical problem *if* it is raised or comes up in the context of their work. In some cases contingency plans are made for taking individuals aside to ameliorate racial conflict on a personal level so that the overall work of the organization will not be hindered by the divisive appearance of prejudice or racism.

The second strand is drawn from the fundamentalist scripture of organizing technology, which says that no issue that is divisive or might aggravate differences among the potential constituency should be addressed or actively pursued. Obviously this tenet, especially when combined with the intent to face the issue tactically, can lead to a "good faith" decision that defines racism as a potential problem to be dealt with in the future. The effect is to methodologically subordinate the question of the relationship of the organization to black people—either those who are potentially part of a local or regional constituency or Black America in general—to the sensitivities of the immediate, existing white constituency.

The preponderance of whiteness in the general population and in the organizational constituency and leadership in Appalachia, coupled with the lack of a positive program for dealing with racism, often leads to self-duplicating outreach strategies. All-white organizations may be created in areas or counties that have black residents—particularly when larger groups that began their organizing activities in all-white or predominantly white mountain counties begin moving into more racially mixed areas. Since outreach and expansion often occur as a result of personal contact between active members and acquaintances in the new areas or by invitations resulting from publicity, the initial contact group is quite likely to be white also. This results in a pattern either of de facto segregated targeting or of responding to segregated initiatives of white groups in new areas that may contain more black people. This does not necessarily reflect the desire or intent of the organizers, but rather the natural growth process of an organization that begins with a white constituency and has no structural requirements for racial inclusiveness.

For organizers, activists, and some leaders, the primary mechanism for multiracial exposure and interaction is the regional or inter-area meeting. Examples are the periodic gatherings staged by organizations such as the Appalachian Development Projects Committee of the Commission on Religion in Appalachia, the Appalachian Community Fund, the now defunct Appalachian Alliance, research and educational organizations such as the Highlander Center, ad hoc issue-based alliances, and coalitional organizations such as the Southern Empowerment Project. All have played a vital role in keeping some form of multiracial communication flowing to and from predominantly white Appalachian organizations.

The importance of these ongoing contacts in supplying a foundation for cooperative work should not be minimized. However, the overall effectiveness and impact on local organizational constituencies are surely quite limited, because these meetings are removed from the normal work and life of the organizations and usually involve a relatively few organizational leaders and members. The latter is true even though some organizations rotate the leaders and members who participate in the regional affairs and coalitions or attempt to expose members to these experiences by hosting the meetings or workshops themselves. Further, while such groupings provide an opportunity for interracial exposure, they normally do not address the issue of racism itself or the importance of facing the issue in local organizing work.

Participation in these broader-based regional meetings has been supplemented to a limited extent by leaders' and members' visits to multiracial or predominantly black organizations in other areas of the South. This form of learning, sharing, and building solidarity is encouraging, but still outside the everyday life of the organizations and greatly restricted by time and money constraints.

The newsletters and newspapers published by many Appalachian organizations offer an avenue for exposing their white constituency to black issues, activities, and organizations. But a review of randomly selected newsletters of two of the largest and most effective Appalachian membership organizations reveals little use of this potentially powerful medium for educating members about the destructive effects of racism or about the work and needs of black people and organizations. In eleven issues from 1989 and the first half of 1990, the *SOCM Sentinel*, the newsletter of Save Our Cumberland Mountains, did not contain a picture of a single black person, even in broad crowd shots, except for one black official behind the podium at a hearing. In two issues the presence of black people at regional meetings of other organizations was mentioned.[2] *Balancing the Scales*, the newspaper published by Kentuckians For The Commonwealth, included pictures of black people in six issues out of the twenty-two examined from 1987 through April of 1990.[3]

Neither publication mentioned issues of race, and each was written from a uniformly "color-blind"' editorial perspective that fails to address the diversity and the economic and cultural contradictions in potential constituencies and among organizations which are potential allies. In this regard the relatively new but increasingly influential newspaper the *Appalachian Reader: An Independent Citizens Quarterly*, which is not affiliated with any organization, is making a significant contribution. The editor of the *Reader* clearly has made a conscious decision to keep the activities of black people and organizations before the readership. Coverage includes reports on meetings of black organizations, articles and information about anti-racism workshops available in the region, and discussions of problems and issues peculiar to black people in Appalachia.[4] Although in its first five issues (fall of 1988 through spring of 1990) the paper did not directly treat racism in editorials or columns, the style of its coverage makes it an important force for promoting racially inclusive solidarity and understanding in the region.

The membership and leadership training and education programs, and the employment patterns of the organizations themselves, are additional areas where racism could be addressed both directly and indirectly. Significantly, the training curriculum of Kentuckians For The Commonwealth, the organization with the most sophisticated leader and member development program in the region, did not as of spring 1991 contain material that addresses racism. While such curriculum materials are not readily available to outsiders, discussions with trainers and organizers and a review of newsletter articles on training sessions indicate that such material is probably missing from most organizational training programs. The Southern Empowerment Project, an organizer-training program sponsored by a broad coalition of membership organizations in the Upper

South and Appalachia, regularly includes a component on personal and structural racism, and the Catholic Committee of Appalachia has sponsored regional workshops by the People's Institute for Survival and Beyond on "Undoing Racism." These are important and laudable initiatives, but they cannot compensate for the general omission of education on racism within the training components of the organizations themselves.

Opportunities for breaching the latent racism of white constituencies and providing occasions to work with black people in a principled relationship are lost when the vast majority of personnel—employees, contractors, organizers, administrators, trainers, and resource people—are white. Having black people in responsible positions and roles within an organization provides direct experience in black-white working relations and to some extent requires white people to begin dealing with their own prejudice and the racism within the organization. While it is admittedly difficult to recruit black staffers to work in predominantly white areas, this structural tactic could and should be pursued by organizations with a commitment to multiracial diversity, cooperation, and alliance. When organizers consider hiring black organizers, inevitably these discussions pertain to hiring for outreach to black geographic areas and constituencies, not for work with white chapters or organizations. More positively, outside the ranks of membership organizations, the Appalachian Community Fund (ACF), which provides small grants to people's organizations in the region, has hired a black executive director and thereby structured a situation in which the white constituencies of funded organizations must to some extent put aside their racism and deal in a principled manner with a black executive. Devising such structural situations in which people's false interest in their white prejudice is put into tension with their real self-interest can be an important component of an overall program against racism.

In sum, the limited exposure of a few members and leaders to black people at regional and inter-area gatherings and through infrequent visits to organizations with black constituencies, and the restricted coverage given to black people and organizations in the newsletters and newspapers of the various Appalachian groups, offer only a semblance of a program against racism. The issue of racism itself is virtually never raised directly, and constituencies are not provided with either structural experiences in working with black people in key roles within organizations or opportunities to learn about the destructive and divisive role of racism in the history of people's movements.

These limitations have several broad and important implications. First, they mean that racism remains a powerful, latent force in the mountains and within the citizen organizations themselves—a force that could burst forth at any time and undermine much of what these organizations have accomplished. Second, the failure of organizers to devise meaningful ways to confront the race issue accommodates their organizations and members to the very fabric of American racism and reaction, leaving them uncritically aligned with the social and economic institutions of racism.[5] Further, failure to confront these institutions and the implicit acceptance of the racist culture undergirds racist practices and inevitably leads to their incorporation into the life and culture of the organizations themselves.

These potentially devastating weaknesses cannot be ignored if community organizing in Appalachia is to be an important ingredient in the creation of a broad, pluralistic, democratic constituency for progressive social change in the United States. For racism—personal, cultural, and institutional—is the single greatest obstacle to achieving hoped-for coalitions and alliances.[6]

From its roots in the late seventeenth century, the role of American racism has been to divide the population into hostile and competing groups. The resulting separation of social forces on the basis of race has proved a critical flaw that time and again has ravaged the popular movements of working people, farmers, and ordinary citizens of this country. Anne Braden, who has devoted most of her working life to organizing southern whites for alliances with black people and organizations, has observed that an essential contributing factor to the failure of southern movements of the past was the fact "that none of them ever really succeeded in bridging the gap between black and white. . . . In the past when the chips were down white Southerners, no matter how oppressed, cared more about illusory privileges of white skin than the unity with their black brothers and sisters that might have changed their life condition."[7] Devising methods and gaining experience in overcoming this reality must become a central concern. As the historian Lerone Bennett, Jr., summarizes the problem, "The formation of a progressive social force cannot be solved until the problem of race is solved."[8]

Ultimately the avoidance of the race issue in Appalachia flows from a deep-seated, cynical belief among organizers that their white constituents cannot and will not change—that their members' racism is so strong that it cannot be challenged and overcome in the ongoing process of organizing and struggle. Braden says that this is one of two myths that victimize white organizers. The other is the ill-founded hope that if the problem is ignored and not mentioned, it will somehow disappear of its own accord. "No white Southerner ever changed his racial views because he was protected from looking at the issue," she reminds us. "Rather change came when events literally forced him to think about it. We must seek to create conditions in which more and more people will be required by their own needs

to face this question."[9] Braden concludes that white people must be organized around their problems but then immediately helped to understand
that the problems of Appalachia, the South, and the nation "will never be
solved unless white and black people unite in common cause. Failing this
our own efforts at best . . . cannot succeed. At worst we may create some
Frankenstein monsters we never intended—new racist groups."[10]

However grim the assessment of the power of racism, this is not
a perspective that lacks faith in the ability of the southern or Appalachian white to change—to understand her or his self-interest in terms of
unity with black people. Quite the contrary, an organizing approach that
insists on dealing openly and systematically with racism displays precisely
such a confidence, while approaches that systematically avoid the issue
most often flow from the doubt and cynicism mentioned above. A realistic
understanding of the latent, destructive power of racism, coupled with a
belief that people can and will change, requires the development of direct approaches to resolving and defusing the issue before it explodes and
destroys another would-be progressive American movement.[11]

The key to a positive program is the inclusion of specific work
against racism as a central strategic component of organizing. The only
way to work against racism is to work against it! At the most general level,
this is a matter of approach, of strategic vision and simple moral integrity. The approach is roughly the opposite of the one being taken now.
Instead of avoiding the issue of racism, organizers and activists must look
for every opportunity to raise the issue in ways that help people come
to grips with it. This requires a systematic, intentional, ongoing process
within each organization. Such a program cannot be deferred until racism
emerges as an issue on its own, but must be prospective and build a base
of understanding *before* racism becomes a tactical issue in an emotionally
charged and polarized situation. The aim of the process is to create a per-
vasive, organizational ethos that is incompatible with racism in any form,
one which helps white people see that putting aside their own prejudice,
opposing institutional racism, and building multiracial organizations and
coalitions is in *their* interest.

The essence of effective educational work against racism is simply
telling white people the truth.[12] This involves using all available media and
organizational forms to expose the historical role of white racism in weak-
ening and defeating organizations and movements—helping people to
internalize an awareness of how American racism was developed, how
and for whose real benefit it functions, and how it is sustained. It involves
developing an understanding of the often illusory and always superficial
benefits of "whiteness" and the necessity of effective multiracial alliances to
the success of one's organizational goals and the struggle for a democratic

future. It involves approaching the issues and planning organizational tactics in such a way that the need for interracial alliances and cooperation is clear, so that personal and organizational goals are in creative tension with the residual racism of the constituency.

This approach will not, of course, lead to instantaneous conversion experiences, and it must not become an exercise in personal attack, self-righteousness, or guilt-tripping. It must be an educational, interpretive, and experiential process that helps the people come to grips with the deeply held cultural preconceptions to which all whites in our society are socialized. It should not involve preaching or moralizing but the creation of an atmosphere of positive reinforcement for thinking through and rejecting self-defeating stereotypes within a practical context of organizational work and political reality.

While there are no hard and fast rules and we all have much to learn about which methods are most effective, the following are some common tactical measures and suggestions.

PERSONNEL: Black people should always be part of organizational personnel. Optimally, black organizers, leaders, and administrators should participate from the very start of any organizing approach. Where lack of a black population makes hiring black staffers difficult, internships and organizational staff exchanges should be used. Organizational resources should be employed to hire black consultants, resource people, and speakers and to strive for maximum organizational exposure to black leadership. White resource people like Anne Braden and others who have a history of anti-racist work with white people should be used. Black organizers should not be hired exclusively for work with black constituencies, but should work with white chapters and the organization at large as well. In addition to the benefits of the working relationships established, this sends a clear message of the organization's anti-racist intent. Throughout, it should be remembered that the burden of working against racism must never be borne primarily by black people. Work against racism must become an organizational agenda that is carried on by white people for white people so that the issue is never portrayed as simply a matter of black interest.

REGIONAL MEETINGS AND CONFERENCES: The contribution of regional gatherings to interracial communication and experience should certainly be continued and encouraged. However, organizers of the meetings should put a much higher priority on including black leadership and resource people in predominant roles. Specific program material on racism, its importance, and ways to work against it in local organizations should be included in a way that involves all meeting participants and not just the faithful few who show up at racism workshops. Organizations should attempt to increase the number of members who attend such meetings.

LEADERSHIP AND STAFF EXCHANGES AND VISITS: Visits to and personnel swaps with organizations that have a multiracial or predominantly black constituency are excellent learning experiences for everyone involved. Although expensive and therefore limited, such visits are important. An excellent example of this type of productive interchange was the October 1990 joint retreat between JONAH and SOCM in Tennessee. The former is a predominantly black community organizing group based in a number of west Tennessee communities; SOCM, predominantly white, is based primarily in the eastern part of the state. The joint retreat was attended by a significant number of the members of both organizations, and workshops were devoted to common, practical organizing problems and issues. Most significantly, the retreat included a session entitled "Celebrating/Exploring Our Differences," which was an "opportunity for both groups to share some uncomfortable experiences stemming from racial and cultural differences."[13] A concluding strategy session, "Getting Power in the State," launched an effective and hopeful working relationship between these important organizations.

NEWSLETTERS AND NEWSPAPERS: Organizational media are a primary tool in work against racism. They should provide maximum exposure to black activities and report on issues of particular concern to black constituencies while emphasizing the importance and commonality of these interests. Successful examples of multiracial alliances, and examples of the need for such alliances, should receive priority coverage. Editorials and columns should examine racism itself as an issue and describe ways to combat racism and racist ideology. Black contributors should be used for articles, reviews, and columns.

EDUCATION AND TRAINING: Organizations do training and leadership development on every conceivable obstacle to organizing success except racism. This potent component of organizational development must be effectively used in overcoming racism. A curriculum must be designed that covers the history and function of racism, the necessity for multiracial alliances, the commonality of black and white interests—all the broad and particular facets of the issue. This is a primary arena for "telling white people the truth" and helping them work through the issues in a supportive situation. Very often it may be helpful to utilize outside trainers for some of these sessions. But care must always be taken to ensure that racism is treated as an organizational, not an outside, issue.

STRUCTURAL REQUIREMENTS FOR RACIAL INCLUSIVENESS: As a matter of policy, all-white groups or chapters should never be organized in areas with a black population. Just as a minimum number of people are required before an organization is formalized or a chapter formed, there should be a structural requirement for significant and effective participation of black people. As organizers work with a potential new group to increase participation, aggressive outreach to black constituents can be done. Often the first move into new territory should be work with a potential black constituency. Otherwise, a period of listening to black people and paying special attention to local black issues and concerns should lead to defining and working on issues of importance to them—and issues where the commonality of interests helps draw the constituencies together. In areas where groups with a white makeup already exist, there should be a program of continuous outreach along these lines.

COALITIONAL EXPERIENCES: While history shows that racism does not magically go away as a result of participating in joint activities, common work in multiracial organizations and alliances within a context of mutual respect and anti-racist understanding is often an essential ingredient in overcoming racial stereotypes. Organizations should define issues and plan tactics in ways that maximize work in these formats. Such mutual efforts, however, cannot always be concerned with issues defined by whites who then ask black people and organizations to work on these predefined campaigns. Joint strategy and issue identification sessions should be held, with full and equal participation in setting aims and directions. White and predominantly white organizations must join in support of efforts initiated by black organizations and must address issues defined from their perspective.

In sum, work against racism within Appalachian organizations has three ultimate goals. The first is to enable members to identify institutional racism in our society as the divisive enemy it is and to make an unqualified commitment to oppose and eliminate it. The second is to promote an understanding of the links between multiracial cooperation and organizational success. The third is to achieve the commitment of all members to thoroughgoing equality within and among organizations and in society at large. This is the fight against racism. Without such an effort there is no principled basis for alliance, and stated opposition to racism becomes sheer rhetoric and self-indulgence. At stake is the viability of Appalachian organizing as part of a progressive social force for change, and perhaps our hopes for a successful people's movement in our time.

Notes

1. For an overview of the role of racism in these popular movements, see Robert Allen (with the collaboration of Pamela Allen), *Reluctant Reformers: Racism and Social Reform* (Washington, D.C.: Howard University Press, 1974); Ted Allen, "White Supremacy in U.S. History: A Speech at the National Guardian Forum," pamphlet (Chicago, 1973); W. E. B. DuBois, *Black Reconstruction in America 1860–1880* (New York: Meridian Books, 1964); Lerone Bennett, Jr., *The Challenge of Blackness* (Chicago: Johnson Publishing Company, 1972); Lerone Bennett, Jr., *Before the Mayflower: A History of Black America*, 5th ed. (New York: Penguin Books, 1982); and Vincent Copeland, *Southern Populism and Black Labor* (New York: World View Publishers, 1973).

2. Issues reviewed were March/April 1989; May 1989; June 1989; July/August 1989; September 1989; October 1989; November/December 1989; February/March 1990; April 1990; May 1990; and June 1990.

3. Issues reviewed were January 1987; July 23, 1987; September 24, 1987; October 22, 1987; November 19, 1987; February 11, 1988; February 18, 1988; February 23, 1989; March 23, 1989; April 20, 1989; May 25, 1989; July 20, 1989; August 24, 1989; September 28, 1989; October 26, 1989; November 16, 1989; January 25, 1990; February 8, 1990; February 22, 1990; April 5, 1990; April 19, 1990; and April 24, 1990.

4. Issues reviewed were Fall 1988; April 1988; Summer 1989; Winter 1990; and Spring 1990.

5. Parallel developments outside Appalachia are traced by Gary Delgado in *Organizing the Movement: The Roots and Growth of ACORN* (Philadelphia: Temple University Press, 1986), 197. Delgado concludes: "With regard to issues of both race and gender, ACORN and the other community organizing networks replicate and reproduce the values of the dominant society and culture."

6. This assertion is not intended to diminish the critical importance of the interrelated issues of class and gender, which require separate treatment, but to posit that the peculiar historical development and socialization process of the United States make racism the central, initial barrier that must be overcome in unifying a broad people's movement.

7. Anne Braden, "Basic Issues in the Movement, Today's Challenge to Organize the White South," *Southern Patriot* 25 (August 1970): 7.

8. Bennett, *The Challenge of Blackness*, 147.

9. Braden, "Basic Issues," 5.

10. Ibid.

11. Michael Ansara and S. M. Miller relate the reality of racism to belief and confidence in people in "Democratic Populism," in *The New Populism: The Politics of Empowerment*, ed. Harry C. Boyte and Frank Riessman (Philadelphia: Temple University Press, 1986), 148: "The association of localism, traditionalism, and populism with a dark side of racism and demagogy is

historical reality. Appreciation of the deep well springs of democratic decency and common sense in Americans should not obscure the continuing traditions and threat of racism, anti-intellectualism, and chauvinism that are deeply imbedded in the political culture in general and that of ethnic blue-collar Americans in particular."

12. Bennett, *The Challenge of Blackness*, 99.
13. *Jonah Story* (newsletter) 11, no. 1 (November 1990).

4

From Fussin' to Organizing
Individual and Collective Resistance at Yellow Creek

Sherry Cable

History will tell you that you can't organize mountain folks. Well, you can, but the problem to be addressed has to be flagrant. It has to be common. And it has to be such that everybody wants something done about it.

Larry Wilson, president of
Yellow Creek Concerned Citizens

The stereotype of the weak-willed, dependent Appalachian is revived each time Appalachians are "discovered" by outsiders. From the comic-strip portrayal of the television series *The Beverly Hillbillies* to the well-intentioned ennobling of Kai Erikson's study of the destruction by flood of a West Virginia coal community,[1] Appalachians have been depicted as meek and apathetic. They are perceived as submissively accepting privations that non-Appalachians would not, and as culturally, perhaps constitutionally, incapable of resistance to unjust conditions.

The stereotype of the docile Appalachian will no doubt remain popular, one more burden laid on by outsiders. But Appalachians are not docile. In fact, they are not all that different from the outsiders who casually blame them for their own poverty and exploitation. If Appalachia and its people are distinguished from other social groups, it is not in terms of personality traits, or even culture. What is significant about Appalachians is their history of systematic, routine oppression. Given that context, their behavior has not been appreciably different from that of other oppressed groups.

The argument that economic oppression produces quiescence—that is, the absence of collective resistance—is presented in John Gaventa's *Power and Powerlessness*.[2] Drawing upon Steven Lukes'[3] thesis that quiescence is a function of power relationships, Gaventa provides a revealing analysis of the lack of rebellion in an Appalachian valley by describing the three dimensions or "faces" of power and how each contributed to the quiescence of the local residents.

Ted and Sue Smith relied on their homegrown vegetables to supplement the family's income until Yellow Creek Concerned Citizens discovered that the soil was contaminated. (*Michael S. Clark*)

Gaventa argues that an elite not only makes decisions that affect the entire community (the first dimension of power), but also prevents certain issues from even entering decision-making arenas (the second dimension), especially when the issues are of concern to non-elites and change is counter to elite interests. Further (in the third dimension of power), elite influence in the socialization process combines with the psychological adaptations that non-elites make to their powerless state to generate in them "an instilled conception of the appropriate relationship between the leaders and the led."[4]

The history of the Yellow Creek valley of southeastern Kentucky mirrors that of most of central Appalachia: a century of economic exploitation by outsiders that left natives land-poor and dependent on industry, primarily coal mining, for their livelihoods. In the new stratification system imposed in the valley, outsiders and a handful of natives with ties to them held positions of power, while the miners and mountaineers were relegated to the lowest positions in the social hierarchy. The welfare of those at the bottom has seldom claimed the attention of those at the top. And with elites controlling the institutions that socialize the young, the power relationships themselves had come to be accepted in a general way. But, at least in regard to one issue, quiescence was not the result. How is the discrepancy to be explained?

Gaventa's focus was on *collective* resistance to oppression, but there is an alternative form: *individual* resistance. Individual resistance is possible in circumstances where collective resistance is not. Thus, a relevant issue in regard to Appalachian resistance is not the infrequency of its occurrence, as many would claim. This volume of essays itself clearly documents resistance. What is important are the conditions under which resistance in Appalachia has been collective rather than individual.

In this chapter I describe individual and collective resistance in the Yellow Creek valley and analyze the transition between the two forms of rebellion. Yellow Creek has been polluted since the late nineteenth century, when a tanning company began operations in the city of Middlesboro and first dumped the waste from production processes into the stream. Over the years, many individuals registered complaints with various city and state officials, but to no avail. In the late 1960s, the tannery's production technology was changed and creek conditions deteriorated even further. Individual complaints increased. By 1976, residents claim, the creek was dead. Despite periodically being driven from their homes by the smell and forced to give up all recreational uses of the creek, residents did not collectively resist the pollution until 1980, when they formed a citizens' protest organization, Yellow Creek Concerned Citizens (YCCC).

Three questions guide this analysis of the resistance at Yellow Creek.

Why was the contamination of the creek met with only *individual* resistance for so long? What conditions facilitated the transformation from *individual* to *collective* resistance? How was the form of collective resistance in the valley shaped by historical conditions?[5]

Individual Resistance at Yellow Creek

Residents' complaints about the creek began virtually with the earliest operations of the Middlesboro tannery. A retired tannery worker and Yellow Creek native recalled:

> That tannery was put up there more than ninety years ago. And as far back as I can remember, somebody's been fussin' about it. People would fuss. Get up petitions. Few weeks would go by and there'd be nothing about what happened or if anybody had done anything about it. Then somebody else would get to fussin'. Sayin' it stinks, their stock won't drink it. A couple of weeks and it would blow over again. On and on and on. Ever since I was a kid.[6]

This periodic "fussin'" was individual resistance, and its character reflected both the values and the history of the residents of the Yellow Creek valley. It demonstrates their recognition that an injustice was being done to them. Traditional rural values sustained an ideology of egalitarianism within this very stratified social system.[7] Their belief in fairness led many residents to feel anger that the tannery was interfering with their normal activities. And so they "fussed" because they could not swim, wade, fish, boat, or even sit near the creek on some days. As one resident put it, "It was so unfair to live with the creek on both sides of my kids and it couldn't be used for nothin'. Wasn't even fit to boat in."

Despite a seldom-voiced consensus over creek conditions, collective resistance was inhibited by a social legacy of the coal companies' economic oppression of the area. The small, isolated communities that dot the valley today are the remnants of the old coal camps, the self-contained communities built by coal companies to house miners. To hinder union organizing in the coalfields during the 1930s, coal company officials induced competition among the camps by encouraging baseball clubs and other sports events. This competitiveness extended into social relations in general, so that hostility and mistrust characterized relationships among residents of the coal camps. Dating across community boundaries was discouraged, and fist fights often occurred when such norms were transgressed. Several activists have recounted incidents of teenaged boys from one camp provoking a fight with their counterparts in another simply by swimming in a spot known to be favored by the others.

The competitiveness of the coal camps outlasted the coal companies themselves and generated a kind of cultural Balkanization. When the major coal companies left the area, intercommunity suspicions remained. An activist explained: "The communities within the valley were separate, didn't have much to do with each other. That's just how we lived and how we did. You really didn't feel comfortable going into another community."

The coal companies had destroyed the "free spaces" that many argue are necessary for the growth of democratic movements.[8] Instead, residents kept to their own small communities, without the wider base of solidarity in the valley that could have facilitated collective resistance to the pollution of the creek. Larry Wilson, the president of YCCC, described this isolation: "People just went to work, to church, and home. We didn't tell each other what we were doing, individually, about the creek because it was private, like religion and politics." Another activist summarized the ethic succinctly: "Whatever a man did was *his* business. If my cow drank out of Yellow Creek and died, that was *my* problem."

Economic oppression and rigid stratification also blocked collective resistance at Yellow Creek in ways attributed by Gaventa to the third dimension of power.[9] Collective resistance in the past had typically been met with physical force, most notably in union organizing, and family histories included accounts of that era. Residents were aware, through either direct or vicarious experience, of the consequences of being on the brunt end of social control efforts. It was not that they were opposed to collective resistance; it was simply not included in their repertoire of behavior. When asked why he thought organizing had not taken place sooner, Wilson paused for a full minute and finally replied, "No one thought of it." Another activist explained: "Nobody I know of had any real strong objections to organizing. It just didn't occur to anyone as a possibility."

The methods of individual resistance that valley residents used corresponded with their generally conservative views. That is, their methods were not radical. Instead of engaging in acts of individual sabotage or terrorism, they went through the proper channels, registering complaints with various levels of government.

Residents first appealed to the Middlesboro city government, which had for decades accommodated the tannery by accepting all untreated tannery waste into the municipal sewage treatment plant. However, plant equipment was inadequate for dealing with such waste. Thus, when effluent from the sewage plant was dumped into Yellow Creek, the inevitable result was pollution: reddish-black foam up to three feet deep, black water the consistency of maple syrup, and a stench that made the eyes sting.

Periodically, the tannery dumped directly into the creek, bypassing even the minimal treatment of the sewage plant. Fish kills were frequent, with dead fish lining the banks of the creek far along its fourteen-mile stretch. After the change to a chromium tanning process in the late 1960s, the pollution problems worsened dramatically. Tannery waste actually destroyed equipment at the sewage treatment plant and rendered the effluent toxic. Fish kills became more common, and many of the fish that survived had ugly sores.

Complaints to the city and tannery were fruitless. An activist spoke of his family's frustration: "My uncle told me in the 1940s that he'd been trying for thirty years to get the creek cleaned up. He told me, 'You can't do nothin' with them scalawags.'"

Nor was the state government responsive to individual complaints. One woman began calling state officials in 1969. Occasionally she was able to get an inspector from the Department of Natural Resources to come to Yellow Creek to collect water samples for testing. She eventually discovered that the samples were provided by either the tannery or the sewage treatment plant: "They [the state inspectors] would pick up the samples that were taken before they even got there. They were supposed to come here and get their samples themselves, but that's not how it was."[10] Later, using the Freedom of Information Act, residents found that state files fully documented this woman's calls. But nothing had been done to clean up the creek. "Nothing's ever come of anything that involved the state," an activist concluded.

One of the co-founders of the citizens' organization had been involved in telephone calls, letter writing, and petition gathering since 1969. He and a cousin instigated a hearing that resulted in the city's obtaining federal funds to renovate the sewage treatment plant so that it could handle the tannery waste. Renovations were completed in 1975, but

> as far as the effect it had on cleaning the creek up—you couldn't tell it. There was no improvement whatsoever. If anything, it came worse. I was tired of it. I was tired of the ninety-dollar phone bills that I was paying. And I was ready to quit. You take on the Establishment one-on-one, you get your head beat in.[11]

The Transformation of Individual Resistance

Individual resistance to the city and tannery was transformed into collective resistance only when relevant conditions changed. Beginning in the late 1960s, changes in the social structure countered historical conditions and opened the way for community mobilization. These changes are discussed in detail elsewhere,[12] so I will merely summarize them here.

At the national level the environmental movement set up an ideological foundation that promoted and framed the definition of environmental grievances. Public opinion polls showed significant levels of environmental concern among the general population, generating and reinforcing a kind of "cognitive liberation"[13] in which environmental grievances were legitimated.

The national environmental movement also contributed to the 1969 passage of the National Environmental Protection Act, which created the Environmental Protection Agency (EPA). A major portion of the agency's funds for improving water quality was directed toward the renovation of municipal sewage treatment plants to better equip them for handling high-technology wastes. With federal aid available for such renovations, Middlesboro officials were less reluctant to admit that there was a problem with Yellow Creek. Their request in 1970 for a federal grant to upgrade the sewage treatment plant was their first public acknowledgment that the creek was indeed polluted by tannery waste. By creating greater legitimacy for claims of environmental injustices and by spurring legislation that allowed Middlesboro to acknowledge the pollution problem, the national environmental movement helped to set the stage for the transformation of individual to collective resistance at Yellow Creek.

Before collective resistance could emerge, however, changes were also necessary at the local level. The first to occur was an increase in residents' distress, which came about through the greater deterioration of the creek. The tannery was bought by a Chicago firm in 1960, and within five years the new owners had replaced the vegetable-based tanning process with a chromium-based technology. As noted above, it quickly became apparent that the sewage treatment plant could not handle such highly corrosive waste. An unprecedented increase in fish kills and visible pollution brought a concomitant increase in individual complaints. It was these renewed complaints that led in 1970 to the city's request for federal funds to renovate the treatment plant.

A much more important local change that paved the way toward collective resistance was a shift in the interaction patterns among valley residents. The cultural Balkanization that was a legacy of the coal camp era was mitigated by the consolidation of the rural public schools in the 1970s. Following a national trend in rural areas at the time, several small schools were replaced with the consolidated Bell County High School. The children of those who had earlier fought over swimming holes now attended the new high school, where localism was not so easy to preserve. The younger generation came to identify much less strongly with their

communities of birth than did their parents. As friendships among teenagers spanned communities, parents were dragged along and community
boundaries soon began to weaken: the potential for a valleywide sense of
solidarity was increased.

The final piece fell into place when Larry Wilson returned with his
family to Yellow Creek. Wilson had worked for the state of Kentucky as
a hospital administrator, dealing with the state's tuberculosis hospitals.
When state officials wanted to close the hospitals, Wilson argued for con-
verting some of them to black lung facilities. The state refused, arguing
that it would hurt private medical practice. After some wrangling, Wilson
resigned and returned to his native Yellow Creek valley to farm, bringing
with him the organizational experience, leadership skills, and knowledge
of political routines that challenges to the Establishment require. The stage
was set for collective resistance in the valley.

The Evolution of Collective Resistance

The citizens' organization that led the collective resistance efforts beginning in 1980 came about through the prodding of two women. Both had
been distressed over the creek pollution for years and had urged their
husbands to do something about it. The women did not know one another
prior to mobilization. They discovered their shared discontent through
their teenaged children. They goaded, teased, and dared their husbands
into meeting with one another. The men finally acceded, and in July 1980
YCCC was formed.

The group began with three married couples who met at a picnic
table in Cumberland Gap State Park, fearing repercussions if the "Clique"
discovered what they were doing. After the initial meeting, the founders
telephoned some trusted acquaintances, and 14 people attended the second meeting. These members then telephoned neighbors and people they
knew who had been fighting the creek pollution for years, and 28 people
attended the third meeting. Feeling less fear because of their numbers,
they went public with membership cards, and within a year YCCC had
over four hundred members. An activist explained the snowballing membership that gathered people who had not known one another previously:
"They saw a concentrated effort coming down the line. And they liked
what they saw, so they jumped on."

The first two years of YCCC's existence were spent in attempting
to get the Middlesboro City Council to enforce a sewer use ordinance that
would impose restrictions on the waste that the tannery was permitted to
send to the municipal sewage treatment plant. The members' most consis-

Don and Dovie Rose examine a glass of their contaminated well water. Don said, "And I'm supposed to drink this water with stuff in it . . . words I can't even begin to pronounce?" (*Michael S. Clark*)

tent tactic was to attend Middlesboro City Council meetings, where two or three men would challenge the mayor to enforce the ordinance, abide by state and federal water quality laws, and clean up the creek. Shouting matches were common, as was the mayor's abrupt adjournment of meetings. The meetings became local media events and attracted spectators, many of whom subsequently became YCCC sympathizers as they witnessed the anger and concern of valley residents and were made aware of creek conditions.

These confrontations in City Council meetings activated social class battle lines that had been drawn when Middlesboro was founded. Activists refer to the local elite as "the Clique" and "the havers" (i.e., those who "have") and identify them as the former mayor, who was not native to the region, the Bell County School Board, which the mayor allegedly controlled, and the City Council, which contained officials from the tannery. The elite came from the families that had always ruled in Bell County. A retired native said: "I got interested in politics when I was six years old. There's no difference today. It's the same people runnin' things. Thank God, one of them died last summer!"

The "Clique," of course, fought back. The YCCC president and another activist were fired on with shotguns while in a pickup truck. Wilson's dog was poisoned. Wilson's children were occasionally harassed by teachers at school. For example, Wilson's son was benched by the football coach, who questioned the boy about Wilson's YCCC activities. The mayor promised Wilson that he would never work for a Bell County employer—and though Wilson has applied throughout the county, he has not been hired.

The bitter fighting between the mayor and YCCC leaders had more to do with power than with money. The city does not collect large revenues from the tannery. Nor are city residents dependent on the tannery for jobs: most of the two hundred tannery employees live in nearby Tennessee and Virginia. An activist explained the city's dogged protection of the tannery in terms of power: "The city doesn't make money off the tannery, except maybe for the [former] mayor. No, they just like being in control. They don't want anyone telling them what to do."

At the end of the first two years of collective resistance, YCCC members had encountered unresponsive officials not only at local but also at state and federal levels. Despairing of any other solution, they finally voted to file a suit against the city. With this decision YCCC entered a new phase of collective resistance.

In late 1983 YCCC filed a $31 million class action suit against the City of Middlesboro. During this stage of fundraising, grant writing, and promotional activities, leaders for the first time established links with external organizations, most notably with the Highlander Research and Education Center. As a consequence of entering a litigation phase, the group lost some grassroots support, as is fairly typical.[14] Leaders lamented the change while acknowledging the necessity of gaining outside funding. As one said: "It simply got too big for us. There was no way we could handle it. But I think we lost a little bit of our strength. It took a little bit of our togetherness away."

Contact with outsiders brought out differences in gender roles. During the litigation phase, women took over the everyday activities of the group primarily because they were available during weekdays when employed men were not. Most hearings and meetings scheduled by state and federal officials took place during their working hours—between nine and five on weekdays. The traditional norm was for women to work at home, tending the house and children, and this left them free for resistance activities when men were not available. Consequently, women attended EPA and other hearings regarding the suit, dealt with the attorneys and the media, and made slide-show presentations to outsiders to enlist support.

A number of studies have found that women who are activists in equity groups often become aware of gender discrimination and take on feminist attitudes.[15] At Yellow Creek, there was a curious split in the women's attitudes: while they clearly rejected the women's movement, they nevertheless described how their activism in YCCC had liberated them from traditional gender roles.

Activism has only somewhat modified the women activists' traditional role behavior. They voice both feminist and traditional views, almost simultaneously, and they recognize the apparent inconsistency—one said, "I know it sounds like I'm talking out of both sides of my mouth." They tend to regard the women's movement as silly, arguing that it does not take a law to make women as free as men, yet they *do* believe that women are exploited in the workplace. They believe that women's feelings go deeper than men's and imply that this is a positive trait, yet argue that total respect for the man of the house is a necessity, that the male is "the most sacred part of the family."

Such seemingly contradictory attitudes among working-class women activists were also observed by Kathleen McCourt, who suggests that most working-class women activists have not changed their consciousness of women's status as a result of their political activity.[16] YCCC's movement networks provided a context for a political interpretation of their pollution problem but did not lead women to generalize that framework to gender inequalities. Why?

Women activists in YCCC believe that the women's movement has been less aware of the needs of working-class women than those of middle-class women. YCCC women are vociferous in their support of equal pay for women, clearly recognizing sexual discrimination in the economy. But their strong sentiments on this issue are consonant with their more general concerns regarding *economic* inequalities and clearly demonstrate the salience of class issues over gender issues. In a region of longtime exploitation, class conflict is a more important issue than gender conflict. Consequently, some of the women activists' hostility and scorn may be directed more toward the middle-class constituents of the women's movement than toward the movement's general goals of gender equality.

In 1985 YCCC's suit was settled out of court with a consent decree signed by the U.S. Justice Department, the EPA, the Commonwealth of Kentucky, the City of Middlesboro, the Middlesboro Tanning Company, and YCCC representatives. The document set limits for discharges into Yellow Creek and established deadlines for construction and compliance. With the suit settled, YCCC's activities have stabilized into a pattern over the past five years. For the residents of the Yellow Creek valley, it is a frustrating cycle in which they document the city's violations of the consent decree, the city appeals to the EPA to weaken the decree, and the EPA threatens to fine or sue the city for noncompliance without actually enforcing anything. In January 1990 the EPA finally conceded to the city and drew up a new, considerably weaker consent decree. In protest, YCCC members refused to sign the new document and are attempting to have the issue resolved in court.

What of the future of YCCC? The group now consists of a small core of highly dedicated activists, still led by Larry Wilson as president, plus a relatively large army of reserves ready to take part as needed. There have been no formal efforts at leadership training in YCCC, but the core activists have learned from Wilson's political and organizing savvy. Wilson was aware of serious snags encountered by other citizen groups in Appalachia and made every effort to avoid them. Moreover, his current job with the Highlander Center requires that he travel frequently, and this has forced others to assume new organizational responsibilities.

YCCC has evolved into a community interest organization, taking on issues besides the pollution of the creek. Group members have been active, for example, in opposing a municipal incinerator, in reporting hazardous waste dumping, and in obtaining a ban on strip mining near an area lake.

Many members have undergone profound personal changes as a result of their experiences in YCCC. These once-stalwart patriots have become radicalized. Their deep anger and resentment at a government they no longer perceive to be "for the people" provide incentive to maintain the struggle. When asked how they manage to keep going, one of the co-founders of YCCC answered: "Bitter resentment keeps us going. I won't quit now till I get full satisfaction. All we've ever tried to do is have the laws enforced. Why should I have to fight to get what's already in the law? I'll tell you why: it's more exploitation of Appalachia."

Reflections

At least at Yellow Creek, the Appalachian stereotype held by outsiders is forcefully countered by a new Appalachian identity, an identity characterized by a self-conscious awareness of the injustices perpetrated by elites and of Appalachia's similarities to the oppressed parts of the world. This is apparent in an activist's reference to the political position of the region: "Appalachia has more in common with some of those countries in Africa than we do with the rest of the United States." Another activist: "I think we are a Third World state—Appalachia. We're low in education, and we're exploited by the bigger cities." This new identity is both a product of the collective resistance effort and a spur to it. Activists' experiences have changed their views—of the past and of the future. Neither they nor their children will accept the decisions of authorities without question.

A striking example of the activists' new perceptions of authorities' abuse of power was offered by a woman whose teenaged daughter was one of several girls ordered by the school principal to cut her hair—specifically, to cut off her "rat tail." She refused, and her parents, co-founders of YCCC, supported her. Their support continued even when the principal called the mother and asked her to help him save face by insisting that her daughter cut her hair, as the other girls had done immediately: "I told him, 'You should have thought of that before you started all this. We're not making her cut her hair.' Now, see, this would *never* have happened before YCCC. Pam wouldn't have thought to refuse and we certainly wouldn't have let her do that way."

The model of individual-turned-collective resistance in the Yellow Creek valley is not a unique one in the history of humankind. It has been observed among a number of oppressed groups, American blacks being but one example.[17] In fact, Richard Couto analyzes the Yellow Creek controversy as "a conflict between repressed and dominant structural interests,"[18] similar to the conflict generated by other community protest groups in Love Canal and Woburn, Massachusetts.[19] The critical point here is that the *similarities* between Appalachian responses to oppression and those of other oppressed groups are more significant than are any *differences*. Consequently, we need not ennoble Appalachians in order to shatter the stereotype. We need only see them as we see others: as more or less decent, more or less intelligent, and more or less able, when conditions are suitable, to resist oppression.

Acknowledgments

For aid in data collection at Yellow Creek, special thanks are extended to activists Larry and Shelia Wilson, Gene and Viola Hurst, and Hotense Quillen, and also to graduate students Lachelle Norris-Hall, Ekem Lartson, and Coreen Broomfield.

Notes

1. Kai T. Erikson, *Everything in Its Path: Destruction of Community in the Buffalo Creek Flood* (New York: Simon and Schuster, 1976).
2. John Gaventa, *Power and Powerlessness: Quiescence and Rebellion in an Appalachian Valley* (Urbana: University of Illinois Press, 1980).
3. Steven Lukes, *Power: A Radical View* (London: Macmillan, 1974).
4. Gaventa, *Power and Powerlessness*, 200.
5. Data for this chapter were collected from 1987 to 1989. Sources include government reports, newspaper and magazine articles, YCCC documents, and many in-depth interviews with sixteen of the twenty-seven most active YCCC members. Unless other attributions are given, all quotations are taken from interviews with activists.
6. Michael Staub, "There's No Quittin: The Struggle to Save Yellow Creek, Kentucky, as Told by the People Who Live There" (manuscript, Vanderbilt University, 1982), 72; and Michael Staub, "'We'll Never Quit!' Yellow Creek Concerned Citizens Combat Creekbed Catastrophe," *Southern Exposure* (January–February 1983): 43–52.
7. Patricia D. Beaver, *Rural Community in the Appalachian South* (Lexington: University Press of Kentucky, 1986); Judith Ivy Fiene, "Snobby People and Just Plain Folks: Social Stratification and Rural, Low-Status, Appalachian Women" (manuscript, University of Tennessee, 1989); and H. K. Schwarzweller, J. S. Brown, and J. J. Mangalam, *Mountain Families in Transition: A Case Study in Appalachian Migration* (University Park: Pennsylvania State University Press, 1971).
8. Sara M. Evans and Harry C. Boyte, *Free Spaces: The Sources of Democratic Change in America* (New York: Harper & Row, 1986). See the discussion and critique of free spaces offered by Stephen Fisher in Chapter 16 of this volume.
9. Gaventa, *Power and Powerlessness*.
10. Staub, "There's No Quittin," 45.
11. Ibid., 67.
12. Sherry Cable and Edward Walsh, "The Emergence of Environmental Protest:

Yellow Creek and Three Mile Island Compared," in *Communities at Risk: Collective Responses to Technological Hazards*, ed. Stephen R. Couch and J. Stephen Kroll-Smith (New York: Peter Lang, 1991), 113–32.

13. Doug McAdam, *Political Process and the Development of Black Insurgency* (Chicago: University of Chicago Press, 1982), 48.

14. Edward J. Walsh and Sherry Cable, "Litigation and Citizen Protest After the Three Mile Island Accident," in *Research in Political Sociology*, vol. 2, ed. Richard C. Braungart and Margaret M. Braungart (Greenwich, Conn.: JAI Press, 1986), 293–316.

15. Sara M. Evans, *Personal Politics: The Roots of Women's Liberation in the Civil Rights Movement and the New Left* (New York: Vintage, 1979); Myra Ferree and Beth B. Hess, *Controversy and Coalition: The New Feminist Movement* (Boston: Twayne, 1985); McAdam, *Political Process and Black Insurgency*; Sheila Rowbotham, *Women, Resistance and Revolution* (New York: Random House, 1972); and Barrie Thorne, "Women in the Draft Resistance Movement: A Case Study of Sex Roles and Social Movements," *Sex Roles* 1 (1975): 179–95.

16. Kathleen McCourt, *Working Class Women and Grass-Roots Politics* (Bloomington: Indiana University Press, 1977), 134.

17. James C. Scott argues that "to the degree that structures of domination can be demonstrated to operate in comparable ways, they will, other things being equal, elicit reactions and patterns of resistance that are also broadly comparable." In *Domination and the Arts of Resistance: Hidden Transcripts* (New Haven: Yale University Press, 1990), xi.

18. Richard A. Couto, "Failing Health and New Prescriptions: Community-Based Approaches to Environmental Risks," in *Current Health Policy Issues and Alternatives*, ed. Carole E. Hill (Athens: University of Georgia Press, 1986), 53–70.

19. Adeline Levine, *Love Canal* (Lexington, Mass.: D. C. Heath, 1982); Phil Brown and Edwin J. Mikkelsen, *No Safe Place* (Berkeley: University of California Press, 1990).

5

Save Our Cumberland Mountains

Growth and Change
Within a Grassroots Organization

Bill Allen

When thirteen Tennessee coalfield residents petitioned their state government to make large coal landholders pay a fair share of taxes, they hardly thought that nearly twenty years later Save Our Cumberland Mountains (SOCM, pronounced "sock 'em") would have grown into one of the strongest citizen organizations in the Appalachian region, with 1,500 families as members. From its roots as an anti-strip mining group, the original members could hardly have envisioned the organization leading a major legislative campaign against the unfairness of employers replacing permanent employees with long-term "temporary" workers. Although SOCM's growth has not been without pain, its willingness to risk redefining its mission has paid off. Many of the organizations born in the Appalachian region in the 1970s and 1980s have disappeared. This chapter explores how SOCM made the changes that enabled it to survive and flourish.

In the late 1960s, citizens in some of Tennessee's poorest and most isolated counties organized health fairs in their communities in conjunction with the Vanderbilt University Student Health Coalition. The fairs were designed to take basic health care and health education to isolated areas because many people could not afford to go to the larger cities for treatment. Some of the local folks asked why they could not get permanent health services in their communities. The answer officials gave—no money—struck a raw nerve because people could see coal trucks hauling the huge wealth of the county out of the mountains every day. A study conducted by the Student Health Coalition revealed that the owners of mineral-rich land in the northern coalfield counties, who leased that land for strip mining, paid very little in property taxes.[1] The failure of government to provide basic services to its citizens because it failed to tax its richest landowners created a cry for change.

The coal economy, which had been the lifeblood of these counties for decades, had switched from deep mining to strip mining during the 1950s and 1960s, in large part because of the growing thirst of industries and city residents for cheap electricity from the Tennessee Valley Authority. This pushed hundreds of union miners out of work in an industry that provided most of the local jobs.

With government providing fewer services and many residents out of work, citizens in five coal counties (Campbell, Scott, Claiborne, Anderson, and Morgan) organized SOCM in 1972 in the hope that such an organization could improve the quality of life there. Because coal dominated the economy in the area, SOCM's targets were coal-related: overweight coal trucks that destroyed rural roads, mining companies that failed to pay property taxes, stream flooding caused by siltation from strip mines.

Many of the early SOCM members were retired deep miners, who saw not only the environmental devastation of strip mining but the economic devastation as well. These oldtimers, many with a strong union background, enjoyed a good fight and recognized the value of organizing. This was, on the one hand, just the right combination for a new organization looking to buck the established system. On the other hand, the primary mission of the organization for these members was to get the federal government to abolish all strip mining—not the classic "winnable" issue that organizers choose to build an organization.

The first two SOCM organizers, Heleny Cook and Jane Sampson, spent months knocking on doors and sitting around chatting with residents about their problems. Both were outsiders;[2] neither had any training or experience in organizing; and they had no organizing model to follow. Their job as they saw it was to bring people from the different communities together to discuss their common problems. Some of the early meetings became confrontations with truckloads of strip miners who were out to intimidate SOCM members. In the beginning members not only fought local strip mine operations that threatened their homes but joined with other groups from around the nation to lobby Congress for a ban on strip mining.

In less than two years, 400 SOCM members had signed up, but the two burned-out organizers had left Tennessee. In their place, two young men, Johnny Burris and Charles "Boomer" Winfrey, who were born and educated in the coalfields, and a former schoolteacher from the Midwest, Maureen O'Connell, were recruited. None had any organizing experience, but they had enthusiasm and a real interest in and ability to talk with rural people. They continued working in communities like Stony Fork, New River, Briceville, Smokey Junction, and Elk Valley. They identified local leaders with anti–strip mining sentiments and through them contacted other people who were concerned about the quality of life in the mountains.

Each of these rural communities had its own leaders. One of the earliest leaders was Millard Ridenour in the White Oak community of northeastern Campbell County. In a place where mining was virtually the only employment for men, his strong opinions against strip mining were not shared by all. But he was known by everyone and commanded their respect. Ridenour had worked in the deep mines for forty years and suffered from black lung disease. Because of his health, he was unable to assume a more important leadership position within the larger organization, but the SOCM staff and other members regularly sought his opinion.

The overall leadership of the organization fell to the most outspoken opponent of strip mining, J. W. Bradley, a former Morgan County deputy sheriff who lived in the small community of Petros, best known as the location of Brushy Mountain Prison. Bradley also had worked in the deep mines and understood first hand what he referred to as the "evils of strip mining." His name was synonymous with SOCM during the first ten years of its existence.

Bradley was a "charismatic" leader who understood only right and wrong; gray was not in his colorbox.[3] He was president of SOCM for its first five years and generally controlled the work of members and staff. However, he controlled not out of a thirst for power but from an implacable desire to eliminate strip mining.

He was obsessed and expected others to follow him in his quest. He was a tireless worker, often working a forty-hour week at his job and another fifty or sixty hours for SOCM. He had so much energy and was so convinced of his position that when he ran, others followed.

Bradley believed in using litigation to bring reform. However, he and other members distrusted local lawyers, who were invariably tied to the coal industry. Thus, in 1974 SOCM established a public interest law firm (East Tennessee Research Corporation), funded by foundation grants, to carry out SOCM's legal work.[4] Bradley had so many ideas and schemes that he could keep a staff of organizers and two or three lawyers busy. He essentially acted as a staff director while he was SOCM president. Unfortunately, that leadership style, along with recruiting professionals to fight the battles, impeded the development of other leaders.

In 1976, as SOCM was working at the state and national levels for a ban on strip mining and fighting individual strip mine operations in the northern coalfield counties, the organization expanded geographically to help residents in the state's southern coalfields fight the largest coal operation ever proposed—before or since—in Tennessee. This decision, perhaps more than any other, set into motion a chain of events that eventually changed SOCM from a staff, service-oriented group to a solid community organization that depends on its members to carry out its work.

J. W. Bradley, the first president of Save Our Cumberland Mountains. (*Karen Kasmauski*)

The decision to expand out of the original five counties was extremely difficult for some members and staff. The issue was compelling: AMAX, Inc., the nation's third-largest coal company, wanted to strip mine about twenty thousand acres in an area just south of Fall Creek Falls State Park. The plan included mining through and relocating streams, practices generally prohibited under Tennessee's water pollution laws. Pressure from such a large, politically powerful company had the potential to change mining practices all over the state, to increase the power of the coal industry in Tennessee, and to destroy water supplies for many SOCM members. On the other hand, SOCM had not yet accomplished its mission in the northern coalfields, so why should it expand? Some members, including Bradley, who was still president, argued that the fight would require an enormous commitment of time—especially from the SOCM staff. After much debate, members decided that the AMAX fight was too important an issue to pass up.

Months of recruiting followed. Meetings were held in the homes of local leaders and in churches. Residents of Sequatchie and Van Buren counties learned how the proposed strip mining operation would change their way of life from northern county members who had suffered already. The fight against AMAX was a huge success. State water pollution regulators denied the necessary discharge permit,[5] and AMAX left the state. The fight was a success from an organizational standpoint, too. For the first time since SOCM's beginning, a large number of new members were recruited. New issues related to strip mining developed as the organization spread into neighboring White, Bledsoe, and Hamilton counties.[6] New leaders also emerged, including two of the next three SOCM presidents.

However, maintaining an organizational presence in the southern counties and tying the northern and southern counties more cohesively into the larger organization became a real challenge.[7] The original model of holding monthly membership meetings where all organizational decisions were made continued. These meetings rotated between communities in the northern and southern areas.

With the AMAX fight over and a federal strip mining law on the horizon, SOCM turned its attention back to Washington. When Congress enacted the federal Surface Mining Control and Reclamation Act of 1977, SOCM was one of the few organizations working on environmental issues that did not rejoice. Urging President Carter to veto the new law because it did not go far enough, Bradley and other oldtime members demanded the abolition of strip mining. Congress incorporated into the new law numerous compromises worked out between national environmental groups and the coal industry. SOCM never agreed to those compromises, and some members felt that they had been sold out by the national groups that had depended heavily on local groups like SOCM to lobby and provide testimony for Congressional study committees.

The passage of the federal act brought an end to SOCM's original dream of banning strip mining. The new law legitimized the industry. Out of necessity, SOCM modified its stance to advocate strict control, rather than a total ban, of strip mining. For some of the earlier members, this was the end of the battle; SOCM had failed in its primary mission, and they dropped out.

The federal enforcement program incubated for months while new regulations were written and inspectors were hired. The years 1978 and 1979 were a lawless period in the Tennessee coalfields as many "wildcat" operations opened. These were usually small operations of less than twenty acres, run by outlaws who made no attempt to obtain a permit or reclaim the land. They operated in open defiance of state regulators, who lacked the political will to stop them. Some previously "legitimate" operators, perhaps frustrated by the slow permitting process and the competition from those who openly operated outside the law during a time of high coal prices, opened new mines without first getting a permit. Although SOCM reported dozens of these operations, more often than not the state belatedly issued the permit anyway. Meanwhile, SOCM's aggressive actions toward illegal operators brought reprisals.

In October 1978 SOCM members were assaulted during a mining permit hearing at the courthouse in Morgan County. One of the most outspoken speakers was J. W. Bradley, who was punched in the face by one of the operators whose permit application was under consideration. A general melee followed, and Maureen O'Connell and Annetta Watson were thrown across a row of pews in the courtroom. Although law enforcement officers attended the hearing, they brought no criminal charges against the offenders. The SOCM members brought a civil lawsuit against four men and won a small jury award.

In 1979 and 1980 the houses of three SOCM families burned mysteriously. For several years, Sam and Roberta Baker had fought off attempts by strippers to mine the extremely steep slopes at the head of Douglas Branch near their home in Campbell County. When an operator moved in and started mining without a permit, the Bakers filed a complaint with regulators, who shut the mine down. Shortly afterward, in October 1979, their house burned to the ground. Less than a month later, another Campbell County SOCM member watched his house burn. At a public hearing just two weeks before, John Johnson, a rather shy middle-aged man who lived alone on Hickory Creek, had spoken out strongly about the effects of nearby blasting by wildcatters. Someone torched his house while he was gone for a couple of hours in the early evening. In

Members of SOCM help rebuild the Bakers' home after an arsonist attack. (*SOCM archives*)

July 1980 Millard and Mable Ridenour's new house went up in flames. Ridenour had been fighting a wildcat operator mining near his old home and had received several threatening phone calls late at night. No one was ever charged in connection with any of these fires. Members of SOCM helped rebuild the Bakers' house and collected new furnishings for the Ridenours and Johnson. This blatant intimidation could have destroyed the organization if members had not shown enormous support for those directly affected.

Staff functions underwent significant change in 1978 when the East Tennessee Research Corporation folded because of decreased foundation support.[8] Although SOCM had urged a veto of the federal law, once the law was signed the group jumped full force into drafting and reviewing thousands of pages of technical documents and regulations. Once, ETRC had performed this role for SOCM; now the task was taken on by an already overcommitted staff and a few members. They worked closely with other environmental leaders to help develop a strong federal regulatory agency. After the federal regulations were adopted, the same few members and staff spent another couple of years working on a state regulatory program for Tennessee. This process developed expertise in drafting regulations, but it did little to expand or even maintain the organization. The process required innumerable meetings that contributed measurably to the burnout of both staff and members. The victories in this process were not easy to measure or celebrate, and the result of the investment made by staff and members was a miserably deficient state regulatory program.[9]

In addition to the time-consuming review of new regulations, the staff responded to almost any call for help from a community fighting a strip mining operation. During this period the coal industry was enjoying a boom, which coincided with the oil "shortage" declared by the federal government. With the increased demand for coal and the rampant lawlessness of the industry, the demand for SOCM's help increased enormously.

The staff's extraordinary expertise in strip mine regulation and its many successes in stopping specific mining operations helped solidify SOCM's reputation statewide and nationally. Yet this emphasis on fighting strip mining operations and pressuring federal and state agencies to adopt strict mining guidelines left the staff without time or energy to build the organization. None of the staff, which by 1979 had grown to six, had any organizer training. More and more, the staff stayed in the office instead of working directly with members. Organizing came in response to requests from communities for direct action to fight a strip mine permit. After that battle was over, win or lose, most of the citizens that SOCM had "organized" dropped out. This rescue-oriented strategy drained staff resources and left no structure to sustain involvement in new communities. The staff had no system for setting priorities and found themselves constantly overcommitted on projects. As one staffer puts it: "The staff was really frustrated. We never decided not to do things; if they needed doing, we did them. As a result, we were just slapping at things—and getting too sloppy."[10]

In 1979 several members and staff recognized the signs of organizational burn-out. Attendance at monthly meetings had dwindled from forty or fifty members to ten or twenty. The staff spent too much time putting out brush fires, leaving too little time for building the organization and developing new leaders. The members had become dependent on staff to formulate positions. A core of ten to fifteen overcommitted and overworked leaders were less willing to carry the burden. "It was the same old tired folks that were meeting every time," says Raymond Weaver, who served for three years as SOCM's president. "That really pointed out the need to broaden our base of leadership within the organization."[11] Staff members were frustrated with the reduced participation of members but did not have the skills to understand the members' disaffection. Decision making had become inconsistent because different members showed up depending on where meetings were held. Members in communities in the southern coalfields had to drive three to four hours to attend a meeting in one of the northern counties, and vice versa.

A handful of active members and staff met in August 1979 at SOCM's first leadership retreat (facilitated by Si Kahn, founder of Grassroots Leadership) to discuss these problems. Some ideas for change came out of this meeting, but when the next leadership retreat came around in November 1980,[12] no progress was apparent. Despite a feeling that the organization had failed in its first attempt, this time a real commitment to explore change took root.

One of the chief complaints expressed at both retreats by members and staff involved the number and length of meetings held to accomplish SOCM's business. The answer, of course, was a series of meetings to discuss that issue—perhaps proving that the substance of the meetings, rather than number and length, was the real problem. A planning group was established to review the overall vision of the organization, consider whether SOCM should remain focused on coal issues or become a multi-issue, membership-driven organization, look at various organizational and decision-making structures, and anticipate the practical implications of changing SOCM.

Members shared a vision of an organization that could become more powerful by adding members and increase its effectiveness by involving more members in its activities. At the same time, members wanted

SOCM to continue to "feel like family." This visionary statement served as a backdrop to discussions of the other points. The recommendation that SOCM become an organization whose primary purpose was to empower its membership was the most significant and most hotly debated issue. In a sense, it admitted defeat on abolishing strip mining; more importantly, it returned control of the organization to the members.

From its beginning, SOCM practiced the purest form of democracy: decisions were made by majority vote of members attending a community meeting. SOCM built on this principle during the restructuring process. Early meetings had consisted of discussions about local problems and state and national developments on strip mine legislation, with suggestions from all members about a plan of action. As the organization expanded into more communities, it took longer and longer to cover all the local issues at the monthly meetings, and eventually the meetings became dominated by endless staff reports. When staff analyzed proposed federal strip mine regulations, many of those attending lost interest because they did not feel directly affected and lacked the technical background to understand the issues. Anyone can get excited about banning strip mining; reviewing the size of sediment ponds and types of vegetation on reclaimed lands is more tedious. In short, the monthly meetings became an unwieldy mechanism for dispensing information and designing strategies. Fewer members were attending; those who did spent little time discussing or planning organizational matters; and, as a result, staff and officers took over much of the decision making.

As models for a new decision-making structure, the planning group researched three other citizen-based organizations with representative boards: the Brown Lung Association in the Carolinas, the Northern Plains Resource Council in Montana, and Minnesota Community Organizations Acting Together (COACT). Drawing on those models, SOCM devised a system of local chapters in counties with more than twenty members. Each chapter would elect a representative to serve on a SOCM board of directors. The board would also include the four traditional officers and three at-large members elected by the entire membership. Four permanent committees—finance, personnel, membership, and legislative—were established to report to the board, with committee members appointed by the SOCM president each year. The chairs of the four committees would form a nominating committee for officers and at-large board members. The board would meet every two months, and members were invited and encouraged to attend. Two general membership meetings would be held annually.

The planning group circulated its ideas to members, who voted on the proposal at a membership meeting in July 1981. The decision-making process was adopted as an "experiment."[13] After a one-year trial period, it was adopted permanently. The process has since been refined. By 1992 the number of chapters had grown from four to twelve, causing an increase in board members from eleven to nineteen. The number of standing committees had increased from four to ten. Only one general membership meeting is now held in conjunction with the annual SOCM picnic.[14] To ensure the development of new leaders, board members and officers are restricted to two consecutive one-year terms.

The other major change that resulted from this reevaluation process was a system for how the staff would allocate its time. A yearly plan approved by the board specifies the percentage of time each staff member will spend with a chapter or committee or on a special project. Internal staff systems provide regular checks on compliance with work plans.[15] In addition, the board now adopts a yearly organizational work plan and a five-year plan to guide its decision making and allocation of staff time.

Efforts are made to educate and train board members on important issues. The staff assists members in preparing presentations and training sessions, but the members do the work at the board meetings. For many years all staff members were expected to attend monthly membership meetings, and they sometimes dominated these discussions. At board meetings now, staff members participate only when asked for a specific piece of information.

In order to continue the creativity exhibited at the early leadership retreats, SOCM holds those events annually. The key difference is that members now conduct the retreats themselves. Unfailingly, the retreats have resulted in new growth for the organization. They provide an opportunity for members to reflect on their history and to dream of the future. For example, at the 1988 leadership retreat held at Fall Creek Falls State Park, SOCM spent half a day discussing its accomplishments over the years. It then spent another day exploring new issues to tackle. Out of that meeting came a commitment to work on toxic waste issues in Tennessee. The board later approved this as a high priority, and SOCM was off and running on a new campaign that has brought in new members, established two new chapters, and allowed SOCM to form new coalitions with other groups in the state.

At its formation, SOCM members protested against their treatment as second-class citizens as they watched their homes and lives in the mountain coalfields sacrificed to strip mining. The same spirit moved the organization to resist the creation of "a second class group of workers" through industry's expanded use of temporary workers.[16]

In 1989 a General Electric plant in Morristown laid off most of its employees, moved the plant thirty miles down the road, and reopened, now using mostly temporary service workers. Employers usually pay temporaries lower wages and provide no medical benefits or the job security enjoyed by a company's permanent workforce. The GE situation was not an isolated occurrence.[17]

The Morristown workers formed a group called Citizens Against Temporary Services (CATS) and requested assistance from SOCM in handling legislation to regulate the exploitation of temporary service workers. "We discovered that no other state in the country had laws restricting the practice, although it was a nationwide problem," says Bill Troy, director of the Tennessee Industrial Renewal Network, a Knoxville-based organization that has focused on problems associated with plant closings.[18] Eventually CATS became a SOCM chapter, and other SOCM members more experienced on the legislative front joined the fight in Nashville. A legislative committee heard testimony from disgruntled workers. "I had no rights," said CATS member Barbara Kirkman, a former temporary worker. "No matter what anyone did to me I had to grin and take it if I wanted to keep working. I felt like a second class citizen and was treated like one."[19] Although the 1990 Tennessee legislature rejected SOCM's bill, which would have prohibited employers from replacing permanent workers with "temporary" ones, a large number of new SOCM members learned how the legislature operates and what influence citizens can have on the legislative process.

Changes in SOCM have generated tremendous growth in members' sense of power in controlling their own organization. A sense of responsibility for the actions of their organization has continued to develop.

"One of the real differences between SOCM and other organizations is how we look at our work and what it is we are trying to do," says Connie White, a past SOCM president. "We don't just care about winning issues; we care more about helping people get stronger. In the long run, that is how you win issues and make real changes. That was actually a pretty revolutionary idea to us until a few years ago. Back in the old days, we thought that getting a strip mine permit denied or getting a tougher reclamation bill passed in Nashville was why we existed. Now we understand that our real success is measured more by how many members participated in protesting the permit or lobbying their legislator and whether they feel empowered by their participation."[20]

Crises within an organization can either destroy it or force change.[21] As stated earlier, many organizations do not survive. Why has SOCM survived, and what can other organizations learn from SOCM's experience?

Most importantly, SOCM was able to redefine its mission after nearly ten years without losing the spirit that originally bonded its members. It still had a core of members in 1980 who cared deeply about the organization. They had courageously fought together against great adversity and were willing to do whatever it took to see SOCM survive. They had developed a sense of a "SOCM community" that was larger than their individual communities, and they still believed that people working together can make a real difference.

In addition, SOCM recognized in 1979 the need for outside assistance. The professional consultants from Grassroots Leadership provided a model for learning that was exciting as well as productive. They helped SOCM identify the crucial organizational issues and created a framework for finding solutions.

The structural changes that evolved from this process opened the door for participation by more members in the work of the organization. Overreliance on staff to find solutions has disappeared. Members take more responsibility. The staff understands and accepts its role and can rely on members. This dichotomy has allowed new leaders to emerge, and a concentrated program of developing new leaders ensures constant revitalization of the organization.

Finally, SOCM continues to address issues that affect the lives of its members. As one longtime member said: "SOCM deals with real problems in the real world by finding real solutions."[22] Toxic waste disposal and loss of jobs affect people's lives the way strip mining did twenty years ago.

Although SOCM's founders did not accomplish their original mission, they did create an organization that has stood for progressive change in one of the poorest regions of the country. Its impressive practical accomplishments have been surpassed only by the power its members have achieved in learning how to participate in a democracy founded on freedom of association.

Notes

1. Researchers found that large companies owning mineral rights in five northern Tennessee coalfield counties held 34.0 percent of the total land there but paid only 3.6 percent of the total property taxes. See John Gaventa, Ellen Ormond, and Bob Thompson, "Coal, Taxation and Tennessee Royalists" (photocopied manuscript, Nashville, Tennessee, Vanderbilt Student Health Coalition, 1971).
2. Heleny Cook is from Massachusetts; Jane Sampson was raised in Chicago, although her family had roots in the southwest Virginia coalfields.
3. Most sociologists recognize the impact of a charismatic leader on a group, especially during its formative years. Studies have shown that most char-

ismatic leaders have trouble either sharing power or administering programs in a way that allows the organization to develop: see Mayer N. Zald and Roberta Ash Garner, "Social Movement Organizations: Growth, Decay and Change," *Social Forces* 44 (1966) : 327–41; and Janice E. Perlman, "Grassrooting the System," *Social Policy* 7 (September/October 1976) : 4–20. When the charismatic leader burns out, the organization often dies. To J. W. Bradley's credit, he gave up the presidency voluntarily after five years and provided much support for the next three. Most importantly, he did not split the organization when he dropped out.

4. One of the first lawsuits brought by ETRC lawyers caused the state to expand its regulation of water pollution laws by requiring strip mine operators to obtain discharge permits. This decision became of paramount importance during the AMAX fight discussed below.

5. See n. 4 above.

6. One of the most important new issues involved legislation in 1976 to protect owners of surface rights from companies owning only mineral rights. Especially in the southern coalfields, many SOCM members owned only the surface and were threatened with indiscriminate stripping of their land. This legislation, which was challenged in court and upheld by the Tennessee Supreme Court, prohibited strip mining without the surface owner's permission. The passage of the act helped solidify the bond between members in northern and southern counties, although many SOCM members still had trouble getting banks to accept their property as collateral for loans. Strategies to reunite surface and mineral interests occupied SOCM for the next decade. Finally, in 1987, the Tennessee Legislature passed a law (1987 Tennessee Public Acts, Chapter 282) that enables the surface owner to claim the mineral interest when the mineral owner has not used it for twenty years.

7. Tension developed between northern and southern members regarding allocation of staff resources to the two areas. As more funding became available in the late 1970s, a SOCM satellite office opened in Pikeville. Problems in coordinating work and training new staff made this arrangement inconvenient, and the office closed two years later.

8. Foundations typically support nonprofit groups for two or three years; ETRC obtained substantial support from the Ford Foundation for five years. In 1978 many of the larger foundations turned away from supporting public interest law and environmental causes.

9. In 1984 the federal government took over primary responsibility for regulating strip mining in Tennessee because the state program did not meet the minimum requirements of federal law.

10. Author's interview with Maureen O'Connell, December 14, 1989.

11. Author's interview with Raymond Weaver, April 24, 1990.

12. The first retreat was held at the Highlander Research and Education Center in New Market, Tennessee; the second, at Camp Cumberland, a Presbyterian church camp in Crossville, Tennessee, was also facilitated by Si Kahn.

13. Adopting the restructuring as a one-year experiment was a compromise

with members who were against drastic changes in the structure. These opponents, led by J. W. Bradley, argued that the representative board was a step away from true democracy.

14. From the beginning the annual picnic was seen as a celebration, not a working meeting. It was a "homecoming" for old and new members and attracted many people who had left the area. Although the picnic now is used as the annual membership meeting, fun is still the major attraction.

15. The SOCM staff is unique among nonprofit organizations in not having a staff director. From the beginning, the staff has recognized all workers as equals. Each receives the same pay regardless of years of service. The only perk for longtime staffers is a paid sabbatical every five years and more vacation time.

16. "CATS Claw Back at the Abuse of Temporary Services," *SOCM Sentinel*, November/December 1989, 2.

17. Department of Employment Security statistics showed a 421 percent increase in the use of temporary workers during the 1980s as many industries, such as assembly plants, replaced permanent workers in the same way offices use "Kelly girls."

18. Author's interview with Bill Troy, April 19, 1991.

19. *SOCM Sentinel*, November/December 1989, 2.

20. Author's interview with Connie White, April 19, 1991.

21. Perlman, "Grassrooting the System," 10, recognizes the "move from protest to program" and the problems inherent in such a move, such as new forms of dependency and the demise of the organization's original participatory structure and mass base. In contrast, SOCM has managed to expand its participation and mass base.

22. Author's interview with Annetta Watson, April 18, 1990.

Members of Kentuckians For The Commonwealth protest against the broad form deed in the Capitol Rotunda in Frankfort, Kentucky, in 1987. (*KFTC archives*)

6

Practical Lessons in Community Organizing in Appalachia

What We've Learned at Kentuckians For The Commonwealth

Joe Szakos

Organizing for change has always been difficult in Appalachia. One of the major obstacles to effective organizing is the fact that the Appalachian economy has long been dependent on coal and other single-industry employers. Absentee owners control much of the land and resources, and decisions about their use are made in board rooms far from the mountains. This situation contributes to the high unemployment that makes workers reluctant to speak out and challenge existing power structures for fear of losing their jobs.

In addition, a long history of local political corruption, along with wrong-headed federal economic development initiatives that favor the already powerful, have bred distrust of government. The strong influence of fundamentalist churches can also discourage participation in worldly matters, by offering instead the hope of justice in the hereafter.

Poor roads, long distances between rural communities, and a lack of public transportation make organizing across county lines difficult. High rates of illiteracy and a poor educational system leave many citizens unaware of their rights and their ability to organize for change.

A lack of good leadership training programs and experienced community organizers, along with meager financial resources and competition between citizens' groups for funding and turf, have rendered many organizations weak and ineffective.

Given these obstacles, it is a testament to the determination of the people in the region that the history of Appalachia is rich in stories of courageous and forceful citizen resistance. But it is not surprising that most of the community-based attempts at social change in the mountains have been piecemeal, temporary, and without long-term vision.

In recent years, a combination of factors has opened up opportunities for people in the mountains to participate in community affairs.

For example, the construction of more and better roads and the advent of more accessible communication media, including local cable television programing and electronic mail, have made it possible for citizens to communicate with one another across community lines.

Open meeting laws and open records laws have made it easier for citizens to learn more about their government and prevent the kind of closed-door decisions that fed corruption in the past.

Churches and charitable foundations have become interested in funding groups working for change in Appalachia, and regional and national groups have become more willing to exchange information and training resources and to work together.

Taking advantage of these and other opportunities, several strong citizens' organizations have appeared in the region that have a solid foundation, work on a variety of issues, cover a wider geographic area, are membership-run, and have developed strategies for continued growth. This chapter examines some of the lessons learned in more than eleven years of community organizing by Kentuckians For The Commonwealth (KFTC), one of the most successful of these organizations.

What Is KFTC?

Started in mid-1981 by a small group of eastern Kentucky residents who joined together to address community problems that crossed county lines, KFTC has grown into a statewide organization of more than 2,350 members in 90 (of 120) Kentucky counties.

From KFTC's early days, people like Gladys Maynard, J. D. Miller, Mary Jane Adams, and Lorraine Slone, among others, had the vision to know that building an organization for the long haul was what would really make a difference in solving the problems they were confronting in their communities. KFTC's work is directed toward achieving broader state and regional changes while emphasizing local leadership development and fostering the ability of local groups to participate in community affairs on a variety of issues. KFTC defines itself as a "citizens social justice group" that uses direct-action community organizing to improve the quality of life for all Kentuckians. "Social justice" implies long-term, fundamental change and avoids the limited scope that a tag like "environmental group" carries. "Direct-action organizing" means that members work together as a group, democratically and nonviolently, to address the root causes of the injustices experienced in Kentucky.

Concerns about social justice have involved the organization in many issues, such as surface owners' rights, inequitable property taxation, toxic and solid wastes, waste reduction and recycling, water quality, legislative democracy, education, utility reform, and the lack of community services. Through such immediate issues, KFTC addresses *longstanding* problems of the use and ownership and control of land and natural resources and the control of our democratic institutions.

In more than eleven years of organizing, concerned citizens throughout the state have built a strong, democratically run organization that is active and effective.

- KFTC led an overwhelmingly successful statewide constitutional amendment campaign in 1988 that stopped strip mining without the permission of the landowner under "broad form" mineral deeds, a practice used by coal companies since the turn of the century to destroy people's homes and land.
- KFTC members pushed through the legislature a law that gives local governments the right to decide whether hazardous waste incinerators can locate in their communities, putting an end to outside interests and insider deals that disregarded the wishes of area residents for a clean, safe, and healthy environment.
- KFTC filed a court case that led to a ruling by the Kentucky Supreme Court that exempting wealthy mineral owners from property taxation was unconstitutional; as a result, millions of dollars in new revenue are now pumped into local school systems and county governments in the coalfields.
- Hundreds of KFTC members have learned new skills and self-confidence in areas such as public speaking, letter writing, lobbying, organizational development, and strategies and tactics for holding government officials accountable.
- KFTC chapters have achieved a long list of local victories, such as stopping unwanted incinerators, preventing industrial water pollution, getting funds for community water systems, and improving county schools.

KFTC's Organizing Goals

Many years of retreats, evaluation sessions, and organizing-training workshops led the KFTC Steering Committee to express the long-term vision of the original KFTC members in terms of five goals. Although the goals may sound simple, few other groups in the region are as systematic about analyzing their work in such terms.

TO EMPOWER PEOPLE: KFTC wants its members to have an effective voice on matters of concern to them, and so the focus of the organization is not limited to acting on issues. KFTC strives to develop members' ability to be leaders in their own communities. Training sessions on the basic skills of community leadership (running meetings, public speaking, developing strategies and tactics, and fundraising, for example) and education on the economy and government are important elements of KFTC's work.

TO BUILD THE ORGANIZATION: KFTC was founded on the belief that individuals are important, but groups get things done. KFTC encourages and enables people to put aside differences in education, religious beliefs, and personal histories, and concentrate instead on specific issues that are common to a group. Time and attention are given to building local community groups as well as the statewide organization.

TO WIN ISSUES: People do not want to keep giving energy to an organization that does not show tangible results. Issues that KFTC tackles are chosen, addressed, and solved through direct actions carried out by, and on behalf of, the membership. Victories that affect the common welfare help build momentum for longer-term social change.

TO FOSTER DEMOCRATIC VALUES: This goal is based on the fundamental tenets that all people are created equal, everyone deserves respect and equal opportunities, and everyone has a right and the ability to share in participation, leadership, power, and wealth. Many groups—even the Ku Klux Klan—claim to have the first three goals, but it is this goal that separates KFTC from many other groups.

TO CHANGE UNJUST SOCIETAL INSTITUTIONS: Unjust institutions include political systems that are corrupt and primarily serve the interests of the powerful few, economic systems that place profits before people and allow widespread unemployment and poverty, and social systems that discriminate on the basis of race, gender, or class. Long-term solutions to major problems are a vital part of KFTC's organizational thinking.

Many groups have a tendency to focus only on winning the immediate issue or building the organization. Yet these aspects of organizing should be seen not as ends in themselves, but merely as vehicles to achieve the ends that are embodied in the other goals. Effective organizations must take the time to build, in clear and deliberate steps, toward achieving the other three goals. Most Appalachian groups have failed to do this. One of the key differences is that KFTC was willing to look to some national organizing networks for training and advice during its initial years of organizing. A great deal was gleaned from Grassroots Leadership, the Industrial

Areas Foundation (IAF), the Midwest Academy, and the National Training and Information Center (NTIC), through training workshops, written materials, phone consultations, and site visits.

KFTC believes that all five goals of organizing are essential and must be built into successful organizing efforts at every step of the way. Balancing these goals is an ongoing process that effective organizations must continually evaluate and refine. The solid waste issue illustrates the way in which KFTC attempts to carry out this balancing process.

The solid waste issue arose from the direct experiences of citizens faced with an alarming increase in the amount of out-of-state waste being transported into Kentucky communities for disposal, a proliferation of proposals for new and expanded solid waste landfills and incinerators, an increase in control of Kentucky land by large corporations, a growing influence by waste companies in Kentucky politics, and a rise in the incidences of water, air, and soil contamination related to waste facilities.

KFTC members quickly realized that the "waste crisis" is a modern-day expression of many of the same systemic injustices they have struggled against for years—the destruction of the land and the environment that people depend upon for water, air, food, and jobs; corporate control of land and natural resources; out-of-state decision making adversely affecting local communities; and the exploitation of people and their communities for the sake of quick profits.

Once faced with the injustices of the waste problems, and aware of the links between issues, members held meetings in their own communities and on a state level as part of KFTC's Environmental Rights Committee. After soliciting and receiving input from local groups and KFTC chapters around the state, the committee developed a document entitled "The ABCs of Environmental Management in Kentucky," which KFTC members presented to the Kentucky Natural Resources and Environmental Protection Cabinet and released to the media as a means of stimulating discussion and encouraging solutions to environmental problems in the state. KFTC used several of the report's major points to develop a series of legislative proposals that were presented to the Kentucky Waste Management Task Force.

KFTC and the Kentucky Resources Council, while serving on the task force and the Kentucky Proposed Solid Waste Regulations Consensus Group, were the only groups that actively demanded affordable solid waste rates, especially for low-income people. On one measure dealing with solid waste billing, KFTC successfully opposed the waste industry's effort to attach delinquent garbage bills to utility bills, since this would have conflicted with KFTC efforts in Jefferson County against low-income utility disconnections. Recognizing that disposal facility costs will inevitably rise as efforts are made to safeguard the environment, KFTC began working to reduce the need for new and expensive landfill capacity by promoting waste reduction, reuse, recycling, and conservation of natural resources. In addition, KFTC strongly pushed for more local control—more democratic participation—in the planning and siting of solid waste facilities. Decision-making power has been shifted from the political wheeling and dealing in the state capital to the local courthouse, which is much more accessible. All of these positions on solid waste issues were developed by KFTC members.

KFTC's Organizational Structure

Kentuckians who support KFTC's goals become members of the organization by paying dues ($10 to $25 per year, based on ability to pay). To provide the greatest number of opportunities for participation and leadership, KFTC's membership is organized into chapters. Chapters are established in every county where KFTC has 15 or more active members (and at least 30 after two years), and they agree to chapter accountability requirements. (See Appendix.) County chapters, rather than groups organized around identified constituencies or issue interests, make the most sense for rural Kentuckians, who typically have a strong identification with their counties. Chapters have the right to petition for the use of KFTC's resources—staff, legal, technical, and financial—and members can attend and offer input at Steering Committee meetings.

When the membership structure was established, the Steering Committee determined that membership should mean more than just paying annual dues. KFTC members have the opportunity to vote each year for the organization's officers, to set the annual platform of goals and priorities, and to select a Steering Committee representative if they live in a county with a chapter. Members are encouraged to use their newly acquired skills in a contagious way. Once they learn how to do something, it is their responsibility to share their skills and knowledge with others: members are student, teacher, mentor, and trainee interchangeably.

The annual platform-setting process is of particular importance. Each September, all county chapters meet to rank the issues that they feel KFTC should work on. Members in nonchapter counties are encouraged to provide similar input. The Steering Committee compiles these rankings into a proposed platform that is circulated among the membership in KFTC's monthly newspaper, *Balancing the Scales*. The final platform is adopted at the annual meeting each October.

The *platform* guides KFTC's work. On the basis of the platform and the activities of the local chapters, the Steering Committee sets priorities for staff time. For example, the platform priorities shape KFTC's decisions on whether and how to respond to requests from local communities and groups for assistance. To help ensure control of the organization's activities by the Steering Committee, these priorities are reviewed and voted on at each bi-monthly Steering Committee meeting.

KFTC does not work on any statewide issue unless the matter cannot be solved at the local level and unless a chapter (or chapters) requests formal statewide action to help deal with it. This policy, plus the platform and continual Steering Committee review, helps keep the organization in line with the needs and energies of its members and prevents a situation common in many other groups in which a few key leaders or staff people have too much influence on the direction of the organization.

As the task of directing the operations of a rapidly growing organization expanded, the Steering Committee established several sub-committees. Executive, Personnel, Finance, and Leadership Development committees share administrative and program responsibilities. An Environmental Rights Committee, a Land Reform Committee, and a Legislative Democracy Working Group have also been formed to broaden and guide work on these issues. Most committee members come from outside the Steering Committee so as to distribute decision-making duties among a larger number of members. Including ad hoc committees (for the annual membership meeting, the annual picnic, the Fall Fundraising Campaign, and special projects like the Tenth Anniversary Campaign), more than seventy people are involved in KFTC's statewide governance structure. Each chapter also has a membership coordinator, a fundraising coordinator, and a correspondent for *Balancing the Scales,* providing additional formal leadership roles.

KFTC believes in "multiple leadership," making sure that new people are constantly given leadership opportunities. Officers can serve only two years in a row, and chapter representatives have a three-year limit. No one person or small group can control the organization, which makes decisions more responsive to the membership. This also makes it harder for anyone to destroy a chapter or the organization because there is no single point of leadership to attack.

The structure and methods that KFTC uses in its governance are flexible enough for anyone to use in organizing, yet restrictive enough so that people cannot use them for their own personal gain.

Strengths of KFTC's Organizing

One of the early lessons that KFTC learned was that to get things changed in Appalachian Kentucky, it was more important to gain the support of people throughout Kentucky than it was to solicit help from people in other Appalachian states, an approach that many citizen organizations in Appalachia have pursued in the past. With major shifts in the early 1980s from the federal to the state level for such things as the delivery of human services, funding for education, and enforcement of environmental policies, KFTC leaders realized that they had to look to the governor and the state legislature for solutions to many of the problems facing eastern Kentucky, and that support and membership had to be organized in Kentucky's non-Appalachian counties to win victories at the state level. This also meant that KFTC had to figure out how to raise money for the long haul, to make sure it was seen as a permanent fixture in the political scene rather than a fly-by-night operation. In addition, strategic thinking had to take a long-term view, and serious thought had to be given to how to integrate all five of KFTC's goals into the organization's development. Issues of concern in other parts of the state and broader training sessions were crucial to this scenario. For example, the goals of the 1988 constitutional amendment campaign were (1) to pass the amendment limiting the abuses of broad form deeds, (2) to increase membership, (3) to have more people learn organizing skills, and (4) to educate the public about landowners' rights, the coal industry, and the economic situation in Appalachia.

KFTC's ability to work on local and statewide issues at the same time is one of its strengths. Unlike organizations devoted to one issue, KFTC is able to work on any campaign in which a significant number of members are willing to participate. Whether it is to be resolved in the bureaucracy, the courts, the legislature, the executive branch, or at a local government meeting, KFTC is willing and able to travel many different routes to deal with an issue.

By using a multi-issue approach, KFTC members can work on each other's issues, giving them a way to learn from each other. For example, through their activities in KFTC, urban blacks working on utility rate reform and rural whites pushing for landowners' rights discovered they had a lot in common when the legislature killed all their bills behind closed doors. Making the legislative process more open and democratic and pushing for long-term institutional change became their common goal. At the same time, such alliances allow the possibility of dealing with racism on a personal level.

Being a multi-issue organization has also allowed KFTC to glean valuable lessons from each issue it has addressed. One of these is that direct-action organizing groups can sometimes get sidetracked into direct service, public awareness, or advocacy. There are so many problems in the world that people try to do too much at once and can forget to stay focused on the five goals of organizing. Another lesson was that direct-action organizing combined with victories did not necessarily produce institutional change. Getting a public water system solves a problem, but may do little to prevent further damage by strip mining. KFTC members also learned that during a slow period in a major campaign on one issue, a multi-issue group can shift its focus in order to maintain members' interest and morale. The multi-issue approach also helps members understand connections between issues. In addition, issues that require a long time to resolve provide more leadership development opportunities.

One reason KFTC is able to work on so many issues is that it trains its members in leadership and organizing skills. KFTC was the first community organization in Appalachia to systematically integrate leadership training into its work. Some organizing schools, networks, and groups in other parts of the country have used these techniques for years, but most groups in the mountains have had more of a "movement" mentality rather than a commitment to the nuts and bolts of building solid organizations.

The heart of KFTC's leadership development philosophy can be found in the preface of its *Leadership Development Training Manual*. Adopted by the KFTC Steering Committee in 1985, the preface outlines the ideal of citizen leadership within the organization:

> Everyone has the potential to lead, but most people are discouraged from taking leadership roles. Our social and economic systems prevent ordinary people from recognizing and developing their talents and skills for leadership by celebrating the rich, powerful and well-educated as leaders. Too often society ignores the contributions of homemakers, retirees, laborers and others in making their communities better places to live. To break these barriers, KFTC's leadership training program is intended to draw out an individual's potential and encourage ongoing skill development by practice and direct application in real situations.

Training sessions consist of practice, role playing, discussion, and evaluations. KFTC's training sessions are not lectures; rather, they draw ideas from the group, with a deep respect for the talents and energies of the participants. Sometimes they are led by staff, sometimes by experienced members. Through this practical and methodical group training, KFTC members learn to lobby legislators, write letters to the editor, raise money, run meetings, talk to the press, and hold public forums. KFTC believes that training is most valuable when it is applied. The leadership training has been so effective that staff control, so common in some citizens' groups, would be difficult to wield in KFTC. At the annual membership meeting, for example, the staff may not speak during the business meeting and elections unless they are asked to respond to a specific question by a member.

Training opportunities, both formal and informal, are continually available to allow KFTC members to expand their skills and leadership potential. Leaders teach skills to new members, and organizers prepare members for events. But it is the group skills training that is the backbone of KFTC's leadership development. Using the training manual described above (which is shared with more than thirty groups throughout North America), workshop topics range from recruiting members to running effective meetings to developing strategies. The workshops, ranging from one hour to an all-day session, are conducted in a variety of settings. Most occur in local communities: in community meeting rooms, libraries, churches, a member's home or backyard.

KFTC also sponsors Kentucky Leadership Schools. Held several times a year, Leadership Schools offer an intensive leadership and organizing training opportunity and are open to members of other citizens groups as well. Three or four topics are covered in one day. In addition, leadership skills workshops are offered at the annual membership meeting and other gatherings, as well as at the chapter level. Gladys Maynard, KFTC's first chairperson, had participated in training by other organizations before she became involved with KFTC. Her comments about the experience reflect KFTC's positions on leadership: "Once I went through the trainings, I realized being a leader was something I'd really been doing all along. Most people are qualified [to be leaders] but it's never having the opportunity that frightens them."

Another reason for KFTC's success is that roles are clearly drawn: members, leaders, organizers, and technical experts.

- *Members* pay dues, identify issues, elect leaders, plan actions, and do the group's work. They support each other, attend meetings and events, and provide a power base.
- *Leaders* are members who develop new leaders, provide direction, motivate and inspire others, coordinate activities, and speak for the organization. They plan meetings and events, implement group decisions, hold members accountable, resolve conflicts, and make emergency decisions when needed. Leaders are not just the elected officers. A successful group has many members with various leadership and organizational skills that may be needed and applied at any given time.
- *Organizers* facilitate training sessions and identify and help to develop leaders. This role is often misunderstood. Organizers do not tell members what to do. They agitate, prod, and push, creating "leadership opportunities" for members to learn new skills while being supportive and offering insights from the experiences of other groups. They produce publications and reports for the organization, but never speak publicly on behalf of the group. They are in the background and not

the forefront, following through on the decisions that members and leaders make as a group.

- *Technical experts* provide advice, information, and credibility. Lawyers, geologists, and land surveyors work for the members to transfer skills to them, teaching them as much as possible so that they can become "experts" themselves. Technical experts help make complicated matters digestible, but they never make decisions for members and leaders. In its eleven-year history, KFTC has had on its staff a hydrologist, who was with the organization three years, a researcher, and first one, then two, part-time attorneys, in addition to technical experts hired for short periods as needed. KFTC's attorneys handle the organization's litigation, give it legal advice, and help draft legislation. The researcher devotes most of his time to working on reports about who mines Kentucky's coal and other issues related to the economy in Kentucky.

Other KFTC strengths include its publishing program. Its monthly newspaper (*Balancing the Scales*) and its other publications (including literacy materials and an annual study on the ownership and control of coal production in Kentucky) are known for their high quality. The newspaper format of *Balancing the Scales* makes it inexpensive to print and easy to distribute to a wide audience. It allows for a variety of coverage: local chapter updates, news of statewide campaigns, feature stories, member interviews, a monthly calendar of events, photographs, cartoons, profiles of mining and waste companies, and articles on broader economic issues and organizing skills.

The organization's members use creative tactics to accomplish their goals—another strength. Some of the best tactics are those that unite and involve many people, have direct impact on the target, have media appeal and high public visibility, and involve creativity, surprise, and, ideally, fun. A full-scale funeral was held in the state capitol building to let the public know that Kentucky was becoming a dumping ground for east coast garbage. When KFTC got tired of the secretary of the Kentucky Natural Resources and Environmental Protection Cabinet's failure to protect the state and its residents, members put up "Wanted" posters with his picture on them all over the state. Knowing that the waste industry was cutting backroom deals with some legislative leaders, KFTC leaders did a live political cartoon that portrayed legislators and industry lobbyists in bed together. The KFTC Toxics Committee staged a rally in front of the Division of Waste Management office in Frankfort, where they hung a clothesline with plastic skeletons and signs declaring this an exposure of the state's dirty laundry. KFTC's tactics have been an ongoing source of organization and personal nourishment. "The worst thing that [state offi-cials] ever did was build roads so that we can get out of eastern Kentucky," said Ruth Colvin at the Frankfort rally described above. "Now we can get up here and raise a little hell."

Providing for the future meant being farsighted about where the money to run KFTC would come from. Besides grassroots fundraising, KFTC depends on donations from foundations, churches, and individuals. Since many of these give money for only a limited period of time, KFTC decided to establish an endowment fund to provide for times when the foundation fountain might slow to a trickle or go dry.

Another very important reason for setting up an endowment was the sense of organizational permanence it gave KFTC's members. "We plan to be around for a long time," said Mary Jane Adams, introducing the campaign. "We've just begun to fight the injustices faced by the people of Kentucky and with a successful [endowment] campaign, we're going to make sure KFTC is here as long as necessary." Endowment funds will also allow the organization to defend its victories in the future and will give KFTC options for additional expansion projects or special campaigns. As of June 1, 1992, the endowment had more than $850,000 in it.

Two final strengths involve leadership and attitudes. KFTC has em-phasized placing women in leadership positions, and twelve of eighteen statewide officers to date have been women. And the organizational men-tality holds that a group can always refine its goals, objectives, process, and methods. KFTC's willingness to use a cyclical process of planning, acting, and evaluating allows for healthy changes and improvements in the organization. Each year, new ideas and methods from other citizens' groups are incorporated into KFTC's system.

Weaknesses of KFTC's Organizing

Although KFTC has been successful, there are still weaknesses in its model, improvements to be made, and obstacles to be overcome.

The major strength of KFTC's structure is that it is member-run and democratic. But that can sometimes pose problems. The democratic pro-cess can be slow, inefficient, and costly. It simply takes longer to make de-cisions in a large membership-controlled organization than it does in more hierarchical groups. Sympathetic lobbyists, legislators, funders, reporters, and others sometimes have a hard time understanding that individual members and staff people cannot make major decisions independently, but must call a chapter or Steering Committee meeting to discuss and vote on new ideas, requests, or changes in strategy.

Another structural problem is that representation is not proportional: the person representing a chapter with 300 members has the same voting power as the person representing a chapter with 30 members. (Nevertheless, limiting counties to one chapter and one Steering Committee representative favors the rural counties and ensures that the Steering Committee will always be composed predominantly of rural representatives, which is a deliberate policy of the organization and keeps it focused on rural issues.) Also, the one at-large member on the Executive Committee is the only voice for the at-large membership, those who live in counties without KFTC chapters. There is no clear way for the at-large membership to communicate their views to the at-large Executive Committee member.

KFTC's membership has increased steadily over the years, but there is reason to be concerned over its composition. Initially, KFTC's targeted constituency was rural, low- and middle-income, longtime residents of the eastern Kentucky coalfields—those most directly affected by the problems KFTC set out to address—as well as anyone else willing to support KFTC actively. For the most part KFTC was successful in recruiting this constituency, but it failed to attract in any significant numbers people with very low incomes, racial minorities, people with low literacy skills, and youth. This has remained true as KFTC has grown into more of a statewide organization. Lower-middle-income people were joining, but the very poor generally were not. KFTC ran up against several obstacles in trying to involve low-income people. Besides a lack of money, transportation, and child care and health care services, some had no telephones, while others had no utility services at all. Low reading levels often compounded these problems and made meetings and mailings appear intimidating.

To address these obstacles, KFTC offered a sliding dues scale and full dues waivers on request, travel cost reimbursement for attending regional meetings, car-pooling, scholarships for workshops and conferences, and other types of financial assistance. The organization made a more conscientious effort to be sensitive to non- or low-level readers by using less written material in leadership training workshops. In 1987 KFTC launched a three-year project staffed by a volunteer through the Mennonite Central Committee U.S. Appalachia Program to develop materials about KFTC issues specifically for those who read at low levels. Despite these efforts, few low-income people got involved.

The barriers were not only logistical. KFTC's issues may have had less appeal to those with very low incomes, even though they would have benefited if some of those campaigns were won. Why worry about getting more tax money for local governments and school systems when your own household budget is insufficient to meet basic needs? Why be concerned about strip mining's destruction of the land and displacement of people from their homes if you do not own land or a home?

In its early years, few blacks were involved in KFTC activities. This was due, in part, to the lack of racial diversity in the eastern Kentucky coalfields. Once KFTC grew into a statewide organization with urban chapters, the lack of racial diversity became more obvious. Although KFTC had active chapters in Louisville and Lexington, Kentucky's largest cities with substantial minority populations, there was no influx of minority members. Some of the reasons for this included the fact that many of the members in the urban chapters were people who had previously lived or worked in eastern Kentucky, almost all of whom were white. Since much of KFTC's recruitment still took place by word of mouth, the white urban members tended to recruit those closest to them: relatives, friends, and neighbors who were also white. Moreover, why should minorities support an issue platform that they did not develop, or join an organization with few minority members or leaders?

KFTC's staff and leaders became increasingly aware that even though they had made a strong verbal commitment to increase the involvement of minorities and the poor in their organization, this would not happen without a conscious and deliberate strategy. Thus in March 1991 the KFTC Steering Committee voted to allot a designated amount of organizing time each week specifically to work on diversifying KFTC's constituency to include more racial minorities and low-income members. Soon afterward, KFTC hosted a workshop in Louisville on multiracial organizing and began exploring other ways KFTC could be more deliberate about targeting and recruiting a broad-based multiracial constituency. In addition, KFTC's Leadership Development Committee is now required to consider such characteristics as gender, race, income-level, and age when developing nominations for statewide offices and committee positions.

Despite KFTC's sophisticated leadership development efforts, there is still room for improvement. One shortcoming is that leadership skills workshops focus mainly on nuts-and-bolts organizing skills, and there is seldom the opportunity to analyze and critique the political economy or to make the links between local and statewide issues, or between local and state issues and national and global structures and events. KFTC seeks to address this problem with workshops on "Power Analysis." While it provides a very basic and sometimes simplistic picture of who holds the power and why and how to change power relationships, it has proven effective in helping members to think more about root causes and systemic changes. Newer workshops include "Approaches to Change" and "What Would a More Desirable Society Look Like?"

One of the most pressing challenges KFTC faces is to create the time and space to systematically analyze what has happened in the past and to engage in deliberate long-range planning for the future. In its relatively short history, KFTC has achieved remarkable success at the local and state level. Many of KFTC's issue campaigns have been so ambitious and demanding that it has been difficult to step back from the intense action and take time for detailed analysis of its work. This analysis is currently being undertaken by a recently created Long Range Planning Committee and is critical to KFTC's immediate and long-term effectiveness.

In addition, KFTC must pay more attention to how much energy it should devote to maintaining its existing chapters, leaders, and members and how much it should give to developing new ones. Several of KFTC's existing chapters lack focus because they no longer have a burning issue—in most cases because they have won that campaign. Should KFTC spend energy and resources helping these chapters get involved in new organizing activities? Or should KFTC go where the energy is by investing its resources in new groups working on new issues? There is increasing concern that issues may play too great a role in determining KFTC's direction. KFTC needs to develop better ways of community-based organizing (developing relationships that include common interests and promote broad social change) instead of focusing so much on desired change on specific issues.

Finally, KFTC is under constant pressure to meet the needs of the membership with limited staff, financial, legal, and technical resources; the organization sometimes tries to do too much at once, becoming overextended and ineffective with limited organizing tools. For example, finding good staff people to keep up with the expansion needs of the organization is not easy, especially when they have to work in isolated areas. KFTC has joined with other groups to form the Southern Empowerment Project, which recruits and trains new organizers.

Conclusion

The essence of organizing is to shift power relations so that the interests of the many are respected. There are various types of power: political, economic, social, cultural, moral. There is also perceived power, actual power, and potential power. Power, in other words, is often difficult to evaluate and measure.

Economic power clearly has not been KFTC's trump card. Though the organization has done some impressive fundraising and its budget and endowment expanded considerably over the years, the organization's assets pale next to those of the corporations it has challenged and continues to confront.

People power is clearly KFTC's strength—the power of numbers. Yet KFTC's highest membership count during its first eleven years was

2,500, in a state with 3.7 million people. Similarly, the most county chapters KFTC ever had was 16, fewer than 15 percent of the state's 120 counties. KFTC's ability to mobilize people and hold mass public actions has been limited. Its biggest statewide event, a rally in Frankfort, drew fewer than 250 people. So exactly how powerful and influential is KFTC?

If sheer numbers and financial clout alone are used as a measure, KFTC appears relatively insignificant. But such criteria can be deceiving. Almost every KFTC member has wide circles of relationships—families, friends, co-workers, neighbors, fellow church members. Thousands of Kentuckians have benefited from KFTC's work: residents of the coal communities who are receiving millions of dollars in new revenue from the unmined minerals tax; people whose land has been saved from destructive strip mining; citizens who have been spared the horror of unnecessary hazardous waste facilities in their communities; or families who have had their ruined water supplies replaced. All of these are part of KFTC's potential power base.

The campaign for the broad form deed amendment tested the gap between KFTC's perceived and potential power. KFTC made connections with anyone and everyone to ask for active involvement and support. Active members contacted former members and nonmembers who had benefited from KFTC's activity or who had heard of the organization but never joined, creating a ripple effect. Just how far-reaching those circles were became obvious on Election Day when the votes were tallied. The coal industry outspent KFTC three to one and made heavy use of expensive electronic media, yet 868,634 Kentuckians voted to pass the amendment. It received 82.5 percent voter approval, one of the highest winning margins for an amendment in Kentucky's history, and passed in all 120 counties.

KFTC has increasingly earned itself a place as a respected player in Kentucky's local and state political arenas. But as Herb E. Smith, a native of Whitesburg, Kentucky, conveys below, KFTC's greatest impact has been on the powerless of eastern Kentucky. KFTC's broad form deed victory, its staying power, its multi-issue approach, and its focus on democratic empowerment have given the region's people hope and an opportunity to improve and enrich their own lives on their own terms:

> I think twenty years from now people are going to be talking about the broad form deed campaign. Previous to it there was this sense that coal was king. The king would have different squabbles with some of his subjects, but generally the subjects would end up falling in line. That's what the coal industry believed. If it came to spending, they had more money. If it came to court battles, they had more lawyers.

No matter how unjust or wrong the broad form deed was, it wasn't obvious at all that we were going to win. . . . But once it happened and the returns were in, the whole playing field changed. It's not so scary any more. It's one of those times when all the makeup and paint gets washed away.

I don't think there's any question that KFTC will be here in ten more years. . . . I think once it has worked so clearly for people to be an effective part of the democratic process that this country is founded on, I don't think you could ever go back on that.

I think there are a number of things that will have to be dealt with for the long haul. But I guess the point for me is that it's not exactly what's on my list that's important, because what's in place now is an idea. . . . And whether that idea is applied to the kinds of things that it has been today or a whole different set of things, it's a powerful idea.

It's the idea that people have the responsibility and the capacity to deal with the kinds of things that affect their lives. And through coordinated efforts we can actually make some changes in this state. It's really simple, in a way.

I was taught in grade school that that was what this country was about. I was given those words. But what I was really told was, "Be quiet." What you were taught probably more than anything was the power of money. Families wanted to keep their jobs. Teachers wanted to keep their paychecks even if they weren't really teaching. The idea that people have the power and the responsibility—whether that's true or not, the point is in *acting,* taking action, putting those ideas into effect. That's the radical part, that we would actually believe it enough to try to cause it to happen. Once that is working, then I don't think any of the everyday things can stop it. You know, all of the other stuff is important day to day, but the idea is the power I trust.

Acknowledgments

Many people have offered comments on this chapter. They include Naomi Baer, Linda Brock, Julie Burns, Walter Davis, Steve Fisher, Jerry Hardt, Terry Keleher, Burt Lauderdale, Jenny Bea Lauderdale, Daymon Morgan, June Rostan, Ellen Ryan, Herb E. Smith, Steve Stoltz, Kristin Layng Szakos, Maynard Tetreault, Jean True, Patty Wallace, and Melanie Zuercher. Ideas for the strengths and weaknesses sections were originally discussed at Steering Committee meetings, KFTC Leadership Retreats, Leadership Schools, and staff meetings. Unless otherwise attributed, quotations come from KFTC publications.

Appendix

PETITION TO BE A CHAPTER OF
KENTUCKIANS FOR THE COMMONWEALTH

COUNTY _____   DATE _____

We hereby petition the membership of Kentuckians For The Commonwealth to be accepted as a chapter.

We realize that our rights as a chapter are:

1. to be a formal part of Kentuckians For The Commonwealth, a statewide citizens social justice organization which uses direct-action community organizing methods;
2. to get one vote on all matters brought before the Steering Committee;
3. to ask for an excused absence for our Steering Committee Representative missing a meeting if there is reasonable cause, if the Alternate or another member cannot attend, and if the KFTC Chairperson is notified in advance;
4. to make recommendations on issues and programs in the annual platform setting process;
5. to participate in KFTC statewide events, issues and programs;
6. to request organizational support for chapter activities;
7. to receive preference over non-chapter counties in getting organizational support and resources;
8. to request staff support for chapter activities (organizing, technical, legal, administrative and program staff support);
9. to request organizational assistance for holding local leadership development workshops and issue workshops;
10. to nominate members to serve as KFTC statewide officers and committee members;
11. to receive preference over members from non-chapter counties for chapter members to become statewide officers or committee members;
12. to receive discounts and fee waivers, when offered, for chapter members at KFTC conferences and Leadership Schools, and to receive priority over non-chapter members for attending such events when space is limited;
13. to request the use of KFTC's publicity services (such as media contacts, flyers and mailings to newspapers throughout the state);
14. to request the use of KFTC's internal communication services (such as use of KFTC's mailing list or phone tree for KFTC activities);

15. to request the use of KFTC's mailing services to send notices of chapter meetings and other routine activities;
16. to participate in multi-county fundraisers, if desired, to help raise the chapter fundraising requirement each year;
17. to submit articles and local updates on chapter activities for *Balancing the Scales;*
18. to review all official records of the organization.

We realize that our duties as a chapter are:

1. to elect a Steering Committee Representative and an Alternate;
2. to have a representative attend *all* Steering Committee meetings and the annual Steering Committee retreat (mileage to these meetings is paid by KFTC);
3. to elect a chapter membership coordinator, chapter fundraising coordinator, a chapter correspondent for *Balancing the Scales* and other local officers as needed;
4. to have chapter representatives attend the KFTC Annual Membership Meeting;
5. to have an Annual Chapter Meeting during the month of September, and meet at other times as needed;
6. to make recommendations of issues in the annual platform setting process;
7. to participate in KFTC statewide events and work on platform issues;
8. to set chapter membership goals for the upcoming year at the Annual Chapter Meeting;
9. to begin with at least 15 members; increase to a level of 30 active members within two years; expand chapter membership each year by having an annual membership drive and by assisting in the collection of membership renewals (the KFTC main office sends out a notice at the time each member must renew her/his dues);
10. to set chapter fundraising goals each year, prior to the beginning of the calendar year;
11. to raise a minimum of $500 in grassroots fundraisers (over and above membership dues and individual donations), and preferably to exceed the minumum requirement;
12. to participate in the KFTC Fall Fundraising Campaign by contacting each member in person or by phone to ask for a donation;
13. to develop a chapter phone tree system and activate it when needed;
14. to help chapter members develop leadership skills;
15. to support KFTC's goals and platform and use direct-action community organizing methods.

PROCEDURES FOR ACCEPTANCE, CONTINUING
AND TERMINATING CHAPTER STATUS

ACCEPTANCE/CONTINUING: A petition for acceptance as a KFTC chapter must be made to the KFTC membership at the Annual Membership Meeting in October. In the event that a new chapter is formed between membership meetings, the petition must be made to the KFTC Steering Committee at its next regularly scheduled meeting following the receipt of the chapter petition form.

A chapter has the right to petition for modifications in its duties, but such modifications must be acknowledged and approved at the time of chapter acceptance.

VOLUNTARY TERMINATION: A chapter wishing to terminate its chapter status can simply not petition to continue to be a chapter at the next Annual Membership Meeting or submit a request for termination to the KFTC Chairperson at any time during the year.

INVOLUNTARY TERMINATION: Failure to meet the obligations of a chapter will result in the loss of chapter status and all accompanying benefits.

Failure to have the Steering Committee Representative, Alternate or an active member of the chapter at three Steering Committee meetings in a row will result in automatic loss of chapter status.

The Steering Committee has the authority to declare a chapter deficient in meeting its obligations and either require corrective action or terminate chapter status.

In the event that chapter status is terminated, the Steering Committee will establish a reinstatement process for the chapter to gain back full status.

AGREEMENT

We understand and agree to all of the benefits, responsibilities and procedures listed above.

Steering Committee Representative

Steering Committee Alternate

Approved and accepted by the KFTC Steering Committee on _____ .

(date)

_____

KFTC Chairperson

Please attach a list of members who attended the local meeting where it was decided that chapter status would be requested of KFTC.

Members of the Community Farm Alliance protesting against low farm income compared with high retail profits, 1991. (*Lois Kleffman, CFA*)

7

The Community Farm Alliance in Kentucky

The Growth, Mistakes, and Lessons of the Farm Movement of the 1980s

Hal Hamilton
Ellen Ryan

After he published an eloquent letter about the farm crisis in his local paper, Tom Robertson's neighbors said they were surprised he could write like that. "Shoot," said Tom, "you can't tell how deep a well is by the length of the pump handle." The same could be said of the family farm movement. Many people think of farmers primarily as a special interest group hurt by economic change. But at a deeper level the farm movement contains lessons for us all about the vision and strategy necessary to transform progressive politics as we head into the next century.

The farm crisis of the early 1980s spurred the development of dozens of new farm groups. The media and public paid attention to the symptoms of the crisis: foreclosures and bankruptcies. Meanwhile, farmers and their neighbors have been engaged in a fundamental challenge to prerogatives of those who are now powerful in our society.

The most successful of the new farm groups are adapting lessons of community organizing to their circumstances and becoming multi-issue organizations. This chapter is about the Community Farm Alliance in Kentucky, the people who created it, their struggles to survive as farmers, and the lessons they have learned about organizing. We will set the stage by explaining the farm economy and the politics of farm policy.

Inflation, Bust, and the Farm Crisis

The farmers' financial crisis followed a decade of inflation. During the 1970s, when automobile drivers paid high prices for gasoline, farmers around the world happily received rising prices for corn, soybeans, wheat, and other commodities. Oil money from the Middle East flowed through banks to the producers of raw materials in the Third World and the United States. Farmers increased their debt tenfold during the 1970s, a debt secured with inflated land values.

In the late 1970s and early 1980s, policy-makers in Washington and New York pulled the plug on credit and the money flow. Interest rates soared, raw commodity prices plummeted, and the world's raw materials producers were left holding the bag.

The 1980s farm crisis accentuated forty years of trouble for farmers and further spurred the industrialization of agriculture. Ever since the early 1950s, farm policy has been designed to wean "excess resources (primarily people) out of agriculture."[1] The chief goal of corporations and their government allies has been to secure the production of cheaper commodities by replacing farmers with machinery and chemicals.

The farm movement began as a response to an economic crisis, but the new organizations and leaders also came to confront their basic assumptions about increasingly large, chemical-dependent farms integrated into a corporate economy. Farmers organized because their family livelihoods were threatened, but a significant number of grassroots leaders reached for a broad understanding of their role in history.

Over the past few decades, farmers' operations have been increasingly dominated by an economic logic that measures only the bottom line of Schedule F, a farmer's federal tax form. If farm A can produce a bushel of corn cheaper than farm B, then farm B should be encouraged either to become more efficient or to cease operation. Farm B may be one of hundreds of smaller farms that support vital small towns and carefully steward rolling land. No matter. Schedule F, every farmer's tax schedule, does not measure small town vitality or topsoil erosion. It does not measure sediment or pesticide accumulation in groundwater. It does not measure the public costs of installing municipal water systems in areas where fertilizer and pesticide runoff have made the well water too hazardous to drink. It does not measure the safety or dignity of the work provided by the farm. It does not measure whether the farm nurtures a generation of children who experience the work, the joys and sorrows, and the accumulated wisdom that come from tending the land in a balanced and respectful system.

The issues of the U.S. and international farm movement are economic issues, certainly. But when farm activists talk about fair prices to farmers as their "bottom line," they are not talking solely about the bottom line on Schedule F. They are talking about prices that reflect the costs and benefits of caring for the land, the laborers, and the local communities that make up the natural and social ecology of agriculture. And they are demanding that government officials include these costs and benefits in the economic equation used to set farm policy.

The 1980s, however, were a decade of political withdrawal from economic responsibility. Republican administrations refused to protect people and communities from the economic and environmental fallout of the market economy. Laissez-faire policies originated in a theory that the market operates most efficiently if government refrains from intervening in the economy. Because transnational corporations control the global market, laissez-faire policies leave the corporations free to exercise their power without restraint.

The one sector of our economy still based on family-scale enterprises is agriculture. All of the buyers of farm commodities, however, are large corporations. Farm policy is constructed by a policy-making fraternity among which corporate lobbyists play a leading role. Farm policy is not eternal, however, and can be changed. Farm policy is written by elected politicians, sometimes at the service of the highest bidder, but usually convinced by the power of votes.

Farm policy is enacted in Washington but has been hidden from view. Newspaper editorial writers, agricultural economists, and farm publication propagandists would all have us believe that we are witnessing the inevitable march of progress rather than the calculated result of policy decisions.

Two examples illustrate that farm policy rather than "progress" determines the structure of ownership and control of agriculture. The first is chicken farming. In the United States a few huge corporations (Tyson, ConAgra, Gold Kist, Holly Farms, and Perdue) have vertically integrated the poultry industry so that they control the process from the hatchery to the retail chains. Farmers produce poultry on contract to these major corporations. As part of their contracts, farmers provide capital and labor, and they bear the risks posed by weather, machinery failure, and disease. But the farmers make no production decisions. They receive each flock of chicks on the company's schedule, and they feed, handle, and medicate them exactly as they are told. The farmers turn the birds over to the company when they are told to, for which they receive two to four cents per pound. This system of "contract farming" has developed within a "laissez-faire" political environment. The government has taken no steps to protect poultry farmers from corporate abuses of the contract system.

In Canada, on the other hand, chickens are still raised autonomously on family farms. Farmers determine their own production schedules and practices, taking into account local conditions. When each flock is ready for market, they can choose the best offer for their chickens from among a variety of companies. Why is the Canadian system different?

Canadian farmers organized and succeeded in establishing a public policy administered by farmer-boards that allocate production quotas among farmers and require the processors to pay a fair price for the poultry.

Peanut and tobacco production in the United States is similarly organized, with production controls and price support loan programs established by law and administered by farmer cooperatives. This public policy accomplishes two goals: companies are required to pay prices above a politically negotiated floor, and production is allocated with market quotas to thousands of family farms, thus preventing the concentration of peanut and tobacco farming into larger and larger farms. These programs run at no cost to taxpayers.

Why aren't other U.S. farm commodities covered by similar production allocation and loan programs? At one time, they were. In response to farm organizing during the Great Depression of the 1930s, farm policies covering major farm commodities were put into place as part of the New Deal of the Roosevelt administration. These New Deal farm policies managed the supply of farm products, dispersed production among thousands of small farms, and established floor prices backed by government loans. But the steady increase in the power of grain trading and food processing corporations after the end of World War II has allowed these corporations to shape food policy in Washington.

Corporations engaged in the global trade and transportation of farm commodities, as well as those engaged in processing and marketing finished products, have an economic interest in buying commodities at low prices. The less corporations have to pay for raw materials, the greater their profits upon resale. Congress has for decades set farm policies that determine the lowest price at which the major farm commodities may be sold. Because corporations by themselves do not have the power to determine commodity prices, they have spent millions of dollars on contributions to political action committees (PACs) and direct lobbying in efforts to influence policy-makers. This investment has paid off handsomely. Although farm income plummeted in the 1980s, net returns for commodity trading and processing corporations hit record highs.

During the farm financial crisis years of 1981 to 1987, when more than 20 percent of U.S. farmers had to leave farming, the agricultural processing sector averaged a 14.3 percent profit rate. During those same years Kellogg's return on equity averaged 33.4 percent. RJR Nabisco averaged 22.8 percent, and HJ Heinz received a return of 21.2 percent. Cargill, the nation's largest agribusiness company, reported a 66 percent increase in earnings in the first year following passage of the 1985 farm bill. These profits were being realized by corporate America during the same years that net income to Kentucky farmers fell by more than 27 percent.[2]

During the 1970s and 1980s the federal government moved away from providing a loan program that maintained adequate price floors to farmers, prices that had to be paid by corporate buyers of commodities. As farm income dropped, new policies instituted direct payments from taxpayers to farmers. A low market price is now mitigated by a subsidy check. Corporate buyers are able to purchase commodities more cheaply than ever before, with farm income subsidized from the federal treasury. Farmers are dramatically more dependent upon government checks, but Wes Jackson of the Land Institute remarked, "The government isn't really subsidizing farmers; it is using farmers to launder money to subsidize the agribusiness corporations."

In effect, American consumers pay twice for their food, once at the supermarket check-out counter and once in their taxes. The shift in policy from maintaining price floors to subsidizing farm income has contributed to the federal deficit. And because payments go to farmers rather than to the corporations, the source of the problem—corporate unwillingness to pay a fair price for the products they receive—is hidden from the public. Farmers get milked and food companies get the cream.

Technology and Ideology

Throughout U.S. history family farmers have been faced with two sets of problems—one external to farming and one internal. Externally, farmers have been easy prey for the businesses that sold them inputs (fuel, fertilizer, seed, machinery) and for the businesses that bought their products. Internally, the structured relationships between people within agriculture also threaten what most family farmers find valuable about their own lifestyles and community economies.

Especially since the second world war, farmers have been weaned from a household or community economy and force-fed business values. During the early 1950s corporate executives, government planners, and university leaders issued a report recommending that "the price supports for wheat, cotton, rice, feed grains and related crops now under price support be reduced immediately." This reduction in price supports, they said, would have two results: "the program would involve moving off the farm about two million of the present farm labor force, plus a number equal to a large part of the new entrants who would otherwise join the farm labor force in the next five years . . . [and] . . . the lower prices would induce some increased sales of these products both at home and abroad."[3]

The internal threat to family farming has come from the agricultural trends that Dwight Eisenhower's secretary of agriculture, Ezra Taft

Benson, called, "Get big or get out." Richard Nixon's secretary of agriculture, Earl Butz, used even more graphic words to describe the same set of policies: "Adapt or die."

Low farm commodity prices and the development of export markets have combined to stimulate credit-worthy farmers to increase their capital investment and their efficiencies of production. The "green revolution" of the 1950s, 1960s, and 1970s was fueled by pesticides, fertilizer, hybrid seeds, and sophisticated machinery. We are now in the midst of a new technological push from computer applications and biotechnology.

Sophisticated technology has permitted ever more productivity, even though farms have maintained their small business character. Farms are larger, more industrialized, and integrated into the corporate economy, but production still primarily involves family units. Family farms are not being replaced by corporate farms, except in sectors amenable to the use of migrant labor. Family farms supply cheap family labor willing to work long hours and absorb the risks of weather and disease. The pressure on family farmers to continually reduce their labor value, and the increasing portion of production inputs supplied by technology and petrochemicals, have "industrialized" large sectors of commercial agriculture and yielded a propensity to overproduction. This tendency to overproduction, or, in economists' terms, "excess capacity," is a direct result of the success of a policy that has placed farmers on a technological treadmill in order to supply plentiful and cheap raw materials for the wholesale and export markets.

Farmers' interest in productivity and increasing their family income leaves them vulnerable to being cultivated for the purposes of others. The universities and agribusiness carefully nurture a one-dimensional image of success, an image that relies upon the self-consciousness of farmers as business operators.

The "best" farmers have often come to be defined as the ones who are the most modern, who use the latest machinery and chemicals to produce the largest yield. These "best" farmers are developed as leaders and held up as examples to all of their colleagues. Modern farming methods and modern farming thinking are packaged together. It has become almost a sin for local activists to question free market capitalism or technological progress. The seedbed for this cultivation of a particular world view, however, is every good farmer's justifiable pride in the hard work and care reflected in the productivity of his or her farm.

The Crisis of the 1980s and the Farmers' Response

As the inflationary period of the 1970s collapsed into the farm crisis of the 1980s, farmers were ill-prepared. Farm debt rose from $20 billion in the early 1970s to over $225 billion in the early 1980s as farmers strove for the "efficiencies" that would earn them a living. Farmers did taste relatively prosperous times during the 1970s, only to have the bubble of prosperity burst by falling land values, tight money, and plummeting commodity prices in the early 1980s.

The collapse of commodity and land prices made it impossible for many family farmers to make payments on debts that had accumulated during the inflationary 1970s. In addition to unsustainable debt burdens, falling commodity prices made it difficult for many families to meet immediate needs, because income received for farm products fell below the cost of producing them, leaving no earnings for family living expenses. Many farm families were desperate. Anger turned both inward and outward. Early farm meetings were a combination of counseling sessions and education about farm policy.

Hundreds of thousands of farmers participated in the farm movement of the mid-1980s out of frustration, sometimes desperation, and with a sense of disbelief over what was happening to them. Each farmer's own dream was collapsing. Farmers were losing not only their jobs, but also their homes and land, homes and land that often carried generations of family history.

While farm movement leaders targeted commodity policy, the anger of average farmers was focused on financial institutions. Most of the local, spontaneous farm organizing addressed the issue of farm credit and immediate relief from the pressure of foreclosure.

Movement activists who espoused reinstitution of New Deal policies on farm prices and production control, and those who demanded foreclosure relief, targeted the federal government. This was the critical strategic error of the farm movement of the 1980s. By focusing almost entirely on federal policy solutions, the farm movement as a whole overlooked opportunities to directly target the sources of corporate influence that were causing the farm crisis. In addition, the federal focus overlooked those regional differences in farming which cause federal farm policies to have different impacts in different parts of the country. Finally, the federal focus overlooked the fact that farmers across the country were not united in strong organizations that could communicate with one another to hammer out strategy and agreements on policies for the various farm commodities grown in different parts of the country.

In sum, in its immediate focus on federal policy issues, the 1980s farm movement skipped several organizing steps.

Movement leaders assumed that farmers in general still had a memory of the agrarian populist ideals that enabled their parents and grandparents to forge New Deal policies during the 1930s. The populist call for massive numbers of rural people to storm Washington demanding better policies was usually unsuccessful. For a couple of years during the mid-1980s, rallies and tractorcades drew tens of thousands of people, but this period of peak activity inevitably subsided. A feeling of crisis and desperation had fueled protest activity but was incapable of sustaining the next stage of organizing, the methodical development of grassroots organizational experience and power.

Community issues may have national or global solutions, but actions and the values that motivate actions must be close to home. The farm movement of the 1980s, however, sought to minimize regional differences in U.S. farmers' needs and demands. The overriding goal was to quickly attain a comprehensive federal farm policy. The farm movement might have more successfully used regional and commodity-specific demands to reeducate farmers and gradually build toward comprehensive solutions. For example, midwestern farmers were most immediately concerned with relief from foreclosure by lending institutions. Western livestock producers were more concerned with loss of markets due to corporate concentration in the livestock industry and the resulting depression of prices. Eastern and midwestern dairy farmers were more concerned with corporate manipulation of dairy prices. In the South, farmers faced widespread abuses of the corporate contract system in poultry production; threats to the peanut and tobacco programs; severe loss of black-owned farms due to racial discrimination in lending; and the absence of technologies, crops, and markets suitable to thin soil and rolling land.

The movement also made no serious, concerted effort to rebuild, renew, and revitalize farm organizations that already existed. The National Farmers Union, the National Farmers Organization, many local and regional cooperatives, commodity groups, and production associations are still technically "owned" by farmer members, although governance of many of these institutions has been turned over to "expert" management that often serves interests other than the members'. Farm Credit Services, the major source of farm credit nationally, is also technically owned by its farmer-borrowers, but it too has been undergoing consolidation and increasing control by management.

Some of the traditional organizations supported the movement groups on specific policy goals, but none were internally revitalized. Entrenched leaders protected their own power and per diem fees for attending meetings, and bureaucratic inertia anchored organizational policy. When a recently elected board director of a regional dairy cooperative, Dairyman Incorporated, suggested a change in attitude toward national dairy policy, he was told by the CEO that he would receive no committee assignments until he "toed the party line." New farm groups have yet to build local power sufficient to renew the large traditional organizations.

Despite the need to build the 1980s farm movement on regional and local demands, farm bills became the focus of mass organizing. Farmers trekked to Washington and also organized hundreds of sessions with federal politicians in their home districts. Movement leaders spent much valuable time drafting the "Family Farm Act," a radical alternative to the policies favored by both Republicans and Democrats. The farm movement wanted to dramatically curtail the power of transnational grain companies and food processors to command cheap grain; new farm organizations demanded higher prices from the market rather than from government subsidies. And the demand for allocation of production quotas to family farms challenged the dominant economic logic that bigger is always better.

In response to this challenge, the companies pulled out all the stops and launched a multi-million-dollar public relations campaign to discredit the farm movement bill. This campaign involved both the media and the agricultural universities.

Although the farm movement won as much as one-third of the vote in Congress in 1985, the companies ultimately won the farm bill fights in 1985 and 1990. Farm organizations won significant minor victories on credit and farm programs, but the basic economic issues of price and corporate profit-gouging were lost. Too often framed as an "all or nothing" effort, the farm movement struggle for new policies was considered by many activists and some of the local organizations to have ended in defeat.

Origins of the Community Farm Alliance

The farm movement of the 1980s had this strategy to reform U.S. farm policy already in place when the Community Farm Alliance (CFA) was founded in the summer of 1985. The economic analysis for this national strategy, with the exception of dairy policy, was based primarily on the situation of midwestern farmers who produced major commodity crops such as corn, wheat, and soybeans. In Kentucky, only farmers in the western part of the state were engaged in producing these commodities on a scale similar to that of the Midwest.

Western Kentucky farmers participated in the Washington tractor-cades of the late 1970s and helped to form the American Agriculture Movement (AAM). The Kentucky AAM's strategy was to organize the largest farmers, thinking that a farm organization's power arose from controlling production rather than from large numbers of people. The president of the state chapter of AAM operated one of the largest farms in the state, with more than ten thousand acres in row crops. Kentucky's main AAM organizer, later a candidate for state commissioner of agriculture, bragged that "he was such a large fish [as a farmer] that when he jumped into the pond the water splashed out and there wasn't room for anyone else." The strategy of organizing production rather than people never created a lasting movement in Kentucky and had little to do with the small farms on rolling land in the central and eastern parts of the state, farms that produced tobacco, livestock, and milk on an average of less than 150 acres.

Other major farm organizations with members in central and eastern Kentucky—most notably the Farm Bureau, commodity groups, and large cooperatives—ignored the farm crisis or called it a "business correction" that would weed out the least productive farmers and leave Kentucky agriculture stronger in the long run.

Although the CFA joined the efforts of the farm movement of the 1980s, its roots were in the experiences of central and eastern Kentucky rural activists who had already been organizing around local rural and agricultural issues. For example, in the late 1970s and early 1980s the Kentucky Rivers Coalition (KRC) formed to protect landowners and rural communities from proliferating dams promoted by the Army Corps of Engineers. Functioning as a public interest organization, with staff drafting policy proposals and educational materials and communicating directly with legislators and the press, KRC also organized local chapters and worked in coalition with environmental organizations to halt dam construction and later to fight oil-shale strip mining.

Meanwhile, the Kentucky New Farm Coalition (KNFC) was formed by beginning farmers concerned with environmentally sound agricultural practices. Primarily an educational and social organization, KNFC held conferences on local farms and at the University of Kentucky, and was successful in passing state legislation to protect farmland from conversion to nonagricultural purposes.

Prior to the emergence of the CFA, most Appalachian organizations had ignored agriculture. Community organizers had assumed that although farming was vital to the flatlands, coal and manufacturing underpinned the economy of the Appalachian region. Less visible were the thousands of tobacco, cattle, hog, and dairy farms. Of Kentucky's fortynine Appalachian counties, at least twenty depend on agriculture as the principal source of income and jobs.[4] The collapse of livestock and crop prices in the early 1980s launched Kentucky into the beginnings of a farm crisis like that in other regions of the country.

When the first wave of farm foreclosures and protest groups developed in the upper Midwest in 1982, Kentucky activists from KRC and KNFC traveled north to meetings with these groups in Minnesota and Iowa, and returned to form the Kentucky Farm Survival Association (KFSA). The first Kentucky hotline for farm families with credit problems was run out of the KRC office for the KFSA. The Kentucky Farm Survival Association was short-lived, however. The attempt to replicate an upper-Midwest strategy of building a protest movement around forced farm sales did not work in Kentucky because foreclosures had not yet hit in large numbers.

The small circle of Kentucky farm activists, all full-time farmers or staff for local nonprofit organizations, continued to speak at dozens of meetings and attended farm movement events in other states during 1983 and 1984. In April 1985 a group of farmers took a bus trip organized by Barren County members of the National Farmers Organization (NFO) to a rally of fifteen thousand farmers in Ames, Iowa. When they returned, this group led an effort to establish a new farm organization in Kentucky, and about twenty-five people participated in the initial organizational meeting of the Community Farm Alliance in the summer of 1985.

Held at the Holiday Inn in Bardstown, with "Welcome Community Farm Alliance" on the marquee, the group polished a mission statement drafted by Baptist preacher Mike Thomason and approved a plan of action drafted by Tim Murphy, director of the Kentucky Resources Council. The remaining members of the founding board were farmers from Henry, Marion, Barren, and Green counties.

Caught Up in the Movement

The new organization formed local chapters and also sought out existing organizations with which it could work in coalition. The coalition-building strategy was not successful, however. Again, Kentucky farm activists tried to replicate upper Midwest organizing strategies, this time following the example of Iowa activists who had built the Iowa Farm Unity Coalition from existing farm organizations, including the American Agriculture Movement, the National Farmers Union, and Rural America. While CFA sought the participation of Kentucky AAM and NFO leaders, neither was focused on organizing small and modest-scale farmers to take action on farm policy issues.

The differences in scale and commodity between AAM grain farmers in the western part of the state and the small farmers of central Kentucky were great. AAM's membership served primarily to give financial support to the national organization's Washington, D.C., lobbying office.

NFO's strategy, on the other hand, was to pool farmers' production and bargain collectively with processors. NFO organizers tended to blame farmers for their own problems; the litany has been repeated since NFO's peak in the late 1960s: "Farmers are their own worst enemies. They won't organize. If only they'd join NFO, we would have the power to set our own prices." Neither AAM nor NFO added momentum to CFA's founding goals of organizing grassroots family farmers to rewrite farm policy.

Church activists proved more important to the early development of CFA than did existing farm organizations. Joe Fitzgerald, then director of Kentucky Catholic Rural Life, helped organize the first CFA support group meetings in Marion County, a predominantly Catholic area. Marion County started the first chapter of CFA, and Fitzgerald served on the first CFA board before moving to Iowa to direct the National Catholic Rural Life Conference. Kentucky leaders in the Christian Church (Disciples) similarly provided early leadership, particularly in the formation of the Henry County chapter and in the eastern Kentucky counties served by Ben Poage of the Kentucky Appalachian Ministry. For two years the Quaker American Friends Service Committee provided a staff person who recruited CFA's first significant numbers of African American members. CFA's membership and board has been bi-racial ever since.

Like other farm movement organizations, CFA was effective as a catalyst in mobilizing large numbers of farmers to protest and lobby on federal farm policy issues. But there were some contradictions between the goals of the "movement" and the goals of CFA as an organization. For example, the movement, represented by its National Family Farm Coalition, went to Congress in 1986 with a comprehensive package of credit reforms. Among CFA members, the question arose: do we work on the whole package, or do we work on those pieces of the package that affect our own situation? The question was answered in practice. CFA members organized letter-writing campaigns and meetings with members of Congress on those issues that appealed to their own self-interest. The whole package was eventually watered down, but CFA members won most of their specific objectives. The credit issue was then translated by CFA members into local campaigns ensuring Kentucky farmers' access to capital, and eventually produced a winning campaign in 1990 for a new state lending program. One later outgrowth of the credit work was a local campaign to improve the Kentucky National Bank's compliance with the Community Reinvestment Act.

Another contradiction for CFA arose from the movement's central goal of reinstituting support prices and supply management programs for major commodities. Aside from dairy farmers, most CFA members do not produce major commodities. Most produce tobacco on small-acreage allotments. Support prices and supply management still operate in the tobacco program, and the movement often used the tobacco program as an example of how to shape programs for other commodities. Meanwhile, Kentucky farmers were acutely aware that the tobacco program was under severe pressure. Most Kentucky farmers see saving the tobacco program as an economic necessity, but the adverse health effects of smoking make tobacco a tough commodity to defend. A key policy need for Kentucky farmers, therefore, has been to develop alternative crops and the infrastructure and markets to make alternative crops profitable. The policy goals of the "movement" did not take account of the policy needs of Kentucky tobacco farmers.

In addition to tensions between the movement and CFA around the choice of policy goals, another organizational need became apparent over time: the need for a process to integrate immediate issues with a larger strategy for power. Like most other farm movement organizations, CFA was built primarily on the efforts of progressive activists with an analysis of the social, political, and economic forces stacked against them. Drawing on their religious and cultural traditions and previous political experiences, the founding activists assumed certain principles as given: racial and gender solidarity, the responsibility of government to correct the abuses of corporate interests, and a healthy irreverence toward the "powers that be." The experiences of new members, however, are varied and primarily based on immediate threats to their everyday lives. Constant mobilization on issue campaigns leaves little time for members to analyze, act, and reflect together on their experiences in order to understand their immediate self-interests within a larger analysis of the way the society works.

What was needed was an organizational form that allowed for the following: (1) recognition of the immediate situations, experiences, and self-interests of the members as the starting point of building power; (2) a process to help members see how their immediate interests and values are threatened by major institutions and historical forces; and (3) a step-by-step organizing plan by which members learn to analyze and change institutions, thereby learning to make history.

The Shift Toward Community Organizing

CFA found considerable inspiration for and examples of rural community organizing in the Appalachian region. Save our Cumberland Mountains (SOCM) and Kentuckians For The Commonwealth (KFTC), organizations described in other chapters of this book, have successful histories of rural community organizing. These organizations devote as much attention to internal process—strategic planning, research, evaluation, leadership training, grassroots fundraising, communications—as they do to developing strategies and acting on public policy issues.

Attention to internal process that nurtures new leaders is probably the key distinguishing characteristic of these groups after which CFA was modeled. The grassroots membership base of SOCM, KFTC, and CFA is organized in a local chapter structure. These local chapters enable members to identify, address, and resolve local issues, and chapters offer the skills training and leadership education that enable members to participate effectively together in public life and develop an analysis of the connections between local concerns and broader public policy issues.

Chapters maximize member participation and ownership of these rural organizations because many members are unwilling or unable to go to events far from their homes; they facilitate recruitment and grassroots fundraising; and they enable an organization to become part of the life of a community and undertake local campaigns—to challenge, for example, a bank's lending policies. When statewide or national campaigns are underway, chapter phone trees are quickly activated, and large numbers of people can take action. Chapters are effective for bringing constituents before their legislators and can be a source of community support for statewide leaders. Chapters also provide for representative democracy within CFA, with chapter delegates to the statewide board of directors directly accountable to members.

Yet chapters present a variety of challenges and can be developed in different ways. Most community organizing is done around "hot" issues. During the summer of 1989, the Montgomery County CFA chapter fought a proposed landfill for out-of-state waste. This campaign drew hundreds of people to meetings, dozens to active leadership, and thousands to sign a petition and tie red ribbons on mailboxes. This county chapter ended the year stronger than it began, and it then successfully took the campaign to change solid-waste policy to the state legislature. Later, after the issue faded, local CFA leaders struggled to keep the chapter together, searching for a new issue.

Immediate and emotional issues permit a burst of recruitment, and new members learn fast in the heat of the moment. Done carefully, issue campaigns prepare people to attack other issues and link up with other constituencies. There are disadvantages, however. Maintaining a number of local issue campaigns can disperse organizational energy. Another problem is that an issue campaign naturally attracts that group of people who care most about the issue. Sometimes this group is unrepresentative of the interests of the larger community. The most difficult task for an organizer is to build a diverse leadership with broad vision that lasts past the immediacy of the campaign.

CFA staff and leaders have developed an organizing method that is less dependent upon hot issues. The CFA board chooses counties to organize, not because they have particular farm problems or a landfill or toxics threat, but because they are politically strategic, lying within an important state or federal legislative district. A staff organizer, with member help, spends as much as three months assessing the organizing potential of the county by interviewing dozens of local citizens. Interviewees are divided among the categories of "gatekeepers," "grassroots leaders," and "grassroots." Gatekeepers are those community leaders who can open or close doors to large numbers of other people. Grassroots people are the ultimate constituency of the chapter, but CFA staff have found that a chapter is most solidly situated in the community if it has the support of as many established opinion-shapers as possible.

The goal of this less issue-dependent form of organizing is to build a chapter that becomes a self-sustaining, permanent institution in the county, capable of developing a vision of a revitalized rural economy, and patiently changing larger institutions that affect the local economy. CFA staff recruit a diverse leadership from the beginning, chosen from among the dozens of interviewees. Each person on the "organizing committee" must have a wide circle of relationships and must be committed to working on a variety of issues. Each organizing committee member holds small meetings in his or her home or community; the committee uses these meetings to test different issues; and the chapter is initiated at a public meeting after a long process of interviews and small meetings.

In early 1991, while CFA members across the state were engaged in hot issue campaigns to win an environmental bill in the state legislature and to change dairy policy, one of CFA's field organizers was also organizing a new chapter in Harrison County. As the hot issues swirled about them in adjacent counties, members of Harrison County's organizing committee held small meetings in their homes and spoke to civic clubs and a young farmers' group in preparation for choosing their own issues. They debated and agreed on a statement of local goals and values in the areas of agriculture, local government, and rural development; and out of a preliminary list of eight issues, they picked three to research and pursue. As new member Sue Bradford said at an early organizing committee meeting, "Let's pick something first that we can win!"

CFA chapter organizing is staff-intensive: staff members are expected not only to initiate the chapter, but also to keep it going. Even though staff organizers always stay in the background in public, their supporting role is important. Organizers prod and encourage, helping members prepare agendas, plan events, and practice their public statements. CFA staff encourage self-sufficiency in local chapters, but this goal is elusive. Some rural organizations are experimenting with part-time member-organizers, but when a few members are paid to do what other members do as volunteers, resentment and divisiveness sometimes result.

At best, chapter leaders take the responsibility for developing their own reinforcements. When Bath County leader Dorothy Robertson told CFA organizer Deborah Webb, "What we need is some ready-made leaders," Webb talked Robertson through a process of listing other potential leaders in the county. They then picked the most likely people, and Robertson evaluated each one for personal strengths and for skills that needed improvement, such as ability to chair a meeting or speak in public. Webb then helped Robertson develop a plan for nurturing strengths and improving weaknesses so that Robertson herself could "make" new leaders.

When a chapter-based organization takes on a statewide issue campaign, a potential dilemma emerges. To win a statewide (or national) issue, support is needed from regions where the organization may not have chapters. CFA often recruits members in nonchaptered counties, but these members are not structured into the internal democratic process of the organization. They also miss the leadership-development opportunities of chapters. Sometimes these nonchaptered members are elected as at-large board representatives, and sometimes they are involved in issue committees, but as a whole they are outside the core of the organization until a chapter can be developed in their area. And chapters require a lot of organizer time.

CFA evaluates its progress in three ways. One criterion is commonplace: is the organization winning issue campaigns? CFA leaders also ask themselves how they are doing at building an organization that empowers members to win further victories, and they ask if the organization is continually enlarging its members' understanding of how the world works.

There will always be some people who join an organization like CFA out of concern with a problem that threatens their everyday life and then, after the problem is solved, return to everyday life and drop out of active participation. The real goal of community organizing, however, is not so much to help people solve these immediate problems as it is to recruit new leaders for long-term change.

Because the national farm movement depended upon the charismatic leadership of a few people, it suffered when those individuals burnt out or died. CFA slowly became grounded in new leadership emerging from its county chapters.

CFA also developed a competent staff. During its early years (1985–86), CFA was staffed by leaders, often working as independent operators, running on their best hunch about what to do. By 1989, with some new staff and a much clearer understanding of community organizing, CFA was in better shape. Organizers now see themselves as professionals, accountable to each other and to the board, responsible for slowly building county chapters rather than running around trying to mobilize people for events. The key to the professionalization of CFA's staff was CFA's willingness to emulate the experience of successful rural organizations around the country. When necessary, CFA contracted for staff and leader training from experienced organizers, and CFA staff managed to be short on ego and long on self-criticism when it came time to ask other organizers for advice.

CFA was also fortunate in developing fundraising and administrative skills. Many farm movement organizations never weaned themselves from financial dependence on Willie Nelson's Farm Aid. Farm Aid passed out money raised at concerts, usually with little accountability and few requirements. Many organizations were wholly funded by Farm Aid and never bothered with bookkeeping. When the Farm Aid money began to be exhausted, so were dozens of farm groups. CFA instead broadened its funding base and learned to raise more money from its own members and communities. And CFA staff learned to keep books and write financial reports, a set of skills essential to enable a board to manage its own organization.

CFA's core of leaders also matured enough to invest time in organization building and training. Once or twice a year, CFA leaders gather in a weekend retreat, sharing experiences, learning from each other, and organizing sessions that explore new directions for rural organizing. Building relationships became as important as planning what to do next.

In late 1988 CFA's board decided at a leadership retreat to begin a long-term planning process. Six leaders met for a whole day each month for a year, produced a long-range plan piece by piece, and led the board in engaging and adopting each piece of the plan. The Planning Committee studied maps of legislative districts, farming areas, and population densities. They made decisions about CFA's constituency, where they lived, and how to recruit them. Not leaving organizational growth to chance, or to whatever activists popped up, they charted a chapter development strategy from the first "cold" contacts to permanent local groups.

CFA as a Living University for Leaders

Work on federal farm policy during the 1980s exposed the power of corporations over farm policy, and many CFA members were awakened to the complex and often hidden power relationships that shape their lives. Kentucky farmers won some credit reforms, but they did not win the battle to wrest control over price policy from the corporations. As a result, rural communities still face a chronic attrition of farmers. Fewer and fewer people own the land. Farm kids are lured away to jobs with higher pay and shorter days. The farmers who remain are told by government and university "experts" to value their neighbor's farms more than they value their neighbors.

These are the realities in rural Kentucky of a world lurching toward a "New World Order" ruled by a few dozen transnational corporations. Farm commodity policy in Washington is still dominated by the exporting and processing corporations. These corporations have vast resources, a global vision, and a plan to realize their vision. How much space exists in the New World Order for community organizations to shape public policy in their members' interests? As the world economy becomes more integrated and national governments matter less and less, what is the arena for citizens' organizations to exercise power?

As the Community Farm Alliance becomes a mature organization, CFA leaders are asking themselves where the organization will go in the future. They have learned how to build an organization that can win political victories. Dozens of new local leaders have learned organizing skills and can analyze the society around them, but CFA members sometimes feel as if they are standing in the path of a stampede called "progress." They know, however, that their future, their neighbors' future, and their children's future depend upon changing the power relationships that determine who gets to define progress.

The burning issues for CFA members are the same ones that confront rural people around the world. Eventually the goal of "saving the family farm" will evolve into land reform. A central concern of CFA members is that few young farmers are getting started. Looking to other countries for examples and inspiration, CFA leaders are beginning to develop policies that would broaden land ownership.

On the local organizing level, the practice of holding politicians accountable will be transformed into a plan for governance. Community organizations can win toeholds of local power. Accountability will always be a fundamental principle and goal, but governance also becomes possible as community organizations gain strength. Electoral strategies are more and more on the minds of CFA leaders.

But issues are only part of what CFA is about. In addition to winning political victories, some large and some small, community organizing is a school for popular leadership. Community Farm Alliance leaders work long hours to run their own organization: raising money and supervising staff, helping county chapters with local issues, and designing goals for state and federal policy. The organization has become a sort of adult university for these leaders. They are enticed and rewarded by the prospect of shaping the world to be more just and more democratic.

The impact of this leadership training is best illustrated through excerpts from an interview with CFA leaders Tom and Dorothy Robertson, a farm couple from Bath County. Dorothy was CFA's board chairperson in 1991. The interviewer was an Antioch College student intern, Ira Rodd.

Ira: How did you start the CFA chapter here?

Dorothy: Tommy got involved immediately. He went to that first organizing meeting that they had in Montgomery County. I said at the time that I didn't have time to get involved. It could be his project, because I had other things to do. So he went, and he got elected to the board. He was going to board meetings, and I went along with him, but I wasn't taking any part in it. It was a very gradual process that I got involved.

Ira: How did you find more time to get involved?

Dorothy: Well, CFA just became so important to me that I found the time. I started to cut corners maybe on other things, because CFA became the most important thing that I did. I've been a volunteer all my life, but this is the most fulfilling work that I've ever done. CFA comes first with me now.

Tommy: You know you've seen these signs on wreckers—"23 *HOUR SERVICE, WE HAVE TO SLEEP SOMETIME.*" Well, we just kind of live it about twenty hours a day.

Dorothy: CFA opened up all kinds of doors for me. I mean, there was work to do on the state level, which I had never done before, and on the national level. I mean, it was so exciting! All the travel that I've gotten to do that I didn't even know I was capable of. It's just been one great experience for me.

Ira: Have you seen that in other members?

Dorothy: Yes, it's a very broadening experience. In 1989 when we had our National Family Farm Coalition meeting and we were working on the 1990 Farm Bill, CFA made it possible for about sixteen people from CFA to go to Washington. It was really money well spent because we took members up there and it broadened their horizons and let them see how you lobby with congressmen and see a broader picture of things. It's made our organization a lot stronger. I see so many of these people growing in CFA. They say, "Oh, I can't do that," and you do develop leaders through it. I see members coming on all the time that a few years ago would have said, "I can't do this." Now they're doing it, because they believe in the organization, and they think it's the only chance we've got to change farm policy and to keep farmers on the farm.

Tommy: We've met so many interesting and smart people . . .

Dorothy: We had all those seminary professors come out to our house for us to explain what was going on in the rural area. We had that sociologist from Poland.

Ira: Why do people join CFA? Is it because of self-interest? Are people generally one issue, or are they willing to work on many issues?

Dorothy: Well, yes, some do and some don't [work on more than one issue]. You bring a lot of people in around issues like we did around this medical waste incinerator in Bath County. Now, a number of those people who worked so hard on that issue and who contributed money and went out and got names on petitions have not been to our last two chapter meetings, although they joined the organization, and they get the postcards. But we may not be able to hold those people, because they were working on that one issue. They were very grateful that CFA had an organization in the county and that we were able to get on top of this thing. Through the resources of CFA, we were able to bring in the experts, and we were able to set up this panel. And we got on it. We got on it really fast. You know, we had three hundred people at that meeting.

Tommy: Now see, I was over at the restaurant a while ago to get a sandwich, and one fella in there says, "How's CFA doing?" Well, he's not a member, but he's a contributor, a donor. He says, "How's CFA doing?" I says, "Doing pretty good!"

Dorothy: So even though we don't always get members, people know what we're doing, and they care about what we're doing. It's very hard to get members to work on multi-issues.

Tommy: Just like that big crowd we had up at the courthouse. Some people were amazed that we could get people there so quick.

Dorothy: And we really got a lot of credibility out of that. We have gotten a lot of members in Bath County, and even though they're not there for every meeting, we can call them. We've got them on the phone tree if we need to make calls to Frankfort [the state capital] or to work on something. We can call them and they'll write letters for us.

Ira: So did the phone tree work during the special session?

Dorothy: The phone tree worked great! See, we had read in the newspaper on Sunday that Don Blandford [Speaker of the Kentucky House of Representatives] had said he hadn't gotten a single call on waste issues. We got that phone tree going on Sunday, and he had to retract that statement, because hundreds of calls went in on Monday. We generated a lot of them. Sometimes our members will get their mother or their sister or somebody to make a call when they really feel strongly about it. The hardest thing we have to do is to bring in committed members. People are busy. They're involved in lots of other things. I really feel like it takes a special kind of person to give that kind of commitment. I mean, it has to be people that really care about other people. It can't just be that selfish interest, where you work on one issue that just concerns you, to have good members that stay over the long haul.

Part of the learning process for CFA involves confronting issues of race, which, as Don Manning-Miller makes clear in Chapter 3 in this volume, are frequently ignored in community organizing efforts among a largely white constituency. CFA is struggling to become a truly bi-racial organization, and its leadership is committed to addressing the particular needs of black farmers.

Black farmer Mattie Mack is the leader of one of CFA's chapters. Mack's charismatic presence and bubbling humor have helped the state-wide board develop a community of interest between farmers of different races, economic levels, and cultural experiences. Another of Mack's leadership contributions was her dogged pursuit of a CFA bill in the state legislature in 1990. With little time left for the new farm loan program to pass through the state Senate, CFA nevertheless succeeded in passing it. Mattie recounted some of her activities:

> We held a firm, positive attitude and exercised a lot of staying power. I grabbed Joe Wright [Senate majority leader] in the hall and said, "Joe, we've got to have this [Bill] 557; where is it?" Joe said, "Mattie, I don't know, I'll find out." And I said, "Well, I'm staying right here until you do!" And I did, too. I waited out by the door from one until three-fifteen. My feet just about went numb, but there was no way he was going to get out of that room without me seeing him. When he did come back out, I pressed a note into his hand, and he said, "Mattie, I've seen your farm. You don't need this loan program." I said, "No, I don't need this loan program myself, but I'm concerned about my less fortunate neighbors, aren't you?"

Joe Wright was the key to winning Senate approval, and the bill finally passed during the last day of the session.

John Botts is one of the few black farmers in the Bath County chapter, and in the county itself. Through involvement in CFA, John has found opportunities to speak out about the loss of black-owned farms, and he and his wife have been featured in the local paper. His chapter, primarily composed of white farmers, persuaded their congressional representative to become an original sponsor of a Minority Farmers Rights Act, portions of which became part of the 1990 farm bill.

CFA members are also working to forge links with urban consumers and low-income groups. Out of a couple of local farmers' markets organized by CFA members in 1986 has grown a new marketing cooperative called the Family Farm Growers. The Family Farm Growers sell chemical-free produce in the city of Louisville and provide fresh produce to low-income people through a pilot coupon program that they hope to persuade the state legislature to adopt on a permanent basis. They work together with representatives of church-based low-income advocacy organizations, and the ties between CFA and urban people have grown as a result. Grower leader Kathy Aman explains the importance of community organizing this way: "People can have ideas, but if they don't know where to go with their ideas or who to ask to get help to implement those ideas, they may never do anything with them. CFA helped to bring the right people together and also helped motivate and give us the opportunity and helped us learn the needed skills to achieve our goals."

Community organizing is sometimes criticized as parochial because issue objectives are often achievable without fundamentally changing power relations. This criticism rings true if our view of social change is revolutionary or apocalyptic. Lasting change in power relations, however, can occur incrementally. Probably the most important contribution of organizations like CFA is the nurturing of new leaders with experience, vision, and commitment. Many new members and participants in local issue campaigns return to their everyday lives without becoming leaders. But an important group of people emerge from these campaigns with a vision of democracy that extends from local communities to the world economy.

Can citizens' groups really democratize the New World Order? We think the answer is yes, and we think the examples are all around us.

Building on the successful experience of the Family Farm Growers, CFA members began in 1990 to develop a comprehensive plan for diversifying the agricultural economy of Kentucky. County chapter discussions, interviews with neighbors, and local research are being used to create a platform for state institutional change. The unifying theme of this project is that rural development should be homegrown and that the state can help build the infrastructure for local development with the same money state government now spends on recruiting outside corporations.

Although rural Kentucky needs to reach for economic conversion because its farm income comes disproportionately from tobacco, public officials put the burden of change on individual farmers. These officials often lack the imagination and will to envision systemic solutions. CFA chapter organizing is now attempting to enable rural citizens in their own counties to analyze the causes of rural impoverishment and develop their own plans for institutional accountability and community revitalization.

Each county group is going through the following steps, with coordination by a statewide committee: interviewing dozens of their neighbors and holding small meetings in their communities; assessing the roles

John and Margaret Botts of Owingsville, Kentucky, are among the four black dairy-farm families left in Kentucky. (*Lois Kleffman, CFA*)

of public institutions in their local economy; assessing corporate involvement in those institutions and in their communities; investigating current research, education, and investment priorities of those institutions; profiling the county economy from census data, Development District information, financial figures, and an analysis of decision making; learning to envision alternative development paths; developing specific suggestions for research priorities, programs, and community oversight; and selecting appropriate strategies to accomplish these suggestions.

Even local rural development, however, exists within a global economy. Because the market and corporate structure of agribusiness are international, CFA members have become increasingly international in their focus. During 1989 and 1990 CFA members worked hard to rally opposition to an international trade proposal that would globally deregulate farm policy. The Reagan and Bush administrations championed this proposal to remove farm programs from the purview of Congress, phasing out all price supports, import controls, and pesticide standards on imported food. CFA members voted at their 1989 Annual Meeting that this General Agreement on Tariffs and Trade (GATT) proposal was CFA's most important issue.

Kentucky farmers wrote stories for their papers, met with their congressmen, spoke to environmental groups, signed on a wide variety of organizations, and earned the support of several members of Kentucky's congressional delegation. In the fall of 1990, a delegation of CFA members traveled to Europe to meet with leaders of other rural organizations who have also been working on trade policy, and then the CFA delegation met with farm groups in Poland and East Germany to talk about grassroots organizing. By organizing opposition to their government's trade proposals to deregulate world agriculture, these farmers have come to realize that their allies are rural groups in other parts of the world. After the trip one of the participants wrote:

> As a member of Community Farm Alliance and a farmer, I have worked with other farmers in trying to understand and change policy that is forcing our people off the land. Now I understand that the problems are not ours alone but common to farmers around the world. That is the message I will talk to groups about in the coming months. The culmination of our trip was Brussels, Belgium, where the GATT negotiations are being held. We met with farmers from around the world in the shadow of the building where Clayton Yeutter [U.S. secretary of agriculture] and Carla Hills [U.S. trade representative] and five hundred people from the U.S. were trying to force a GATT agreement on the world. On December 3rd, we joined a march to oppose an agreement. Forty thousand strong, farmers representing many nations marched through downtown Brussels. There were banners and flags, and it was exciting to be a part of a worldwide effort.

From local organizing and discussions with colleagues around the world, a new world view is emerging, a world view that counterposes a vision of community economies with the transnational corporations' vision of a global workforce, freely accessible resources, and a global shopping center. Rural leaders instead envision a democratic and communitarian economy that is diverse, self-reliant, accountable, and respectful of the natural world. Homer Hecht, CFA member and Christian Church pastor in Liberty, wrote:

> I have been a member for some four years. CFA is the one organization of which I'm aware in our area which makes, or is trying to make, the connections between stewardship of God's earth and concern for the state of farming in our land. It has also given concerned farmers a renewed sense of community and has provided the land with the leadership which comes from people being given and accepting the power which is theirs.

Some people believe that grassroots community organizing is a feeble effort to resist history, to recreate a mythical time when communities actually existed and the deepest community values were shared. But grassroots community organizations, with all their flaws, demonstrate just the opposite. They are living proof that society can be better than it is now, and is better than many of us give it credit for. Appalachia's grassroots community organizations articulate and demonstrate a collective vision, not only of the world as it might be, but of the world as it is, a world of ordinary, dignified, courageous people who do not resist history, but who create it.

Notes

1. Quoted from the Committee for Economic Development in Mark Ritchie and Kevin Ristau, *Crisis by Design: A Brief History of U.S. Farm Policy* (Minneapolis: League of Rural Voters Education Project, 1987).
2. Testimony by former Texas Agriculture Commissioner Jim Hightower before the U.S. House Agriculture Committee, Washington, D.C., March 31, 1987.
3. Ritchie and Ristau, *Crisis by Design*, 5.
4. Ben Poage, "The Rural/Farm Crisis in Kentucky Appalachia," in *The Land and the Economy of Appalachia: Proceedings from the 1986 Conference on Appalachia* (Lexington, Ky.: Appalachian Center, University of Kentucky, 1987), 37.

PART II
NEW STRATEGIES IN LABOR STRUGGLES

8

Appalachian Women Fight Back

Organizational Approaches to Nontraditional Job Advocacy

Chris Weiss

In 1982, what did a coal miner in Tennessee, a carpenter in Charleston, West Virginia, and a highway construction worker in Kentucky have in common? They were all women who got their jobs because of women's organizations that fought for their employment rights. From 1977 to the early part of the 1980s, nontraditional job advocacy affected the lives of hundreds of Appalachian women who had never before had the opportunity to work in the jobs that their husbands, fathers, and boyfriends had taken for granted for generations. For these women, the promise of Title VII of the 1964 Civil Rights Act guaranteeing nondiscrimination in employment finally came true.

Starting in the late 1970s, there was a window of opportunity for women who wanted to break out of stereotypical occupations and get "men's" jobs that paid more and had greater benefits. In a resource-based economy dominated by coal, oil, and gas, Appalachian women have traditionally had few occupational choices. But because of the enforcement of various civil and employment rights laws and executive orders under the Carter administration, and a modestly expanding economy, women began to cast covetous eyes on jobs held by the men in their families and communities.

Three very different women's organizations were created and took advantage of this window. Each of the three was formed by leadership coming out of a tradition of organizing and advocacy, and each of the three faced almost insurmountable obstacles, including a cultural tradition that dictated passivity and acquiescence for women, active hostility from men to new employment roles for women, lack of government and private financing for women's organizations, and absence of organizational role models. Despite these obstacles, the Coal Employment Project (CEP), which targeted coal mines, the Southeast Women's Employment Coalition (SWEC), which focused on highway jobs in the region, and Women and Employment (W&E), which took on the building trades in West Virginia, have provided models for other organizations in the United States for the last ten years.

As the founder of Women and Employment, I was an integral part of this nontraditional job advocacy. In this chapter, I take a retrospective look at all three organizations, examining their successes and failures, the role that race and gender played in their growth, the changes in the organizations as the context of the job advocacy changed, and their regional and national impact. I offer a perspective on the role of citizen resistance in Appalachia as it was played out in the employment arena by women, who not only challenged job segregation, but created new organizational models of resistance. Finally, the chapter contains some reflections on the future of women's economic development organizations in creating an institutional base for economic justice for women.

In the later years of his administration, President Jimmy Carter put his mark on anti-discrimination regulation by issuing his Executive Order 11246. This order required equitable hiring practices by contractors who do business with the federal government. Enforcement was assigned to the Office of Federal Contract Compliance (OFCCP), and a set of goals and timetables was created. The philosophy behind this Executive Order was that women and minorities had a right to jobs paid for by their taxes. The precedents for this action went back to World War II, when black men organized and pressured President Franklin D. Roosevelt to ensure that military contractors hired blacks for the war effort.

The late 1970s also saw the rise of the women's movement, and history repeated itself when women demanded a share of the jobs created by government spending. Gloria Steinem, one of the "mothers" of the movement, reflected in later years that each of the founders of the three organizations "caught an epidemic of rebelliousness that is feminism," and she pointed out that the change in government policy happened because of a women's movement.[1] I agree with her in that I believe women in the Appalachian mountains caught the rebelliousness and saw it as an opportunity to come together to advocate for jobs and opportunities we never had.

Whatever the cause, Executive Order 11246 and OFCCP were tools that were (and still are) used by women in Appalachia to claim jobs that their tax dollars created. They were helped by another federal program, the Comprehensive Employment Training Act (CETA), which encouraged programs to train people in "nontraditional occupations," defined by the U.S. Department of Labor as any occupation in which men or women represented fewer than 25 percent of the job holders. Thus men could be trained as nurses, and women could be trained as carpenters. The combination of Order 11246, OFCCP, CETA, and the women's movement created a climate favorable to the previously unheard-of notion of women coal miners, highway workers, and carpenters.

The Coal Employment Project was the first of the three organizations that "fought back" against occupational segregation. In 1977 Betty Jean Hall, a lawyer from Kentucky, heard about an employment discrimination case while working for a public interest law firm in Washington, D.C. A tour of the coal mines had been arranged for a group of lawyers, and the one woman among them had been denied access to the tour because of her gender. The law firm figured that if a woman lawyer could not even go down into the mines to observe, a woman did not have much chance of getting a job there. Yet, although there appeared to be good grounds for a law suit against coal companies for employment discrimination, Hall was skeptical that any women actually wanted to work in the mines.

In September 1977 Hall met Mavis Williams in Letcher County in eastern Kentucky and forever changed her mind about the availability of women who wanted to work in the coal mines. Mavis had been in the military and was divorced, with four kids to support. She had heard that the coal mines were going to have to hire women, and she figured that the work could not be any harder than washing diapers in the creek in the dead of winter with two babies in her care. Williams told Hall that if she had known the lawyer was coming, she "could have had fifty women here tonight."

Once convinced, Hall spent the next six months putting together the strategy that ultimately worked for women coal miners as well as women carpenters. The elements of the strategy included filing administrative complaints under Executive Order 11246, recruiting women to apply for the jobs, filing law suits based on the women's experiences, and waging a well-orchestrated media campaign. The legal strategy included research and documentation from all appropriate sources, including the Equal Employment Opportunity Commission (EEOC), which enforces Title VII of the Civil Rights Act, and the Bituminous Coal Operators Association. The media campaign included well-thought-out press releases to national and regional newspapers and television appearances by women job applicants wearing hard hats and work clothes. Articles on women who wanted to work in the mines appeared in the *New York Times* as well as papers across the region. As the word spread, the numbers of women in the coal mines went from .015 of 1 percent of new hires (one woman in West Virginia) in 1974 to 4.2 percent of all new hires by 1979. By 1980 in West Virginia alone there were 1,100 new hires who were women.

Organizationally, the Coal Employment Project, as it came to be called, grew almost as fast. Once the media campaign established the notion of women coal miners in the minds of the public, some New York foundations were quick to support the fledgling organization. The Ms. Foundation for Women and the John Hay Whitney Foundation were the first of many. CEP had two main program strategies. The first was dictated by the sheer number of women who came forward to claim jobs in the mines. Support groups of women who wanted jobs or who had jobs but suffered from sexual harassment (a common complaint) were formed in various Appalachian areas. According to Hall, the philosophy of the support groups was to bring women together who had difficulties in getting or keeping jobs. Prospective miners were told that CEP "will come and help organize you into support groups to solve your own problems. Then we will help you in those areas that you can't solve by yourselves." These latter problems included recalcitrant coal companies that refused to hire women at all. In 1979 the support groups and individuals came together for the first Coal Mining Women's Conference in Charleston, West Virginia, creating a tradition of annual conferences that continues today.

CEP's second major strategy involved a training program for women, supported under CETA. It became clear to CEP that women who went into the mines would pave the way for other women. CEP needed to create a trained applicant base and, as a result, designed an effective training program under a special grant from the U.S. Department of Labor (DOL). The Women's Bureau, an agency of the DOL, acted as an advocate and resource for this program, as it did for nontraditional training programs for women in other parts of the country. By 1982 all the staff as well as hundreds of women had gone through a forty-hour training program that provided them with the certificate required by the coal companies for entry-level miners.

The second women's organization to make a splash in Appalachia followed in CEP's footsteps. In 1979 Leslie Lilly, while still operating the Southern Appalachian Leadership Training (SALT) program in Kentucky, traveled the mountains of Appalachia talking to women who were working for change in their communities. SALT had been created with private foundation money to increase leadership skills among people in the mountains who sought to alleviate poverty and improve living conditions in their communities. In addition, many new CETA programs popping up in the mountains were designed and created by women for women. Several of these programs emphasized nontraditional jobs. Leslie, herself a product of SALT from northern Georgia and a friend of Hall's, roamed Kentucky, West Virginia, Tennessee, and other parts of the Appalachians in the late spring of 1979 to recruit these women leaders to come to a meeting in July at the Highlander Center. I was one of these women, as was Betty Jean Hall.

Lilly was inspired by CEP's success and by other victories around occupational segregation. Karen Nussbaum in Chicago had just created an organization called 9 to 5, which drew national attention to the problems faced by women working as secretaries and file clerks. "We started giving a name—occupational segregation—to what was going on" said Lilly. Once named, the problem could be addressed, and "as an advocate you did have some power" to change things.

The meeting at Highlander was important. It brought almost sixty advocates together for the first time to compare stories on programs, on the harassment that we and other women were facing at home, and on the struggle to find and create answers for the economic desperation of women in our communities. When the need for an organizational base to call home became clear, another meeting was scheduled for the fall, and the Southeast Women's Employment Coalition was born. Betty Jean Hall and I and ten others agreed to serve on the first board of directors.

Lilly cites three conditions as critical to the formation of SWEC and other advocacy organizations in 1979–83. The first was the leadership of the women themselves and their willingness to be risk-takers, to stick their necks out for the principles of equality in which they believed. This involved not only organizational risks, but also some personal ones for themselves and their families. This leadership was encouraged by the women's movement and the "epidemic of rebelliousness" referred to earlier. However, the national women's movement had not produced economic gains for blue-collar workers at this point, and women in the mountains saw themselves as pioneers in the movement to include women in the blue-collar trades.

A second condition was an atmosphere of regulatory reform and an increasing body of legal precedents that were being created by the federal courts. Equal employment hiring guidelines were being upheld by the courts, and goals were being met. Women felt that they could flex their muscle with the law behind them. Tied to these legal developments was a public policy—the Carter administration's commitment to contract compliance and equal employment hiring practices. State human rights commissions, especially the one in Kentucky, were active in promoting Title VII and in processing claims of employment discrimination.

Last, but certainly not least, was support from private foundations such as the Ms. Foundation for Women, which provided key seed money for women's organizations designing programs for economic reform. Church foundations provided small but critical amounts of money toward salaries and organizational development, and the Women's Bureau of the DOL also steered resources to these fledgling organizations. Later, the Ford Foundation and its Rural Poverty program played a key role in stabilizing these organizations.

But in 1979 and 1980, this was all a gleam in Lilly's eye. Twelve women representing as many organizations from six Appalachian states joined the initial board of SWEC. From the outset the Center for Community Change in Washington, D.C., and staff member Eileen Paul played a key role in helping Lilly and the rest of us understand how organizations grow and develop, how to plan programs and write proposals, and how to gain access to financial resources. The SWEC board became a place where leadership was developed and nurtured. In those days "leadership" was defined as support for risk-takers doing organizing work for change in their communities. The work that we did came out of a deep personal commitment to values, and we rarely thought of ourselves as leaders in the sense in which that word is defined today. Our models were Mother Jones and Martin Luther King, Jr., two people who came out of the union and civil rights movements, where many of us had our roots.

Lilly reflects that the women on the first SWEC board "were ultimately changed by the experience. We had a deep sense of appreciation of the risks that we took, not only in how we did the work, but also in how we brought issues of diversity and equality in decision making back into our own organizations." There was some initial struggle around program strategies, with some board members lobbying for support for the "80 percent"—women in traditional jobs. However, SWEC decided to adopt, as its first major program, advocacy for jobs for women in the highway construction industry. The reasoning was that we could open jobs to rural Appalachian women—especially those jobs funded by the Appalachian Regional Commission—through the same strategy that CEP had used. More basic to the decision, though, was the fact that several board members, including Betty Jean Hall, had experience in nontraditional job advocacy programs. The decision was clinched by a presentation to the board by the chief compliance officer in charge of equal employment hiring for the Federal Highways Administration, who was particularly arrogant and condescending.

After much planning and discussion, in the fall of 1980 an administrative complaint was filed in Washington, D.C., complete with a press conference attended by hard-hatted women, against all fifty states and their departments of transportation for not enforcing equal employment hiring guidelines for women. The initial states targeted were Kentucky and Virginia, with Ohio coming in later.

The results of the complaint were mixed and seemed to depend on the presence of a local advocacy organization to put pressure on the state highway system to hire women. The best results were obtained in Ohio, where SWEC, in partnership with local employment and training programs, raised money to help train women and place them in the Ohio Department of Transportation. Because of problems in collecting employment data from private contractors, however, SWEC was never able to track new hiring as CEP had, instead relying on "sightings" of women on the job.

A third women's organization whose birth was influenced by the Coal Employment Project and SWEC was Women and Employment in Charleston, West Virginia, born out of a CETA project that had been shut down by the state because of controversy. I founded Women and Employment in the fall of 1979. The SWEC/Highlander meeting occurred at a time when I and other women in a CETA project in Charleston were under fire from local building trade unions and contractors for trying to get women hired on a large, federally funded project. When W&E was started, I was a VISTA volunteer, as was Leslie Lilly in pre-SWEC days.

Conditions for women in Charleston in 1979 were very similar to those elsewhere in the mountains. The Department of Housing and Urban Development was funding a development that included a mall, parking garage, and hotel, a project subject to contract compliance and other equal employment guidelines. But there were no women and few minority men in the building trades unions in 1979, and the building trades had a monopoly on the labor supply for Charleston. Women in Charleston were inspired by the same conditions as women looking for coal mining or highway construction jobs, so we adopted the same strategies. Women were recruited who wanted the jobs, administrative complaints were filed with OFCCP and EEOC, press conferences were held, and eventually, in 1982, a law suit was filed in federal court, attacking the way in which the City of Charleston, as the main contractor, was enforcing equal employment hiring guidelines. One major difference in the legal strategy was that W&E was joined by two other groups, the Minority Open Forum and the Concerned Citizens of the Kanawha Valley. These groups included sizable numbers of black men and women, ensuring that the benefits of a legal settlement would come to minority men as well as to all women.

The resulting out-of-court settlement required the building trades unions to issue work permits to women and minorities to enable them to work on a union job. Only a few of the women were absorbed into the trade unions themselves, because the Laborers Union and the Operating Engineers were the only two unions that accepted women in any numbers. But the result of the settlement was that between thirty and forty West Virginia women worked on a large building construction project for the first time in the history of the state.

In 1980 a new president was elected and the Reagan administration began systematically to close the window opened under the Carter administration. Yet CEP, SWEC, and W&E survived, adapting to new conditions and gathering new resources, notably from the Ford Foundation.

The foundation had just gone through a major reorganization and gave staff the go-ahead to design a new program for domestic rural poverty and women's economic issues. The program was to concentrate on employment and economic development and had some autonomy to develop innovative ways of responding to new program initiatives from the field. Kate McKee, the program officer, who had previously worked with women in West Africa, faced the challenge of applying what she had learned there to the Third World conditions in Appalachia and the South.

McKee commissioned a study of conditions faced by women in the Southeast and met with the leaders of many women's organizations. She was instrumental in providing program and core funding support for several organizations, including CEP (which had already received some support from Ford) as well as SWEC and W&E. The Ford money gave these three organizations the leeway in the next five years to develop new programs and to expand their leadership, steps that proved critical to their longevity.

Ten years later, two of the three organizations still exist under different leadership. Grants from the Ford Foundation and other foundations and churches have continued, and each organization has broadened its constituency base. CEP organizers moved west to include women in deep mines and strip mines in Utah and Colorado. W&E, moving out from its Charleston base, now works with women all through central and southern West Virginia. W&E has changed to a dues-paying membership base to define its constituency more clearly, and CEP announced in a 1991 newsletter that women miners who pay dues to CEP will now vote for their representatives to the CEP board of directors. SWEC's board decided in 1991 to close down operations because of a combination of lack of funding and internal disagreement on program strategies.

Several factors explain why CEP and W&E continue to operate, and why SWEC lasted ten years, when many other organizations go out of business within a few years of their founding. Although the founders' vision and commitment were vital initially, adaptability and program diversity proved to be the keys to prolonged existence. The nontraditional jobs advocacy that had been the initial organizing impetus could no longer be the sole thrust of the organizations, for two reasons. First, the Reagan administration began systematically to close off avenues to equal opportunity. At the OFCCP, travel budgets were cut and investigators were laid off. At the EEOC, a limit was placed on the number of cases that could be litigated. Employers began to feel that they could with impunity deny jobs to women and minorities. It was clear that these agencies could no longer be counted on as partners in the struggle against job discrimination. Second, the economy began to decline in the coal fields; there were massive layoffs of miners as a result of new technology and a declining market for domestic coal. Women were the last hired and so were the first fired.

As the context of the struggle for equal employment opportunity changed, the organizations used similar methods to develop new programs in order to survive. The methods involved research, analysis, and action, and the goal in each case was to broaden the nontraditional jobs advocacy to include other strategies that would give women additional choices in the job market.

Research meant telling the story and documenting women's experience in the economy. In 1979 there was little or no information, except anecdotal, on women's employment histories, their function in the economy, and the effect of legislation and public policy on their lives. SWEC changed all that with its 1986 publication, *Women of the Rural South*, a research project on the economic status of southern women.[2] Using participatory research and targeting West Virginia, South Carolina, and North Carolina, SWEC documented women's experiences in finding and getting jobs, supporting their families, and facing poverty and its consequences. Starting in 1983, W&E used a law intern from the National Lawyers' Guild to research and write a paper on a different topic each summer. In 1985 "Towards Self Sufficiency: AFDC Mothers and Self Employment in West Virginia" by Antoinette Eates established a basis for legislation by demonstrating that women on welfare were capable of creating their own small businesses. In 1986 "Women and Minorities Last: An Analysis of the Internal Hiring Practices at the WV Department of Highways" by Danita Haskins played a key role in a law suit brought by four women, two black and two white, with the assistance of the NAACP Legal Defense Fund, against the West Virginia Department of Highways and Civil Service System.

In these and other cases, research, analysis, and action led to new programs. For example, W&E began to assist women with self-employment and credit alternatives when jobs in the coalfields and funds for federal construction projects disappeared. SWEC moved further into research and leadership training programs, and CEP was instrumental in persuading the United Mine Workers to include a clause on family leave in the new contract with the Bituminous Coal Operators Association. The recent move of W&E and CEP toward a dues-paying constituency indicates a maturing awareness of the value of members to an advocacy organization and a willingness to mobilize that constituency for social and economic change.

The organizational growth and development of the three groups over the last ten years did not occur without mistakes and internal struggles. In the beginning the founders lacked administrative skills. Betty Jean

Hall confesses to hiring a secretary who had the correct political line but could not type; and I admit to hiring a newsletter editor who could not write, for the same reason. Each organization had to struggle through the learning phase of its founder, who knew about organizing but not about personnel policies. This lack of administrative interest and know-how eventually influenced the decision of each of the founding executive directors to turn the leadership of her organization over to new talent.

Other internal struggles concerned diversity and race. Since the SWEC board of directors was the arena where the executive directors of the three organizations and many others came together, SWEC board meetings came to be the place where the women confronted racism, their own and others', and discussed other "isms" in the context of social and economic change.

The first SWEC board was made up of white women, and the initial attempts to recruit black women onto the all-white board were only partially successful—some black women came to meetings sporadically but did not engage in dialogue on program development. In the spring of 1982, however, three black women who were to be key in the organization joined the board. Sophia Bracy-Harris, Sara Davis, and Gardenia White were instrumental in starting organizations in South Carolina, Alabama, and West Virginia. They had a common agenda with other SWEC members, mainly around economic concerns, and were willing to stick with the organization as it grew and expanded. Despite a rocky start, all the board members settled into the struggle to define racism and determine how it was to be dealt with in the context of SWEC's practices and programs.

The discussion was very deliberate. On the agenda for each quarterly board meeting was space for a discussion of racism, in the form of either a workshop (with a facilitator) to explore racist attitudes or a power analysis to explore institutional racism as it was experienced by those in the room. The work was painful and enlightening, and each of the board members was changed by the experience. Leslie Lilly describes it as "spending forty days and forty nights in the wilderness." But she also feels that SWEC lost some focus as an organization while discussing these issues, partly because of the amount of time it took, diverting attention from SWEC business. Kate McKee of the Ford Foundation also believes that there was too much time spent on process, possibly at the expense of the practice: "It was always a question of balance."

The fact remains, however, that participants in the process were forever changed. Board members took the principles of a nonracist society home to their own organizations and had similar discussions there. Over a period of years, the women who were leaders of organizations touched by SWEC contributed to the discussion on racism and moved it forward to include other issues such as homophobia and disabilities.

The discussions on racism helped SWEC and other organizations develop new programs that took into account the differences in the employment history of black and white women. For example, it became clear that a strategy focused on nontraditional jobs advocacy was not going to include large numbers of black women. For them, having been confined to domestic work for much of their employment history, a nontraditional job could be secretarial. It was important then for SWEC, through the process of research and analysis, to document the racism that had segregated black women into even fewer job categories than white women and make recommendations for change. This focus led to a specific set of recommendations to public policy-makers, churches, and grantmakers in *Women of the Rural South*. One recommendation was "to allocate 50% of state economic development funds to projects benefitting primarily women and additional funds to projects benefitting people of color in direct proportion to their representation in the state population."[3]

In the second half of the 1980s, each of the organizations modified its focus on nontraditional job advocacy. These modifications and the adoption of new program strategies coincided with the resignation of the founders and a transition to new leadership. CEP had the most difficult time, in large part because of an internal struggle between membership and staff. Since its beginning CEP had a legal strategy, using the courts to force coal companies to hire women and treat them equitably. In early 1988 the board of CEP faced a dilemma. The staff felt that the organization should move the legal strategy to other workplaces, such as construction, and they were encouraged by funders to do so. The women coal miners, who wanted the organization to continue to focus on them and their needs, were unhappy with this direction. Even though some of them had been laid off for years, they still regarded themselves as miners and had a strong sense of ownership in the organization. There was also a feeling that there were limitations to litigation as an organizing strategy, and women who were members of the United Mine Workers wanted to see labor organizing techniques used to strengthen the role of women miners.

The struggle to broaden the use of successful advocacy strategies resulted in staff resignations, including that of its founder, Betty Jean Hall. In retrospect, Madeline Rogero, who accepted the board's appointment as the new executive director, says, "To take the [advocacy] model somewhere else was appropriate, but it was also appropriate for CEP to hang on to who they were—an organization of coal mining women." Rogero herself has since moved on, and CEP appointed a woman miner as its new executive director in 1991.

SWEC went through a similar transition when its founder left in 1986. W&E's transition was relatively smooth. Pam Curry, who was the next director of W&E, says, "Now the structure is there, people within the organization can move on." W&E has continued to attract the support of funders from outside the state, and even has some support within the state.

According to Wendy Johnson, who was on the staff of SWEC and became the director when Leslie Lilly left, "There was a lot of concern about program direction, which became sharper in the transition period. The question was always how to move the organization forward." After Johnson left, there was a long gap between directors. The board of directors decided to move the office from Kentucky to Atlanta, and things seemed to go downhill after that. After struggling for years with different programs going in many directions—leadership, advocacy for nontraditional jobs, grassroots organizing—SWEC's board decided to focus on research on issues of employment for women in the South, particularly on federal programs and the effect of welfare reform and the Job Training Partnership Act. But this strategy failed to attract support from funders, who questioned the effects of this program on SWEC's constituency, and a decision was made to close the organization at the end of February 1991.

Margo Smith, the last director of SWEC, said that part of the problem was that funders wanted to see "new, strong program initiatives" and felt that SWEC was no longer on the "cutting edge of the issues." SWEC maintained that the problems for women in the South were still the same and argued for research that would support a public advocacy voice for women's employment. But major funders were not convinced, and the board of directors, lacking a clear constituency to support them, gave up.

As the decade of the nineties unfolds, the future of the movement for economic justice for women is unclear. A dismal economic climate clouds the horizon, and the prediction of the feminization of poverty seems destined to come true in many parts of rural Appalachia and the South. Much of the fight against sex and race discrimination in employment that was begun in the late 1970s has yet to be won. The Bush administration continued the legacy of its predecessor, and no national rural economic development policy exists except as it relates to agriculture.

What then did SWEC, CEP, and W&E accomplish over the last ten to twelve years? Leslie Lilly reflects that although the barriers have not changed and we have even less leverage than in the past, there is now new leadership. More education and training are available; there is more recognition for women in leadership roles. There are mentors and resources and a history for people to build on. The women who have done it are still accessible and serve as a resource base for the new leaders. Betty Jean Hall works for the Occupational Safety and Law Center, still advocating for women coal miners; Leslie Lilly is the vice president of the Foundation for the South in Mississippi; and I am still in West Virginia, working for the Ms. Foundation for Women and running my own consulting business. Each of us continues to work with grassroots women.

It is also true that even though the economy has slowed, when there is hiring for the coal mines and for highway and building construction, women are able to claim some of those jobs. There is still much work to be done to change the attitudes of educators and employers, but with some determination young women can and do go into nontraditional fields. Slowly, the figures are rising. And some women are now starting businesses and employing other women.

The national and regional impact of the nontraditional job advocacy of the three organizations profiled in this chapter has been substantial. Even though equal employment opportunities narrowed in the 1980s, the struggle continues in the 1990s to formulate new civil rights legislation. Organizational strategies have moved from narrowly focused job advocacy to the exploration of economic development alternatives for women. As Alice Kessler-Harris puts it when speaking of debates about access and choices: "New material conditions have shifted the content of equity from a demand for equality with men to a challenge to male structures. The altered terms of the debate no longer ask how women can achieve equality in a predominantly male work world so much as how to revalue the world of work and workers in a way that incorporates female self interest."[4]

I believe that the most important result of the struggle is that there are now institutions owned and operated by women for women to continue the struggle against economic injustice and to revalue the world of work. Over the last ten years, the Southeast Women's Employment Coalition, Women and Employment, the Coal Employment Project, and similar organizations in Appalachia and the South have continued to provide an arena for new leadership to develop and be supported as well as models for emerging organizations.

In the last analysis, however, the job advocacy strategies that began in the late 1970s happened in large part because federal public policy and the women's movement provided the opportunity for those strategies to grow and develop—with the help of female leaders and the organizations they formed. The government was a partner, through the law, training programs, and administrative regulations. The federal partnership ended when the Reagan administration slammed shut the window of opportunity opened under the Carter administration.

The chances that the federal government will reverse its current antipathy to affirmative action and equal employment opportunity with proactive programs seem slight. Women will continue to have to battle against the barriers of race and sex discrimination in employment without federal help and with other allies. Fortunately, they now have some help in that struggle. Across this nation, women are replicating the models of the three organizations profiled here, and new grassroots leaders are emerging. The "epidemic of rebelliousness" continues.

Acknowledgments

Thanks to the following who were interviewed for this article: Pam Curry, Betty Jean Hall, Wendy Johnson, Leslie Lilly, Kate McKee, Eileen Paul, Madeline Rogero, and Margo Smith. Thanks also to Gardenia White and Gloria Steinem for reviewing the manuscript and making suggestions.

Notes

1. Gloria Steinem to Chris Weiss, September 1, 1990.
2. Barbara Smith, *Women of the Rural South: Economic Status and Prospects* (Lexington, Ky.: Southeast Women's Employment Coalition, 1986).
3. Ibid., iv.
4. Alice Kessler-Harris, "The Just Price, the Free Market, and the Value of Women," *Feminist Studies* 14 (1988) : 244.

9

The Memory of Miners and the Conscience of Capital

Coal Miners' Strikes as Free Spaces

Richard A. Couto

We attribute a range of human characteristics to capital. For example, we say capital has a nose for profit and a heart for charitable contributions and philanthropy. Capital distributes its benefits with an invisible hand. Just like humans, capital also has foibles and contradictions. The eyes of capital are fixed on the future, on the lookout for what is new. The mind of capital, however, brims with nineteenth-century Darwinian concerns about competition and survival. Memory and conscience are curiously missing from the stock of capital's human parts.

If capital had a conscience, the excesses of the coal industry would trouble it. Fatalities and disabling injuries on the job, unemployment, and occupational illness are all apparent, common, and direct consequences of the conduct of the coal industry in Appalachia. The Buffalo Creek area of West Virginia had three communities literally destroyed by the industry in which its residents worked. The conditions in the Appalachian coalfields are so severe that they establish measures of human need that occasionally prick the conscience of America.

This chapter suggests that coal miners have provided capital, in the coal industry at least, with a memory and a conscience. Most recently, miners reminded capital of the costs of debilitating competition and the benefit of industrywide standards for wages and working conditions. Memories of these hard-won lessons undergird the long and bitter strikes against the A. T. Massey Coal Group and the Pittston Coal Company, in 1984–85 and 1989–90 respectively.

In addition to explaining the explicit memories that supported miners during the strike, this chapter treats the strikes as free spaces. Sara Evans and Harry Boyte, who have developed the concept, explain free spaces as

> public places in the community . . . the environments in which people are able to learn a new self-respect, a deeper and more assertive group iden-

tity, public skills, and values of cooperation and civic virtue . . . settings between private lives and large-scale institutions where ordinary citizens can act with dignity, independence, and vision.[1]

According to Evans and Boyte, free spaces foster the discovery of new democratic potential among people and new political facts about the world, the construction of networks and contacts with other groups, expanded identities, and control of a space that is relatively independent of elite control.[2] This chapter will interpret both strikes, and distinguish between them, using these characteristics of free spaces.

This analysis of the strikes suggests additional features of free spaces. In particular, as we shall show, memories of past democratic efforts are fashioned within free spaces into tools to renew those efforts in different times and circumstances. In the simplest terms, strikers within the free spaces of both strikes recalled the efforts of former union members and their families to curb the excesses of competition within the coal industry and to achieve the benefits of industrywide standards to protect the position of workers. The memory of these efforts strengthened the miners' resolve to apply the lessons that these memories impart to new conditions of a changed, global economy. Thus, free spaces have a time dimension. In them, narratives refresh memories of past events. Narrators survey past struggles and, avoiding customary detours and tangents, fashion a linear history that runs directly from previous democratic efforts to their own. Another distinguishing quality of the free spaces, this chapter suggests, is the synergism created by combining local leadership with organizational resources, such as those of the United Mine Workers of America (UMWA).[3]

Miners' Memories of Hard Lessons

The lessons applied by miners in the Massey and Pittston strikes are central in the history of the UMWA. By the mid-1920s, John L. Lewis, the leader of the UMWA, concluded that the central problem of the coal industry was excess capacity—the industry's ability to produce more than it could sell at a profit. Operators invariably expanded production in profitable times, which exacerbated the problem of excess capacity when prices fell and profits disappeared. In order to acquire a competitive advantage in those times of bust, operators lowered labor costs by reducing wages and laying off miners.

Coal miners in the central Appalachian coalfields remember, in direct and personal terms, how low labor standards fell when operators searched for a competitive edge and profit. At Massey, strikers reflected on conditions before the UMWA, a time when "the coal companies treated the miners any way they wanted to."[4] Joe Johnson, an eighty-year old miner and Freewill Baptist minister, recalled during the Pittston strike: "I worked in water up to my knees for a dollar a day loading coal by hand, and if I said anything about it the boss would tell me, "If you don't like it, there's a barefoot man waiting outside ready to take your job."[5]

Lewis made repeated efforts to convince operators of the need for an industrywide agreement that would improve and preserve the standards of labor, assure uninterrupted production, and provide profits for reinvestment and improvement in the industry, including mechanization. By the mid-1920s Lewis had lost faith in the coal operators' ability to learn the lessons of excess capacity and to regulate themselves: "It is utterly absurd even to entertain the thought that the time will ever come when the bituminous coal industry can establish sane business relations through corrective measures brought about of its own free application." Miners, he concluded, organized in an industrywide union, would have to compel managers to adhere to the lessons of excess capacity and rapacious competition.[6]

Lewis succeeded in imparting his lessons after severe conflict and only through the intervention of the federal government. In the 1920s "wars" raged in the coalfields. Violent strikes led by the more militant National Miners' Union ushered in the 1930s and established such historic markers as Matewan and "Bloody Harlan."[7] Eventually, the New Deal gave vitality to labor unions in general and the UMWA and Lewis in particular. The National Labor Relations Act of 1935 made it the policy of the United States to encourage collective bargaining by organized labor groups.[8] The UMWA moved from ebb to flood tide. By the end of the 1930s, it had about 90 percent of coal production organized. Lewis and the UMWA also led a social movement of labor in the 1930s, and specifically the formation of the Committee for Industrial Organization (which later evolved into the Congress of Industrial Organizations). Coal miners benefited further during World War II when the federal government, in order to ensure continued production without labor strife, took charge of the mines and negotiated generously with Lewis.

After the war, with the mines restored to private owners, Lewis faced the prospect of restored cutthroat competition in a leaderless industry that now had the most organized and best-paid blue-collar workforce in America. Indeed, Lewis' initial negotiations with the restored owners immediately after the war resembled times past. In 1946 Lewis placed a major new demand on the table: a royalty on every ton of coal produced to support a fund for the health, welfare, and retirement of miners and their dependents. Miners struck to achieve it. When the operators would still not come to terms, Lewis left the negotiating table with a rhetorical wish "that time, as it shrinks your purse, may modify your niggardly and anti-social propensities."[9] President Truman placed the mines under federal control, negotiated the royalty that Lewis sought, and did more. Truman, and the federal courts, levied unprecedented fines of $3.5 million against the UMWA, and $10,000 against Lewis personally. Moreover, Truman invoked the Taft-Hartley Act three times between 1948 and 1950. These federal actions made clear that the federal government no longer provided leverage with which Lewis could move the operators.

By 1950 the coal operators were looking for their own leverage to move the industry. Coal was losing traditional markets, like railroads and home heating, to oil and natural gas. To compete for new markets, such as electrical utilities, the coal industry needed to supply customers reliably, without interruption by strikes. They also needed to modernize and mechanize production. This required a capital investment that they hoped would come from higher profits and uninterrupted production. Peace with labor became important to major producers.

Some operators, mainly those in the northern Appalachian region, who were tied to steel companies and led by Consolidated Coal and Island Creek, proposed an association, the Bituminous Coal Operators Association (BCOA). The BCOA would negotiate a multiple-employer contract with the UMWA to establish a high industry standard. In exchange for this uniform higher standard, Lewis was to provide the members of the BCOA with a labor force that would not interrupt production with strikes, the key factor for reliable supplies of coal and a good return on their investment in capital-intense mechanization.[10] This accord expressed the lessons that Lewis had been preaching for twenty-five years.

As part of the higher standard for labor, the BCOA agreed to establish two funds, from royalties paid on each ton of coal produced, for an industry-sponsored welfare system. One fund financed pensions for miners, many of whom would be forced out of work by mechanization. The other fund financed a health plan that exceeded that of any other American union. Both funds were industrywide, and miners remained eligible for them at any company under contract with the UMWA. In an industry marked by the frequent appearance and disappearance of coal companies, the industrywide nature of the funds safeguarded the benefits of miners from the failures of individual companies.

Trading improved standard wages for mechanization cost most miners dearly. The unemployment and distress that mechanization caused in the coalfields exceeded anyone's calculation. Between 1950 and 1960, a quarter of a million miners, almost 60 percent of the workforce, lost their jobs. The funds were inadequate to mitigate the severe social consequences of mechanization: unemployment, migration, community deterioration, and a decline of social services. Payments for the intended beneficiaries—retirees, widows, and disabled miners—taxed the funds' limits. Lewis controlled the trustees of the funds and kept the coal royalties modest in order to keep the price of coal low. When the demands for benefit payments exceeded the revenues of the funds, Lewis whittled benefits and ratcheted eligibility criteria to reduce the number of beneficiaries.

Whatever its unintended consequences, the BCOA-UMWA accord brought some changes to the coal industry that Lewis assiduously sought. The accord forged cooperation among a set of producers, mostly large ones, who agreed to set a limit on their competition by accepting a standard cost of labor. This industrywide standard led to higher wages for the miners left employed in the mechanized sector of the industry, and it removed labor costs from the calculation of competition. Observers at the time described the accord as consistent with the industrial finance theory of bargaining. It established and imposed a uniformly high wage scale that both required capital investment in mechanization and protected that investment. Mechanization encouraged higher wage rates, and higher wage rates encouraged still more mechanization.[11]

The BCOA-UMWA agreement was also a deliberate attempt to eliminate a competitive sector of small operations in the coal industry. Lewis and the BCOA agreed that meeting the generous terms of the labor contracts was a condition of remaining in business. If only large mechanized companies could afford the contracts and small operators had to drop out of the industry, that was acceptable—in fact, preferable. The demise of small, unmechanized operations would diminish the excess capacity of an industry faced with a cataclysmic decline in demand.

All did not go as planned, however. The spiral of benefits was interrupted by forces that kept the competitive sector of small operators alive and well. In particular, in the 1950s the Tennessee Valley Authority (TVA) encouraged small, unmechanized operations and new, large, strip mine operations.[12] This was precisely the competition that Lewis had fought his entire career. He complained to Congress that TVA's coal purchasing practices "beat down small isolated producing units to a starvation wage, ignoring safety standards and health conditions, taxes, compensation obligations, and so forth." TVA, Lewis continued, then called upon companies like those in the BCOA "to meet the intolerable and unjustifiable price" it had extracted from the smaller units.[13] Lewis literally went to war with these smaller, TVA-supported mines. Secretly, he financed new mechanized mines that undersold production at smaller UMWA mines. Some district leaders used violence to stop the small producers' supply of labor. The UMWA became, one account suggests, "the only union in

American history to undertake a concerted, directed, planned, financed and calculated campaign, over a sustained period of time, of violence, terror, dynamite, and killing of other men."[14]

Lewis devised another, less overtly violent, tactic that shut off the supply of labor to non-UMWA mines but sowed the seeds of later reform. As part of the restrictive criteria Lewis adopted to decrease the number of the funds' beneficiaries, a miner and his dependents were ineligible for retirement benefits if he had ever worked in a nonunion mine. In response to these and other restrictions, some intended but now ineligible beneficiaries organized and protested against their loss of benefits in the 1960s. Later, this protest movement and others like it developed into the black lung movement, which contributed, in turn, to the Miners for Democracy and the democratic reform of the UMWA.[15]

The contract of 1977 presented UMWA miners with a new test of the lessons they had acquired and the reforms they had conducted. In the late 1940s the American economy and transportation system slowed and then stopped without coal. Railroads interrupted their schedules because of fuel problems. Steel plants closed without coke. Automobile manufacturers shut down without steel. In addition, if the strike was in winter, heating homes and offices became a serious concern. By the mid-1970s, however, railroads no longer used coal. Smokestack industries had declined, and most heating requirements were now met by natural gas and oil. Coal's expanded vital link to electricity was circumvented regularly as utilities without coal supplies bought electricity from other utilities and maintained their service without interruption. Only the ailing steel industry remained vulnerable to a UMWA strike.

Along with this shift in demand came new competition for the BCOA companies and changes in areas of production. Surface and non-union producers in the central Appalachian coalfields, first financed by TVA, increased. The growth of demand for coal among the midwestern utilities spurred a new set of coal operators, primarily sub-bituminous producers, in the western states. In the contract year of 1977, western miners produced 22 percent of all bituminous and sub-bituminous coal. Sixteen of the nation's 25 largest mines were in the West; only one was in Appalachia. Of those 16, 9 had opened since 1970. By 1988, another contract year, 33 percent of all bituminous and sub-bituminous coal was mined in the West; 80 percent of that amount was sub-bituminous. Twenty-four of the nation's 25 largest coal mines were operating in the West. All but three had opened since 1970. And producers in South Africa, Columbia, and Venezuela had entered utility markets in the southern and Gulf states.[16]

These changes in production further hindered the ability of UMWA miners to shut off the supply of coal. By 1977 UMWA miners produced only 50 percent of the nation's coal, compared with 90 percent in 1947. Mines without UMWA contracts continued to produce during the 1977–78 strike, and even some mines with UMWA contracts did so. The UMWA, in an effort to win support in the new and expanding coalfields of the West, did not strike UMWA mines there. The union had its strongest hold on the frail eastern coal producers, and that proved inadequate for victory. The 1977–78 strike was the longest industrywide strike in the union's history and its least successful since the BCOA accord.

The miners continued to strike against difficult odds chiefly because their full-coverage health plan was at stake. To settle the strike, the UMWA eventually conceded it and the industrywide benefits plan as well. Employers became directly and individually responsible for the health care and nonpension benefits of miners who retired as their employees, and for their dependents.[17]

As the 1970s ended, UMWA members could look back on a complex history. The violent, bloody organizing efforts of the 1930s and new federal legislation had brought high, industrywide standards for coal miners, which by the 1950s included a comprehensive health benefit plan. The price of that victory was drastically reduced employment in coal mining, migration out of the Appalachian coalfields, and union violence against miners. Another cost was the increased isolation of UMWA leadership from the rank and file and retired miners, with the result that retirement benefits and protective legislation for health and safety were placed beyond the members' reach. Consequently, the miners' efforts to build the UMWA in the 1930s and 1940s were followed by the efforts of the 1960s and 1970s to compensate former miners for their disabling black lung disease and protect working miners from the corruption and indolence of their own union.

Forward to the Past

The strikes at Massey and Pittston pitted miners' memories of industrial competition and the benefits of the BCOA agreement against the calculations of some coal companies that the BCOA agreement undermined their competitiveness in the coal industry. The strikes came when excess capacity in the coal industry stimulated new competition and miners' memories of its related problems. At the same time, new managers of the American coal industry were addressing their new competition with little commitment to an industrywide standard for coal miners and few memories of the standard's origins and the sacrifices made to achieve it.

By 1977 the coal industry resembled Lewis' design for fewer, larger mechanized operations in a greatly expanded coal market, but his plan had gone awry. The industry had grown and become concentrated in the West, where the UMWA has had trouble organizing because western miners view themselves more as heavy equipment operators than as coal miners. They do not share the traditions and memories of miners in the East.[18] Likewise, the founding members of the BCOA, steel-related coal mines, played a smaller role in the coal industry. The strike of 1977–78 demonstrated how greatly these changes had diminished the capacity of UMWA members to win a strike against the BCOA. In the 1980s, new foreign producers competed with American coal at home and abroad and further imperiled the UMWA-BCOA accord.

At the same time, some companies in the BCOA, like the new companies of the West, became subsidiaries of parent corporations with less memory of the importance of industrywide agreements and stable floors of labor standards in the industry. Initially, oil corporations bought into the coal industry. As oil profits dwindled and cash flow problems beset these companies, they sold assets, including coal companies, to prevent being bought themselves.[19]

This infusion of capital from outside the coal industry unraveled the frayed remnant of the UMWA-BCOA industrial finance theory. In a swift palace revolt, new capital managers took "return on investment," whose acronym (ROI) is the French word for "king," and enthroned it in Appalachian economics, where, in plain English, coal had once been "king." These capital managers had less stake in a high-wage, stable coal industry and greater concern for ROI in any field. Amoco's coal operations, for example, were profitable but fell below the company's goal of 13 to 15 percent of ROI, and so the operations were put up for sale in 1985. Under the rule of ROI, coal companies compete with the parent company's other investment opportunities, and not only with other mining ventures.[20] This new competition placed new downward pressure on miners' wages and benefits. New managers proposed to reintroduce labor costs into the calculation of competition, a proposal that suggested a future with which miners were already familiar.

The Massey Strike

E. Morgan Massey, president of the A. T. Massey Coal Group, had intergenerational ties within the coal industry. Renewing an anti-union sentiment barely dormant in some sectors of the coal industry, he blamed unions and industrywide standards for "putting this country out of business."[21] Massey sought a separate contract for each of his company's subsidiaries. This meant, he insisted, that the UMWA had to bargain on a company-by-company basis with his subsidiaries and tailor labor terms and trim labor costs to fit each company. Massey's effort to Balkanize the coal industry aroused miners' memories of a standardless industry where competition would fracture labor arrangements. In company-by-company negotiations within a competitive market, a standard was no longer a floor but a ceiling, no longer a guarantee but a point from which to begin concessions.

Massey's insistence that its subsidiaries were actually independent employers also clashed directly with the major new UMWA effort to expand employment opportunities for its members, especially the 30 percent who were unemployed. The BCOA contract permitted laid-off miners to place their names on panels of job applicants at the employer's other mines and wholly owned or controlled subsidiaries or affiliates. The UMWA complained that union producers like Massey were creating new operations or leasing coal land and subcontracting production to nonunion operations.[22] By insisting that each of its subsidiaries was a separate, independent company, Massey was dissolving the bonds that made panel rights transferrable for UMWA labor. Thus, whether the A. T. Massey Coal Group was one employer or many became the narrow, litigious, contentious issue of the strike. Behind it was the question of maintaining industrywide agreements, creating companywide opportunities for work, or reverting to an industry of many employers and cutthroat competition for labor.

The strike ended after fifteen months. The National Labor Relations Board (NLRB) finally upheld the UMWA's allegation that Massey's refusal to bargain as a single employer was an unfair labor practice.[23] Richard Trumka, president of the UMWA, accepted that decision as a victory and called an end to the strike. The UMWA and Massey then began another set of legal battles over the single-employer issue. By 1988, four years after the strike began, another agreement ended the dispute without resolving the issue of corporate structure. The UMWA won panel rights among Massey subsidiaries; in exchange, the Massey companies reduced their royalty payments to the 1950 Pension Fund.[24]

The Pittston Strike
The Pittston Coal Company also attempted to abandon the industrywide standard of the BCOA contract. The company stressed its need to compete in a global market for metallurgical coal; 75 percent of its production went to foreign markets, especially Japan, in 1988. To be more competitive in its coal markets and more profitable in general, Pittston aimed to save five to six dollars a ton from the costs incurred under the BCOA agreement[25] and also to change UMWA work rules. However, the company's most serious action, in the miners' estimation, was its cessation of payments to the industrywide benefits and pension funds that Lewis won in 1946 and that had been part of the BCOA pact since 1950.[26] In addition, the miners

contested Pittston's attempts, like those of Massey, to circumvent the costs of its UMWA contract by contracting with nonunion companies within a new corporate division it had established for that purpose.[27]

Pittston's action had serious consequences for the remaining members of the BCOA, which were left with higher costs for the industry's past promises to its workers. In fact, the situation got worse. Pittston absolved itself of the industry's debt to its workers and their families just as that debt was increasing. A 1987 court decision determined that retirees of companies that went bankrupt were eligible for benefits. This decision nearly doubled the beneficiaries of the 1974 Benefits Trust to 7,000.[28] To meet the increased cost of benefits to former workers of defunct companies, BCOA contract signatories were faced with increases of 44 percent, up to $3.23 per hour, on royalties paid to the 1974 Trust. Pittston's withdrawal meant that the remaining BCOA members would face larger costs from a dwindling base. Thus, its action cut two ways: it improved its own position and placed the other BCOA companies in a worse one.[29]

Paul Douglas, chairman of Pittston, described the company's action as forward-looking rather than a shirking of past promises. He spoke of establishing a "modern" medical plan at Pittston that would double deductibles and require miners to pay 20 percent of remaining costs. This was part of Pittston's effort "to get back the management of the mines," according to Douglas. Similarly, Pittston president Michael Odom resolved "to pull the union into the future." According to a U.S. Senate subcommittee staff report, these measures would have established a labor contract more in line with those outside the coal industry.[30]

Pittston's actions, like Massey's, placed labor costs back at the center of competitive calculations at a time of expanding production and profits in the American coal industry. The unusual timing of their decision is explained in part by the changes in the companies and the industry, which obscured the memory of corporate managers and focused their attention on higher rates of profits within their own corporate structures.

Labor provided capital with the memory that its calculation for profit obscured. Miners remembered these Funds as benefits they had earned and as partial payment for the individual and common sacrifices they made in the industry shakedown of the 1950s. Company officials spoke of the benefits as time-limited elements of competition, "just like your American Express is dated."[31] In contrast, strikers spoke of enduring rights and obligations. Joe Cocoran, UMWA Pittston strike organizer, explained the obligation miners felt toward others:

> What these people in Greenwich [Pittston's Connecticut headquarters] don't realize is that the company pensioners are not an amorphous, un-

identified bunch of people in Miami. They're these guys' [Pittston miners']
fathers and widowed grandmothers and they've been living in some hol-
low of these mountains. To use pensioners as a stick to beat at working
people has really appalled Appalachia.[32]

A miner in southwest Virginia explained the strike in terms of what
the company owed his family, even if changes in name and ownership
fostered ignorance of the past among its present managers.

My father, my grandfather, and I have over 100 years of coal mining with
Clinchfield Coal Co. [now owned by Pittston]. And the company took
away my father's hospitalization. My mother-in-law's a widow and they
took her hospitalization, too. So I decided I'd fight 'em 'til hell freezes over
to see 'em do right by these people.[33]

Pittston restored benefits to the post-1974 retirees during the strike.
In the contract that ended the strike, the company contributed $10 million
to the 1950 Benefit Trust fund and agreed to pay the amounts stipulated in
the BCOA 1988 contract into the 1974 Pension and Benefit Trust funds. In
exchange, it was allowed to duck its obligations to the 1950 Benefit Trust.
The company also made gains in work rules. The UMWA agreed to ten-
hour shifts, a four-day work week, and Sunday operations, measures that
permit the company to operate around the clock, an important step to cost
savings in a capital-intense industry. The UMWA acquired more employment opportunities and job security for its members. Pittston agreed to
hire UMWA unemployed miners for 4 out of 5 positions at its nonunion
mines and for 19 out of 20 positions for any operations subcontracted,
commitments that went beyond the 1988 BCOA contract.[34]

The Strikes as Free Spaces

Within free spaces of family and union, coal miners and their family members had continued the memories of the conduct of the coal industry and
cultivated the lesson that they had the primary responsibility to see that
coal companies "do right." The strikes took those memories and lessons
to more public space. In this sense the strikes extended the free spaces
of the miners. This is clearer if we examine the strikes in terms of the
characteristics of free spaces that, according to Evans and Boyte, change
social protest into democratic movements. This examination also creates
a context for the dismay over the outcome of the Massey strike and the
euphoria over the outcome at Pittston.

New Political Facts About the World

The Massey strike involved hard lessons for miners about new political realities—lessons that the UMWA would apply at Pittston. The Massey company was connected by a web of international capital to other sources of profit. Opportunities for profit, within and outside the coal industry, determined the company's future within its corporate structure. In a sense, the Massey company did not compete in the coal industry; it competed in its own corporate structure for capital investment. Its successful competition required the promise of an equal or greater return on investment than other opportunities offered.

Massey managers invoked competition from foreign, western, and nonunion producers to justify the need for company-by-company agreements. Yet Massey's own corporate structure illustrated the ambiguity of "competition" in the industry. The Massey Coal Group was literally a subsidiary of a joint venture of joint ventures of subsidiaries of parent corporations, Fluor and the Royal Dutch/Shell Group. The Royal Dutch/Shell Group owned mining interests in South Africa, and Fluor was developing coal mining in China with Massey's assistance.[35] Some of Massey's subsidiaries in the Appalachian region were nonunion competitors of union mines. In fact, Massey estimated that his company was the largest nonunion underground mining company in Appalachia, if not the country.[36] Part of the UMWA's grievance to the NLRB concerned the company's practice of subcontracting the work of UMWA mines to its other, nonunion mines. In effect, Massey supplied some of its own competition, and its parent corporations supplied some more.

In a new global economy with changed corporate structures, the UMWA devised a new strike strategy. Rather than striking all coal producers for the violation of a BCOA member, the UMWA would strike companies selectively. Selective strikes permitted the union to discipline one producer, such as Massey or Pittston, for straying from contract standards without disrupting other companies' production. The selective strike helped the UMWA to negotiate two BCOA contracts in 1984 and 1988, without a nationwide strike. This has helped preserve the BCOA. Thus, the selective strike responded to new political facts about the world of coal. It also solved a dilemma of maintaining a tradition of militant resistance within a frail segment of the coal industry.[37]

Within the strategy of the selective strike, the UMWA developed the tactic of corporate campaigns. This tactic was not entirely new: the Brookside strike in the early 1970s—a tense and severe labor conflict that harked back to "Bloody Harlan" of the 1930s—also involved a corporate campaign. At Massey and Pittston, the UMWA worked with bankers, citizen groups, stockholders, and an array of other actors to slow down the supply of capital to the companies. In addition, corporate campaigns challenged the financial as well as moral conduct of the companies in the strike. The UMWA's brochures resembled glossy corporate publications and used the language of "long-term viability," "profitable divisions," "share of revenues," and "operating structure" as fluently as the most profit-conscious stockholder might. Finally, the UMWA's corporate campaign also attempted to persuade customers to pressure the companies to comply with union requests by threatening to curtail business with them. During the Pittston strike, for example, the UMWA approached the steel firms of Japan in this way, while getting Australian miners to agree to produce no extra coal to help Pittston meet contracts with Japanese steel firms.[38]

A demand for lower standards for labor that resulted from new competition within a global economy provided a familiar lesson for miners at Massey and Pittston. In addition, the 1980s brought a decline in what Richard Titmuss described as the welfare system tied to work, health care, pensions, and security in employment.[39] In its place, workers found less employment at lower wages and fewer benefits. A simultaneous decline in the public welfare system prodded displaced workers to enter work at lower wages and with fewer benefits. Massey, as a subsidiary of Royal Dutch Shell, was an obvious reminder of the competition between American workers and those in other countries working for lower wages and benefits and in oppressive conditions, including apartheid. Massey's and Pittston's practice of transferring contracts and assets to their nonunion subsidiaries occurred in other industries and eroded the employment security and conditions of workers there.

Exacerbating the declining standards of labor was another new fact of the world of labor—the increased determination of capital to replace workers who struck or protested against the decline in their standards. President Ronald Reagan set a dramatic example for the nation when he fired and replaced 12,000 air traffic controllers at the beginning of his administration. Hiring replacement workers soon became common. The National Football League's 1988 season provided the most visible effort at worker replacement, while the Eastern Airlines and Greyhound strikes were other prominent examples that occurred at about the time of the Pittston strike. Massey began hiring replacement workers five months after the strike began. The tensions between striking miners and replacement workers and the security guards who escorted them provided a backdrop of real and possible violence to the strike.

Massey and Pittston miners renewed former lessons on how courts and federal agencies enforced laws to protect the companies' interests. Miners' actions to impede production brought swift and extraordinary court action; management's efforts to elude contractual obligations toward miners brought slow response through ordinary, cumbersome channels. The NLRB took six months to reach a preliminary determination that A. T. Massey was a single employer, and another eight months to issue a complaint against the company—at which point the UMWA called an end to the strike. In the Pittston case, the NLRB took fourteen months to uphold the UMWA in twenty-three grievances that it filed.[40] In contrast, the NLRB issued a temporary restraining order within days when the Massey company complained of strikers' misconduct, and acted within forty-two days of the start of the Pittston strike to prohibit union action that state court orders already enjoined.[41]

Additionally, the courts had two standards of punishment. Union actions at Pittston brought incredible fines, but company actions brought leniency. After just two months on strike, the union incurred initial fines of $3 million from the state courts and several hundred thousand dollars from the federal courts, and three union organizers were imprisoned within two weeks of the court order for failing to prevent the blocking of roads by mass sit-downs and slow-moving cars. By contrast, in 1983 Pittston was fined $47,500 for violating Mine Health and Safety Act regulations and negligently contributing to the deaths of seven miners.

The selective strike expressed lessons that miners derived from the new political facts about the world. The Massey and Pittston strikes incorporated and expressed the same lessons, but the cost of the Massey strike, the recurring threat of violence, and its ambiguous outcome offered additional lessons for the UMWA. These lessons prompted union leaders to conduct the strike at Pittston far more deliberately as a social movement than a labor conflict, borrowing strategies and tactics from other social movements and making the strike more of a free space than its effort at Massey had been.

New Democratic Potential

Many of the strategies of the Massey strike undermined the democratic nature of social movements. For the first five months of the strike, union lawyers, not miners, addressed the central issue of the strike, which was a legal and technical one—the nature of Massey as a single employer. A congressional subcommittee staff report described the strike as "a classic example" of a labor dispute that had degenerated into a series of legal battles.[42]

In late February strikers briefly took charge of the strike. In response to increased security forces and the hiring of replacement workers, miners without much forethought used the tactics of nonviolent civil disobedience to prevent renewed production. Hundreds of miners and their family members blocked roads near Massey mines with marches, sit-down demonstrations, and parked vehicles, halting production, generating the most favorable publicity to that date, transforming the strike, and bringing the company to the bargaining table for the most serious negotiations of the strike. But the miners' actions also caught the attention of the courts. From mid-March to mid-April, several judges levied fines for violations of past injunctions or issued new injunctions lowering the permissible number of pickets. The UMWA, fearful of large fines, complied. Organizers dispersed fewer pickets to many different sites and returned control of the strike's resolution to the lawyers.[43]

The court's action had several ramifications. Negotiations stalled and then stopped, sending the strike into protracted litigation. The injunctions, coupled with the emphasis on legal action, limited the miners' participation in their own strike. Without roles for them to carry out, the union had less control over the miners' actions. In the face of provocation and violence, some striking miners reverted to their own traditions of violence. Company and union spokesmen exchanged charges and examples of violence. A U.S. House subcommittee staff report found that "neither the union nor the company did enough" to keep the strike peaceful. It also suggested that court action, such as that at Massey, which reduces "the ability of strikers to legitimately express their grievances increases individual frustrations and diminishes the influence of responsible leaders." The report quoted one strike organizer's complaint, "The worst problem we have is when the men have nothing to do but stand around . . . these court injunctions are just taking us out of the picture."[44] Selective strike tactics were new, but other facts about the world that miners faced evoked traditions of violence that reduced the democratic potential of the Massey strike.

At Pittston, UMWA leaders deliberately incorporated elements of other social movements, releasing the democratic potential first glimpsed at Massey. Consultants from social movements for peace and against nuclear weapons trained union leaders in civil disobedience.[45] The massive civil disobedience campaign to block operations at Pittston involved striking miners in a form of resistance that Massey strikers had spontaneously conducted. At Pittston, the union also depended heavily on family members, community residents, church leaders, and other supporters to circumvent court orders on the union, to conduct the campaign of massive civil disobedience, or to support those people who did.[46]

The union's tactics at Pittston did more to permit people to discover the democratic potential in their power to say "No" to corporate power. Two events that expressed this power sent the strike in a profoundly different direction from the Massey strike. On April 18, 1989, two weeks after the start of the strike, thirty-seven women—wives, daughters, and widows of miners—entered the Pittston company offices in Lebanon, Virginia, and began a two-day, nondisruptive occupation of the offices. When asked their names, the women invoked their traditions and answered, "Daughters of Mother Jones," the labor organizer of the early twentieth century. Their sit-in won statewide media coverage for the strike and demonstrated early on the power of civil disobedience and the role of people other than miners in the conduct of civil disobedience.[47]

Six days after the women's action at Pittston's offices, miners sat down on access roads to three major operating sites of the Pittston mines. Like the women, the miners sang, "We Shall Not Be Moved." Unlike the women, the miners were dealing with state police, who had less training in civil disobedience than the miners and less presence of mind than officials in the Pittston offices. The police reacted to the sit-down with force and mass arrests. Stories of the arrests and harsh treatment spread through the community, and sympathy and support for the strikers increased. Local officials proved uncooperative with the state police, local merchants refused to sell them gasoline for their vehicles, and eventually students at the county's three high schools walked out of class to protest against the arrests and treatment of the miners. By late April the strike had mobilized the community, and many local people were mesmerized by their newly discovered power to stand up for what they thought was right.

Late in the strike, strikers and supporters flexed their new political muscles again. In November UMWA District 28 President Jackie Stump ran for the Virginia House of Delegates as a write-in candidate. With massive UMWA support, Stump won with a stunning two-to-one margin in a long-shot campaign against an incumbent of twenty years. It was an especially satisfying victory because that incumbent was the father of the state court judge who eventually fined the UMWA $31 million.[48]

The Contest for Free Space

The central element that distinguishes the two strikes is the contest for and the creation of free spaces. The sit-in at the Pittston office defied the authority and control of the company in its own space. The Massey strike had no comparable feature. Massey's office was far from the coalfields, and Massey himself made a point of the firm's remoteness in explaining its apparent indifference to the welfare of the strike-bound region: "Multinational corporations do not have a great deal of national loyalty and even less loyalty to southern West Virginia."[49] Yet the Massey strike provided a dress rehearsal for Pittston in other ways. The sit-downs at Pittston, just like those at Massey, blocked the company's operations and defied its right to use the roads to conduct business as usual rather than negotiate. At

Massey, miners learned the importance of continuing this tactic, a lesson other miners applied at Pittston.[50]

The contest over free space at Pittston extended to the courts. Without directly violating any laws, the UMWA challenged the role of the courts at Pittston—as it was unable to do at Massey. Eventually one judge pushed the courts' action to absurd proportions. The state court levied fines of $5 million on the union for violations of injunctions on the number of pickets and impeding the company's operations. It then went one step further and levied a fine of $500,000, to be doubled every day as long as the campaign of civil disobedience continued. In 12 days, this reached $1.2 billion. In 22 days, this fine would have totaled about $1.2 trillion, more than the national budget.

The corporate campaign at Pittston entailed another contest over space. Miners and coalfield residents confronted Pittston officials about their obligations to former workers at the corporation's annual stockholders' meeting in Greenwich, Connecticut, on May 10, 1989. Predictably, the company's calculation of present profitability had clouded its memory of debts to past workers. When reminded, company officials responded with cynicism. For example, when a Pittston official suggested that miners resisting the company's demand that they work on Sunday were using religion as a crutch, a miner replied, "I use church to get through work during the week. That's my crutch in life, the whole meaning of it, because I hope to go to a better place when this is over." His stark, solemn declaration brought the retort, "Come to Greenwich," from one Pittston official and laughter from others. This exchange and others left one miner's wife examining capital's body for missing parts: "I think they have lost their ears—and I wonder how they live without hearts."[51]

In September local UMWA strike organizers directed another contest over space: the takeover and sit-in at Moss 3, the Pittston coal cleaning plant. (Jim Sessions and Fran Ansley recount the details and human emotion of that event in Chapter 10, offering an inside look at the creation of a free space.) The takeover breathed new life into the strike. Once again, a union action drew upon traditions—the great Flint sit-ins, for example—to give strikers and their supporters energy for their present struggle.

In addition to these challenges to the company's control of space, the Pittston strikers and their supporters created their own clearly autonomous space. Camp Solidarity was one such free space; the Binns-Counts Community Development Center in McClure, Virginia, was another. The presence of both helped make the Pittston strike different from the one at Massey. These two spaces also differed from each other. Like the local people, the Binns-Counts Center had a history preceding but transformed by the strike. The center was named, in part, for Mary Kathleen Counts, one of America's first women miners and the first woman to lose her life in a mining accident. (She was one of seven miners killed in the 1983 Pittston mine explosion.) The center provided meals and meeting space primarily for local miners and supporters.

The center, as a free space of the strike, offered family members, bound by the intergenerational ties of common work, and community residents, bound by the common economic foundation of the coal industry, public spaces to share views and experiences previously exchanged in less public places. Stories were exchanged of different times and different places, but with lessons applicable to local and current events. Those stories enabled miners and their families to draw parallels between the 1930s and their own time: from the gun thugs of the 1930s to the Vance International Asset Protection Team of a half-century later, from coal operator justice then to coal operator justice now. In these spaces, coal officials' positions and statements were analyzed and found wanting. Paul Douglas claimed, "This is 1989, not 1939. The era of company towns, of violence and confrontation, is long gone. Good riddance. We [Pittston] cannot and never would return to the practices of the past."[52] People in free spaces rebutted such statements: "Pittston would love to take this community back to the '30s and the '40s," observed one woman, the daughter, sister, and wife of coal miners.[53] She had memories of times past acquired in the free spaces of family, community, and union. She also had a determination to act in the free spaces that the strike offered her to prevent the conditions of times past from returning.

Camp Solidarity was created explicitly for the tens of thousands of visitors who came to support the strike. Formerly a swim and tennis club, this free space was a rare instance in a coal county of Appalachia of land beyond the control of coal companies and available to strike supporters. The lessons and history preserved in families and union locals found more public and wider expression at Camp Solidarity. It also offered miners and their visiting allies a place to interpret and analyze the forces arrayed against them, and the analysis of police and court intimidation fostered the power to resist it.[54] In Camp Solidarity and the Binns-Counts Center, court injunctions and the massive police presence became new measures of the state's willingness to substitute force for the memory and conscience of capital. One visiting miner from Indiana observed, "They [the police and courts] seem just like another Pittston subsidiary to me."[55]

Building Networks and Establishing Broader Identities
Within these strikes, as in all free spaces, individuals found common bonds and took strength from each other's example and support. They

were spaces in which people could reclaim the past and make a claim on the future. As one miner's wife explained:

> The camp [Camp Solidarity] is a reminder of our roots. When the UMWA was first organized, miners were forced to live in tent cities, but even under those conditions, our parents and grandparents had the courage and strength to stick together to win a better life. Now it's our turn.[56]

The UMWA, especially at Pittston, borrowed from the civil rights movement symbols and tactics that helped strikers identify with broader issues. Taylor Branch's history of the civil rights movement[57] bonded with the miners' own memories as the intellectual foundations of the Pittston strike. The campaign of nonviolence, the stark division of evil and good, the commitment to overcoming evil with good, and the dedication to civil disobedience against unjust laws described on the pages of Branch's book were used to rewrite the Massey tactics at Pittston. The similarities between the Pittston strike and the civil rights movement prompted Jesse Jackson to assert, before a crowd of twelve thousand, "We look around today, we see the tradition of John L. Lewis and Martin Luther King, Jr. have come together *and we will not go back!*"[58]

Both strikes galvanized new ties between the UMWA and other organized labor groups because the issues epitomized developments in the American economy and government that affected other groups of workers. The UMWA began to work with those groups apart from the strikes to address those issues. For example, UMWA officers led the AFL-CIO anti-apartheid campaign in part because of Shell's ties to both Massey and South African coal mines. The UMWA participated in the Jobs With Justice campaign to protest against the labor and economic policies of the 1980s.[59] Reciprocally, leaders of other unions and the AFL-CIO, and other striking workers, like those at Eastern Airlines, came to southwestern Virginia to demonstrate support for the miners at Pittston. Capping a decade of rapprochement, the cooperation of union leaders during the strike promoted the reaffiliation of the UMWA with the AFL-CIO.

Strike organizers carefully related the strikes to issues facing American workers and workers of other nations as well. They were more successful at Pittston, where the issues—benefits to old and retired miners and their dependents—were expressed in personal terms. The legal issues of the Massey strike, however important, were not easily conveyed to the general public. Miners at Pittston reached back in time for precedents like the Flint sit-ins and reached around the world for counterparts to their own struggle. Camp Solidarity evoked organizing struggles of other times and places and the contemporary Polish liberation movement. During Lech Walesa's visit to the United States in October 1989, a member of Solidarity explained to the miners in southwestern Virginia that their strike was "the first time in the history of our movement that the workers of Poland have been able to support a labor union in the United States."[60] In the Pittston strike, as noted above, the UMWA also reached out to labor organizations in South Africa and Australia, and to the International Confederation of Trade Unions. This attention to international cooperation distinguished the UMWA's strike at Pittston from business unionism as usual and embellished the traditions kept in the memories of miners.

It also won the attention of Secretary of Labor Elizabeth Dole. The day after meeting with labor representatives of Solidarity and other nations, Dole announced that she would visit the coalfields. About a month later, Dole arranged for talks between the UMWA and the company to resume. William Usery, the mediator whom Dole selected, found that for all the publicity and turmoil, the issue, for the miners, remained the conscience of capital. Everything "kept leading us back to Pittston withdrawing from the [health care] funds."[61]

Free Spaces, Memory, and Conscience

In the free spaces of recent strikes, miners continued to function as the conscience of capital. As John L. Lewis traced that conscience to operators' purse strings, miners followed optical fibers and satellite communications to a global host of subsidiaries in a space-age web of capital flow. Still, as in Lewis' times, it takes someone else—policy-makers and organized groups—to fashion from those strings something resembling a conscience. Government was not interested in this task in the 1980s: it trusted more in the invisible hand to redress the imbalances of wealth and power that capital created. Coal miners were therefore required to take up this role once again, using the lessons acquired in free spaces, some of which were their own and some of which other social movements provided.

Evans and Boyte maintain that free spaces, as the base of democratic movements, draw their strength, vision, and power, as well as their limits, from communitarian settings.[62] These strikes seem to confirm this. Both strikes brought to bear in specific places a world of new facts about global economics and American labor relations in the Reagan era. The strikes also suggest, however, that the media influence the public perception of the communitarian setting. Coverage of the Massey strike drew on violent themes of coalfield wars, like those of nearby Matewan, whereas coverage of the Pittston strike drew on romantic notions of dignity and hard work in coalfield poverty. The latter images garnered much more support for the UMWA nationally and for the Pittston strike as a free space.

Evans and Boyte also suggest that when large-scale organizations like trade unions lose their organic connection to local communities, they lose their role as actors in social movements.[63] Again these strikes seem to bear their observation out, with a corollary. The UMWA succeeded at Pittston, in part, because it personalized the strike issues more there, directly involved larger numbers of people over a longer period of time, and explicitly modeled its action on earlier democratic movements. The UMWA's role suggests that however local communities may enhance the role of organizations as actors in social movements, those organizations may also increase the capacity of local communities to participate effectively in social movements. Strikers at Pittston might have replayed the events at Massey had the UMWA not used its organic connection to their communities to introduce traditions of other free spaces. The transformations of people and the UMWA in the free spaces of the Massey and Pittston strikes were symbiotic and synergistic.

There are obvious limits to free spaces. It is doubtful that the strikes, for example, will transform American labor. The coal industry illustrates in an unusually clear way the relationship between industrial conduct and community welfare—a connection that uniquely catalyzes the formation of free spaces in the coalfields and that is difficult to replicate in other settings.[64] As one Massey miner described the situation, "Our families are here, our homes, our jobs. There's no place else to work. They're trying to take everything away from us."[65] The victory at Pittston may not even transform the UMWA as much as the dubious outcome at Massey did. The UMWA changed its tactics after Massey, whereas discussions between local community leaders and UMWA officials since the Pittston strike have left participants without a clear idea of how the UMWA can now contribute to a community to which it owes so much. Having won a major labor struggle over a company's debt to a community and its residents, the UMWA is not sure how to pay its own debt.

Social movements, or strikes, seldom produce clear-cut institutional change, however. Rather, the clearest and perhaps most significant, but least tangible, outcome of social movements, including strikes, is the personal transformation they engender: bright, shining moments when democratic imaginations are stirred and people dare to take organized action for the benefit of the group. Actions at Massey stirred imaginations at Pittston. Actions at Pittston will undoubtedly stir the imaginations of other people in future free spaces. These people will recount the strikes, and those memories will preserve a spirit of democratic resistance and express, once again, a conscience for capital.

Acknowledgments

I am grateful to the Appalachian Studies Fellowship Program of Berea College and the Faculty Scholars Program of the University of Kentucky for the support they provided me for the research for this chapter.

Notes

1. Sara M. Evans and Harry C. Boyte, *Free Spaces: The Sources of Democratic Change in America* (New York: Harper & Row, 1986), 17.
2. Ibid., 188.
3. The differences between the analysis of free spaces in this chapter and that of Evans and Boyte are matters of degree. To be sure, Evans and Boyte integrate history into their discussion of free spaces, and their heavy emphasis on the communal basis of free spaces implies the history of local places and conditions. Yet in defining free spaces, Evans and Boyte do not include a sense of connection with past or other current efforts to achieve democratic change. The historical aspect of free spaces permits us to understand efforts at democratic reform as related and not isolated. Indeed, much of the personal transformation that occurs in free spaces happens precisely because people there expand their identification with a historical process of change, and with past and future events in that process. Similarly, this analysis differs, in degree, from Evans and Boyte's suggestion that centralized organizations lose the vitality of democratic movements when they lose their communal basis. Much of the history of the UMWA bears this out, but the strike at Pittston illustrates the vitality that a labor union can inject into a strike and thus transform it into part of a democratic movement.
4. Nicolaus Mills, "War in Tug River Valley: A Long and Bitter Miners' Strike," *Dissent* 33 (1986) : 52.
5. Quoted in Charlie D. Thompson, "The Pittston Strike," *Southern Changes* 11 (December 1989) : 1–6. One leader of the 1979–80 UMWA strike at Stearns, Kentucky, also connected his memory of the past with his efforts in that strike: "My greatest fear after all is for the young people. I can remember way back when. My father was a miner and he was mashed up in the mines and died a couple of months after that accident. At that time it was this way—you did the job management told you or you had no job. And I can see what will happen without the unions. What will happen is that the bosses will continue to go as far as they can until they go too far and where there won't be a safe place for anyone to work with decent pay. . . . You don't have to believe how bad it will get if you've seen it. I can remember working all day, 14 hours, coming home in wet clothes and sleeping behind the stove and getting up the next day and going back. That's the way it was, if you were going to keep your job." In Richard A. Couto, *Redemptive Resistance: Church-Based Intervention in the Pursuit of Justice* (Whitesburg, Ky.: Catholic Committee of Appalachia, 1981), 25.

6. Lewis quoted in John Peter David, "Earnings, Health, Safety, and Bituminous Coal Miners Since the Encouragement of Mechanization by the United Mine Workers of America" (Ph.D. diss., West Virginia University, 1972), 52. See also David S. Walls, "Central Appalachia in Advanced Capitalism: Its Coal Industry and Coal Operators' Associations" (Ph.D. diss., University of Kentucky, 1978), 123–69, for a discussion of the industry during this time. For Lewis' views in the 1920s, see John L. Lewis, *The Miners' Fight for American Standards* (Indianapolis: Bell, 1925).

7. These conflicts coincided with a low point in union membership and in the influence of the UMWA and Lewis: Melvyn Dubofsky and Warren Van Tine, *John L. Lewis: A Biography* (New York: Quadrangle/New York Times, 1977), 170–72. For descriptions of Lewis and the union during this period, see David Alan Corbin, *Life, Work, and Rebellion in the Coal Fields: The Southern West Virginia Miners, 1880–1922* (Urbana: University of Illinois Press, 1981); Ronald D Eller, *Miners, Millhands, and Mountaineers: Industrialization of the Appalachian South, 1880–1930* (Knoxville: University of Tennessee Press, 1982), 199–224; John Gaventa, *Power and Powerlessness: Quiescence and Rebellion in an Appalachian Valley* (Urbana: University of Illinois Press, 1980), 84–116.

8. Curtis Seltzer, *Fire in the Hole: Miners and Managers in the American Coal Industry* (Lexington: University Press of Kentucky, 1985), 52–53.

9. Dubofsky and Van Tine, *John L. Lewis*, 459–60.

10. For background to the 1950 agreement, see Richard A. Couto, "Changing Technologies and Consequences for Labor in Coal Mining," in Daniel B. Cornfield, ed., *Workers, Managers, and Technological Change: Emerging Patterns of Labor Relations* (New York: Plenum Press, 1987), 175–202; David, "Earnings, Health, Safety, and Bituminous Coal Miners"; and Seltzer, *Fire in the Hole*, 61–84.

11. For contemporary assessments of the industrial finance theory, see Morton S. Baratz, *The Union and the Coal Industry* (New Haven: Yale University Press, 1955), 72; and C. L. Christenson, *Economic Redevelopment in Bituminous Coal* (Cambridge: Harvard University Press, 1962), 275–76.

12. Lewis disparaged TVA for these practices and for buying coal on the spot market from producers who had no alternative in a depressed market but to sell coal at prices below costs. TVA defended its practices as stimulating competition and offered them as evidence, in a politically conservative decade, that this New Deal agency had adopted the gospel of the market with the zeal of a new convert. Richard A. Couto, "TVA, Appalachian Underdevelopment, and the Post-Industrial Era," *Sociological Spectrum* 8 (1988) : 323–47.

13. Lewis quoted in Richard Harshberger, "TVA Coal Buying Policies" (Ph.D. diss., Indiana University, 1964), p. 32. For an overview of TVA's coal-buying policies at this time, see Couto, "TVA, Appalachian Underdevelopment, and the Post-Industrial Era."

14. Joseph F. Finley, *The Corrupt Kingdom: The Rise and Fall of the United Mine*

Workers (New York: Simon and Schuster, 1972), 154. For this period in the UMWA's history, see 136–58. Lewis was not on a new path in the 1950s: he had employed terror and deception against union insurgents in the 1920s. See Dubofsky and Van Tine, *John L. Lewis*, 127–28, 163–65.

15. Seltzer, *Fire in the Hole*, 90–93; and Dubofsky and Van Tine, *John L. Lewis*, 519–20. See also Paul F. Clark, *The Miners' Fight for Democracy: Arnold Miller and the Reform of the United Mine Workers* (Ithaca, N.Y.: New York School of Industrial and Labor Relations, Cornell University, 1981); George William Hopkins, *The Miners for Democracy: Insurgency in the United Mine Workers of America, 1970–1972* (Ann Arbor, Mich.: University Microfilms International, 1977); Richard J. Jensen, *Rebellion in the United Mine Workers: The Miners for Democracy, 1970–1972* (Ann Arbor, Mich.: University Microfilms International, 1977); Paul J. Nyden, "Miners for Democracy: Struggle in the Coal Fields" (Ph.D. diss., Columbia University, 1974); Barbara Smith, *Digging Our Own Graves: Coal Miners and the Struggle Over Black Lung Disease* (Philadelphia: Temple University Press, 1987), 75–86.

16. "Some Southern Utilities Find It Cheaper to Import Coal," *Coal Age* 89 (May 1984) : 19; "Lawmakers Grow Wary of Colombian Coal," *Coal Age* 90 (June 1985) : 11–13; "Imports: The Growing Threat to U.S. Coal," *Coal Age* 90 (May 1985) : 11–13; "U.S. Utilities Buy More Inexpensive Foreign Coal," *Coal Age* 93 (January 1988) : 13.

17. Barbara Berney, "The Rise and Fall of the UMW Fund," *Southern Exposure* 6 (Summer 1978) : 95–102.

18. For a discussion of the UMWA's relations with the Progressive Miners Union, which is active in the West, see Finley, *The Corrupt Kingdom*, 72–73, 86, 112.

19. The increase of large western coal producers also led to greater concentration of coal production among the giants of the industry. In 1950, the fifty largest coal companies produced 45.0 percent of the nation's bituminous coal. By 1977, their share increased to 65.0 percent, and in 1988 it reached 74.6 percent. Indeed, by 1988 the fifteen largest coal companies were producing more of the nation's coal—46.7 percent—than the largest fifty companies had in 1950. See "Big Oil Sells Off Some of Its Coal Interests," *Coal Age* 90 (March 1985) : 11–12; "Basic Changes Underlie Recent Acquisitions," *Coal Age* 91 (November 1986) : 11–13. Shell and Fluor ended their joint venture at A. T. Massey in 1987. Fluor gained control of the company and, despite early speculation that it might sell Massey, retained it. In early 1992, Massey acquired Island Creek holdings, thus increasing Fluor's stake in coal. Leslie Berkman, "Shearson Hired to Study Fluor's Unit's Options," *Los Angeles Times*, March 10, 1990; "Fluor Unit Buys Two Mines from Occidental," *Los Angeles Times*, February 19, 1992.

20. Occidental Petroleum, for example, invested in China's largest open-pit mine, which had a capacity of 15 million metric tons. This investment sent it looking for cash and led it to consider the sale of its subsidiary, Island Creek, a founder of the BCOA: "Pact Reached on U.S.–Chinese Mine Project," *New*

York Times, May 19, 1985; "Big Oil Sells Off Some of Its Coal Interests," *Coal Age*, 13. Peabody's prospective buyer in 1990, the British corporation Hanson PLC, also had a reputation for buying and selling companies for cash flow purposes or profit. Like Fluor, however, Hanson expanded Peabody in the early 1990s. "Peabody's Sale to Hanson Causes Concern in U.S. Coal Industry," *Coal Age* 95 (April 1990) : 9; "Hanson's Plans for Peabody Appear Serious After Recent Acquisition of Arch Reserves," *Coal* 96 (February 1991) : 23.

21. "Six-Month-Old Coal Miners' Strike Grows Bitter," *New York Times*, April 2, 1985.

22. "Talks Will Focus on Job Security, Work Rules," *Coal Age* 92 (November 1987) : 11–12, "The Union Adopts an Aggressive Stance," *Coal Age* 91 (October 1986): 11; "UMW Promises to Take a Tough Stance in Negotiations," *Coal Age* 91 (December 1986): 15.

23. "NLRB Says Massey Must Negotiate As a Single Employer," *Coal Age* 90 (June 1986) : 19.

24. Bill Keller, "Mine Workers and Coal Operators Reach Agreement on Pact," *New York Times*, September 22, 1984; "Massey Strike Ends," *Coal Age* 91 (January 1986) : 11. For information on the strike, see U.S. House Subcommittee on Labor-Management Relations, "Report on the Massey Strike Prepared by the Majority Staff," Washington, D.C., January 24, 1986 (hereinafter cited as House Subcommittee Staff Report on Massey); "UMW, Massey Hold the Line as Strikes Enter Sixth Month," *Coal Age* 90 (March 1985) : 21; "UMW Selective Strike Against A. T. Massey Mines Spreads," *Coal Age* 90 (April 1985) : 23; Kenneth B. Noble, "Miners Call End to Coal Walkout," *New York Times*, December 21, 1985; and "The Massey Strike: A Chronology," *United Mine Workers Journal* 96 (October 1985) : 14–17.

25. Richard Phalon, "Miscalculated Risk?" *Forbes* 142 (June 12, 1989) : 41.

26. The Pittston Coal Group left the BCOA in 1986. In 1987 company officials informed the Funds' trustees of their intent to reduce substantially their contribution to the 1950 Welfare Fund: "Lawsuits Filed in 1950 Pension Fund Controversy," *Coal Age* 92 (June 1987) : 18. Some 118,000 retired miners and their dependents were covered by the 1950 funds in 1987. The 1950 Pension Trust fund, with set costs, was fully funded in May 1987. The 1950 Benefit Trust fund, with escalating costs for health care, had a deficit of about $50 million in the same year. In 1988, when the 1984 contract ended, Pittston walked away from its share of the cost of these funds. The company ended its payments to the 1950 Benefit Trust Fund and canceled the health benefits of 1,500 pensioners, widows, and disabled miners for whom it was responsible under the 1974 Benefit Trust Plan. This action added an estimated $10 million deficit to the already financially strapped 1950 fund. By these actions, Pittston reneged on obligations to its former employees. It had renewed this obligation in 1984 by signing a BCOA agreement that required each company to protect the beneficiaries without leaving some companies with more of the past cost of the industry to bear than others.

For conflict within the UMWA over the fund, including a proposal for higher pensions as incentives for miners to retire earlier, see "Internal Union Dispute Centers on Pension Fund Payments," *Coal Age* 91 (June 1986) : 19.

27. United Mine Workers of America, "Betraying the Trust: The Pittston Company's Drive to Break Appalachia's Coalfield Communities" (Washington, D.C.: United Mine Workers of America, 1989), 8.

28. "After Months of Contract Talks, UMWA Strikes Pittston," *Coal* 26 (June 1989) : 9–10; Joel Chernoff, "Miners Fighting for Health Plans: Management Backs Asset Transfer," *Pensions & Investment Age*, October 30, 1989, 1; Trudy Ring, "Withdrawal Sought: Pittston Proposes Single-Employer Plan," *Pensions & Investment Age*, January 9, 1989, 3.

29. Chernoff, "Miners Fighting for Health Plans," 1; Ring, "Withdrawal Sought: Pittston Proposes Single-Employer Plan," 3.

Pittston's effort to leave the debt of the coal industry to the miners and dependents who had developed the industry and to other companies who stood by earlier agreements bothered the editors of *Business Week* as well as UMWA miners. They wrote that Pittston had a "moral obligation" to continue benefits that were "promises . . . made in exchange for concessions by the very people whose benefits are threatened." The adverse consequences of Pittston's actions for the coal industry seemed clear: "If Pittston is allowed to avoid the benefit payments, other operators will make a mad dash to abandon the fund when the BCOA contract expires in 1992. . . . Abandoning the funds could also mean death for the BCOA and industrywide bargaining which has helped stabilize the coal industry since 1950." "Pittston Should Stand by Its Promises," *Business Week*, October 9, 1989, 182.

30. Richard Phalon, "Miscalculated Risk?" 41; U.S. Senate Subcommittee on Labor-Management Relations, "Report of the Majority Staff on the Strike at the Pittston Coal Company," Washington, D.C., August 3, 1989, 7 (hereinafter cited as "Senate Subcommittee Staff Report on Pittston"). Odom is quoted in John Bookser Feister, "Crisis in the Coalfields: The Church Calls for Justice," *St. Anthony Messenger*, December 1989, 25.

31. William Byrne, Jr., Pittston director of financial public relations, quoted in Joyce Hollyday, "Amazing Grace," *Sojourners* 18 (July 1989) : 20.

32. Denise Giardina, "Strike Zone: The 'Appalachia Intifada' Rages On," *Village Voice*, August 29, 1989, 32.

33. Emilie Stoltzfus, "Solidarity Triumphs: Pittston Miners Return to Work with a New Contract," *United Mine Workers Journal* 101 (March 1990) : 6.

34. "Summary of Changes in the Pittston Contract," *United Mine Workers Journal* 101 (March 1990) : 8–9.

Assessments of the strike's outcome differ, of course. The *Wall Street Journal* found important gains by the company: Alecia Swasy and Albert R. Karr, "Pittston, UMW Tentatively Set Labor Accord," *Wall Street Journal*, January 2, 1990; Alecia Swasy, "Pittston Accord, If Ratified, May Bring Work-Rule Changes, Productivity Gains," *Wall Street Journal*, January 5, 1990. Most others scored the strike as an important victory for the UMWA and organized labor: Laurent Belsie, "Labor Gains in Labor Strife: Health, Pensions Are Key Issues in Contract Negotiations," *Christian Science Monitor*, February 20, 1990; and Susan Dentzer, "A Healthy Settlement for Mine Workers: Pittston Strikers Won Big, but the Fight Over Retiree Benefits Has Just Begun," *U.S. News and World Report*, January 15, 1990, 45–46.

35. "The Massey Connection: Company Documents Reveal a Corporate Shell Game Designed to Avoid Responsibility," *United Mine Workers Journal* 96 (April–May 1985) : 10–11; "Slave Labor: America's Newest Import?" *United Mine Workers Journal* 96 (July 1985) : 14–15; Maude P. Brunstetter, "Major Resource Capabilities of the United Mine Workers in Its Selective Strike Against the A. T. Massey Coal Company, 1984–5," paper presented at the annual meeting of the American Political Science Association, Atlanta, Ga., August 1989, 17.

36. William Serrin, "Miners' Strike in 9th Month Is a Test of Union Strategy," *New York Times*, June 9, 1985, 26.

37. Bill Keller, "The Strike: Union Adjusting Tactics," *New York Times*, September 24, 1984, 9; "Trumka on Strike Program: The Membership Made It Work," *United Mine Workers Journal* 96 (June 1985) : 14–15; "UMWA Gives Trumka Selective Strike Powers," *Coal Age* 89 (January 1984) : 11–13.

38. UMWA, "Betraying the Trust." For discussions of the tactics of the corporate campaign, see David Moberg's coverage of the Pittston strike in *In These Times*, May 10, 1989, 6; November 15, 1989, 8–9; and January 17, 1990, 7; Thompson, "The Pittston Strike," 6; Nicolaus Mills, "Solidarity in Virginia: The Mine Workers Remake History," *Dissent* 37 (1990) : 241–42.

39. Robert Kuttner applied Titmuss' 1955 analysis to current matters in the *Boston Globe*, June 19, 1990, 13. See Richard Titmuss, "The Social Division of Welfare," in *Essays on the Welfare State* (Boston: Beacon Press, 1969), 34–55. UMWA Vice President John Banovic also placed health care high on the list of the union's concerns and noted that it is both a national problem and a problem for the union: "It Takes More Than a Picket Line to Beat a Multinational Corporation," *United Mine Workers Journal* 101 (April–May 1990) : 8–9.

40. The UMWA alleged that Pittston had abandoned the arbitration system, unlawfully contracted work out to nonunion firms, threatened people who pursued grievances, refused to provide information necessary for collective bargaining, and discriminated against union supporters. It was only after the NLRB found merit in these allegations and fourteen months of working without a contract that the UMWA began its strike at Pittston.

41. A Senate subcommittee staff report on the Pittston strike observed what miners had noticed as well: "While they await the disposition of the charges which initiated the strike, the miners are subject to the swift and extensive sanctions imposed by the courts largely for acts of non-violent civil disobedience": "Senate Subcommittee Staff Report on Pittston," 13.

42. "House Subcommittee Staff Report on Massey," 16.

43. For accounts that stress these aspects of the Massey strike, see Mills, "War

in Tug River Valley"; and "Thunder in the Coalfields: The UMW's Strike Against Pittston," *Roanoke Times & World-News*, April 29, 1990.

44. "House Subcommittee Staff Report on Massey," 16.

45. "Thunder in the Coalfields," 3. This eighteen-page special report offers the most in-depth and comprehensive coverage of the Pittston strike.

46. For an account stressing the community mobilization within the strike, see Giardina, "Strike Zone," 31–36. For accounts stressing the churches' role in the strike, see Hollyday, "Amazing Grace," 12–22; and Tena Willemsma, "Strike Reflections from SW Virginia," *CORAspondent*, Spring 1990, 1, 4–5.

47. "Thunder in the Coalfields," 4.

48. Ibid., 14–15. There were election victories for the Massey strikers as well, but these occurred after the strike, unlike Stump's victory.

49. E. Morgan Massey quoted in Mills, "War in Tug River Valley," 50.

50. Eventually Pittston strike supporters from outside the area would conduct rolling roadblocks. Driving slowly along narrow county roads, the visitors pitted their leisurely use of the roads as tourists against the company's right to swift movement of its trucks, which sometimes violated the law without punishment.

51. Gay Martin quoted in Hollyday, "Amazing Grace," p. 21. The exchange on religion can be found in Denise Giardina, "The Pittston Strike: Solidarity in Appalachia," *Nation* 249 (July 3, 1989): 14.

52. Paul Douglas, "Letter to the Editor—Best Deal at Pittston: Profitable Togetherness," *Wall Street Journal*, December 8, 1989.

53. UMWA, "Betraying the Trust," 9.

54. The U.S. Senate subcommittee staff that investigated the Pittston strike reported that the presence of approximately one-third of Virginia's state police force and a large number of federal marshals created "a sense that the coal fields are occupied by a massive security force from outside the southwestern Virginia region." The report also found that the federal judge who presided over cases related to the strike took unprecedented action to enforce a stipulation of the NLRB against the UMWA before the NLRB asked for it: "Senate Subcommittee Staff Report on Pittston," 17. Miners striking in the Soviet Union at the same time elicited less show of force than the Pittston strike but more attention from the American press: Alexander Cockburn, "Their Miners and Ours," *Nation* 251 (August 28, 1990) : 195.

55. "Work, Family, Union: Pittston Attacks a Way of Life," *United Mine Workers Journal* 100 (July–August 1989) : 7.

56. Gene Carroll, "Camp Solidarity: The Heart of the Pittston Strike," *United Mine Workers Journal* 100 (November 1989) : 17. For comparable memories of miners at Massey, see Mills, "War in Tug River Valley," 51–52.

57. Taylor Branch, *Parting the Waters: America in the King Years 1954–63* (New York: Simon and Schuster, 1988).

58. "Thunder in the Coalfields," 6. The UMWA could relate the Pittston strike to the civil rights movement because African Americans and Appalachian miners share fundamental grievances. To cite just one example, capital

underestimated the social costs of the mechanization of both row crop agriculture in the South and coal production in Appalachia. As a result, African Americans in the rural South and coal miners in Appalachia bore the costs of this economic transformation individually and within families, primarily in the form of migration or high rates of unemployment and poverty if they remained at home. African Americans are prominent within the coal mining tradition, some of which countered the prevalent racism of America, and some of which replicated it. African American miners provided leadership in the insurgent movements of the 1930s but lost employment disproportionately from mechanization in the 1940s and 1950s. Ronald L. Lewis, *Black Coal Miners in America: Race, Class, and Community Conflict, 1780–1980* (Lexington: University Press of Kentucky, 1987), esp. 174–90. An early study that established a parallel between the problems of the rural South and those of the Appalachian coalfields is Tony Dunbar, *Our Land Too* (New York: Pantheon, 1971). See also William H. Turner and Edward J. Cabbell, eds., *Blacks in Appalachia* (Lexington: University Press of Kentucky, 1985).

The Pittston and Massey strikes also resemble the civil rights movement in their local nature. We are slowly coming to the realization that the civil rights movement was an aggregation of local efforts of resistance, protest, and reform by ordinary people inspired by the vision of democratic freedoms and economic opportunity. It was not a movement orchestrated by the leadership of a group or organization but a thousand movements in response to myriad local injustices that a few people came to symbolize. Nor did the civil rights movement occur at one time. It stretched back in history, and efforts built one upon another. The ultimate significance of the Massey and Pittston strikes will be their part in the equally long history of protest against the inadequate conditions of labor.

59. This increased cooperation improved the UMWA's leverage to work on issues common to all labor union members and other working men and women. One such issue is the reform of work-related health and benefit plans. Health and benefits were, of course, central to the Pittston strike, but such problems extend beyond a single company or even industry. The ability of producers to pass on increased production costs to consumers diminishes with increased competition. Consequently, employers look to cut the costs, like health insurance, that they cannot pass along. In addition, health care costs are increasing rapidly and are difficult for employers to contain. In 1989, four out of every five workers who went on strike did so in a dispute that included health care benefits. Joan O'C. Hamilton, "Health Care Costs Take a Turn for the Worse," *Business Week*, October 31, 1988, 120; Laura Zinn, "Ouch! The Squeeze on Your Health Benefits," *Business Week*, November 20, 1989, 110–22; Service Employees International Union, *Labor and Management: On a Collision Course Over Health Care* (Washington, D.C.: SEIU, 1989); Erich Kirshner, "Health Benefits a Top Priority for Striking Workers," *Healthweek* 4 (February 26, 1990) : 1.

Similarly, the efforts of companies to avoid the costs of pension plans extend beyond Pittston. The coal industry had an industrywide agreement to which both the union and the other companies wanted to hold Pittston. In other industries there is no such agreement, and thus there is less pressure on one company to hold another to a common liability. This suggests to some that, however severe the Pittston strike was, it may be a modest prelude to the storm that will hit workers of other declining smokestack industries who have fewer protections than the UMWA-BCOA accord provided. See Susan Dentzer, "Benefits Shock," *U.S. News & World Report*, March 28, 1988, 58–60. One element of the Pittston negotiated settlement was the creation of a blue-ribbon committee to report on health and retirement benefits in the coal industry. In creating the committee, Secretary of Labor Dole explained that these problems extended beyond the Pittston dispute.

60. Thompson, "The Pittston Strike," 6. See also Mills, "Solidarity in Virginia," 242.
61. Usery quoted in "Thunder in the Coalfields," 15.
62. Evans and Boyte, *Free Spaces*, 201.
63. Ibid.
64. For a discussion of coal mining communities and the solidarity they engender, see Jonathan and Ruth Winterton, *Coal, Crisis, and Conflict: The 1984–85 Miners' Strike in Yorkshire* (Manchester: Manchester University Press, 1989), especially 102–8.
65. Mills, "War in Tug River Valley," 51.

10

Singing Across Dark Spaces
The Union/Community Takeover
of Pittston's Moss 3 Plant

Jim Sessions
Fran Ansley

Like many people in the Appalachian region and throughout the country, we found our lives touched by the 1989 United Mine Workers strike in the southern Appalachian coalfields. During that last year of a decade that brought such hardships to so many poor and working people and such debilitating reverses for even the mildest efforts at a progressive political agenda, the mineworkers' strike challenged and inspired us to look again at what people might achieve as we move into the next century. We hope to share something of that challenge and inspiration in this personal memoir.

Each of us had reason to be interested. As director of the Commission on Religion in Appalachia, Jim was involved in organizing support for the miners' strike from the time it started in April. He worked to explain the aims of the strikers to media and church people who often lacked basic information about the contemporary labor movement or life in the coalfields. After almost twenty years as an activist in Appalachia and the Southeast, he knew the bloody history of the rank and file's struggle in the 1970s to win back control of the UMWA from the corrupt leadership exemplified by Tony Boyle, and he fully appreciated the UMWA's crucial role in bending the economy of central Appalachia to better meet the needs of miners and other working people in the region.

Fran also had a history of studying and being involved in issues of justice in the coalfields. As the strike wore on, she had kept her students at the University of Tennessee Law School posted on developments. Both of us and the children (our then fifteen-year-old son, Elisha, and twelve-year-old daughter, Lee) participated in strike support activities organized in Knoxville. Then, in September, all of us were swept up in the strike in a new and more immediate way when union leaders decided to attempt an occupation of Pittston's mammoth Moss 3 coal preparation plant near St. Paul, Virginia, and Jim accepted an invitation to join the action as a sympathetic but "unaffiliated" witness to the takeover.

Miners and supporters mass outside the Moss 3 preparation plant during the four-day occupation. (*Earl Dotter*)

When Jim was approached afterward about writing down his experiences, we talked it over. It seemed to us that even his single "insider's" view of the occupation of Moss 3 would be incomplete without some mention of those "outside," the people from the community and the union who took over the roads, bridges, and gates to the coal plant during the occupation, and who prepared to defend those who were inside. But if you were in one place, you could hardly imagine what it was like in the other. So we have decided it takes both of us to tell this story as it should be told. Jim will relate his experiences as a member of the takeover team, and Fran will describe something of the remarkable scene that developed among those who massed outside the plant during the four-day occupation. But first we will explain the background of the strike and what was at stake for the miners, their families, and the communities that supported them.

Background

Two years before the dramatic coal strike of 1989 began, the Pittston Coal Company unilaterally pulled out of the Bituminous Coal Operators Association. The BCOA had been negotiating industrywide contracts with the UMWA since 1950, but Pittston, the largest exporter of coal in the United States, claimed that it needed special union concessions in order to compete in foreign markets (principally Japan), and that it would therefore no longer accept the bargaining framework or the agreements worked out in the BCOA forum. Like so many employers in today's economy, Pittston invoked global competition as a reason why coal miners should agree to a lower standard of living and less control over their own workplaces. In recent years the company had also steadily shifted increasing amounts of its coal reserves from its union operations to new, nonunion subsidiaries.

As the time drew near for the existing contract between Pittston and the UMWA to expire, the company—which then owned Brinks, Inc., Burlington Air Express, and other subsidiaries in addition to twenty-five coal mines—began pressing for the right to schedule irregular shifts, to mine coal on Sundays, to eliminate a number of other hard-fought work rules, and to subcontract mining work to nonunion companies. All these issues were important to the miners, but it was the issue of health and retirement benefits more than any other that truly galvanized the coalfields.

When Pittston pulled out of the BCOA in 1987, it stopped paying into an industrywide fund that supports miners who retired before 1974 and their widows. When the existing contract expired on February 1, 1988, Pittston canceled the health and insurance benefits of an additional 1,600 miners who had retired *after* 1974. Most of the retired miners were fathers or grandfathers of active miners, so that retirees and working miners were well aware of each others' problems. The company's actions could not have said more plainly that Pittston had no compunction about reneging on prior commitments, and that it was unhampered by loyalty to the communities where its past and present workers lived.

Still the union hoped to avoid a strike. Despite a long tradition of refusing to work without a contract, the Pittston miners stayed on the job for fourteen months after their contract ran out. Only four years earlier, a UMWA strike against the A. T. Massey Coal Group in West Virginia had ended in a stalemate. A series of violent clashes between desperate miners and the company had resulted in heavy legal penalties and political isolation for the union.

This time UMWA leaders intended things to be different. They were wary of being baited into a strike, and were determined to be cautious and patient.

Caution did not mean inaction, however. The union and a range of supporting community-based organizations mobilized during the fourteen-month period, using the time to organize support for the miners' demands. The union hired Cosby Totten and Katherine Tompka, two women with past experience as underground miners, to work with miners' wives and other women in the community to raise awareness of contract issues. (These two were part of a select sisterhood of strong women who began in the 1970s to break down gender barriers in underground mining. Like similar efforts by blacks in certain U.S. industries, their progress has been crippled by the recessions and economic restructuring that followed the advent of equal opportunity laws.)

In June 1988 this women's network organized a memorial service for the seven miners killed in the 1983 explosion at the Pittston-owned McClure mine. They held fundraisers, staged convoys, and established a regular presence at local company headquarters in Lebanon, Virginia. Their role during this preparatory phase was crucial.

At last Pittston made a "take it or leave it" demand and refused to bargain further. The miners did not take it. On April 5, 1989, twelve hundred union miners in Virginia and five hundred more in West Virginia and Kentucky walked out. The strike was on.

As events unfolded, and the strikers mounted their extraordinary campaign, the strike's significance spread far beyond the coalfields. It became a rallying point for the labor movement in this country and abroad. In the weeks before the plant occupation we describe below, over twenty thousand union, religious, and community supporters from across the country marched at Pittston. The strike, and the takeover in particular, brought into sharp focus the desperate situation in which many American workers find themselves, but also showed the potential for broad and deep resistance to the increasingly brutal strategies of today's global corporations. The strike forcefully challenged prevailing ideas about whose "rights" should count for what in labor-management conflict. It demonstrated more eloquently than words ever could that American labor law has become an instrument that blunts and contains worker rights more than it protects or extends them, and that unions will sometimes have to defy the law if they want to survive with the strength to defend the interests of their members in any meaningful way.

The Takeover of Moss 3

The occupation of the Moss 3 coal preparation plant happened only after the courts and National Labor Relations Board had effectively closed off an entire range of peaceful, nonviolent tactics the union was attempting to pursue. With injunctions blanketing the coalfields, mass actions had ceased, and coal production was picking up again. Local citizens risked arrest merely by traveling their own roads. Astronomical fines and increasingly stiff sentences against the union and individuals were handed down by state and federal judges, who confusingly claimed simultaneous jurisdiction over the strikers' conduct. State troopers were everywhere. Frustration and indignation were setting in as the coalfields faced the winter under what amounted to martial law.

It was becoming clear that the miners could not win unless they could somehow retake the initiative, slow coal production, and challenge the legitimacy of the legal rules that were being used to cripple the strike. Against this background the union decided to take the dramatic move of physically seizing Moss 3. Only too aware that Pittston would attempt to cast the miners as violence-prone thugs, local leaders asked Jim if he would join them as a witness to the nature of the action. Jim's personal account begins the night before the takeover.

September 16

JIM: Sleep does not come easily. My anticipation and apprehension are both at a high pitch. Hours from the coalfields, safe and sound in my own bed in Knoxville, my images of what may be coming seem almost unreal. I know that tomorrow I will be joining a group of miners in the unprecedented step of attempting to take Pittston property and to stay for as long as we can manage a productive way to dig in. But I do not know where the action is to occur, whether we will be in a building or a coal mine, how many others will be with us, or how we will gain entry.

Security is tight, to say the least. For months southwest Virginia has looked as though it were under military occupation. The heavy-handed police presence is designed to ensure that coal production continues in spite of the creative disorder the mineworkers have managed to bring about through massive civil disobedience and community mobilization. The union's use of this strategy is one of the main things that makes the Pittston strike unique.

An early indication for me of the depth and seriousness of the UMWA's new resolve to mount a nonviolent and community-based strike came on June 7 when I was asked to go to Roanoke to visit three union leaders who had been jailed for contempt. They had refused to promise a federal judge that they would tell UMWA members to stop engaging in civil disobedience, and they were consequently sitting in jail. After being allowed to visit these local leaders, I realized that something extraordinary was going on.

The three men had begun a hunger strike to protest their treatment by the judge. During our time together I urged them to be mindful of their health and relayed a message from the union that community support was strong. As we talked, the three reflected on the union's strategy for this strike. They reported that they and other union staffers had committed the time to read *Parting the Waters*, Taylor Branch's book on the civil rights movement in the South, and that they were devoting special study to the thought and the political practice of Martin Luther King, Jr. They were drawing lessons from the mass mobilizations mounted during that era by black students and community members.

Though union leaders had been uncertain how the membership would receive the idea of civil disobedience, the members and their families had responded en masse. On April 18 women broke the ice. Some had been miners themselves. Others were wives, widows, daughters, other kin, and friends of miners. They staged a sit-in at Pittston's local headquarters in Lebanon, Virginia. A week later, two hundred union members sat down in the road at the Lambert Fork mine to block passage of coal trucks. They were arrested by state police. Another three hundred sat in at the McClure mine, and a thousand more outside the Moss 3 preparation plant. Rough handling of arrested demonstrators by state police shocked and angered many participants and community people, but did not dampen people's resolve.

Day after day, the miners took to the roads and streets to make their voices heard. As family members and friends of the miners began to join them in civil disobedience, the police became visibly nonplused. Soon over three thousand people had gone to jail. By the time the three staffers were jailed for contempt, the strategy of massive civil disobedience had won broad community support and appeared to be spreading.

At this point, in fact, on the eve of the takeover, the commitment has become strong enough that union orators sense they can speak forcefully at gatherings without fear of provoking undisciplined responses. The strike has begun to carry an air of simultaneous nonviolence and militance that is extraordinary.

The strikers' favorite speaker, UMW vice-president Cecil Roberts, a fourth-generation West Virginia coal miner, was originally sent by the union's president, Richard Trumka, to head the strike when the local leaders were thrown in the Roanoke jail, and has been here directing the strike ever since. He has developed a ritual opening for his frequent speeches at mass meetings: "Welcome to class warfare in southwest Virginia!" Cecil pronounces this greeting, and the crowds roar. He often continues in something like this vein: "All you need to know about this war is this: You work; they don't. You ought to be on our side, because working-class people have been taking it on the chin for the past ten to fifteen years. It's time to stop being quiet. Every major union in this country has taken a stand and recognized this battle for what it is. It's class warfare."

Cecil's other oratorical claim to fame is his unabashed use of the word "love" and his admiration for Dr. Martin Luther King. He has begun quoting entire passages of King's speeches from memory, and his Appalachian audiences have listened in rapt attention.

It is Pittston's own actions that have set the stage for the community to embrace both sides of this militance/nonviolence coin. The company took on new management, which entered the scene with guns blazing. The newcomers first engineered Pittston's withdrawal from the BCOA. Then they refused to enter into serious negotiations with the union over a new contract, leading many to conclude that they were in fact trying to provoke a strike and break the union. When the miners did go out, Pittston responded by throwing down the gauntlet eighties style: it announced that the mines would stay open, operated by replacement workers. With the strike focused on the survival of the union itself and continuation of health-care benefits for pensioners, entire communities—three and four generations deep—have now mobilized to support the striking miners.

If coalfield communities are committing themselves to broad-based nonviolent disruption, the state and federal authorities now appear equally committed to stopping them. As the strike has worn on, the miners and their families have been hauled repeatedly into court. Overlapping layers of injunctions from both state and federal courts are now imposed on the miners and their communities. If a picket line already has nine people on it, a person wandering too close on some related or unrelated errand may get arrested on the grounds that he constitutes the forbidden tenth picketer. Out-of-state strike supporters have been astounded to find themselves pulled over to the side of the road and searched for no apparent reason. Law enforcement personnel escort coal trucks loaded with coal mined by strikebreakers from the mines to their destinations. As a part of the evolving nonviolent strategy, "rolling roadblocks" have developed almost spontaneously, and now numerous people have been arrested for driving too slowly on the curvy mountain roads, because they are thereby impeding the movement of nonunion coal.

As time passes, and thousands of arrests and millions of dollars in fines have piled up, people's inventiveness has been increasingly taxed to find anything effective they can do that won't land them in jail. Despite the union's unprecedented and courageous willingness to keep on in the face of staggering legal penalties, morale has begun to wane. Many families have reached the end of savings and are beginning to lose houses and cars when payments cannot be met. Fall is approaching, and people know from experience how hard it is to be on strike during the winter. Some have begun to question the wisdom of nonviolent civil disobedience.

The union is receiving support from community groups, labor unions, and church organizations around the country. It has developed a creative "corporate campaign" that has tried to take the hardships and issues of the strike to the company's affluent home in Greenwich, Connecticut. Bake sales, soup kitchens, singing groups, quilting raffles—everything anybody can think of is being done.

But the company is still mining coal, and court injunctions continue to narrow the miners' alternatives. It is out of this sense of crisis that the action for tomorrow is being planned. But the crisis atmosphere itself makes me wonder as I lie here whether we will get very far with our plans.

In addition to the state and federal law enforcement presence, Pittston has hired its own private troops. Where local residents often take a moderately tolerant attitude toward the state troopers and even the federal marshals, their hatred for Pittston's private guards, the Vance Asset Protection Team, is clear and unqualified. The Vance guards are seen by union families as modern-day successors to the gun thugs hired to terrorize mountain communities when the union was first trying to organize. These "professionals," with their bright blue jumpsuits and their high-tech hardware, are another important element in the increasingly militarized atmosphere in the coalfields.

Given this highly charged, security-saturated context, it is hard to envision how we might actually be able to "take over" Pittston's property. I have told Fran in strictest confidence the general outlines of what I know, purposefully downplaying the significance of what we may achieve. "Realistically" I expect to get promptly arrested, and then to be out on bond and home again by evening tomorrow or the next day. Still, I have grown to respect the savvy and the seriousness of the strike leadership, and I secretly harbor romantic notions that we might actually be able to take a position, hold it long enough to affect coal production, and gain a wider audience for the miners' demands. Finally I drift off to sleep.

September 17

JIM: I get up early and set out for Virginia. It is the 170th day of the strike, a sunny, summerlike Sunday. My destination is Camp Solidarity, a tent community that has sprung up during the strike on land donated by a local union sympathizer. It has become a gathering place for local strikers and community members and for the constant stream of visitors who come to offer support and to witness for themselves what is happening in this amazing strike.

The preparation of communal meals at Camp Solidarity is an important contribution by local women. Role-stereotyped or not, this assignment puts them in the thick of strike activity and creates an opportunity to meet with neighbors, find out the latest strike news, and participate in group plans and discussions about evolving union and community strategy. Sitting around a table one evening over sausage biscuits and pinto beans, you might find an auto worker from Michigan, an Eastern Airlines flight attendant from California, a British labor journalist, a Free Will Baptist preacher, and a Jesuit priest discussing the future of the U.S. labor movement and its relation to justice for unemployed workers in Latin America. It is a pretty amazing atmosphere.

Complementing the activity at Camp Solidarity are the efforts of women at the Binns-Counts Community Development Center on the McClure side of the mountain, where hundreds of miners are fed each day, and where many formal and informal gatherings take place. (The Center is funded in part by church groups and is named for Deaconess Margaret Binns, a longtime mountain minister, and for Mary Kathleen "Cat" Counts, who died in the McClure explosion of 1983, the first woman coal miner to be killed on the job in Virginia.) The Center is less isolated than Camp Solidarity and has therefore been more vulnerable to official and unofficial harassment: as the strike has worn on, the Center's doors have been shot out three times, workers have arrived to find the carcass of a dead dog at the doorstep, a bomb threat has been received, and the oppressively close police presence has kept everyone's nerves on edge. None of these stresses have succeeded in cowing those who labor to keep the Center open and vital.

As I approach Camp Solidarity, I think of all the people who have helped to keep it and the community center flourishing. I soon realize that

I have joined a thin but almost constant stream of traffic moving toward the camp. We all pass through a system of checkpoints set up along the public road, before finally emerging into the open bottom land of Camp Solidarity. There I meet the camouflage-clad figures who will take part in the action planned for today.

The camouflage clothing has become a signature of the strike. The idea grew primarily from the experiences of UMWA strikers in the ill-fated A. T. Massey strike, where men were frequently arrested and convicted on the strength of descriptions of the clothing they had worn on a picket line or in a demonstration. Someone got the idea that the strikers should all try to look alike, and the notion caught fire. Practically everyone in the coalfields already owned some camouflage, since hunting is popular, so it was a natural choice for generic strike wear. Local stores (at least at the beginning) could easily supply more. And people soon discovered that the wearing of their colors helped their morale and provided a spirit-lifting way to show solidarity. Between camo regalia and the yellow "hostage" ribbons that soon appeared on car antennas, mailboxes, and the doors and windows of local small businesses, the towns of the area have come to wear a look that is somehow dead serious and festive all at the same time.

As I join the gathering crowd, I learn how others have come to be there. Very few know as much as I do about the plans for the day. Those invited to join this brigade were selected with care. The primary criterion was that each man (and all were men) must have demonstrated a personal willingness to accept the discipline of a nonviolent strike and an ability to keep cool under pressure. Planners took the particular situation of each man into account. Each had been asked if he would be willing to help do "something serious" on that day, and each had said yes. Over the weekend each man got a short phone call with the code words: "Kiss the wife and kids goodbye." They knew only that those words meant they were to be at Camp Solidarity at 2 p.m. on Sunday, packed to be gone "for a while."

There are 125 of us assembled. The leadership holds discussions about and with each miner, culling those with pending court cases because of strike activities or with critical family obligations. When this process is completed, a hundred men are left: ninety-five miners, four union staff members, and me. The strikers are divided into "Red," "White," and "Blue" teams, based primarily on each one's state of origin. They have been purposefully selected from West Virginia, Kentucky, and Virginia, so that each state with Pittston miners on strike is represented, even though the focus of the action will be here in southwest Virginia, the most active area of the strike. Eddie Burke (the union staff member with primary responsibility for the occupation) and I are not assigned a team, but are to stick together and help each other and the teams as needed.

A big U-Haul truck pulls up, and the back opens. As we look inside, we begin to realize the scale of what we are involved in, and the level of planning and preparation that has already taken place. The U-Haul is filled with 105 backpacks and bright orange vests. Each pack has ten days' worth of rations and supplies. The union has already bought a share of Pittston stock in each of our names, and when we arrive at our destination, we will announce that we are there "to inspect our property." Accordingly, we begin to call ourselves the Stockholders Brigade. The entire scheme is finally laid out in an old army tent. We learn that the plan is to take over the third-largest coal preparation plant in the world. Not one man backs out.

The giant Moss 3 facility is near the small town of Carbo in Russell County, Virginia. It is Pittston's largest coal preparation plant and ordinarily handles about 22,000 tons of coal a day. When it is shut down, every Pittston mine in the area ceases production. If the men can occupy this plant and stop coal from moving through it, they will be successfully pursuing a strike "the old-fashioned way"—by stopping production. Wall Street has at several important junctures cheered Pittston on in its effort to roll back longstanding agreements with the UMWA and has been quite sanguine about Pittston's power to have its way. Hurting Pittston's ability to process and deliver coal would surely send a message in a language these players could understand.

We pull out of Camp Solidarity packed into two U-Haul trucks and an old school bus with the seats removed, our pulses racing and hopes high. As we head toward Carbo, additional inconspicuous caravans of striking miners are also winding their way through the mountains from a number of assembly locations. They do not know where they are going or what they will find when they get there, but most people apparently suspect (and hope) that it is something big. The strike *needs* something big. The caravans stop periodically while leaders open their next set of sealed instructions to learn which fork in the road to take. At the same time a decoy group is sent ostentatiously to a mine in McClure, Virginia. Fake leads and deceptive rumors about an action in McClure are put out over car radios to be picked up by "the Vance" and the state troopers. Trees mysteriously fall across roads after the false leads are followed, significantly slowing the process of retreat.

Meanwhile the various caravans heading for Moss 3 are converging. They are to pass certain checkpoints at given moments along the way. Timing is critical, not only for the sake of surprise and successful entry, but also so that supporters will arrive immediately after our entrance, to secure the gates against attempts to evict us. Although there are some tense moments, we arrive on schedule at 4:10 p.m.

The road leading to the preparation plant is beginning to fill with hundreds of supporters and some media representatives, alerted at the last moment. We pile out of the vehicles, and everything begins to happen very quickly. We see the giant plant looming up before us. Amazingly, the gates are wide open. Eddie picks up his bullhorn and urges us on our way. We walk quickly through the open gates as planned, team by team, our hands high in the air to indicate we are unarmed. Two Vance Security men are the only guards anywhere in evidence. They take one look at our group and run to the shelter of their pickup truck, where they roll up their windows, hunch down in their seats, and stare out at us with hostile eyes. To see the swaggering Vance bullies cowed and surprised is a tremendous boost to everyone's spirits.

No reinforcements appear in time to hamper our entrance. The timing has been planned to catch the state troopers during a shift change. As things turn out, the troopers are caught six miles away from Moss 3 and are forced to tail after the train of supporters who are by now streaming toward the plant. The troopers are the last to arrive.

As we actually step through the plant gates, a huge crowd behind us is cheering us on. We are concerned about a panicked overreaction from the guards, and Burke keeps announcing over and over on the bullhorn, "This is a peaceful action. . . . We are an unarmed group. . . . I repeat, we are unarmed. No person or property will be harmed. We are simply here to inspect our property." We have been told that if shots are fired, we are to kneel and hold our ground until told to proceed.

The union has done everything its leaders could think of to prevent any of us or anyone else from being harmed. One man in each team is equipped with a gas mask and heavy gloves; these are "chuckers," who are to handle tear gas canisters if any are used. A helicopter hovers overhead, in radio contact with us and ready to help if anything unexpected happens. But it turns out that more contingencies were planned for than actually develop. We have caught them completely off-guard. There are a small number of supervisors inside the plant. We ask them to leave peacefully, assuring them that they will not be harmed in any way, and they quickly comply.

The gates we enter open directly onto County Road 600. From there a narrow bridge crosses a creek onto the Pittston property. From the bridge to the plant is a span of about two hundred yards with two giant silting ponds between. The plant is six stories of ramshackle steel plates and girders that enclose massive coal crunching machinery. Narrow steel stairs wind up through the machinery and connect the six floors of the plant. As we enter the plant, we climb single file up four flights of those stairs to the central control room.

The last man mounts the last step, and we look at each other and grin. Incredible: we are inside, and in control. The entire takeover has taken about twenty minutes, and has gone thus far without a hitch. Quickly everyone is deployed to secure the doors; watches are appointed to scan in every direction. Communications are set up, using two-way radios, with prearranged posts on the outside. In fact, throughout the occupation we are in constant communication with numerous checkpoints. (The union's expertise in communication is only one of several ways in which the Vietnam experience common to many of the miners will prove relevant during this nonviolent occupation.)

Soon after we enter, strike leaders speak to us about the great Flint sit-down strike that gave birth to the United Auto Workers and the CIO during the Depression. Auto workers took over and occupied the Fisher body plant in Flint, Michigan, in 1937, and the event marked a turning point in the development of the industrial union movement. Organizers give the Moss 3 takeover the code name "Flintstone" to honor that historic event and claim lineage from it. The men begin to challenge one another to break the Flint record of a forty-four-day occupation (later we learn that union press releases mentioned that record as well). In our hearts, though, we are hoping mainly to make it until nightfall.

We try to make ourselves at home, despite the fact that the environment is far from inviting. A coal preparation plant is a dirty place. Coal dust is literally everywhere. We become smeared with black coal dust, seemingly without touching a thing. There is also the—for me—unnerving combination of electricity and trickling water everywhere. We pick up trash and begin what will come to seem like an eternal sweeping at the ever-present coal dust.

Some men come back from scouting to report that they have discovered a way to the roof. This turns out to be important, because on the roof there is a balconylike area big enough for us to gather in such a way that we can see back down toward the bridge and the road where the crowd of our supporters is still growing, as it will continue to do throughout the occupation.

Someone checks his watch and lets out a whoop. *We have been in for an hour: victory!* But how soon will the troopers move to take us out? There is a good crowd out front, but are there enough to stop an evacuation? And will our supporters be willing to engage in civil disobedience to prevent or delay our removal? (Later we will realize that we were probably at our most vulnerable point at that moment, just barely settled in the plant, with many strikers and potential supporters not yet aware that anything was afoot. But the numbers were increasing, and it would soon become clear that the response of other rank-and-file miners and the surrounding community would play a crucial role in determining how long the occupation would last.) We have made a dramatic move and have important work yet to do, but the initiative now is shifting from us to the company and to other miners and the community.

If the men have doubts about whether their fellow unionists and neighbors will support them, our first visit to the roof removes them. We emerge into the light and squint across the distance to the bridge and the road beyond. One of the men spray-paints "UMWA FOREVER" in huge letters on the side of the building behind our walkway on the roof, and an enthusiastic cheer goes up from the crowd. Even at our distance we can tell the crowd is growing, and the surge of feeling in that cheer is powerful.

As dusk falls, we have our first visit from representatives of the company, escorted by UMWA vice president Cecil Roberts. From the beginning of the occupation, the men have assured the company that the coal plant is safe in their hands, and that the union will be happy to arrange inspections so that management can confirm the safety of its equipment.

Nevertheless, when Cecil enters the facility with two troopers and the Moss 3 superintendent, the latter is visibly tense and hostile. It is funny to watch his surprise when he is introduced to one of our number, Chuck Blevins. Chuck was specially recruited for this action because he had been the plant operator at Moss 3 for twenty-two years. Two years earlier Pittston had shifted him to a small one-man plant on top of a nearby mountain, but Chuck is still minutely familiar with the operation at Moss 3. Six or seven other members of the takeover team are employees from the plant as well. The union was serious when it assured Pittston that it could take proper care of the plant and its equipment.

The Pittston supervisor relaxes visibly once he realizes the expertise on hand. Throughout the plant occupation these orderly inspections continue, each time revealing that the facility is being kept in perfect working order.

As the light fades from the sky, we are summoned out to the roof again and have our first exposure to what will become a nightly ritual: our evening serenade. A mass of enthusiastic supporters have gathered just on our side of the bridge connecting the plant to the county road, getting as close to us as the union's own security team will allow. They are equipped with bullhorns, as well as just plain strong voices, and soon we are trading chants:

"We are!"
"Union!"
"We are!"
"Union!"

The crowd is singing to us, yelling to us, chanting to us, and roaring its approval. It seems to us that if we were state troopers, we would not want to try to wade through that particular crowd on that particular evening. Maybe we will be spending the night after all.

As true dark is coming on, we check our flashlights in readiness for the night. We soon learn that the water to the plant has been cut off. We, of course, have brought water with us in our packs. But the loss of the bathroom is a serious hardship. Back inside the plant we begin to explore our packs in greater detail. Each of the three teams has been provided with checkers, cards, a Bible, a small television. Everyone's individual pack has flashlights, extra batteries, hand lotion, dried food and fruit for ten days to two weeks, two bottled drinks, five canteens, toilet paper, soap, cleaning cloths, and notebooks and pens for keeping personal journals (the notes from one of which you are now reading). All of us take delight in the loving precision with which all these things have been planned. People start autographing the team Bibles.

I decide to try to sleep in the transformer room under constantly blinking red and green control panel lights. It is like bedding down under a giant 4,160-volt Christmas tree that I hope may hum me to sleep. But first Eddie is holding a crackling radio signal next to my head. The message is garbled, but I understand them to be saying that they are trying to get through to Fran, Elisha, and Lee to let them know that I am okay.

FRAN: All day long on Sunday, I feel on edge. For all we knew when Jim left this morning, he might end up with a handful of other hardy souls somewhere down in a coal mine in the wilds of southwest Virginia. Somehow a coal mine does not seem like the kind of place you'd like to be caught by a group of state troopers or Vance security guards. By five o'clock, though, a staff person at the District headquarters in Castlewood, Virginia, has called to say that the men are above ground inside the Moss 3 coal preparation plant, and everything is all right.

Next we start monitoring the news media and calling friends to alert them to what is happening. The children and I are proud and excited to be even indirectly involved in this important action. It is hard to put my full weight down all evening.

At about 9:30 the telephone rings, and I jump. When I pick up the receiver, a friendly voice says, "Hello, I am John Hawks with the United Mine Workers of America. I'm calling to tell you that your family member is safe tonight. Everything is going fine." It was almost like being tucked into bed. We would receive nightly calls for the duration of the occupation. They symbolize for me the care and attention to human-scale details we experienced throughout the takeover.

September 18

JIM: I try hard for sleep this first night, but without much success. I am just too energized. There is a ground cloth in my pack, but it and the sleeping bag are not much comfort on the steel-plated floor. About midnight I finally fall asleep, but awake about three and again at five, and finally get up. I wander out onto the roof. The company has big flood lights trained on the plant, and their glare blinds me so I can't tell much about the crowd. Scores and scores of state police headlights move endlessly back and forth to no apparent purpose. I expect we will be removed at dawn by the troopers and try to scan the scene for any sign that they may be about to make their move. After all, it can't be in the state's or the company's interest for us to stay here long.

At dawn, as the mists begin to lift, I can discern people on the roads, now stretching as far as the eye can see. It is a beautiful sight. The men begin to rise and clean up. We pack all our gear so we can be mobile at any time, a pattern we are to repeat each morning.

As I pull my things together, I look around at the collection of men who have ended up in this odd position together. The oldest is sixty-one; the youngest, twenty-seven. There are members from all three states where Pittston miners are striking. Two black miners are in the group. There are 1,400 years of mining experience represented among the group.

One of the miners from West Virginia is a handsome black man named Doug Johnson. He is thirty-three years old and lives two miles from historic Blair Mountain in Logan County, scene of some of the most protracted and violent episodes in UMWA history. Doug tells me that when he was sixteen, he and his family lived just below the defective dam that collapsed in the 1972 Buffalo Creek disaster. One hundred and twenty-seven people died in that disaster, seven were never found, and 4,000 were left homeless. They were victims of gross negligence when the coal refuse dam, created by Pittston and owned by its subsidiary, Buffalo Mining Company, gave way and poured 130 million gallons of water through the narrow, crowded valley of Buffalo Creek in the worst flood in West Virginia history. Doug went to work for Pittston four years later when he was twenty. He now has a three-year-old son. He shakes his head, "That Pittston, it's got me coming and going."

Another member of the Moss 3 brigade is the Reverend Johnny Fred Williams of Dripping Springs Free Will Baptist Church. He lives in Haysi, Virginia. I ask him about his family and he tells me that his wife works. He also has three daughters: two are already married, and his "baby" is to be married this coming Friday. She wants him to perform the ceremony, but he assures me that if he is still in Moss 3 or in jail on Friday she will understand. He says his church is split between union and nonunion, but he feels certain that even the nonunion people will understand what he is doing and support him in standing "for what is right" by his own lights.

Rayford Campbell also talks about his family. He tells me that his father is Travis Campbell, a seventy-eight-year-old Free Will Baptist preacher with black lung disease. Rayford's grandfather also had black lung, and he died of it. Rayford says, "A man who won't take care of his family is worse than an infidel." He follows with a remark I will hear echoed many times: "It's a shame we have to go through this for a job."

T. Larry Ford, Jr., is the oldest of five boys. The other four all live nearby. Their father is a minister who died at the age of fifty-one on the first day of the strike, back in April. Larry thinks the company will fire him after the strike, no matter what. He is thinking of taking some other job when this is over. He has two kids: the one in the third grade is gifted and scores in the ninety-ninth percentile on tests she has taken. She loves music and science. He was in the process of getting her a piano by trading a calf for it, but the deal fell through when the takeover began. He will sell the calf and get her the piano when he gets out of Moss 3, he says.

A brother and I concoct a game of horseshoes or quoits, tossing scrap gaskets and rubber belts over machinery parts that are lying all over the place. By radio a dozen roses are sent to the wife of one of the miners for her birthday, compliments of the union, since her husband won't be home tonight to celebrate it. Blood pressure medicine is ordered for another miner and arrives promptly.

Late in the afternoon the troopers and plant superintendent return. The troopers formally ask Eddie Burke if we will leave voluntarily. Eddie replies that he will not. The trooper asks then if that is true for everybody, and the answer comes back loud and clear: "Yes!" The troopers dutifully go on to inform us that we are trespassing. We figure the stage is set, and we had better be prepared. Some of the men begin to spray-paint the numbers of union locals on the outside wall of the plant, where our support crew can see them, along with "UMWA FOREVER," until every local represented in the takeover is honored. Even "Rev. Sessions" eventually makes it onto the wall, an unwitting reminder of the solitary individualism of professional clergy, maybe, but also a sign of the men's unfailing courtesy and inclusiveness toward me during the events of the week. The American flag and a camouflage flag are raised from the roof. If we have to go, we will go down with colors bravely flying. However, as evening falls once more, we are still here: we have made it through a second day and are facing another night and hopefully another dawn.

September 19

JIM: I am up by 5:30. Soreness from my steel mattress is setting in along with the routine of being in the plant, so sleep has become a goal that must be achieved, not a natural activity.

Anticipation about what might be coming next is also becoming routine. Maybe they will move today, but we said that yesterday. All the formalities have been completed and the orders have been given. What do they have to wait for? What is there to gain? The longer we stay, the greater the benefit for the strike, but also, everyone is realizing, the greater the potential personal consequences.

In the late afternoon, standing on the roof with a bunch of other men, I learn that Fran is here. I am surprised, because we had not talked about her coming up. She is somewhere over there among the perpetual knot of people near the bridge. We talk over the radio, but I cannot make out which little figure she is.

FRAN: By Tuesday, I just can't stand it any more. I know that the site of the building occupation is only three hours from home, and I have no classes to teach on Wednesday. When Rich Kirby volunteers to drive up to Carbo with me after my last class on Tuesday, that settles it. (Rich is a temporary neighbor, staying in Knoxville for a year. His home is in southwest Virginia, and since the strike began he has donated much energy and his considerable musical talents to innumerable strike gatherings of all kinds.) We take off about two-thirty in the afternoon and drive straight to Virginia, not knowing what in the world we will find when we get there. For all we knew, an evacuation might be launched at any time. We also have no idea how close we can get to the plant, and we fear we will be stopped at some point short of our goal by a roadblock of state troopers.

As we go deeper into the coalfields, Rich points out the signs of the growing mobilization that has seized the area since the start of the strike. There are signs in store windows (such as "We respectfully refuse to serve state troopers during the period of the UMWA strike"), slogans spray-painted on walls (such as "We won't go back"), bumper stickers everywhere (such as "Our Jobs, Our Kids, Our Union"), yellow hostage ribbons on antennas and mailboxes.

As we drive out of St. Paul and hit the last stretch before the coal preparation plant, things begin to change even more. We notice little clumps of men standing beside pickup trucks or parked cars at certain points on the road. They look relaxed but alert, as if they are planning to stay where they are indefinitely. Nobody is in any hurry. As soon as they see our yellow ribbon, these men wave and smile or give a thumbs-up sign. Still no troopers or Vance. As we continue, the clumps of people begin getting closer together, and pretty soon the isolated knots of vehicles became more like a broken line and then an unbroken one. Eventually it is as though both sides of the road have become a parking lot.

As we draw nearer to the plant, we get the feeling that we have stumbled into a giant cultural event, something like a cross between a bluegrass festival, a turkey shoot, and an oldtime revival. People are everywhere, standing and talking in quiet groups, strolling side by side down the road, or sitting on tailgates, drinking soft drinks and whittling.

We squeeze our car between two other bumper-stickered, yellow-ribboned cars beside the road, and begin to walk toward Moss 3. The excitement in the air is simply electric. As we cross the small bridge connecting the road with the Pittston property, we are finally stopped by two men in camouflage, each sporting a walkie-talkie and a big grin. "Sorry, we're not allowing anybody beyond this point. Can we help you?"

Suddenly it dawns on us. There *are* no troopers, no Vance, no police. The *union* is in control here. It is as though we have entered another country, another time, another dimension, right here on the ground that was forbidden to the miners by the company and the courts a few short days ago. Now it is UMWA territory.

One of the most extraordinary sensations is looking into other people's eyes, young and old, black and white, men and women. As gazes meet, even between total strangers, there is irrepressible pride and a kind of harnessed elation. I have the impression that *all* of us are thinking, "This is one of the most important experiences of my life. I will remember this until I die."

The boundary where we find ourselves, the line maintained by the union, turns out to be an amazing contact point, a permeable membrane connecting and separating the "inside" and the "outside." From this position, you can see across to a kind of balcony on the preparation plant, and many of the men occupying the plant are lined up gazing out at us. Someone has spray-painted a huge, bigger-than-life "UMWA FOREVER" on the side of the building. The two union sentries explain that they are in radio contact with the men on the "roof," and that if we want to wait our turn, we can talk to Jim.

I look around me and realize that I am not the only family member who has come to visit. At my left stands a woman in full strike regalia. She is covered in camouflage, all of it spanking clean and sporty. Her brand new camo T-shirt is topped off with a bead-fringed camo bandanna at her neck, and a pair of jack-rock earrings dangle from her ears. ("Jack-rocks" are the bent and joined nails that have shown up on the road since the company reopened the mines. They have been sprinkled in the path of union caravans as well as coal trucks, but they have come to symbolize union resistance to the company's provocative decision to run the mines with nonunion workers.)

The woman's young daughter is standing beside her with a camouflage bow in her neatly curled hair. The woman is squinting intently into a pair of binoculars at the roof across the way. Suddenly she begins to laugh. "He's got me in his glasses, and I've got him in mine!" she says. For a couple of long minutes she gazes through the binoculars, chuckling now and then in pure delight. Then the sentry makes radio contact for her. "Stockholder, stockholder, we've got a family member here. Can we talk to Lonnie Evans?"

In a minute Lonnie is on the other radio, and the woman next to me is talking to him at top decibel while the mob of us other miners and supporters appreciatively listen in. She tells Lonnie she is sending in a bag of fresh-baked brownies donated by a neighbor, that his brother has called from out of town to wish him well, that the dog's ailment is better, that she loves him. Next the daughter takes her turn, yelling into her end while her eyes are trained on the tiny figure of her father on the balcony. "Daddy, we're proud of you." Mother and daughter stand and wave for several minutes.

As they turn to go, replacements step up to the line. This is the Students' Auxiliary, a group of middle and high school students who have joined in strike activities to support fathers, brothers, uncles, grandfathers, friends, and neighbors on strike, and to make a statement for themselves about the kind of place they want to live in, the kinds of jobs they want to have when they get out of school.

The mobilization of this younger generation is one of the new developments in this strike, and one of the indications that the support of the community is more than superficial or passive. In the spring, students had staged a walk-out of classes at all three Dickenson County high schools to protest the troopers' rough treatment of the miners in the civil disobedience at the McClure mine. In the summer, kids had walked picket lines, written irreverent songs about particularly hated figures in Pittston management, and staged strike support rallies. On this evening they are there to sing to the Moss 3 brigade, and sing they do, at the tops of their voices. They sing the Appalachian labor hymn "Which Side Are You On?"—written by Florence Reece during the miners' strike in Harlan County, Kentucky, in the 1930s. They sing "We Shall Not Be Moved." They sing new songs about the strike against Pittston.

In a few more minutes, I get my chance on the radio, and with the help of intermediaries and lots of instructions about which button to push, I am soon talking to Jim and hearing his voice come crackling back into my ear. He waves his white hard hat in the air, and suddenly I can pick him easily out of the line-up of men on the roof. It is odd, being helped by strangers to establish this connection to my own husband, at once so intimate and so glaringly public. He seems utterly familiar and utterly transformed, like the liberated grass under our feet, like the occupied building across the way, like "Which Side Are You On?" in the throats of the teenagers of the Student Auxiliary.

Rich and I stand around a while more, watching the parade of visitors who come to pay their different kinds of respects. Then we decide to take a wider tour. We go back across the bridge and out onto the road, walking and mingling with the jubilant, almost dazed crowd. At one point I look around me and realize how many more men there are than women, how many more whites than blacks. Under most circumstances, a woman vastly outnumbered by a crowd of men on a rural road with night coming on would be seriously nervous about her own safety—for good reason. And under most circumstances, a black person vastly outnumbered by whites in that same situation would feel the same. But this is not "most circumstances." And I never felt safer in my life. These people are here to take care of each other and of the men inside, and one consequence of the bond they are feeling is that we all get a glimpse of what a less oppressive set of race and gender relations might one day look like.

This period just before dusk has a little of the feeling of visiting hours at a hospital. Clearly most people are there for the duration—like Jim's co-worker Tena Willemsma, who is out on the road, busy organizing food, helping to guard one of the gates, and holding down other tasks as well. They will be sleeping in the backs of cars and pickups, or maybe not at all. But others have come to pay their respects and will go home at nightfall: elderly women in Sunday clothes, tiny babies wrapped in blankets and passed from hand to hand or held up in the air and pointed toward the "UMWA FOREVER" sign on the side of the plant, older siblings pulling younger ones by the hand through moving streams of people.

In its own chaotic way, the instant city that has sprung up along this road is well ordered. Food is being provided to the crowd for free—purchased, organized, and kept moving by many of the same tough, overworked, and chronically underappreciated women who have provided the backbone of community support throughout the strike. One man tells Rich and me with obvious pride about his wife, who had gone home on Sunday evening and stayed up all night. She cooked five hams and took them to Camp Solidarity, where she met her comrades, and, "Those women had 1,700 ham biscuits here at Moss 3 by seven o'clock on Monday morning." (Later we will hear tales of women working round the clock at Camp Solidarity to feed the occupation support crowd, of women at the Binns-

Counts Center cooking hot dogs and hamburgers for one thousand and bussing them over to Moss 3 when it looked as if food was running short.) Port-a-johns have been hauled in and set up. In all the sea of camouflage and pickup trucks, not a single beer is anywhere to be seen.

String musicians are scattered through the area making all kinds of music, along with various groups of supporters making films, shooting video, taping interviews. One of the bridges in the area is being held by members of the Amalgamated Clothing and Textile Workers Union from Pennsylvania. They arrived at Camp Solidarity for a visit just before the building occupation and have allowed themselves to be drafted into the effort. Now they say they wouldn't *think* of leaving while the men are inside. They have never been part of anything like this in all their lives. Neither have the rest of us.

Night is falling, and as we look across at the coal plant, we can see that the guys on the inside have come out on the roof again. This time they have their flashlights with them, and they look like a little swarm of radiant fireflies on the building opposite. A crowd has already gathered for the nightly ritual of chanting and singing back and forth across the no-man's land between the bridge and the plant itself. With bullhorns or enough raw voices, each side can make itself heard by the other.

A group of Kentucky miners arrive, and they have their own contribution. They get on the bullhorn, introduce themselves, and say they have planned a song they want to sing to the men in the plant. One of their members, a gifted singer, lines out "Amazing Grace" in the old style, for all those on both sides of the empty space to hear and join.

There is a resonant pause as we hear our own echoes fall away, and in a minute the musicians have launched us into "Solidarity Forever." As we on our side join raised hands and sway to the rhythm of the grand old song, we look over at the plant roof and see that the lights of the men across the way are also held high and are swaying in time to the music. Tears fall free and unashamed down many faces around me.

When the song is over, people on our side light matches and cigarette lighters and hold them up, so we can send light back across the space to the glowing beams on the roof across the way. Suddenly we realize that the flashlight beams are no longer swaying to the music or bobbing randomly. The men on the roof have trained their lights on the side of the coal plant, and the glowing ovals spell out in huge wavering letters "U-M-W-A." The crowd around me goes crazy. We are stomping and cheering and waving.

(After the occupation was over, the company would be quick to paint over the spray-painted slogans and local union numbers that the occupying miners had put on the side of the building. During an interview with Paper Tiger Television, however, James Hicks, president of Local Union 1259, would remember the night the men used their flashlights to spell out the name of their union. He said, "I can drive up there now after dark and the visualization of those flashlights shining on that tipple is still there. They can't paint over them. . . . And it's something to be proud of.")

Next a member of the Kentucky local asks everybody to kneel. All around me, men and women in camouflage kneel in the gravel road, and the miner-preacher from Kentucky calls down his God's blessing on this just fight.

The true night watch begins then, with a rally and brief speeches from the back of a pickup truck by the union leaders responsible for things on the "outside." Their themes are to welcome all newcomers (UMWA members and representatives of other unions are streaming into Virginia, and each person we talk to seems to have heard of some other caravan on its way from Michigan or Ohio or Texas), to restate again and again the union's stringent commitment to nonviolence (with cordial but clear instructions for any who cannot accept that discipline to leave the scene), to commend the men inside for the personal risks they are incurring by their action, and to urge upon the crowd that the fate of those inside depends largely on the staying power and solidarity of those outside.

Rich and I take one more lingering look at the astonishing scene and head out to where we are to spend the night. We will come back for one quick visit in the morning (assuming, of course, that the men are still here!), but we won't be able to stay long. I have to get back to my job and to the children, though all that seems a thousand miles away.

And of course things will be like that for everyone. "Life" will still go on. People's normal preoccupations and everyday concerns and warts and pettiness and racism and sexism and in-fighting and fearfulness and inertia and weariness are all perfectly real and powerful factors in their personal and political lives. That was true before Moss 3, has been true during Moss 3, and will without a doubt be true after Moss 3 is over, however this specific action turns out. Even a victorious strike will have its bitter side; even dazzlingly right choices will be followed by murky dilemmas with no clear solutions. The coal industry in particular and the American economy in general will still be in deep trouble. The press is likely to continue its shamefully sluggish and niggardly coverage of the strike. None of this can be denied.

But neither can it be denied that there are moments of transcendence that are capable of teaching us, of making us *feel* the possibilities that reside in us, in the people around us, and in the groups of which we are or can be a part. Walking the road and the bridge in front of Moss 3 tonight has been such a moment for me.

Many ingredients leading up to this night were just right: strong leaders who were subjected to the continuing tough and well-informed scrutiny of rank-and-file miners; a cumulative set of decisions by those leaders that convinced workers and communities step by step that the leaders were worthy of trust and respect; a membership knit closely together by kinship and cultural tradition; a union with a long history of militant struggles against management; a recently demonstrated ability to take repeated militant actions and to resist corporate and state authority over and over again; a similarly demonstrated ability to accept the discipline of nonviolence; brilliant tactical planning; adequate resources and a willingness to spend them; growing acknowledgment by union members that they could not win the fight by themselves, but needed the support of their spouses, children, elders, and other people beyond the coalfields; families and communities and outsiders who were willing to respond to the miners' call for support; and finally a decision to tap into two powerful American traditions of social struggle: the industrial union movement of the 1930s and the fight against racial injustice of the 1960s.

But on the road that night, I want to tell you that it didn't feel like correct ingredients. It felt like a mysterious and unexplainable gift of great love and power. I will never forget the look in people's eyes that afternoon or the sound of that singing across black space to and with the sparks on the other side.

The Night of September 19

JIM: New worries begin: the word is that misdemeanor charges are now felonies for us, and that (federal) Judge Williams in Abingdon may be vindictive. The amounts of fines and the length of jail terms are debated. Two or three men are smuggled out of the plant for personal reasons and are replaced with two or three new recruits. (Nothing is said about this silent transfer. It seems as though it is intentionally unnoted as part of our collective discipline. For all anyone knows, the new guys might have been there all along.)

In the mists of evening, people are winding down, going to their watches and dispersing, thinking about the rest of the evening. One very young miner is left on the edge of the roof with a now soft-sounding bullhorn. He is listening for a word from a barely visible lone figure on the bridge:

"Bobby, I love you."
"Connie, I love you."
"We're proud of you."
"I'm proud of you."

"Goodnight, honey."
"Goodnight."
Like two whippoorwills.

September 20

JIM: When the mists clear in the morning, the crowd can see that we have painted "Day 4" on the plant, and a roar goes up. Around eight o'clock in the morning, Fran and Rich make their way across the bridge. I spot them right away, and I interrupt Eddie, who is telling me how he became a Catholic because of the pastoral letter on labor. Fran is beautiful in a blue sweater over an amazingly white shirt. What a treat. We talk over the walkie-talkie. Lee and Elisha are fine and send their love. Friends and family have called. Sentiment and feelings are so much closer to the surface for all of us. Tears come easily.

At morning prayers, which have become a part of our routine, I ask Reverend Williams to pray. He is eloquent, but he pretty much breaks up before he can conclude. I take over the task then and ask for silent prayers for POW-MIA's, as a miner has requested, and for the casualties and sacrifices of all wars, including this one; I bid us to remember that all wars are in some ways class wars like this one. We end together with the Lord's Prayer, so our voices are together.

Water has been turned back on for the sake of the silting ponds. A brother tells me that he has fixed up a hose on the sixth floor, if I want to take a good cold shower in some privacy. I wash my shirt and socks while I am at it.

In the early afternoon a federal marshal and four troopers serve us with the federal judge's order to leave. Seven tonight is the deadline. There is no formal announcement; the court order is not read aloud, but everyone knows the deadline nevertheless. Word is that the state has a fleet of buses parked up the road at the power station, poised to take us to jail. We have a group meeting and Burke updates us. He thinks they will come tonight or in the morning. Be ready. They may try tricks. Watches are set for all night on all sides, and everybody is fully packed and ready. No resisting arrest. We feel strong, almost immune from police action. There is an incredible sense of security because of the giant crowd outside who have pledged that they will have to be taken first before the troopers or National Guard can get to us. All of us are aware of the moment when the seven p.m. deadline passes and still we have not moved.

There is the nightly serenade outside from our folks across the way. A beautiful female voice is singing original songs for this occasion. I murmur, "How beautiful," and Earl, standing next to me, says: "That's my wife,

Jean." I know of Jean because she is one of the many women who have invented a new kind of leadership in this strike. She participated in the women's sit-down at the Pittston office. She and other women formed support squads for arrested demonstrators after mass actions. (They would scour the countryside to find out which jails demonstrators had been taken to, then set up a constant vigil outside those jails until people were released.) She has spoken at miners' rallies and traveled outside the coalfields to help build support. She has written songs about the strike and sung them with other women and alone on countless occasions.

As I listen to her that night, she stands in my mind for all the women who took up the new challenges posed by this strike, who cooked biscuits, wrote poems, traveled to strange cities, met totally unexpected new friends from far-away places, who threw themselves into the strike for the sake of those who had gone before, for those who would come after, for their men in the mines, and for the exhilaration of feeling and using their own new powers. Her voice is as clear and pure an Appalachian voice as you could hear anywhere, and carries like a bird across the space from the bridge.

But as we look in that direction, we realize that the flood lights on the road have been taken down. Is that to allow the night to cover their moves? Or ours?

After seventy-six hours our personal, family, real-life needs and loves have begun to focus again in our minds. Why do we have to do this? Why can't all this struggle and risk-taking be a dream? Why can't peace and justice, covenants and contracts, family and loved ones, home and work, be present realities, instead of being across "over there" and "not yet"? We and the crowd pray together over bullhorns and sing and chant, and we think our fourth night in Moss 3 has begun.

But the night is young. Cecil is especially worried about the supporters outside as the crowd has grown, night has fallen, and the troopers are preparing to move. Convoys of supporters and union members are headed into the state, with some people predicting fifty thousand supporters for the next day. The injunction deadline has passed. Law enforcement is going to have to move. But how can they?

Cecil and Eddie call a meeting of all of us. The announcement comes: leadership has decided that the time has come to end the takeover. At the present moment things are incredibly favorable for the union. Support from the community is at a peak. Discipline has been maintained. The plant is in perfect condition. No one has been hurt. The advantages of leaving on our own terms and during a high point are beginning to look significantly more attractive than the dangers of staying.

Nevertheless, the proposal is difficult for us to absorb. There are strong but quietly held feelings. Some want to stay: make *them* move; force *their* hand; why take them off the hook? We are doing fine—better and better, in fact. But there is also a corresponding sense of relief. The men know that the next move threatened by the court would strip them of their tie to the union and take away all their membership rights, including the right to union legal representation. Commitments, desires, ambivalence, and emotions are deep throughout the group. All of us would like to shed the tension of anticipating the personal consequences that will probably flow from continuing the occupation, but we also resist the idea of leaving before we are forced. We have dug into the place.

There are strong talks by Eddie and Cecil. The Moss 3 takeover has achieved its goals: it has reestablished the direction and momentum of the strike; it has dramatically reaffirmed nonviolent, militant civil disobedience as a commitment that works and strengthens the union. With the occupation of Moss 3, the union shut down Pittston's mines and halted production. By reviving a tactic that recalled the great sit-downs of the 1930s, the takeover has reinvigorated support, retaken the initiative, and accelerated the momentum of the strike; it has delivered a dramatic message to Pittston about the miners' seriousness and the depth, breadth, and militancy of their community support. Cecil stresses that this is not the final act of the union's strategy for the strike but only the beginning.

In the end, the same trust, solidarity, and discipline that brought these men here lead them to accept the decision proposed. Acting on the belief that the union leadership has earned their trust in matters of strategy, the men stand firm. The decision is made and reinforced by ninety-nine men moving together to leave, as well and as tightly and in as high spirits as when we entered.

Cecil asks me to close the occupation with prayer. It is hard. Despite all the prayers I have undertaken in this occupation, this one seems different. "I'm all prayed out," I joke, and it's really true. When I finally begin, though, I am blessed with the most heartfelt words that have ever come to me. They fly from my lips. None of us want to part.

But we do, and we are quick down the stairs once we begin. Eddie and I link arms, and we all move together, quickly across the open ground and bridge, with an American flag flying in the lead. We are immediately enfolded into the startled bosom of our favorite mob. Our hats and packs mysteriously vanish as we enter the crowd. Someone hugs me and says, "This isn't a union, it's a movement." Another grabs me and whispers, "This shows we can lead with our head as well as our heart."

There is a short rally of celebration that ends with one more pouring out of "Amazing Grace," and then we are gone. Eddie, Rick, and I pile into the back of a pickup truck that carries us along darkened roads lined for miles with people, cars, and trucks. We duck down like fugitives as we ease through a police roadblock, then happily encounter our own checkpoints, where we are greeted by friendly, fire-lit faces, and finally come safely to Camp Solidarity, where magically our packs, hats, and belongings are waiting for us. The occupation has ended.

Afterword by Jim

At a briefing for stock analysts the month after the takeover of Moss 3, Pittston president Paul Douglas admitted that the company had overestimated the ability of the courts to control the UMWA's strike activity. All Pittston coal production in Virginia had stopped for almost a week. That could happen again and again. But could Pittston ever know where or when?

Twenty-four days after the takeover, U.S. Secretary of Labor Elizabeth Dole stood in front of Moss 3 announcing that she had asked UMWA president Richard Trumka and Pittston president Paul Douglas to meet in her office the next day. There, after only ninety minutes, an agreement was reached to appoint a mediator, who eventually helped to negotiate an end to the strike.

The settlement was not perfect. Months after the settlement, as Fran and I write this memoir, some miners are still laid off. Some may never return to work. The company won more "flexibility" on work rules, thus eroding hard-fought union victories and shifting more control over the work process back to management. But the terms of the agreement were vastly more favorable to the union than anyone dreamed would be possible when Pittston first set out to break the union, to drop all health care obligations to retirees, and to bust up the BCOA. Although the coal industry in America and the UMWA are still in trouble and still in great conflict, the victories won in this strike, and the methods that won them, stand as a beacon and challenge to the entire U.S. labor movement and to all those in churches and in communities who care about the future of American working people, their families, and their communities.

That tense, emotional last meeting together inside Moss 3 is etched deeply in my memory, as I know it is in the hearts and minds of the other men. As I search for what the future may hold, and as I try to think about how we should move toward that future, I remember Cecil's closing words to us as we stood together in a circle for the last time: "We'll stay just one step ahead of the law. Effective actions don't get bogged down. The question can never be, 'How can we hang on?' but, 'What's next?'"

Acknowledgments

With gratitude to Tena Willemsma, Eddie Burke, Rich Kirby, Sam and Florence Reece, and the people of the United Mine Workers of America and the coalfield communities of southwest Virginia.

The names of all rank-and-file miners who participated in the takeover and those of their family members have been changed to protect their privacy.

Hobart Grills, president of the Harlan County Black Lung Association. (*Earl Dotter*)

11

The People's Respirator

Coalition Building and the
Black Lung Association

Bennett M. Judkins

The struggle for occupational health in America today owes much to the efforts of retired and disabled miners in the coalfields of Appalachia. In the late 1960s they created an organization that served as a model for occupational health battles in several industries in the 1970s and 1980s. Called the Black Lung Association (BLA), it was part of the broader black lung movement, which sought recognition of, and compensation for, a disease referred to medically as "coal workers' pneumoconiosis." A chronic dust disease of the lungs arising out of employment in an underground coal mine, it is known to the miners as "black lung."

The BLA still exists today, but the movement was at its peak in the late 1960s and early 1970s. Arising in West Virginia out of a conflict over state workers' compensation, it quickly spread to several Appalachian states after the passage of the federal Coal Mine Health and Safety Act of 1969. This act, among other things, established the Black Lung Benefits Program, a federally supported plan to compensate miners who contracted the disease. Problems in the early management of the program by the Social Security Administration encouraged the formation of several new BLA chapters.

The BLA did battle with the Social Security Administration, and then the Department of Labor, which took over the program in 1974. Although the movement died down in the late 1970s, it was revitalized somewhat in the early 1980s when the Reagan administration attempted to alter eligibility standards and cut funds from the benefits program.

The history of the black lung movement has been chronicled elsewhere.[1] My purpose here is to provide a brief overview of the origins of the BLA as a prelude to the efforts made in the later stages of the movement to build a coalition with two similar organizations outside Appalachia: the Brown Lung Association in the southern textile industry and the White Lung Association in the asbestos industry.

The Black Lung Association

It is not surprising that one of the most successful movements to come out of Appalachia would involve rank-and-file miners. The United Mine Workers of America (UMWA) have a long tradition of struggle and resistance. Ironically, the BLA's battle was not just with industry, the government, and the medical profession, but also with the union, which had for years downplayed health and safety issues. With the 1950 Bituminous Coal Wage Agreement, John L. Lewis, then president of the UMWA, ended large-scale warfare between labor and management in the coalfields, established an intricate collaboration between union and management, and created the UMWA Welfare and Retirement Fund, which was financed by a royalty on each ton of coal. Although the fund provided pensions and free medical care, it also gave the union a vested interest in production, which some suggested resulted in collusion, rather than just collaboration, between the UMWA and the major coal companies.[2]

This partnership also resulted in the mechanization of the mines and a subsequent drop in the number of miners employed—from 415,000 in 1950 to fewer than 130,000 in 1969. Those union miners who remained employed were well paid, received a pension, and had access to free medical care. Unfortunately, mechanization also made them more likely to contract black lung, since the new continuous mining machine, with its enhanced speed and motion, increased the amount of coal dust circulating in the mines.[3]

Tensions increased in the 1960s when then UMWA president Tony Boyle neither proposed new legislation regarding mine safety nor applied pressure to enforce existing regulations. In 1968, 9,000 men were injured in mine accidents and another 307 men were killed. Seventy-eight of these died in a disaster in Farmington, West Virginia, over the Thanksgiving holidays, which, through television, brought to the nation's attention the plight of coal miners in Appalachia. This disaster was the catalyst for the first phase of the black lung revolt, which sought changes in the West Virginia workers' compensation system. Successful action in West Virginia was, in part, also responsible for the inclusion of a federal black lung benefits program in the 1969 Coal Mine Health and Safety Act.

The hasty inclusion of this program and the failure to plan for its implementation by the responsible agency, the Social Security Administration, created new problems. The frustration of disabled miners and their widows with the application process resulted in a revitalization of the West Virginia BLA and its expansion to several states in the Appalachian area.

The movement owed its success to the efforts of many people in and outside the mines. Perhaps most significant was a coalition of doctors who worked in the late 1960s to raise the consciousness of Appalachians about pulmonary diseases among underground miners. Less well known were a cadre of young activists who came to Appalachia with an ideology of social change and a willingness to challenge the prevailing power structure of the region. Many came to work with the BLA through a non-profit organization called Designs for Rural Action (DRA), an anti-poverty group that had begun to shift its initial focus on welfare rights to a broader concern for economic power in the Appalachian region.

The core of the movement, however, was the rank-and-file miner, often retired and disabled, who had filed a claim for compensation with the local office of the Social Security Administration. Countywide BLA chapters formed the foundation of the black lung movement. Barbara Smith notes the chapters' triple function: "they offered assistance through lay advocates for individuals pursuing federal black lung compensation claims; they pressured the Social Security Administration and the Congress to reform the compensation program; and they organized a network of dissident UMWA members."[4]

The BLA was seen by many of these dissidents, and most of the young activists in DRA, as a vehicle for union reform; but the miners and their widows who came to the organization seeking help simply wanted assistance, at least initially, in obtaining compensation.

Initial efforts of the BLA remained at the local level with campaigns to put pressure on SSA officials. Demonstrations, aimed primarily at the media, were effective in embarrassing the authorities. It became clear early on, however, that local SSA offices were simply relaying information to the Baltimore offices of the SSA, where final decisions were made. Chapters reluctantly came together for meetings to plan a regional strategy. Eventually, the battle moved to Washington, where frequent marches and testimony at Congressional hearings helped to change both the law and the procedures for implementing the Black Lung Benefits Program. The impact on Congress was reflected in the words of Senator Richard Schweiker from Pennsylvania:

> One cannot have a hearing on a disease that is the largest occupational killer in the world today without it having some impact on him. . . .
> One cannot attend committee hearings, see the pictures, and hear the witnesses including miners themselves, without getting the message that these Americans have been neglected for years. Only belatedly are we beginning to realize that we all have a responsibility, the industry, the unions, and most important of all, the country.[5]

Kelly Buchanan, a West Virginia coal miner, protests in the early 1970s at the National Bank of Washington, which was owned by the United Mine Workers of America. (*Earl Dotter*)

The miners had offered themselves as evidence, and the end result was the passage in 1972 of amendments to the original black lung law that greatly liberalized the requirements for obtaining compensation. It was a major victory for the movement and its supporters.

The struggle was not over, however. In 1974 the *Black Lung Bulletin* prophetically recognized that "without a continuing fight against abuses and a continuing fight for immediate compensation, miners who are now working won't have black lung benefits when they quit or are forced to quit work."[6] Yet it was another group of retired miners who carried on the next phase of the struggle, and in an unlikely location, the city of Chicago. The unemployment caused by technology and mine shutdowns that began in the 1950s sent many coal miners to Chicago and other cities to work in factories and foundries. Few of these coalfield migrants found adequate employment, and many became "part of that mass of humanity, the urban poor, who have been defined by those who try to run their lives as a 'problem,' the unemployables to be moved out by 'redevelopment plans' to bring the middle class back to the city."[7] As time went by, many fell victim to pulmonary problems resulting from their years in the mines. When applying for benefits in the 1970s, they were confronted with a medical and governmental system that knew little about their disease.

The Chicago Area Black Lung Association (CABLA) was formed in 1976. In addition to its work with migrant miners in Illinois, the CABLA linked with BLA chapters in Appalachia to form the National Black Lung Association, which was instrumental in the passage of the 1977 amendments to the Black Lung Benefits Act. This act further liberalized the criteria for benefits and altered the regulations about how claims were to be processed and financed. For the next few years, over 80 percent of claims were approved.

In 1981, however, the Reagan administration dramatically cut eligibility for black lung benefits, and thereafter only a small fraction of those who applied had their claims approved. As the CABLA lamented in a letter to miners:

> They made it so that in the future there will be very little about a *Federal* black lung claim that will be any different from the way a *State* compensation claim would be handled. The masterplan is to wipe out the present debt the Trust Fund owes the government and then say, "why not give it back to the states?" That will leave miners once again at the mercy of the operators and state officials that the operators pay off. . . . [The law] has laid the groundwork to destroy the Federal Black Lung Program.[8]

The Brown and White Lung Associations

In 1974 coalworkers in Appalachia were involved in a strike against a mine in Harlan County, Kentucky, which was owned by Duke Power, an electrical company based in North Carolina. Many supporters, who had also worked with the BLA, came to North Carolina to collect funds for the strikers and their families. The fundraising trip provided the opportunity for several meetings to be held at the Highlander Center in Tennessee, a research and education hub for grassroots organizations, between BLA representatives and labor activists in North and South Carolina. Out of these meetings emerged, as one staff member later indicated, "a direct translation or application of what was going on in the coal mines into the rest of the south, where textiles was the dominant industry."[9]

What was "going on" in the South was byssinosis, a lung affliction caused by the inhalation of cotton dust. The workers called it brown lung. Because millworkers did not have the benefit of a free medical examination (which was provided to coal miners through the Black Lung Benefits Program), organizers set up screening clinics. For workers unaccustomed to unions or other worker organizations, the clinics provided a nonthreatening environment in which to come together. The realization that they were not alone in their pulmonary struggle had a strong empowering effect. They began to translate their personal trouble into a public issue.

Out of these clinics emerged the Carolina Brown Lung Association (CBLA), which had expanded by 1980 to fifteen cities in five states.[10] Unlike the BLA, which depended primarily on member contributions, the CBLA was blessed with substantial funding from foundations and the federal government, primarily through the Comprehensive Employment Training Act (CETA), the Occupational Safety and Health Administration (OSHA), and the Volunteers in Service to America (VISTA). By 1980 the organization had a $300,000 annual budget and more than forty staff members. Its goals—to educate workers and the public about the disease, to obtain compensation for those afflicted, and to clean up the workplace—were similar to those of the BLA, but it had to approach them differently.

Like the original West Virginia BLA, the textile workers focused on reforming the state workers' compensation systems. A federal benefits program was not a viable option for the brown lung movement, in part because of the success, and cost, of the black lung program. What was originally expected to cost a total of $50 million was by 1980 claiming over $1 billion a year from the federal budget. Few legislators were willing to duplicate such a program for other occupational groups. In addition, textile workers, at least in North Carolina, perceived that the compensation system in that state was basically sound; reform was all that was needed.

By 1985, around $23 million had been paid for claims in North Carolina, the state with the largest number of textile workers. The 1,554 claimants who received these awards represented only 51 percent of those who applied, compared with a success rate of over 80 percent for miners and their widows prior to the 1982 amendments. Perhaps more important is the fact that those awarded compensation represented only 20 percent of those who, according to research, actually had the disease.[11] There was also a significant drop in the number of claims filed after 1981, when the CBLA lost most of its funding. Direct cutbacks in OSHA, CETA, and VISTA, as well as a more conservative mood among foundations, resulted in a substantial and relatively quick drop in the budget and, consequently, staff. Although industry argued that the mills were cleaner, CBLA representatives stated that the drop in claims simply reflected a reduction in the efforts to persuade sick, and often reticent, workers to file them.

At approximately the same time that southern textile workers were organizing the CBLA, asbestos workers were also having their consciousness raised about their own occupational health. Unlike Appalachian coal miners and southern millhands, these workers represented several types of industries all across the nation and were the victims of a product introduced by a third party, the asbestos manufacturer. Extensive exposure to the dust of asbestos can cause either cancer or asbestosis, a lung disease similar to pneumoconiosis and byssinosis. The workers called it white lung.[12]

Because of the prevalence of shipyards (where asbestos has been used in shipbuilding) and the strong occupational health movement of the previous decade, the first White Lung Association (WLA) was formed in Los Angeles, California, in 1979. Recognizing the need to be organized across the country, the WLA expanded to Maryland in 1980 and to New York and Alabama in 1981. By the late 1980s chapters had been opened in Illinois and South Carolina.

Unlike miners and millhands, those who worked with asbestos shared little by way of work experience, culture, or history. In addition, bringing people together from all over the country was difficult and expensive. However, creative people in the movement were able to translate the asbestos removal process, which was sweeping the country in the wake of information about the effects of the material, into a profit-making venture. WLA representatives, intimately familiar with the use of asbestos in construction, designed plans and trained personnel in asbestos removal, transferring some of the profits back to the organization.

The purpose of the WLA (like that of the BLA and the CBLA) was to organize and aid the victims of asbestos exposure and to educate the general public about the dangers of asbestos. While victims often filed state worker compensation claims against their employer, they also filed third-party suits against the asbestos manufacturer. These claims were hampered when many asbestos companies filed for bankruptcy in 1982. Although a trust was established in 1986 to handle the claims of the Manville Corporation, the largest asbestos producer, the money available would not come close to paying off the 17,000 claims prior to 1982 and the approximately 100,000 claims since. *Asbestos Watch*, the newsletter of the WLA, lamented: "The Trust is also legally responsible for payments to Manville, the government and other asbestos companies, their insurers and distributors. Unfortunately for victims, these claims take precedence over—and have to be paid before—the victims' claims."[13]

The Breath of Life Organizing Campaign

By the early 1980s, many involved in these occupational health movements recognized that there had to be a better way to compensate victims of occupational diseases. They were also concerned about the increasing inactivity on the part of the federal government with regard to occupational health, even though a 1979 government study had revealed that one of every five people receiving Social Security Disability Benefits had become disabled through working conditions, and that only 5 percent of all occupational disease victims ever received state compensation from their employers.[14]

A National Commission on State Workmen's Compensation Laws had concluded in 1972 that state programs did not adequately compensate the victims of industrial diseases. By 1979, no state was in compliance with the commission's nineteen essential recommendations, and no federal legislation that dealt directly with state workers' compensation laws had come close to passage in Congress.[15]

The Breath of Life Organizing Campaign (BLOC) was begun in Kentucky in August 1981 when members of the BLA convened a meeting of representatives of their own group, the WLA, and the CBLA. Two motives attracted the coal miners to a coalition with other occupational disease groups. First, they recognized that it would be difficult to maintain the Black Lung Benefits Program indefinitely. The Black Lung Benefits Reform Act of 1977 made coal companies responsible for full payment of black lung benefits directly to miners. A Trust Fund (financed by a royalty of $.50 a ton on underground coal and $.25 a ton on surface coal) was set up for those miners who had the disease but could not identify one responsible operator. The intent was to hold coal companies responsible for their past neglect and to build an incentive for operators to hold down dust levels in the mines.[16] However, the vast majority of claims approved (about 85 percent from 1977 to 1981) were challenged by the companies, which meant that the payments to the claimants, by law, had to be picked up by the Trust Fund. In addition, many of the companies were remiss in paying what they owed the Fund, resulting in serious shortages that required the Fund to borrow money at high interest rates. In effect, the companies were able to shirk their responsibility and to put the burden of paying claimants on the taxpayer.

The second motive for building a coalition was simple concern for other workers. According to Paul Seigel of the CABLA, members were aware that achieving a Black Lung Benefits Program was part of the fight for all working people. This was especially emphasized in Chicago, where the association was linked more closely to the struggles of the working class and poor in the Uptown region of the city. Bill Worthington, former BLA president from Kentucky and chair of the BLOC board of directors, had stressed for years that the black lung struggle was to be part of a broader occupational health movement. The Black Lung Benefits Program was targeted for attack by the Reagan administration precisely because it was an example to other workers. Consequently, the miners recognized the need for a broad-based movement on the national level. The only way to save the plan was to broaden it.[17]

Several 1981 planning meetings for BLOC led to the first Congress of Disabled Workers, held in North Carolina in 1982. More than 150 disabled workers from fifteen states, representing the coal, textile, and asbestos industries, as well as medical and legal professionals supportive of the broader occupational health movement, were in attendance.

The potential problems of bringing such a diverse group together were evident in the opening prayer:

> We face a difficult task. We are each limited by our own individual desires and experiences. Yet we are pulled toward oneness by the desires and experiences we share as a class. Lord, this is your world; we know you have called us to this struggle and we thank you for giving us what we need to overcome. . . . Help us together to resolve who are our real friends and who are our enemies. Help us to discover those ways in which we can unite all our brothers and sisters and keep us from being fooled and divided by our enemies.[18]

However, most anticipated differences failed to materialize. As one observer noted, "It was remarkable to see how people clicked together."[19]

Some in the BLA thought that such a coalition might siphon off energy and resources from their own group, but these fears were quickly dispelled. All present had similar stories to share about their breathing difficulties, about problems with lawyers and compensation hearings, and about efforts to improve health conditions in the workplace. Although the settings were different, the stories had a familiar ring. A bond was established, with their common experiences providing the glue.

They also shared a common ideology, believing that, as a class, they bore the major burden of occupational disease in the United States. The economic and political environment of the early 1980s resulted increasingly in the sacrifice of workers' health, safety, and compensation programs to save, or perhaps even increase, corporate profits. The significance of a class-based struggle was evident throughout the meetings of BLOC, as reflected in the following resolutions from a political action workshop:

> If we are to achieve our goals—a safe, healthy workplace and guaranteed compensation for victims of occupational disabilities—we must undertake mass political action built on the broadest political base. The value of this approach has been proven by our history. For example, miners won the first federal law which recognized and compensated victims of occupational disease through this mass collective action—thousands of miners struck and stopped coal production in many Eastern states. It was this type of action that forced the politicians to pass the Black Lung Act.[20]

A "unity" workshop was established to build cohesion between the representatives of the three associations. Participants proposed a system of intercommunication between both the leadership and the members, utilizing such means as a BLOC directory, newsletters, joint publications, and press campaigns. With the exception of one newsletter, however, none of these proposals were implemented. Nor has the coalition, as yet, mobilized the national class-based political movement that was originally envisioned. Only one subsequent Congress of Disabled Workers was held, and two meetings of representatives from each association were held in 1985 and 1987 to finalize a plan formulated in the two congresses for the most visible product of the coalition—a federal occupational disease compensation program.

A Federal Compensation Program

The early years of the Reagan administration witnessed a serious attack on the working population of the United States, especially those who were disabled. With regard to black lung benefits, Reagan wanted to restrict eligibility to those who were "truly medically disabled." Rather than blame the insolvency of the Trust Fund on the failure of companies to meet their financial responsibility, the new administration argued that lax statutory and administrative procedures had turned the coal miners' benefit program into an "automatic pension." The charge stemmed from a 1980 study by the General Accounting Office, which argued, based upon a medical report published in the *Journal of the American Medical Association*, that 88 percent of all black lung claimants certified as eligible "were either not disabled or could not be proved to have black lung."[21] Although both studies were heavily criticized for their research methods, they influenced new amendments passed in 1981 that significantly reduced the number of claims approved for black lung benefits in the 1980s.

Attacks on disabled workers in general were based on a similar report completed in 1980. The Disability Insurance National Pilot Study claimed that one-third of the beneficiaries of Social Security programs for the disabled should be denied benefits, and it recommended a review of many of these cases. This is significant to the occupational health struggle because only one out of eight injured or diseased workers ever receives workers' compensation; most apply for some other type of transfer payment, often Social Security Disability Insurance. Between 1981 and 1982, SSA removed from the disability rolls almost 50 percent of the million or so cases it reviewed, primarily by changing the definition of "disabled."[22]

In response to this onslaught, BLOC developed a Toxic Substances Disease Compensation and Prevention Act to educate the public about the plight of diseased and disabled workers and the features of a just compensation system. The act was based primarily on several lessons that emerged from the struggles of the BLA and secondarily on the experiences of southern textile and asbestos workers. First, state and federal workers' compensation laws governing occupational disease failed in many cases to provide prompt and equitable compensation. Second, federal action was needed to relieve the burden this situation placed upon the victims of exposure to toxic substances and their families. Third, the health of American workers and citizens was dependent upon linking adequate compensation for victims of toxic exposure to the prevention of work-related diseases in a comprehensive nationwide system. Finally, a fair and efficient program of federal compensation was necessary to reduce the uncertainty for victims inherent in the litigation system.[23]

Several aspects of the proposed system not only deviate from current programs but also address many of the problems experienced over the past two decades by retired and disabled workers trying to obtain compensation. These problems fall into four categories: the overall administration of the compensation system; funding of compensation claims; the filing and processing of claims; and the evaluation of claims.

First, the program of compensation established by this act would be administered by a nonprofit corporation, tentatively titled the National Workers' Occupational Disease Compensation Corporation. Of the thirteen members of the corporation's board of directors, seven would be disabled workers covered by the provisions of the act. Three would be medical doctors trained in occupational disease caused by toxic substances, and no more than two board members could be representatives of private industry. The board would also appoint a medical panel to consider medical questions raised in claims filed under the act. The dominance of disabled workers on the proposed board reflected the BLA's long and arduous struggle with the bureaucratic heads of the Black Lung Benefits Program, the Social Security Administration, and the Department of Labor. It was assumed not only that disabled workers would be more sympathetic to the plight of other victims of occupational disease, but that they would also be less susceptible to the dictates of the bureaucratic system. Similarly, the requirement that physicians on the board be trained in occupational health reflected the fact that few physicians had such training (from 1960 to 1968, only thirty-eight physicians in the United States had completed three years of residency in this field),[24] so that decisions about compensation were often influenced by doctors with little experience in the area.

Second, the act would establish a National Workers' Compensation Pool for Victims of Toxic Substances. The basic idea for the pool came from the Black Lung Benefits Trust Fund, but with some important additions. Participation in the pool would be mandatory for any business that was engaged in the manufacture, sale, use, or handling of a material that contains one or more listed toxic substances. Assessments for funding would be based on the number of employees exposed in each of these industries and businesses. Where applicable, assessments would also be based on Social Security Disability and workers' compensation benefits paid, as well as any other evidence of disability or disease resulting from exposure to toxic substances.

Third, a key factor in eligibility would be a rebuttable presumption. If a worker had been exposed to a toxic substance and developed a disease known to be associated with that substance, it would be rebuttably presumed (meaning that the company would have to prove otherwise) that the disability resulted from the exposure. Although the Black Lung Benefits Reform Act of 1977 established a rebuttable presumption for coal miners, most workers must prove the association between their disease and exposure at the workplace. There would be no deadline or time limit with regard to the filing of claims, and claimants would be entitled to a representative of their own choosing, who could be a lay person or an attorney. Recognizing that much of the money paid to victims over the last two decades, between 25 and 35 percent, has in fact gone to lawyers, the proposed program would minimize, if not eliminate, the need for legal representation.

The claimant's treating physician would be given primary weight in evaluating claims, and the claimant would be entitled to review all medical evaluations made by any employer and could at any time submit further evidence in support of her or his claim. This provision addresses three fundamental questions in occupational health: who defines an occupational disease, what evidence can be presented, and does the worker have access to all information?

In addition, BLOC proposed fines and/or imprisonment for failure to notify an employee of the potential health hazard from exposure to a toxic substance; failure to notify an employee of disease discovered during a physical examination; failure to correct a hazardous situation within a reasonable period of time; and failure to notify the pool of the use or presence of a toxic substance. All fines assessed would be awarded to the pool, thereby increasing the funds available for compensation.

This federal compensation proposal was finalized in 1989 as the Toxic Substance Disease Compensation and Prevention Act (TSDCPA). As a nonprofit organization, BLOC could not lobby for legislation. But Congress was not the direct target for its efforts; rather, the thrust was to educate the public about the needs of diseased and disabled workers and to illustrate the features of a just compensation system.

Lessons from BLOC

What lessons can be learned from this effort at coalition building by an Appalachian grassroots organization? First, it is increasingly important to link the struggles of workers in Appalachia to similar battles outside the region. The problems of preventing occupational disease and compensating those afflicted are similar throughout the nation: corporations are primarily interested in profits; the government, at both state and federal levels, while sympathetic at times, responds erratically without constant pressure; and the medical profession lacks sufficient knowledge, and technology, to separate work-related from non-work-related diseases. The result is that the struggle for occupational health and safety, like so many other workers' battles, is necessarily a political conflict.

In bad economic times, broad-based coalitions become even more important. As Smith points out, economic despair has settled into the Appalachian region, and the "workplace is being reorganized and new technology introduced at a time of rank and file weakness."[25] Of special significance is the recent use of longwall mining machines, which stir up even more clouds of dust than the continuous mining machinery that many have blamed for the increase in black lung cases in the last three decades.

The political climate also requires a broader-based approach. Not only have attacks on the Black Lung Benefits Program substantially increased the number of claims denied over the last decade; the major government agency responsible for guaranteeing the health and safety of our nation's workers, OSHA, is increasingly unable to do its job. Primarily because of substantial cuts in funding and resources, it inspects only 4 percent of the country's 4.6 million workplaces each year.[26]

A second lesson is that "community," often the foundation for collective action, is not necessarily bound by geographic terrain. Workers' common experiences in the fight for their own health can be an important component of a broader effort for social change. Members of BLOC shared a common experience—a lung disease that profoundly affected each of them and their families. In addition, they shared a common struggle—with the medical and legal professions, the compensation system, the government, and industry—which created a communal bond that cut across occupational boundaries. The Breath of Life Organizing Campaign certainly drew much of its impetus from the failure of state workers' compensation systems to adequately repay the damage done to workers. But it also emerged out of a shared sense of injustice and victimization that bound this group of disabled workers together.

The number of disabled workers who participated in BLOC activities was small, never more than a few hundred. The same could be said of the associations from which BLOC emerged: gatherings of retired and disabled workers from the coal, textile, and asbestos industries rarely attracted more than a hundred people at any one time—and most of these were initially interested simply in getting financial compensation for their affliction. Only a few had their consciousness raised to the point where this individual motivation was transformed into a collective incentive for participation. In addition, age and illness contributed to a high mortality rate for many active and potential participants. Bill Worthington, chair of BLOC's board of directors, died in 1985, and leaders from all three associations, many with valuable experience, became ill and often unable to function. Consequently, much of the work of grassroots organizations like the Black, Brown and White Lung Associations, as well as BLOC itself, has to be carried on by supportive, and often younger, activists and professionals.

All of this suggests a third lesson: that grassroots occupational health struggles, particularly those oriented to addressing issues of compensation for retired and disabled workers, must build coalitions that incorporate the knowledge and experience of both workers and professionals. This was certainly the case with the completion of the TSDCPA, where many of the legal and medical issues had to be worked out by people with expertise in those respective areas. Although at times supported by the collective action of large groups of active miners, the BLA was able to accomplish most of its goals with a relatively small group of retired and disabled miners and a few supporters. Some sociologists call this a "professional social movement,"[27] one composed of a small actual membership but a large group of beneficiaries, with its functions being carried out by various "professional" organizers. BLOC reflected a similar model. Perhaps the complexity of the world of work today mandates that we change our conception of what a "workers' movement" must necessarily look like.

Finally, the BLOC alliance encourages us to consider that outcomes of this type of coalition building may be more "idea"- than "action"-based, sometimes with the ideas emerging out of the action. Even though BLOC was unable to mobilize a class-based political movement for social change, it did create a model for a national workers' compensation program. The core notions of the TSDCPA reflect almost two decades of the struggles of workers in three industries for a healthier workplace and for compensation to those afflicted by occupational illness. The most significant aspect of this proposed change is a shift in the overall responsibility of a compensation program to those most affected by work-related diseases—disabled workers themselves.

Notes

1. For further information on the black lung movement, see William Denman, "The Black Lung Movement: A Study in Contemporary Agitation" (Ph.D. diss., Ohio University, 1974); Bennett M. Judkins, "The Black Lung Association: A Case Study of a Modern Social Movement" (Ph.D. diss., University of Tennessee, 1975); Bennett M. Judkins, *We Offer Ourselves as Evidence: Toward Workers' Control of Occupational Health* (New York: Greenwood Press, 1986); J. Davitt McAteer, *Coal Mine Health and Safety: The Case of West Virginia* (New York: Praeger, 1970); and Barbara E. Smith, *Digging Our Own Graves:*

Coal Miners and the Struggle Over Black Lung Disease (Philadelphia: Temple University Press, 1987). For further information about the miners' reform movement, see Paul F. Clark, *The Miners' Fight for Democracy: Arnold Miller and the Reform of the United Mine Workers* (Ithaca: New York State School of Industrial and Labor Relations, Cornell University, 1981); and Brit Hume, *Death and the Mines: Rebellion and Murder in the United Mine Workers* (New York: Grossman, 1971).

2. Brit Hume, "Coal Mining: The Union," *Atlantic Monthly*, November 1969, 23. See also Chapter 9 by Richard Couto in this volume.

3. Henry N. Doyle, "The Impact of Changing Technology on Health Problems in the Coal Mining Industry," in *Papers and Proceedings of the National Conference on Medicine and the Federal Coal Mine Health and Safety Act of 1969*, June 15–18, 1970 (Washington, D.C.: U.S. Government Printing Office, 1970), 195–97.

4. Smith, *Digging Our Own Graves*, 159.

5. Senator Richard Schweiker, in *Legislative History, 1975*: 2014–15.

6. *Black Lung Bulletin*, February 1974, 1.

7. Chicago Area Black Lung Association, *Disabled Miners in Chicago Tell Their Own Story*, rev. ed. (Chicago: CABLA, 1978), 3.

8. Undated letter to BLA chapters, probably early 1982.

9. Author's interview with Mike and Kathy Russell, early staff members of the Carolina Brown Lung Association, May 24, 1982. For further information about the Highlander Center, see Chapter 2 in this volume by John Glen, and Chapter 12, by Guy and Candie Carawan.

10. For further reading on the Brown Lung Association, see Bennett M. Judkins and Bart Dredge, "The Brown Lung Association and Grass Roots Organizing," in *Hanging by a Thread: Social Change in Southern Textiles*, ed. Jeffery Leiter, Michael D. Schulman, and Rhonda Zingraff (Ithaca, N.Y.: ILR Press, 1991), 121–36; Judkins, *We Offer Ourselves as Evidence*, esp. chap. 7, 8, and 9; and Bart Dredge's forthcoming dissertation at the University of North Carolina at Chapel Hill: "A Modern Social Movement Organization: Byssinosis and the Carolina Brown Lung Association, 1974–1989." Finally, political scientist Robert Botsch is in the final stages of a book for Temple University Press tentatively titled "Organizing the Breathless."

11. Compiled by the author from monthly reports provided by the North Carolina Industrial Commission.

12. For further information about asbestos and "white lung," see Paul Brodeur, *Outrageous Misconduct: The Asbestos Industry on Trial* (New York: Pantheon, 1985).

13. "Healthy Manville Immune from Suits, Victim's Trust Works to Solve Payment Problems," *Asbestos Watch* 6 (November/December 1988) : 1.

14. *People's Respirator* 1:1 (1985) : 4. "The People's Respirator" was the nickname of the BLOC campaign, as well as the name of its newsletter.

15. Peter S. Barth, "On Efforts to Reform Workers' Compensation for Occupational Diseases," in *Current Issues in Workers' Compensation*, ed. James Chelius (Kalamazoo, Mich.: W. E. Upjohn Institute, 1986), 327–45.

16. "Miners Protest Black Lung Cuts," *Mountain Life & Work* (March 1981) : 16.
17. Author's telephone interview with Paul Seigel, Chicago Area Black Lung Association, May 29, 1991.
18. From the invocation by Marilyn Hunter, reprinted in "Resolutions Adopted by the First Congress of Disabled Workers," Durham, N.C., September 17–19, 1982.
19. Author's telephone interview with Milt Gordon, Appalachian Research and Defense Fund, May 27, 1991.
20. Resolutions from the Political Action Workshop, Durham, N.C., September 17–19, 1982.
21. "Miners Protest Black Lung Cuts," 14.
22. "Disabled Workers Lose SS Benefits," *People's Tribune*, January 17, 1983, 7.
23. "The Toxic Substance Disease Compensation and Prevention Act of 1989," developed by the Breath of Life Organizing Campaign at the First and Second Congresses of Disabled Workers and subsequent meetings.
24. Frank Goldsmith and Lorin E. Kerr, *Occupational Safety and Health* (New York: Human Sciences Press, 1982), 36–37.
25. Smith, *Digging Our Own Graves*, 217.
26. "OTA Report Is Critical of Workplace Protection," *Nation's Health*, May/June 1985, 1, 5.
27. John D. McCarthy and Mayer Zald first wrote about this phenomenon in *The Trend of Social Movements in America: Professionalization and Resource Mobilization* (Morristown, N.J.: General Learning Press, 1973). I have discussed this with regard to the Black Lung Association in *We Offer Ourselves as Evidence*, esp. chap. 10.

PART III

CULTURE, CLASS, AND GENDER IN APPALACHIAN RESISTANCE MOVEMENTS

12

Sowing on the Mountain
Nurturing Cultural Roots and Creativity for Community Change

Guy and Candie Carawan

We talk here of sowing. We have had the good fortune to be a part of some intense movements for social change in the American South in our role as cultural staff members since 1959 at the Highlander Center in Tennessee. These include the civil rights movement in the Deep South, the anti–strip mine movement in the Appalachian mountains, the ongoing struggle for equity for coal miners, and the environmental movement currently evolving into a broader movement for social justice. We have lived in communities rich in grassroots cultural expression. What we have tried to sow is support for that important cultural thread that is part of the fabric of struggling for change.

We came to the Appalachian mountains from the civil rights movement, a time of powerful singing and the flowering of real life drama and poetry as part of change.[1] We had lived in the sea islands off the coast of South Carolina, a world in which many layers of African culture remained and flourished, where we participated in a citizenship education program designed to help black residents gain the literacy skills required to register and vote.[2] We had participated in civil rights campaigns in a number of southern cities and in many civil rights workshops at Highlander.

Through these experiences we had learned much about how cultural traditions can sustain and strengthen resistance movements. At Highlander there was a thirty-year history of building music, poetry, drama, into every gathering, and not just at the end of an evening as entertainment. We knew that when people meet to talk about hard problems, singing commonly known songs together—religious or secular—contributes to the energy and hope needed to go on. We had also learned that something enriching happens when older people are present and share stories, songs, knowledge, and skills from their life experiences.[3] We knew that commonly known art forms could be adapted to suit new situations. We had seen dozens of spirituals, hymns, and popular songs adapted in the civil rights movement to speak to both universal goals and very specific events. We were interested to see how many of these lessons would apply in mountain communities.

When we came to the mountains in the late 1960s, Appalachia faced problems of extreme poverty, a low level of social services, a dependency on a personally humiliating form of welfare, and corrupt local politics tied closely to the coal industry and powerful landholding companies. Many Appalachians shared a low level of self-esteem that was fostered by some mainstream institutions. Television in particular, and the media in general, regularly stereotyped and degraded mountain people. Regional schools and colleges failed to promote an appreciation of the unique cultural heritage of Appalachian youth.[4]

Fortunately, traditional cultures and time-tested values are tenacious, especially in communities where people have long had to rely on their own wits to survive. Many "hillbillies" held firmly to their traditions and kept them alive for a time when they would be more widely recognized as special and valuable. But in the mid-1960s, mountain culture was not praised or honored publicly, and these folks were mostly in their own kitchens and back porches or in small gatherings of friends in the local gas station or storefront.

When Gurney Norman, a gifted east Kentucky writer, came back to the mountains after studying in California, he could not *find* the music, though he knew it was going on somewhere. Ironically, he had come to a new appreciation of it while on the west coast.

> It was in California that I learned to appreciate Kentucky in a way I never had before, because people said, "Oh, you're from Kentucky? Tell us about Bill Monroe. Tell us about Bluegrass music," or "Can you pick and sing?" But I was out of touch with it. The thing that was clear to me was that all these people were admiring the very stuff that I had rejected. So this opened up the possibility for me to admire it, too. At a friend's house in Palo Alto, California, there was a Roscoe Holcomb record, *Mountain Music of Kentucky*. And that was the first time I ever heard Roscoe. Well, to make a long story short, I began to open up to what was happening in Perry County, where I'd grown up.[5]

Around that time Appalachia was being "discovered" again by others, including Presidents John Kennedy and Lyndon Johnson. Johnson declared a "War on Poverty," with Appalachia as one of the major battlegrounds. Besides providing some relief—warding off actual starvation in a number of mountain homes—the "war" brought an onslaught of people from outside the region with lots of different ideas and things to try. The mountain people were often challenged to look at themselves anew and to defend their values and their experiences. The last half of the 1960s was a time of ferment and change—a complicated era with very mixed results.

Pike County, Kentucky, 1967

Our first home in the mountains was Hellier, Kentucky, one of the tiny coal mining towns built alongside the railroad in the Marrowbone Creek section of Pike County. Because of the "war" on poverty, there was an "army" of volunteers spending the summer in the mountains—young VISTA workers who were hoping to go into the Peace Corps. Many were assigned to the Appalachian Volunteers, a group of youthful mountain residents working for community improvements, which by 1967 was funded in large part by the federal government. Trying to guide these enthusiastic young volunteers were some seasoned community members who had been concerned for many years about the problems in the area and, while skeptical, were willing to see if this new infusion of young workers and federal funds might accomplish anything.

The Highlander Center was working with these community leaders, helping to clarify issues and collectively strategize about dealing with them. One such leader, Edith Easterling, was hoping to start a folk school based on the Highlander principles of education. She wanted a place where Appalachian people could come together in a democratic atmosphere, discuss their problems, and look for solutions.

Edith invited us to join her in Pike County to see what could be done about enlivening the community improvement campaign with music. We were to learn a great deal from Edith, her husband Jake, and the rest of her family. We initially spent time getting to know people, looking particularly for singers and musicians, good talkers, tale-tellers, dancers, and square dance callers. Once acquainted, we invited these people to share their skills and talents at the community meetings held in a variety of homes and small clapboard buildings. The room would gradually fill with folks concerned about their deteriorating roads, the quality of education for their children, the lack of jobs, the ever-pressing dangers and conflicts around coal mining. Edith and other leaders felt that music and dance helped lift people's spirits at these problem-solving gatherings:

> It makes a big difference to have a whole group of people singing, dancing, clapping together. It gives you more strength and more courage within

yourself. The music is one of the really important things in getting groups together. It puts people's minds at ease and helps them spread their love from breast to breast. It makes a connection.[6]

We organized a series of jamborees—evenings to give people a chance to enjoy each other's music, dance, humor. There did not seem to be public settings for this to happen in Pike County, and later we realized that this situation was common in other mountain communities as well. Once community cultural celebrations were a natural conclusion to a season of farming, a barn raising, a sorghum stir-off. By the mid-1960s, people tended to be watching television in their own living rooms. In some communities, dances had become associated with drinking and violence, and it was simpler just to cancel them and stay at home. People had been out of touch and seemed to enjoy coming out to sing and play for the community. Some of the gatherings were designed to interest people in the Marrowbone Folk School, which Edith hoped would be an important resource for the community, so there would be announcements about upcoming meetings and ways to become involved.

We ran into problems and learned from our mistakes as we came to better understand the mores and attitudes along the hollows. Some community members, active church-goers, were opposed to dancing. Initially there was a bit of disapproval voiced about the jamborees. But gradually more people began to come out as they heard that there was spirited music, singing, informal visiting, and no drinking.

We experimented with group singing at the jamborees and at community meetings. We were interested in the potential of group song in the mountains, thinking of the powerful singing at mass meetings and demonstrations in the Deep South. Here people were used to singing together at church, so that many of the songs they knew in common were gospel and older religious songs. There were also popular country and bluegrass songs that everybody knew and folk songs out of an older tradition, but some of these were to be listened to rather than sung together. There is a strong solo ballad tradition in the mountains, where a story is spun out by the singer. We did find people ready to sing together such songs as "Amazing Grace," "I'll Fly Away," "Somebody Touched Me," and a mountain version of "We Shall Not Be Moved."

We were curious about whether new songs had been written, or older ones adapted, to talk about current concerns. In 1967 this seemed to be a new idea to most people, though Michael Kline, a talented songwriter working as an Appalachian Volunteer, was traveling the region singing with people and beginning to rework familiar songs and write new ones.

One of the first experiences we had in the mountains of this process of adapting songs was on a long bus ride with people from Pike County going to Owensboro to protest against strip mining at a statewide hearing. People sang hymns and gospel songs on the bus and as the group assembled in front of the motel where government officials were meeting. We had the good fortune to sit next to a disabled coal miner with a big, powerful voice and a wide repertoire of songs. When he sang "Sowing on the Mountain," Guy started supplying verses about strip mining: "stripping on the mountain, pollution in the valley . . . look at what your greed has done to the mountain . . . you're going to reap just what you sow." The singer was George Tucker, a banjo-player and an expressive singer of coal mining songs, religious songs, humorous songs, and stories. By the time we got back from the long ride, several other songs had been adapted and sung many times by the group on the bus, and we had begun a friendship with George that would span many years.

The Anti–Strip Mine Movement

Strip mining was a major problem for mountain families by 1967. The kind of destruction it brought to homes and farms was increasingly evident. Appalachian Volunteer Joe Mulloy put it this way:

> Strip mining is polluting our streams, ruining the surface of the land for farming, creating slides that destroy homes and property, causing the floods in the hollows to get worse, and sapping the wealth of the region. It just isn't right to undo in six weeks what it took nature thousands of years to do. The only way to end it is to organize people, to get them together to voice their demands.[7]

Organized opposition to strip mining in eastern Kentucky had been underway since 1965, when a group of neighbors in Knott County banded together to stop the destruction of land that had been in their families for generations. Calling themselves the Appalachian Group to Save the Land and People, they took strip mine operators to court and held off bulldozers with their bodies and, finally, with their guns.

As the demonstrations and protests increased, songs began to be a way of communicating about strip mining. "Strip Away, Big D-Nine Dozer . . . coming for to bury my home" was an adaption of "Swing Low, Sweet Chariot" by Michael Kline and Tom Bethel, two Appalachian Volunteers. Jean Ritchie, who periodically returned to her home place in Viper, Kentucky, wrote "Black Waters," describing the devastation that became more obvious to her on every trip. Billy Edd Wheeler, who grew up in the

West Virginia coalfields, wrote the angry "They Can't Put it Back," and Bill Christopher in Tennessee wrote "Nature's Lamentation": "Stripper, stripper, spare that tree / alas he would not heed / Perhaps a tree shall grow again / but a mountain has no seed." John Prine, whose people came from western Kentucky, graphically told what happened to their home town of Paradise. Other ballads and poems were written for the emerging folk heroes and heroines who stood off the bulldozers.[8]

An important person in this songmaking process was the aforementioned Michael Kline, who came from eastern West Virginia with a sharp wit and satirical hand at song writing. In the late 1960s he wrote a number of songs and adapted others that captured the spirit of the times in the Appalachian hills, and he encouraged others to do the same. He helped spread the songs written by other people as he traveled by jeep from one community to another. He also sought out and encouraged local musicians—the oldtimers and the youngtimers. He introduced us to many regional musicians and community leaders during our first months in the mountains, and later we planned workshops and gatherings together.

As the anti–strip mine activities intensified, so did the opposition. There was no problem as long as the VISTA volunteers and the AVs worked on painting schoolhouses or filling holes in the narrow little roads going up the hollows. But as soon as they began to support the local people in their protests and demonstrations against strip mining, they came under attack from local officials, many of whom were coal operators or closely tied to the industry.

In Pike County a group of local business and government leaders strategized on how to deal with what seemed to them a threatening situation, and the result was a midnight raid and the arrest of three poverty workers, who were charged with sedition. This charge was eventually dropped and the relevant law declared unconstitutional, but the arrests and the accompanying publicity (along with the bombing of one of their homes) created suspicion about the AVs and the VISTA workers.

In other counties, too, attempts at systemic change were thwarted and poverty workers undermined. Eventually the federal funding for the War on Poverty would come under the control of local officials who had a compelling stake in the status quo. As one mountain philosopher expressed it: "The poor people lost the War on Poverty. Congress forced them to lose it. They don't want poor people to organize and they don't aim for them to organize. But until they do organize, they'll never do no good."[9]

In this atmosphere we explored the uses of music. As the antipoverty work came under attack, the community more or less chose sides. Those who continued to come out to meetings and gatherings became more determined to really change things—to remove from office the entrenched "court house gang." Edith Easterling, who remained an out-spoken critic of the inequities in Pike County and the strip mining that was by now threatening her own home, was asked to leave her church and was called before the newly established Kentucky Un-American Activities Committee. She wore a bright red dress for her appearance and called the legislators by their first names, just as they addressed her.

But at the community meetings there would sometimes be a rumble from the back of the room and questions asked about whether some of the outsiders (ourselves included) might be communists. Thomas Ratliff, who was running for lieutenant governor in Kentucky, had this to say about the VISTA volunteers in Pike County:

> What you had was a bunch of damn long-haired barefoot beatniks and hippies running around town up to no good and setting up this High-lander folk school right in Pikeville. Why, they had a plan for infiltrating the schools and churches. They tried to start a Red Guard like in China with our teenagers. We don't want them. Let them go back to Berkeley where they belong.[10]

In some ways the cultural expression of this period increased as Michael Kline and others put together new satirical songs and musicians came out to local gatherings in the face of criticism, but the fear and sus-picion and overall tension worked against a feeling of unity and optimism in the community. Some of the meeting places were suddenly no longer available, including the large building Edith and her supporters were using for the Marrowbone Folk School. They decided to build a cinderblock community center on Easterling property, and did it with donated labor and materials.

By January 1968, after six months in Pike County, we felt we had gained a rudimentary understanding of the coal-dominated social and political realities in Appalachia, and some closer knowledge of its cul-tural traditions. We had ideas about the kind of cultural developments that might take place over a period of time. We definitely felt that singing and music could play a role in community improvement campaigns and in challenges to the inequitable social order—already new songs were being written and singing was becoming a part of local struggles. We were inter-ested in organizing workshops and gatherings that would bring together cultural workers and tradition-bearers on a regional basis.

A Cultural Affirmation

> It was clear to me after seeing the struggles on Clear Creek in Knott
> County in '65 and '66, that sheer force and muscle weren't going to win
> the War on Poverty or any other war. And that another way to go at it
> was through some sort of cultural affirmation in which people were en-
> couraged to sing their songs and tell their stories and maybe get some
> sort of vision together. I knew what had happened with the civil rights
> movement, and that vision-building was a very important part of that—
> much more important than arming people.[11]

Isolation was a problem in the mountains. People in one community often
did not realize that the same problems were being addressed in a neighboring area. Highlander is a networking center that has always tried to bring
together people who could benefit from the contact over shared concerns.
Beginning in the early 1970s, we held a series of workshops focusing on
various aspects of regional culture.

The first, in October 1972, was entitled "Mountain Movement Music" and gave special emphasis to the history and contemporary uses of
cultural expressions growing out of struggle—something often neglected
by the mass media and the educational institutions of the region. Together
with Michael Kline, we planned and organized a three-day meeting at
Highlander, making sure to invite strong culture-bearers who had written
hard-hitting songs during the union organizing days of the 1930s: Tillman
Cadle, Sarah Ogan Gunning, Florence Reece, Nimrod Workman. We also
invited younger people around the region who were writing songs about
current conditions in Appalachian communities, or who enjoyed providing music or dancing at community meetings or protest gatherings. From
Washington, D.C., we brought Hazel Dickens, who had grown up in the
West Virginia coalfields and written some of the most descriptive songs
yet heard about mining and its effects. George Tucker came over from
eastern Kentucky. Community leaders who had organized around strip
mining, welfare rights, and black lung took part. We took care to include
organizers and musicians from black communities in the mountains: Bill
Worthington, coal miner from Harlan County and pioneer in the black
lung movement, and Earl Gilmore, a gospel singer and song leader from
Clinchco, Virginia. There were also people who would, within the next few
years, be in a position to influence regional cultural developments through
their work with Broadside TV, the Foxfire Project, and Appalshop.

A Highlander workshop generally begins in a circle, with each participant speaking a little from his or her own experience. The understanding is that each person comes with experiences that are valid and from

Top: Hazel Dickens and Florence Reece at the Highlander Center. Florence celebrated her eighty-fifth birthday at the Center in 1986. (*Gary Hamilton*)

Bottom: Nimrod Workman speaks at a Highlander cultural workshop in 1972. The theme of the workshop was "Mountain Movement Music." Also in the circle are Hazel Dickens, Sparky Rucker, Sarah Ogan Gunning, Tillman Cadle, Myles Horton, George Tucker, Shelva Thompson, and Guy Carawan. (*Doug Yarrow*)

which others can learn. In cultural workshops people often sing of their experiences as well as telling about them, or they have put their thoughts into a poem or a story.

For the younger people this workshop offered the first opportunity to meet Nimrod, Sarah, Florence, George, and Tillman, and to be moved by their experiences, stories, and songs, and to come to know Hazel, who would become a role model for younger musicians. Some of those writing songs of struggle in the 1970s were unaware that they were joining a long tradition of protest in the mountains, though they had probably heard "Sixteen Tons" and "Dark as a Dungeon." Neither radio and television, the public school system, regional colleges, nor even the United Mine Workers at that time made it a priority to pass on the songs and poetry of struggle to people coming of age in the mountains. In turn, the younger people offered expressive material about contemporary issues.

There was spirited string music, dancing, and group singing, mainly of well-known hymns and union songs. Joe Begley, community leader and activist from Blackey, Kentucky, threatened to send us a bill for a new pair of shoes, claiming he had danced holes in his. Ted Carpenter, close friend and colleague of Mike Clark, the director of Highlander, brought to the workshop a small video camera, which he passed around during the weekend. Workshop participants recorded a vivid tape of singers, dancing, and conversations. Carpenter and Clark were instrumental in establishing Broadside TV, a video network that for several years used tapes to create dialogue between mountain communities and keep people informed and in touch with one another.

By the time the weekend was over, it was clear that a large number of new songs were being used to focus on problems in the mountains— a real contrast to the situation in 1967, when this process was just beginning. There were songs about the union struggles of the 1930s, the more recent organizing around strip mining and black lung, the "War on Poverty" period, the mine disasters still so prevalent in the coalfields, a reform movement in the United Mine Workers Union, and the feelings of people forced by economic need to migrate out of the region; there were also songs expressing hopes and dreams for the future.[12]

Many of us look back to that workshop as a starting point for a network throughout the mountains of people who would continue to work culturally and support each other in many ways. Appalshop, now a creative and vital center for the arts in the mountains, was in its formative years. It began as a collective of young people making films about the life they saw around them. Most were high school students in Whitesburg, Kentucky, though Appalshop would soon attract young people from throughout the region. Jack Wright, a singer, musician, and songwriter from southwestern Virginia who attended the workshop, was instrumental in starting June Appal Records as part of Appalshop. Its goal was to record and make available regional music, both old and new. The Foxfire Project in Rabun County, Georgia, building on the notion that young people can learn a great deal by spending time with the oldsters of the community and recording what they think and know, was another fledgling project. The musical heritage in Rabun County was yet to be discovered and tapped, but George Reynolds, a musician and a recent graduate in folklore who was at the workshop, would later add this dimension to the Foxfire work. A loose grouping of area musicians formed the Mountain Musicians' Co-operative following that weekend. The Cooperative was short-lived, but as Rich Kirby explains, "It was an indication of people who were musicians beginning to think collectively and regionally." [13] Rich himself is a long-term cultural worker, supporting regional artists and organizing gatherings as well as playing music. He currently manages the radio station at Appalshop.

The 1972 workshop at Highlander occurred against a backdrop of cultural ferment in the mountains that some have described as an Appalachian renaissance. A number of regional colleges began offering Appalachian Studies courses in the early 1970s, thanks to the work of some pioneering teachers and students. Helen Lewis, who would later join the Highlander staff, organized meetings of students and others to pressure for courses that offered an appreciation of regional culture and history and looked at social and economic issues in the mountains. There was also a coming home of people who had left the mountains: veterans returning from Vietnam, workers returning from urban centers in the North as one more coal boom began. Many would look with renewed interest and appreciation at mountain values and traditions. There was a cultural resurgence in public gatherings. A whole series of regional festivals grew up—at Pipestem, West Virginia, where Don West had an Appalachian Folklife Center; in nearby Ivydale, where Dave and John Morris designed a family and neighborhood music festival; at High Knob in southwestern Virginia, where Jack Wright and friends put on a festival that included bluegrass and country rock as well as folk music; the John Henry Memorial Festival, organized by Ed Cabbell with some help from Sparky Rucker, which paid tribute to the music and culture of black Appalachians. A group of Appalachian writers began meeting annually at Highlander to critique each other's work, and a group of theater activists came together to form a southern collective called Alternate Roots. Ron Short, working at Highlander at the time, was instrumental in bringing both of these groups together and would later join Appalshop's Roadside Theater as a writer, musician, and actor.

There began to surface a new determination to stay in the mountains and an Appalachian pride in the cultural expression, values, and
lifestyle of mountain people. This Appalachian renaissance provided an
underpinning to the social movements in the mountains in the 1970s.

Much of Highlander's educational work throughout the 1970s was
with miners and in communities greatly affected by coal. The staff worked
with groups on coalfield health and safety issues, environmental concerns,
and land ownership. Music usually played some part in the workshops at
Highlander and in much of the work in the field.

Appalachian coal communities have a distinctive culture. In addition to ballads, tales, and folk songs, string music, and religious songs
associated with the southern mountains, songs, stories, and poems have
been written to describe the specific dangers, working conditions, joys,
and sorrows of coal. Black people, bringing their own cultural heritage,
came from the Deep South to work in the mines and to build the railroad.
European immigrants came as well, and gradually the groups influenced
each other.

Between 1972 and 1982 Highlander hosted cultural workshops to
explore this history and focus on movements for change in the coalfields.[14]
Each was reflective of events in the region. Women, who had always
been deeply involved in coalfield struggles, organized to win jobs in the
mines. Women musicians, poets, and photographers flowered as well.[15]
Major strikes took place at Stearns and Jericol in eastern Kentucky, and
several disasters of the early 1980s reminded us that mining is still the
most dangerous occupation in America. At these workshops Myles Horton,
Highlander's former director, would remind participants that telling and
retelling coalfield horror stories—both past and present—is valuable only
if you go on to analyze the reasons for such occurrences and strategize
about what can be done.

We made an effort to increase the participation of black coalmining
families in the workshops. We were aware of the richness of black history
in the coalfields, but most African Americans tended to keep a low profile
in the community at large. Through our field work we got to know people
like community organizer Mattie Knight; Bill Turner, who knew the history of black mining communities through personal experience as well
as academic study; Lorenzo and Mary Ann Childress, both miners, who
with their children formed a gospel singing family; and Hugh Cowans,
a UMWA officer and preacher/activist, and Julia Cowans, both active in
fighting the Ku Klux Klan in Harlan County and both powerful singers
and talkers. In workshops at Highlander, away from the patterns of segregation in mountain communities, blacks and whites were able to share

common experiences and gain a new appreciation of each other's history and culture.

Affirmation in the Field

From 1976 through 1979 the people of Stearns, Kentucky, were on strike— the coal miners and their families pitted against the Blue Diamond Coal Company in a struggle for representation by the United Mine Workers of America. The major issues were safety and rank-and-file representation on a mine safety committee, rather than higher wages. Music was one element of the campaign at Stearns.

A few months into the strike, a delegation of miners and their families came to Knoxville to picket the Blue Diamond office. John Gaventa of the Highlander staff videotaped the demonstration and then put together an edited tape to show at a community meeting in Stearns. He dubbed in some songs about coal mining and struggle, including a song about the Blue Diamond Coal Company by Jean Ritchie. When the striking miners and their families viewed the tape, they were excited to see themselves confronting the company and to hear songs about coal—they had been unaware that such songs existed. John arranged for us to bring some musicians to the next rally at Stearns.

We invited Phyllis Boyens, Hazel Dickens, Sonny Houston, Rich Kirby, and Jack Wright, who introduced the miners and their support- ers to such songs as "Which Side Are You On?" "They'll Never Keep Us Down," and "We Shall Not Be Moved." Phyllis had a stirring version of "The Blue Diamond Mines," and some local musicians sang gospel and religious songs. The music lifted people's spirits, and the songs related to coal drew enthusiastic cheers. After the rally, the visiting musicians and singers went out to the picket site and helped spark an hour-long session of singing and dancing. It was the first time that women had been to the picket site, and it set a precedent for women to begin participating in the picketing.

This was the first of many visits to Stearns. We mimeographed songsheets with all the appropriate songs we could think of and distrib- uted a box of albums: *Come All You Coal Miners* from the 1972 Highlander workshop and Jean Ritchie's *Clear Waters Remembered*, which contained "The Blue Diamond Mines." People began to learn the songs and sing them at meetings and demonstrations. They came again to Knoxville and sang at the company headquarters and at its owner's home. Soon they began to adapt the songs to speak more specifically to their particular situation.

Phoebia Bowman, a Stearns high school student, wrote several long narrative ballads about the strike, naming names and covering the local scene
in great detail. The people in the community loved these songs, which
made them laugh, cry, and get angry. Now when we attended the rallies
and meetings, people would listen to the visiting musicians and join in
on some of the songs, and then would cheer and rise to their feet when
Phoebia sang her songs. Their movement was producing its own cultural
expression and telling its own history.

The people at Stearns became teachers and communicators. After a
particularly violent confrontation in which the miners and some of their
wives were arrested by state troopers for blocking the cars of scabs going
into the mines, representatives from Stearns began to travel and speak
to raise support for the strike. John Gaventa had been alerted to the
upcoming confrontation and was there with his video camera. No news-
people were at the scene, but his tapes were shown on national news. More
importantly, they were made into a documentary tape that traveled with
the miners when they went out to describe their situation.

As the women were shoved into paddy wagons to follow their husbands to jail, they sang, "We shall not be moved / We want a union
contract, / We shall not be moved / . . . Tell Blue Diamond, we shall not
be moved." The miners, who stayed in jail for many weeks, sang together
and were visited in jail by musicians. Singing was crucial to the network
of support around these men and their families.

During this period, whenever there was a cultural workshop at
Highlander, people from Stearns were invited to come and share the music
that had grown up around their struggle. They met sympathetic musicians,
who then came to Stearns for rallies and programs. Some of them organized concerts in their own communities to gain support for the miners.
The workshops at Highlander were among the places where solidarity was
built with groups from around the region, where people from Stearns felt
themselves a part of a long history of struggle.

In 1979 the union decided it was not possible to win at Stearns and
withdrew its support for the miners. The wounds in the community would
be a long time healing, but there was a group within it who had struggled
together for three years, had gone to jail together, had raised money and
support together, had sung together, and who would be united in spirit
even though the union was gone. They maintained their support for one
another until each family found new work, sometimes in a new location.
And they passed a lot of what they learned on to others. For example,
when UMWA miners struck Jericol in Harlan County, many Stearns families visited the local union office and the picket site, and in the mid-1980s,
when the union took on the A.T. Massey Coal Company, veterans from

Stearns crossed the mountain into West Virginia to strategize and add their wisdom.

When the Pittston strike came along in 1989, it was apparent that a lot had changed in the mountains, and that cultural confidence was now recognized as a requirement for standing up for your rights. The UMWA for the first time identified the musical resources available in the community as an important tool for rallying energy and support. The union made use of Harold Dutton, Curtis Franks, and others, who became the Picket Line Pickers, the Rabbit Ridge Pea Pickers, Edna Sauls and the spirited women of the Daughters of Mother Jones, the high school students who became the UMWA Youth Auxiliary, Pam Kane, Bill Mullins, Hoyt Kiser, and many more. The ten-month Pittston strike had a strong cultural underpinning: not only music, but camouflage fashion, whittling and dancing at the picket sites, large puppets, a theater piece on Mother Jones, and the establishment of Camp Solidarity, where supporters gathered every night for food, humor, string music, and singing as well as strategizing for the next day's events.[16] A group of women has put together an oral history of the strike so that its many lessons will not be lost. For us, it seemed a great evolution since the late 1960s. Cultural pride and expression had flowered and were taken for granted as part of community life and struggle.

You're Gonna Reap Just What You Sow

Our experience has taught us that music and other powerful cultural forms have a lot to do with resistance and survival. Resistance movements are strengthened by building on their own heritage and adding contemporary expressions from the new struggle. Singing together, even in the face of terrible difficulties, can be empowering. As the Reverend C. T. Vivian, a longtime friend from the civil rights movement, puts it:

> Music picks up people's spirits. Anytime you can get something that lifts your spirits and also speaks to the reality of your life, even the reality of oppression, and at the same time is talking about how you can really overcome—that's terribly important stuff. I don't see anyone having struggle separate from music. I think that a movement without music would crumble.[17]

Acknowledging history and learning from elders are equally crucial. It is important to feel you are part of a long line of fighters if you mean to stay involved and fight yourself. We are mindful of Myles Horton's warning: you must do more than just remember the hard times; you must also analyze the reasons and plan the resistance. And in doing so, it is essential to weave a cultural thread throughout gatherings and workshops because, as we have tried to show, cultural expression is unifying and empowering.

In two decades we have witnessed a cultural flowering in Appalachia—not only a renewed interest in traditional forms, but a powerful evolution of contemporary mountain culture for the 1970s and 1980s—a "hillbilly pride." There are more community workers who identify themselves as cultural workers. For this we are gratified. There is a tendency to underestimate the importance of cultural work, to feel that music and poetry, dance and humor, will naturally be a part of community life and attempts to challenge oppression or inequality. In our experience, this is not the case. The seeds for cultural expression are there, but cultivating and nurturing those seeds are also necessary. Not only is it important for individuals to seek out and encourage the richness of cultural expression; there also have to be organizations and institutions that recognize and support this work. We have been fortunate to be a part of one.

Notes

1. See Guy and Candie Carawan, eds., *Sing for Freedom: The Story of the Civil Rights Movement Through Its Songs* (Bethlehem, Pa.: Sing Out Publications, 1990).

2. See Guy and Candie Carawan, eds., *Ain't You Got a Right to the Tree of Life? The People of Johns Island, South Carolina—Their Faces, Their Words, and Their Songs* (Athens: University of Georgia Press, 1989).

3. Bernice Reagon, whom we met as a teenager in Albany, Georgia, and who went on to become director of the Program in Black American Culture at the National Museum of American History at the Smithsonian Institution, wrote to us that meeting Doc Reese, a survivor of the Texas prison system, Bessie Jones from the Georgia sea islands, and other older black folk artists at Highlander workshops during the civil rights era changed her life.

4. James Branscome, "Annihilating the Hillbilly: The Appalachians' Struggle with America's Institutions," *Katallagete* 3 (Winter 1971): 25–32.

5. Authors' interview with Gurney Norman, 1983.

6. Authors' interview with Edith Easterling, 1983.

7. Joe Mulloy, quoted in Guy and Candie Carawan, eds., *Voices from the Mountains* (Urbana: University of Illinois Press, 1982).

8. For additional information on local resistance to strip mining during this period, see Chapter 1 by Mary Beth Bingman in this volume. For more in-

formation on the anti–strip mine songs, see Carawan and Carawan, *Voices from the Mountains.*

9. Everette Tharp in Carawan and Carawan, *Voices from the Mountains*, 98.
10. *National Observer*, August 28, 1967.
11. Authors' interview with Michael Kline, 1984.
12. See Carawan and Carawan, *Voices from the Mountains*, and Rounder Records, *Come All You Coal Miners*, 1973. Both products grew out of the 1972 workshop.
13. Authors' interview with Rich Kirby, 1984.
14. See issues of *Highlander Reports* (the Highlander newsletter) from this period for further information on these workshops.
15. During this period an album of songs from the coalfields performed by women was produced: Rounder Records, *They'll Never Keep Us Down*, 1984.
16. See Jim Sessions and Fran Ansley's chapter on the Pittston strike in this volume (Chapter 10) and Richard Couto's description of Camp Solidarity (Chapter 9).
17. Authors' interview with the Reverend C. T. Vivian, 1983.

Resources

The following books and publications have been helpful to us in our analysis of cultural work in Appalachia.

BOOKS

Green, Archie. *Only a Miner.* Urbana: University of Illinois Press, 1972.
Whisnant, David E. *All That Is Native and Fine: The Politics of Culture in an American Region.* Chapel Hill: University of North Carolina Press, 1983.
Whisnant, David E. *Modernizing the Mountaineer: People, Power and Planning in Appalachia.* Boone, N.C.: Appalachian Consortium Press, 1981.

ONGOING PUBLICATIONS

Appalachian Journal, Appalachian State University, Boone, N.C. 28608.
Appalshop Notes, 306 Madison Street, Whitesburg, Ky. 41858.
Foxfire, P.O. Box B, Rabun Gap, Ga. 30568.
Goldenseal: West Virginia Traditional Life, Cultural Center, Capitol Complex, Charleston, W.Va. 25305.
The Mountain Eagle, Whitesburg, Ky. 41858.
Now and Then: The Appalachian Magazine, East Tennessee State University, Johnson City, Tenn. 37614.

13

Engendering the Struggle

Women's Labor and Traditions of Resistance in Rural Southern Appalachia

Mary K. Anglin

By class I understand an historical phenomenon, unifying a number of disparate and seemingly unconnected events, both in the raw material of experience and in consciousness. . . . I do not see class as a "structure," nor even as a "category," but as something which in fact happens . . . in human relationships.

E. P. Thompson,
The Making of the English Working Class

In examining the lives and labors of working-class Appalachian women at the close of the twentieth century, my concern is to illustrate the importance of analyses of gender to the study of waged labor and, further, to broaden the terms through which we think about labor and dissent. If economic conditions have rendered problematic not only the quality, but equally the prospect, of employment in the 1990s, they also serve to motivate activists and scholars to reexamine our assumptions about the location and meaning of waged work for members of the working class.

The study of work and protest in Appalachia involves an analysis of regional culture as a force that informs the construction of class consciousness, gender relations, and community life.[1] In this reading, regional culture is not construed in simple terms as the locus of folk ideology or a set of doctrinal structures underwritten by traditional authority. Rather, regional culture encompasses material resources, systems of kin/community ties, and pragmatic information about how to live in specific settings, in addition to perspectives on what is a life well-lived. It reflects a particular history and set of socioeconomic conditions, and is the means by which individuals come to terms with, or contest, these particularities.

This approach stands in contrast with prevailing schools of thought that have either romanticized Appalachian culture or dismissed it as the locus of exploitative policies imposed by agents of industrial capitalism.[2]

In this chapter I seek to establish a middle ground wherein Appalachian traditions are examined in light of the history of the region but are not reduced to the logics of capital accumulation.[3] Recent analyses that present southern and central Appalachia as regions with complex histories offer useful illustrations and resources.[4] From this vantage point, we can study the ways in which women and men, individuals and communities, remake tradition in the wake of deindustrialization and its attendant phenomena: plant closings, unemployment, inflation, and intensified expropriation of labor. Further, we can resurrect terms such as "dissent" and "class consciousness" while at the same time recognizing contradictory dimensions in the survival strategies employed by working-class women and men.

This approach to the study of culture(s) does not reject the possibility of hegemony, the appropriation of cultural forms under the aegis of the state and/or dominant classes.[5] Equally possible, however, is recourse to tradition by working-class and marginalized peoples as part of their efforts to contest the authority of elite groups. The study of regional culture in Appalachia thus involves an examination of forces in opposition: the (re)construction of culture to advance and to protest against capitalist relations. In other words, embedded within the constellation of practices and perspectives that constitute the cultural traditions of southern Appalachia is a history of interactions and struggles between inhabitants of the region and those who have sought to capitalize on the mountains.[6]

All these issues emerge in research on women's work in the mica industry of western North Carolina—a little-known industry whose history is largely chronicled in the annals of the U.S. Geological Society.[7] Our primary focus is on the reconfiguration of local custom within the mica factory through which women workers orchestrated their participation in factory labor. Women's activities did, on occasion, serve the interests of management, obscuring class interests through the language of kinship and presenting obeisance to management directives in the form of personal obligation. Nonetheless, women invoked tradition equally to legitimate their own authority in the factory and to contest particular practices in an industry whose cyclic history and steady decline in recent years offered laborers minimal job security, much less bargaining power.

Western Carolina Mica

The mountains of North Carolina contain a variety of minerals of sufficient quantity and economic value to attract the attention of local entrepreneurs and travelers to the region. Chief among these is mica, a nonmetallic mineral whose translucence and pliability once made it an object of trade and ceremonial use by the aboriginal inhabitants of the mountains.

Trade in mica by white settlers commenced in earnest in the late nineteenth century, when Edison's invention of the electric motor created a need for insulating materials.[8] Mica was ideal for this application, insofar as the mineral could be split into thin sheets that resisted currents of electricity. For these purposes, furthermore, small pieces of mica—the form most readily obtainable—were more than adequate.

With the establishment of this important market, prospecting and mining efforts escalated in the mountains of North Carolina. By the turn of the century, "mica houses" dotted the landscape, factories where blocks of mica were brought to be cleaned and split into sheets and then cut into patterns. Although western North Carolina was still largely oriented toward farming in this period, revenues from mica became increasingly important to household economies, and families sent young, unmarried daughters to labor in the mica houses.

Demand for the mineral was never constant, however, and banner years were followed by years of decline. Not only are mica veins unpredictable and mica mining an extremely risky venture, but orders were generated by the dictates of the electrical industry, which required only small amounts for purposes of insulation. World Wars I and II created greater demands for mica, and its use expanded to include airplane instrumentation and radio equipment. The mineral was designated a "strategic resource" by Congress in 1939, and federal programs were created to stimulate domestic mica production. At the same time, the U.S. government intensified efforts to find international sources of mica and subsidized research on synthetic alternatives.[9] These efforts notwithstanding, domestic stores of mica remained vital.

For more than two decades, western North Carolina, recognized as the primary source of domestic mica, was host to a succession of federal agents and programs.[10] Funds and equipment were made available at different times to encourage mica prospecting, and federal programs established artificially high prices for mica, the better to mobilize local populations for intensive production.[11]

Local response to these incentives was enormous. Companies were started to take advantage of lucrative government contracts, while families and individuals engaged in mining and processing as cottage industries. The ending of government subsidies in the 1960s had an equally dramatic effect on the mica industry of western North Carolina. Mining operations ceased, small companies went under, and unemployment rates soared in an already impoverished area. The collapse of the federal program did not destroy the mica industry in western North Carolina, however. Several companies established prior to the mica boom of the mid-twentieth century continue to produce mica parts on contract to the federal government and to electronics firms.[12]

This brief description of the mica industry suggests several observations. First and foremost, the history of mica makes evident the need to tie any analysis of labor relations to an examination of the economic cycles, past and present, within the industry. Given the problematic history of the industry in general and its depressed state in recent years, it makes sense that workers' demands are tied to their perceptions of the viability of their respective companies. Far from capitulation, this approach may be considered a form of pragmatism.

Second, as will become more evident, the mica industry has historically relied upon informal labor relations organized around seasonal cycles and households as units of production. Even during periods of intensive production, when government agents and factory entrepreneurs attempted to streamline labor processes, the force of this history served to counterbalance their efforts. In addition, the nature of mica itself—coming out of the ground in pieces of irregular shape and uneven quality—necessitated that workers exercise some initiative in labor processes.

Finally, analyses of labor relations in mica factories cannot be reduced to technological factors and economic formulas. Workers brought family ties and local history into the factories, in interactions with co-workers (many of whom were recruited through kin and community networks) and through expectations of work settings responsive to the conditions of rural life. Definitions of, or disagreements over, fair and just working conditions were framed in accordance with notions of regional tradition and based upon generations of experience in working in mica. Factory owners and local elites likewise traded upon regional custom, appropriating the languages of kinship and of Christian fundamentalism when it suited their purposes. All of this must be taken into consideration in analyses of work and protest.

Engendered Subjects

Throughout its history the mica industry relied on women to process raw mica as well as to cut it into various shapes and sizes with punch presses. Reasons cited by factory owners are reminiscent of explanations typically offered for women's work in other labor-intensive industries: women's legendary patience and fine motor skills, their willingness to work hard and for lower wages. Of equal interpretive value, it would seem, were the gendered divisions of productive labor in farm households, where women commonly engaged in skilled labor to craft produce for household consumption and for local markets.[13]

Such an argument seems particularly applicable to the mica industry of the mid-nineteenth century, which consisted of individual prospectors mining mica for sale to outside buyers. As the market for mica expanded in the late nineteenth century, more mines were opened by elites and by individual families, some of the latter becoming quite wealthy through this venture. Not only were some of the early mica houses an outgrowth of family operations, but individual households continued to process mica for sale to neighborhood merchants and mica concerns throughout the twentieth century.[14]

In household operations, men were responsible for mining and overseeing activities while women split and sorted the mica thus obtained.[15] Processing mica required knowledge and skill, and was of considerable economic importance, since the grading of mica was directly tied to its value on the market. If women were hard-working and long-suffering, they also performed skilled labor whose value was recognized by merchants and entrepreneurs, as well as heads of households.

It is not surprising, then, that the early factories employed a division of labor wherein women were responsible for the processing while men served primarily as overseers and machine-fixers—similar to the gendered divisions of labor employed in the textile mills of the North Carolina Piedmont.

Given the strong bonds between the planters and textile magnates of the Piedmont and the elites of the mountainous portion of the state, and the ties between northern capitalists and regional elites, such similarities seem far from coincidental. Rather, they suggest the exporting of paternalistic methods of labor control from the mill villages of the Piedmont to factories and other enterprises in the mountains.[16] Mica workers were governed by constant interaction with factory owners, whom they knew personally, and by the authority of supervisors who were kinsmen as well as bosses.[17]

Technological innovations of the twentieth century altered processing operations and displaced workers without completely offsetting the gender-based composition of the labor force. Women continued to make up the bulk of the workforce in mica factories, but their jobs were deskilled. Mica processing was mechanized where possible and governed by the principles of stretch-out and speed-up well known in the textile industry.[18] In the streamlining of the mica industry, in other words, women's labor became more expendable and more easily controlled.

In the factory where I conducted field research in 1988, roughly two-thirds of the workers were female, and most of them had been initiated into their work regimens under the auspices of kinswomen who had worked there previously. June Robbins and Zona Watson, for example, found employment through aunts who gently prodded them to look for work in the mica factory. June's story is characteristic of this passage:

> I was about twenty-three years old, and my aunt come over and said, "Let's go down to Moth Hill and ask for a job." I said, "What do you mean?" I wasn't even wanting a job, you know! We went down there and she asked for a job. I didn't even ask, but they told us to come in to work at nine the next day. (Interview no. 5, 1987)

Even though June Robbins confused "mica plate" (sheets of laminated mica) with dinnerware in her initial assessment of her new job, and was clearly less than enthusiastic about the prospect of working for a wage, she went to work the next day and remained at Moth Hill for more than forty years.

Zona Watson's aunt had previously worked at Moth Hill and introduced her niece to the "old hands" in the factory. Zona's aunt preferred the older methods of "laying mica plate," which involved hand labor and greater worker control. Zona, however, went to work on the machines— again, under the auspices of the "old hands" who trained her and supported her claim to that assignment:

> And this woman from Cove Creek, she was cutting off [mica] plate on that machine, there where I've worked on all these years. She wanted me to cut off for her, and I would. And she'd sometimes rest and go over there and patch [the machine-made mica plate]. When she told [the son of the factory owner] that she was quitting, she said, "Let Zona have that machine." And they did. Junior Willis was there then, so that's how . . . I got started. I didn't know a lot of them [at first] but I learned a lot of people, a lot that's dead now. (Interview no. 7, 1988)

Women at Moth Hill Mica Company thus confronted two contradictory tendencies: the legacy of women's productive labor reflected in both family histories and the continuance of women as the primary workforce in the mica factory and, on the opposing end, their experience of marginalization in a declining industry. This dual context informed women's daily work lives, and they responded to it through departmental networks that asserted kin and community ties over and against the alienation of factory labor.[19] That was not all, as Annie Burleson explained: "Whenever anyone [at the factory] gets sick, we take up a collection and look out for each other. It's our family. Whenever you've been together for twenty-six or thirty years, it's [y]our family" (Interview no. 29, 1988). Equally important, workers looked out for each other *on* the job. The old hands recruited neighbors and kin for new work assignments in the factory, as had been the case with Zona and June, and trained them in the processes and politics of Moth Hill.[20]

When I met June Robbins in the late 1980s, she taught me the importance of such political expertise. Not long after my arrival in the factory, she and a co-worker from her department decided to pay a visit to Royce Payne—one of the factory owners, long since retired from active supervision of the factory. Subsequent to that visit, she suggested that I, too, call on him. As it turned out, Royce was less than pleased with reports of me from other workers, and my visit provided an occasion to clear up this controversy.

Had I not listened to June Robbins, and had she not interceded on my behalf, I would have been compelled to leave the factory at that point—and the force behind my hastened departure would have been the complaints of other factory workers who did not understand my presence there.[21] For June's part, my assumption is that she wanted me in her debt. As part of her departmental network, I was rendered harmless and at the same time made privy to her conversations with Royce and others of the Payne family. Through such means, June and her colleagues on the "lower end" shaped departmental routine.[22]

Moth Hill employees lacked any formal means to press for changes in working conditions, especially given the current status of the mica industry. Moth Hill Mica Company had declined from a labor force of three hundred workers on three shifts to a skeleton crew of some fifty workers. Work orders fluctuated from one week to the next, and with them plans for individual departments. The status of one's employment at Moth Hill was always in question and conveyed in informal, personal terms by one's supervisor at the end of the work week.

The bottom line for Moth Hill workers was "the mica business," known to be on the wane.[23] In this context union drives and strikes would have proved fruitless at best.[24] Permanent unemployment, indeed the demise of the company, was already too real a possibility. A strike would likely have prompted a factory lockout much like the bouts of temporary unemployment workers routinely experienced, along with the firing of whoever was suspected of organizing the protests. In this respect the experience of mica workers may well be emblematic of wage laborers encountering deindustrialization.

As unskilled laborers at Moth Hill, the lowest-paid and most susceptible to unemployment, women turned to informal means, underwritten by local tradition, to establish a vocal presence within the factory.[25] Through departmental networks, women contravened the plans of supervisors and articulated their own concerns about work processes and job assignments, prompting one supervisor to claim that he could not "boss" anyone in his department save his daughter.[26] Women likewise voiced their protests over working conditions, especially about the contamination of the air by mica particles and lacquer fumes.[27] And they kept up a running commentary on the directives of the Payne family, the better to mediate factory policies.

In their interactions with male co-workers, women openly contested the gender politics set in motion by the Paynes. If men were paid more and given more autonomy, even in semiskilled positions, they were not allowed to use this as leverage against female workers. It was not only that male employees looked to female kin for food and sociability during work breaks. Equally important, women used public reprimand and informal sanction to keep male colleagues in line.

When one supervisor teased me publicly about being a single woman, the women were equally aggressive in offering rejoinders. "Tell him we don't take the culls," one suggested loudly.[28] The next day the supervisor apologized and stopped his teasing.

Such actions did not undo formal policies excluding women from supervisory power, but they outlined the limits within which such power could be wielded. Male supervisors responded to women's requests for steady employment by maintaining productive processes even in the face of dwindling orders and by reassigning workers to processes for which there was a constant demand. They acceded, wherever possible, to women's demands for decent working conditions—for example, they rigged safety equipment when none was provided by the Paynes. Further, they acknowledged workers' autonomy in the performance of their duties.

Calling upon each other to support their claims as workers and to celebrate life passages such as weddings and birthdays, women "humanized the workplace" at Moth Hill and made it a nicer place to be. Kinspeople came to visit Moth Hill employees at work, further cementing community bonds. Women kept in touch with co-workers outside the plant, offering financial aid and other resources in times of crisis.

However, insofar as workers identified their own interests with those of their factory departments, women's work cultures also served to benefit the factory owners.[29] For example, worker solidarity easily translated into efforts to maintain the profitability of respective departments for the sake of one's co-workers and oneself.[30]

Gertie Russell noted her own efforts to this end and exhorted her colleagues to join her: "The hands have to work harder to make more money for Moth Hill so the company will keep going." By the same token, she criticized working conditions at Moth Hill, describing stretch-out practices that forced her to work too quickly and without adequate attention to the quality of output: "If I save ten dollars worth of [mica] plate [because it meets technical standards for quality], that's ten dollars for the company and ten dollars for me."[31]

Defective merchandise was generally recognized to be a major problem at Moth Hill, a mark of the lack of concern displayed by current management and a flaw that might cause the collapse of the company. Thus, even though Gertie Russell was considered by some of her colleagues to be a little too compliant with management's wishes, her concerns about productive processes that overworked laborers and yielded defective products were shared by all.

Apart from the issue of quality control, workers exercised prerogatives underwritten by local custom: leaving work to tend to families, gardens, and household duties or because the weather threatened to be bad; taking unscheduled breaks and/or slowing down work, especially on Friday afternoons; recruiting neighbors and kin for the limited job openings; and conferring with each other about work-related problems and community issues. The women I interviewed were vocal about the importance of exercising these rights, lest supervisors or factory owners gain too much control over the shop floor. Moreover, they were clear about the tradeoffs involved in working at Moth Hill, where, to paraphrase one worker, "they don't pay you much but they leave you alone." As another woman noted, "I mean it's, it's close home. They don't pay that much, but if you're sick or if you have to be out, nothing is ever said. That makes it good." These comments were linked to discussions of other factory settings where employees "worked production" and labor policies were considered more rigid and oppressive.[32] By comparison, Moth Hill offered no benefits and salaries were tied to the state (as opposed to federal) minimum wage, but it recognized the force of local tradition in its dealings with employees.

The term "close home" is significant in that it suggests the tension between opposition and complicity that Moth Hill workers themselves demonstrated in departmental work cultures. On the one hand, the notion of working "close home" emphasized the importance of worker solidarity, based on loyalties that extended beyond the factory, and legitimated women's agency within the factory inasmuch as they were recognized to be important kin/community members.

"Close home" also meant working with "good, Christian people" who valued the traditions of evangelical Protestantism, its radical morality, and its call to individual witness.[33] At Moth Hill, workers used the language of evangelical Protestantism to set up an oppositional discourse that criticized factory owners as sinful and corrupt, and reaffirmed the importance of church-based networks over and against the authority of factory management.[34] One expression of this dissent was the lack of attendance by Moth Hill employees at the church founded and supported by the Payne family.

At the same time, the imagery of being "close home" in the factory was used by management to underwrite its paternalistic labor policies. Adherence to company policy was framed in terms of personal obligation to the family who owned and managed Moth Hill. As mentioned earlier, workers were on a first-name basis with factory management. By the same token, Royce Payne, the aged head of the Payne family, could recite the names of bygone generations of workers to illustrate to their descendants the various ways in which the Moth Hill Mica Company had served their families and the community. Equally important, the Paynes counted upon Moth Hill employees like June Robbins for reports on shop floor activities and worker concerns.[35]

Moth Hill employees also provided household labor and taxi and childcare services to the Payne family. One factory worker tended the herd of cattle owned by a member of the Payne family as part of his work routine. Factory workers supplied the Paynes with food and attended them in illness. In short, workers were protective of the factory head and his family even while they criticized company policies.

In other words, "close home" is evocative of the struggle over the terms of local tradition that was played out in the mica factory. The owners of the Moth Hill Mica Company usurped cultural imagery in their efforts to instill a sense of accountability and conviction in their work force and present the company as a "family business" that was itself loyal and trustworthy. Although workers were responsive to this rhetoric, they also recognized human fallibility, especially in those who presented themselves as authority figures. Moreover, because kin connectedness was reflected in deed, not rhetoric, departmental networks and community relations outside the factory were taken as the measure of closeness—not the verbiage of owners, whose self-interest was evident to all.

The imagery of kinship was, in other words, appropriated by workers *and* management to clarify loyalties and to assert rights. Through departmental networks underwritten by kin and quasi-kin bonds, coworkers offered each other material resources as well as political solidarity and emotional support. Familistic symbolism emphasized the importance of negotiated authority and conflict mediation, as opposed to the unilateral claims of factory management.[36] Even supervisors were kinspeople as well as overseers, and answerable to claims made outside the factory.

Last but not least, kin networks provided a vehicle by which boundaries were established between those who were known and trustworthy and those who stood outside. Notwithstanding the fact that renderings of kin connectedness were highly selective at best, their assertion was a powerful statement of interdependence—of fellowship and reliability. The lines thus drawn were not as sharply or indelibly defined as those created by union cards and pickets, but they were the means by which workers' rights were advanced amidst the chaos of economic restructuring.

These are the political-economic conditions within which mica workers have labored in southern Appalachia. Clearly, workplace struggles in industries like this involve increasingly limited terms. Our enthusiasm for working-class heroism has prompted us to look for dramatic confrontations within the workplace, to read defiance into workers' complaints, or to decry workers for failing to do more. Instead of this either/or position, I suggest we explore both the economic and political constraints that operate on factory relations and, equally important, workers' perspectives on what is desirable and feasible.

Consideration of the latter takes us beyond the factory per se into community networks and cultural perspectives on the place of waged labor in working people's lives. What do the residents of western North Carolina want—as women and men in the late twentieth century, as members of family lineages and settlements, as participants (and nonparticipants) in evangelical churches, as part of a rural workforce in southern Appalachia, as citizens of a state and country in economic recession? How do women, and men, negotiate these concerns in daily interactions at the Moth Hill Mica Company?

It was late in my study of Moth Hill that I realized how much my research questions reflected a set of class and cultural perspectives divergent from those of the workers I interviewed. Perhaps I had succumbed to the paternalistic rhetoric of the factory owners, or maybe it was my own middle-class vocationalism, but I assumed that waged work in the mica factory formed the center of employees' lives. The workers themselves helped me revise my analysis, as when Hazel Roberts declared, "Mountain women are strong! We could scratch a living off a rock if we had to."

This, in combination with the litanies of alternative occupations and subsistence activities recited by workers, helped me better understand how they perceived the mica factory. For Moth Hill workers, the primary issue was one of finding work in a marginal economy. What made Moth Hill a viable choice was its long history in the rural community in which many of the workers lived. Not only was Moth Hill thus "a known quantity"; it was a workplace where generations of workers and owners had arrived at a set of expectations about factory life that spoke to important parameters of workers' lives. If the wage packet it offered was minimal, such was the case with many other jobs located farther away.

Workers recognized that the company's perilous status and wage scale made it less than suitable for younger workers, who were conspicuously absent from the mica factory. The children of Moth Hill workers for the most part looked to other factory jobs or to educational programs that would move them out of the venue of institutions like Moth Hill. In the glory days of Uncle Dan Payne, however, Moth Hill was a place to sell mica as well as one's labor. It was a place where aunts took nieces to find work in a money-tight economy, a place where women—married and unmarried—performed hand labor vital to a burgeoning industry. If these days were long gone, they offered a yardstick against which workers measured current conditions and strategies.

The women of Moth Hill were not quiescent, as theorists like John Gaventa might have predicted.[37] They did not simply defer to the Paynes or accept a marginalized position within the factory, given the unsettled economic conditions.[38] Rather, women called upon departmental cohorts, neighbors, and kin to question factory policy and secure control over their own labor processes. Hazel Roberts summed it up nicely: "I guess you've already figured it out. Around here, the hands boss themselves."

Acknowledgments

This research was funded, in part, through an Appalachian Studies Fellowship from Berea College, a James Still Fellowship in Appalachian Studies from the University of Kentucky, and a National Women's Studies Association–Pergamon Press Scholarship in Women's Studies. I would like to thank Steve Fisher, Carl Hand, and the anonymous reviewers for their insightful comments on an earlier draft of this chapter.

Notes

1. For a more detailed discussion of the concept of culture, see Mary Anglin, "'A Lost and Dying World': Women's Labor in the Mica Industry of Southern Appalachia" (Ph.D. diss., New School for Social Research, 1990).
2. Community studies such as John Stephenson, *Shiloh: A Mountain Community* (Lexington: University of Kentucky Press, 1968); George Hicks, *Appalachian Valley* (New York: Holt, Rinehart, and Winston, 1976); and, more recently, Patricia Beaver, *Rural Community in the Appalachian South* (Lexington: Uni-

versity Press of Kentucky, 1986), present Appalachia as an enduring folk society, much as the local colorists of the nineteenth century eulogized this "land that time forgot." For descriptions of the local color movement, see Allen Batteau, "Appalachia and the Concept of Culture: A Theory of Shared Misunderstandings," *Appalachian Journal* 7 (Autumn–Winter 1979/80) : 9–31; Henry D. Shapiro, *Appalachia on Our Mind: The Southern Mountains and Mountaineers in the American Consciousness, 1870–1920* (Chapel Hill: University of North Carolina Press, 1978); and David E. Whisnant, *All That Is Native and Fine: The Politics of Culture in an American Region* (Chapel Hill: University of North Carolina Press, 1983).

On the opposite end are those who emphasize political-economic relations over and against the "Appalachian subculture." See, for example, John Gaventa, *Power and Powerlessness: Quiescence and Rebellion in an Appalachian Valley* (Urbana: University of Illinois Press, 1980); and Helen Lewis, Linda Johnson, and Donald Askins, eds., *Colonialism in Modern America: The Appalachian Case* (Boone, N.C.: Appalachian Consortium Press, 1978).

3. See Christine Ward Gailey, "Culture Wars: Resistance to State Formation," in *Power Relations and State Formation*, ed. Thomas C. Patterson and Christine W. Gailey (Washington, D.C.: American Anthropological Association, 1987); William Roseberry, *Anthropologies and Histories: Essays in Culture, History, and Political Economy* (New Brunswick, N.J.: Rutgers University Press, 1988); and Eric Wolf, *Europe and the People Without History* (Berkeley: University of California Press, 1982).

4. See John Inscoe, *Mountain Masters, Slavery, and the Sectional Crisis in Western North Carolina* (Knoxville: University of Tennessee Press, 1989); Helen M. Lewis and Suzanna O'Donnell, eds., *Ivanhoe, Virginia: Remembering Our Past, Building Our Future* (Ivanhoe, Va.: Ivanhoe Civic League, 1990); Gordon McKinney, "Subsistence Economy and Community in Western North Carolina, 1860–1865," paper presented at the annual meeting of the Organization of American Historians, Reno, Nevada, March 1988; and "The Other Victims: Women in Civil War Western North Carolina," paper presented at the annual meeting of the Southern Historical Association, Norfolk, Virginia, November 1988; and Altina L. Waller, *Feud: Hatfields, McCoys, and Social Change in Appalachia, 1860–1900* (Chapel Hill: University of North Carolina Press, 1988). Cf. Rhoda Halperin, *The Livelihood of Kin: Making Ends Meet "the Kentucky Way"* (Austin: University of Texas Press, 1990), for an analysis of agrarian traditions in eastern Kentucky and resistance to industrial capitalism.

5. Hegemony is read here as an inherently historical process, not a structural relationship. As Raymond Williams writes, hegemony does not connote the unidimensional construction of cultural meanings by those in authority: "At any time, forms of alternative or directly oppositional politics and culture exist as significant elements in the society. We shall need to explore their conditions and their limits, but their active presence is decisive, not only because they have to be included in any historical (as distinct from epochal)

analysis, but as forms which have had significant effect on the hegemonic process itself. That is to say, alternative political and cultural emphases, and the many forms of opposition and struggle, are important not only in themselves but as indicative features of what the hegemonic process has in practice had to work to control." See *Marxism and Literature* (Oxford: Oxford University Press, 1977), 113. See also James C. Scott, *Domination and the Arts of Resistance: Hidden Transcripts* (New Haven: Yale University Press, 1990), for an account of the elaborate interplay between the practices of the dominant and their subversion by those ostensibly without power.

6. See Mary K. Anglin, "A Question of Loyalty: Nationalism and Regional Identity in Workers' Narratives," *Anthropological Quarterly* 65 (July 1992) : 105–16.

7. All proper names pertaining to field research in North Carolina are my invention.

8. Mica, or isinglass, had been used for stove windows, gas lamps, and curtains in the first automobiles. However, because mica was rarely found in sheets large enough to be used for these purposes, the early phase of the industry was beset with material shortages, waste, and unfruitful mining efforts. Mines were typically closed down when seams of mica were lost. The risks of investigating further simply proved too great relative to the market for the commodity. See Douglas B. Sterrett, "Mica Deposits of the United States," U.S. Geological Survey, Bulletin 740 (Washington, D.C.: Government Printing Office, 1923); and Jasper L. Stuckey, *North Carolina: Its Geology and Mineral Resources* (Raleigh, N.C.: Department of Conservation and Development, 1965).

9. International procurement programs were established under the Combined Raw Materials Board, which included Great Britain and other allies. These programs were implemented in Angola, Argentina, Brazil, India, Madagascar, Peru, and Tanzania, to name the more significant locations. India, in particular, was known as an abundant source of the highest grades of mica, and had been since the nineteenth century. See Milford L. Skow, "Mica: A Materials Survey," Information Circular No. 8125, U.S. Department of the Interior, Bureau of the Mines (Washington, D.C.: Government Printing Office, 1962).

10. Another dimension of the federal policy was the establishment of a research program, undertaken by federal and state geological surveys, into domestic sources of mica. The purpose was to establish the location, abundance, and quality of mica seams. See, for example, U.S. Geological Survey, Notebooks No. 1394, 1398, 1405, 1406 (1940–53); and U.S. Tariff Commission, *Mica: Prepared in Response to Requests from the Committee on Finance of the United States Senate and the Committee on Ways and Means of the House of Representatives*, War Changes in Industry Series, Report No. 21 (Washington, D.C.: Government Printing Office, 1947).

11. See Anglin, "'A Lost and Dying World,'" for a more detailed account of legislation and policies concerning the stockpiling of mica for wartime use.

12. Mica has continued to be of importance to the electronics industry as the

insulating material that meets the most exacting specifications in terms of voltage sustained. Mica is used in such high-tech applications as CAT scans and radiation therapy equipment, as well as in transformers used in radio and television transmission. See Alvin B. Zlobik, *Mica: Mineral Facts and Problems*, Bulletin 671, U.S. Department of the Interior, Bureau of the Mines (Washington, D.C.: Government Printing Office, 1980); Fred Block and Wilton Johnson, *Mica*, Bureau of Mines Minerals Yearbook, U.S. Department of the Interior, Bureau of the Mines (Washington, D.C.: Government Printing Office, 1982); and Wilton Johnson, *Mineral Commodity Summaries*, U.S. Department of the Interior, Bureau of the Mines (Washington, D.C.: Government Printing Office, 1983), for their estimates of the demand for mica in the United States through the year 2000.

13. This argument is based, in part, upon field research on women's labor in farm households in southern Appalachia, with particular attention to the raising of burley tobacco as a cash crop. Although some tasks—for example, driving tractors and preparing fields for the transplanting of tobacco seedlings—were clearly demarcated as "men's work," women performed other roles and were considered an integral part of tobacco production. For example, women helped prepare and tend seedbeds, transplant seedlings, water and hoe tobacco plants, and process the harvested tobacco. Although men took the tobacco to market and publicly assumed ownership of the crop, production rested upon the collective efforts of the household. See Mary Anglin, "Field Notes," 1979–1981. This interpretation is substantiated by McKinney's research on nineteenth-century western North Carolina: "Subsistence Economy and Community" and "The Other Victims."

14. A number of the women who worked at Moth Hill Mica Company—among them Zona Watson, Gertie Russell, and Annie Burleson—remembered their mothers "cobbing" mica for trade to local merchants as part of household patterns of production.

15. The first reference to women as laborers in the mica industry comes in the U.S. Census for 1900. Prior to that date, the vast majority of women are listed as "keeping house," if wives, or "at home," if daughters—thus obscuring their productive labors. See U.S. Census, *Schedule One: Population* (Washington, D.C.: n.p., 1900).

16. See Thomas Lanier Clingman, *Selections from the Speeches and Writings of Hon. Thomas L. Clingman of North Carolina, with Additions and Explanatory Notes* (Raleigh: John Nichols, 1887); Jacquelyn Dowd Hall et al., *Like a Family: The Making of a Southern Cotton Mill World* (Chapel Hill: University of North Carolina Press, 1987); Harriet Herring, *Passing of the Mill Village* (Chapel Hill: University of North Carolina Press, 1949); and Inscoe, *Mountain Masters*.

17. Recruitment stories (see below) told by Moth Hill employees typically referenced Royce Payne or his father, "Uncle Dan," who founded the company. In these stories, Royce or Uncle Dan was frequently placed in a local store where he struck up a conversation with, or was approached by, the relative of a potential employee, whom he knew on a first-name basis. Recruitment

       stories make clear the force of the Payne men as personalities and authority figures in the community.

18. Gertie Russell and other workers noted changes in labor processes, particularly after the federal contracts were withdrawn from the mica industry and the region: "When the low wages went up, they took [the extra workers] away. . . . Oh!!!! They was four more working on that machine. They were . . . two, four, six, . . . seven worked down there then." In place of seven workers, there were three or even two, so that Gertie or her sister, Annie Burleson, had to run between two machines to keep them both in operation. (Interview 12A, 1988.)

19. My analysis of departmental networks draws from feminist research on work cultures, the perspectives and practices that ground workers' identities and workplace social relations. Work cultures are not only a vehicle through which ethnicity, gender, and class relations are articulated, but, equally, a potential force for dissent. See Mary K. Anglin, "The Dialectics of Kinship: Wage Labor and Ideologies of Resistance," *Southern Women: The Intersection of Race, Class and Gender*, Working Paper 4, Memphis State University and Duke–University of North Carolina Centers for Research on Women (1991); Maria Patricia Fernandez-Kelly, *For We Are Sold, I and My People: Women and Industry in Mexico's Frontier* (Albany: State University of New York Press, 1983); Louise Lamphere, "Bringing the Family to Work: Women's Culture on the Shop Floor," *Feminist Studies* 11 (Fall 1985) : 519–40; Karen Brodkin Sacks, *Caring by the Hour: Women, Work, and Organizing at Duke Medical Center* (Urbana: University of Illinois Press, 1988); Karen Brodkin Sacks and Dorothy Remy, eds., *My Troubles Are Going To Have Trouble With Me: Everyday Trials and Triumphs of Women Workers* (New Brunswick, N.J.: Rutgers University Press, 1984); Rosalyn Terborg-Penn, "Survival Strategies Among African-American Women Workers: A Continuing Process," in *Women, Work and Protest: A Century of U.S. Women's Labor History*, ed. Ruth Milkman (Boston: Routledge and Kegan Paul, 1985); Sallie Westwood, *All Day, Every Day: Factory and Family in the Making of Women's Lives* (Urbana: University of Illinois Press, 1985); and Patricia Zavella, *Women's Work and Chicano Families: Cannery Workers of the Santa Clara Valley* (Ithaca, N.Y.: Cornell University Press, 1987).

20. Louise Lamphere discusses the importance of this kind of "worker training" in *From Working Daughters to Working Mothers* (Ithaca, N.Y.: Cornell University Press, 1987). New workers are taught how to deal with floor supervisors and company bosses, how to work without rate busting, whom to trust on the shop floor, and—I would suggest—how to express dissent.

21. I was never accused of being a labor organizer, but rather of being an "industrial spy." However ludicrous the charge, it speaks to the longstanding concern for the continued profitability of the company as well as to the experience, a decade or more ago, of someone covertly investigating work processes at Moth Hill.

22. The "lower end" was the department with the most reliable production orders, and members of that department exercised great care in selecting

and shaping new recruits. As a Moth Hill employee from another department put it, "It's the best place to work, and they know it." Workers who did not meet the standards of "that bunch on the lower end" were hazed, and were either transferred to another department or left Moth Hill.

23. As one worker noted, "When my mother and Zona went to work, Moth Hill was really something. Now, it's just a job in the neighborhood."

24. The only evidence I have to date of unionization efforts by mica workers comes from a review of a case taken by the National Labor Relations Board in the late 1940s/early 1950s against a small company that produced ground mica, a product of less value than sheeted mica. While employees narrowly voted the union in, the plant superintendent fired the workers who had organized the effort and did so in a manner that pitted customary privileges, such as those exercised by Moth Hill employees, against the authority of the union. The NLRB eventually prevailed in contesting the legality of the superintendent's actions, but the union was broken. See National Labor Relations Board, Case No. 34-CA-168, NLRB 92, No. 118: 766–90 (1950); and *Federal Reporter* (2d series), National Labor Relations Board No. 6393 : 986–7 (1952).

25. One of the models for this vocal presence comes from women's participation in community churches, wherein they teach classes, hold office, and present individual testimonials to the church body. While women, for the most part, are excluded from the office of deacon or preacher, they nonetheless shape church policy and are regarded by all as vital to the well-being of the church. In the local church I attended, women's active dislike of the preacher helped cause his departure from office.

26. Within the factory, all the departments had a male supervisor, save the hand-laid mica plate operation within the "upstairs" department. Even the supervisor of that department ultimately coordinated her activities with a male supervisor, who was arguably head of that department. Why this one division had a female supervisor was never explained to me, but I presume it is a holdover from the past. In the current scenario, the hand-laid plate division was the most susceptible of all plant operations to temporary layoffs, and the division supervisor had limited authority except to delegate duties based on production orders.

27. On one occasion a manager stepped from his office into the factory proper to close a door and protect himself from the heavy odor of the lacquers used in laminating mica. The women in the department derided him, asking, "What do you think we're breathing?" While their comments had no visible impact at the time, they provided the backdrop against which workers could voice the same concerns in more serious fashion and seek some relief.

28. "Culls" are cattle weeded out of herds for their inferior breeding potential, a trenchant metaphor for unsuitability.

29. See Lamphere, "Bringing the Family to Work" and *From Working Daughters to Working Mothers*, for her discussion of work cultures and their potential complicity with management.

30. While this orientation did not necessarily lead to departmental rivalries,

insofar as each department was tied to a separate productive process, it was indicative of the localized loyalties maintained by workers. However, because workers were bound by kinship and church affiliation to members of other departments, departmental loyalties were at times subsumed by other priorities. Celebrations of holidays and life passages such as weddings and birthdays also served to offset divisions between work groups.

31. As Caroline White has noted in her study of workers in British electronics factories, "Why Do Workers Bother? Paradoxes of Resistance in Two English Factories," *Critique of Anthropology* 7 (Winter 1989) : 51–68, women resort to the language of quality control to carve out their own terrain in terms that management could not deny.

32. Of another area factory, it was said: "You work *hard* there. When you get out of an evening, you're *tired*!" The Moth Hill employee who made these observations added that while working in that factory she requested reassignment to a work station more compatible with her skills and experience, and was summarily denied. Her response was to "wait until I had a payday" and leave.

33. Appalachians have called upon these traditions to fuel opposition to oppressive capitalist policies. See Dwight B. Billings, "Religion as Opposition: A Gramscian Analysis," *American Journal of Sociology* 96 (1990) : 1–31; and Dwight B. Billings and Robert Goldman, "Religion and Class Consciousness in the Kanawha County School Textbook Controversy," in *Appalachia and America: Autonomy and Regional Dependence*, ed. Allen Batteau (Lexington: University Press of Kentucky, 1983).

34. This issue is explored in greater depth in Anglin, "A Lost and Dying World." Cf. Mary K. Anglin, "Dissent by Another Name: Regional Culture and Workplace Resistance in Southern Appalachia," paper presented at the annual meeting of the American Anthropological Association, New Orleans, Louisiana, November 1990.

35. After one such visit, June Robbins reported that Royce Payne was worried about efforts to raise the state minimum wage. She told us that, according to Royce, if the minimum wage reached $4.00 as was threatened, Moth Hill would have to close its doors.

36. See Sacks, *Caring by the Hour*, for her discussion of familism as a philosophy underlying the Duke Hospital workers' strike, wherein female leaders presented the collective concerns of their work departments and negotiated differences of opinion between work groups. The power wielded by "center women" was the authority to represent the interests of their cohorts, not to force a centrally ordained perspective upon them. I would simply add that the model for Sacks's "center women," and for negotiators like June Robbins at Moth Hill, comes from women's participation in community churches. See n. 25 above.

37. Gaventa, in his study of central Appalachia, *Power and Powerlessness*, argues that the dominance of coal companies was based on their ability to inculcate an ideology of industrialization that exalted conspicuous consumption and

the value of wage work—in the mines—over and against the traditions of the region. Workers were quiescent not because of defects of personality or socialization but because the massive authority of the coal companies made resistance impossible. Although the mica industry in decline is hardly comparable to the coal companies at their zenith, I would argue nonetheless that Gaventa overlooked struggles by and through tradition, especially insofar as he assumed a union-organizing model of activism with its implicit hierarchies.

38. See Scott, *Domination and the Arts of Resistance*, for his cogent argument about deference as a mode of impression-management used by subordinate peoples in public interactions. Scott suggests that quite a different set of activities takes place "offstage," where the subordinate openly express dissent and plot their revenge. Such an argument seems quite appropriate to the setting at Moth Hill.

14

Appalachian Studies, Resistance, and Postmodernism

Alan Banks
Dwight Billings
Karen Tice

The most informative writing about the economic inequalities of the Appalachian region during the last decade has not come from the circle of academe. Rather, it has come primarily from those outside the academic world—committed journalists, investigative researchers, regional activists, and those individuals who have organized their own citizen groups—who have been directly involved in the struggles against inequalities.
John Gaventa, "Inequality and the Appalachian Studies Industry"

John Gaventa's remarks, made at the first annual meeting of the Appalachian Studies Conference, were a call for a more constructive relationship between activists and scholars.[1] They were a challenge to produce knowledge useful for democratic empowerment. Gaventa's remarks were also intentionally exaggerated. Good writing about the region was never the exclusive property of a small, committed group of nonacademics. But Gaventa's observations were nonetheless important. They helped give identity to the emerging Appalachian Studies Association (ASA) and shape relations among activists and scholars in and around the region.

Designed from the beginning to "coordinate analysis of the region's problems across disciplinary lines" and to "relate scholarship to regional needs and the concerns of the Appalachian people," the ASA has provided an important context for those who seek to overcome the separateness of regional activists, citizens, and academicians. As the program of the sixth annual ASA meeting in 1984 proudly recalled: "The Appalachian Studies Conference was formed in 1977 by a group of scholars, teachers, and regional activists who believed that shared community has been and will continue to be important for those writing, researching and teaching about things Appalachian." At its best, the ASA has provided a social space where oppositional discourse has flourished. Despite tensions between their goals, the ASA has served as a forum where activists and academics can talk with each other, rather than at each other. It has been a meeting place for people with very different daily pressures and role obligations.

This chapter falls into two main sections. First, we examine the emergence of Appalachian Studies and the Appalachian Studies Association. We argue that both have contributed to grassroots dissent in the region, but we also address intellectual and organizational tendencies that threaten to constrain the ASA's role as an important regionwide forum. Then, we explore the emergence of a new direction in Appalachian Studies—postmodernism. Our objective is to focus upon the political implications that postmodernism may have for those of us in Appalachian Studies who want to build upon the activist traditions that have long sustained our work.

Oppositional Discourse and Appalachian Studies

In Appalachian Studies, research and action have always had an important connection. This is not to say that all perspectives on Appalachia contribute equally to an effort to understand or abolish social inequalities in the region. But ameliorative impulses have predominated, rather than scholarly detachment. Put differently, the research carried out by many Appalachian scholars has not come primarily from the intellectual agenda of academic disciplines, but rather from a regional conversation among activists and scholars. Even the much criticized "culture of poverty" musings in *Yesterday's People* were popularized by a minister working to improve the lives of Appalachian people. Though wrongheaded, Jack Weller's book, like Harry Caudill's *Night Comes to the Cumberlands*, had an important audience among educators, church people, and community development workers. Indeed, Weller's book was handed out among young Appalachian Volunteers and Vista workers entering the region in the late 1960s as a sort of handbook for understanding regional woes, a Peterson's field guide for recognizing Appalachian people on the wing. What concerned subsequent Appalachian scholars, of course, was the way Weller's book stereotyped the region's people as backward folk who existed outside industrial America.[2]

Beginning about 1970, many people began to understand the "problem" of Appalachia in a new way—not as "fatalism," as Weller had maintained, but as "the coal industry." Writing in *Mountain Life & Work*, Helen Lewis helped pioneer an alternative discourse on Appalachia as an economically exploited, politically dominated, and culturally denigrated "internal colony." This new discourse was not the exclusive property of any particular audience. Rather, the colonial interpretation of Appalachian problems had great appeal among scholars, activists, and community people within the region. It helped us see ourselves in a larger social context and visualize a path for collective struggle and resistance.[3]

Over the past twenty years, Appalachian scholars and activists have formed an alliance that has yielded some very impressive results. While this alliance, understandably, has had its uneasy moments, Appalachian activists and scholars have documented a complex history of both "resistance" to and "complicity" with capitalist development in the mountains. Some writers have explored how Appalachian coal miners in the 1920s and 1930s grew into one of the most militant and class-conscious workforces in the United States, building a strong oppositional culture in the mountains and providing national leadership for industrial unionism in the CIO.[4] Other writers have examined a different response to domination and exploitation: quiescence and complicity.[5] Still others have provided important analyses of how both these trends developed in specific mountain communities.[6]

In the context of the ASA, such studies institutionalize a memory of resistance and dissent that otherwise would be erased from the region. They provide a link between research and the grassroots that recognizes the importance of historical struggles in our personal and collective growth. These studies nurture an understanding of social change that rejects the attempts of historical winners to justify the losers' fate as the inevitable result of personality flaws or geography or impersonal market conditions. Such an understanding portrays regional inhabitants as actors with history-making potential. Knowledge that leads to this sort of self-understanding is an important part of what has sustained the regional conversation among intellectuals and activists. It is also the sort of discourse that is indispensable if oppositional movements are to flourish.

In addition to helping preserve the region's history of dissent, Appalachian scholars have also worked with community people to expand current knowledge about the region. One important example comes from the late 1970s. In 1977 the Tug River, located on the Kentucky–West Virginia border, flooded and left thousands homeless. Angered at being forced to live in crowded flood plains because of absentee ownership and frustrated by governments' inability to find alternative sites for relocation, local activists called for support from other regional groups to create a federation of grassroots organizations known as the Appalachian Alliance. In addition to providing an important regionwide forum and publishing educational materials, members of the Alliance helped to launch the Appalachian Land Ownership Task Force. The task force, consisting of both activists and academics, trained indigenous researchers to investigate mineral rights, land ownership, and taxation on over 20 million acres of land in eighty counties spanning six states in the region.[7]

The task force's documentation of vast amounts of minimally taxed land and mineral resources owned by absentee firms spearheaded tax reform efforts in Tennessee and Virginia. It also led to challenges to mineral leasing practices in North Carolina, and was used to persuade the state supreme court in West Virginia to rule that inequitable school funding in that state was unconstitutional. In Kentucky, the information, skills, and attitudes gained from the land study helped form the Kentucky Fair Tax Coalition (KFTC). Numbering more than twenty-three hundred members statewide, KFTC (now Kentuckians For The Commonwealth) has helped to reform policy on unmined mineral taxes and won passage of a constitutional amendment prohibiting the use of the notorious "broad form deed" that formerly allowed mineral owners to mine surface owners' property without permission or compensation. Moreover, the indigenous researchers were empowered with new knowledge, new skills, and a new confidence to battle local political and economic elites.

Another constructive example of a scholar-activist partnership can be found in the cultural arena. Many people have worked to overcome the often romantic and contrived characterizations of Appalachian culture and produce an understanding that is supportive of regional identity yet sensitive to the realities of inequality in a world capitalist system. Their general orientation has been to preserve a focus on cultural identity and regional pride while incorporating this understanding into an analysis of the position of Appalachia within a larger political economy.

Knowledge about the region's culture as well as its traditions of dissent and its current problems has been widely disseminated through a proliferating number of Appalachian Studies courses on college campuses across the region. Growing respectability as a multidisciplinary intellectual field has helped to legitimate the development of majors and minors in Appalachian Studies, while student internships have helped to link classroom learning with community needs and realities. The increasing number of Appalachian centers devoted to teaching, research, and service among the region's colleges and universities is another indicator of important new commitments that at least begin to counter the prior neglect of Appalachia by academic institutions.

An off-campus illustration of the benefits of the scholar-activist partnership can be found at Appalshop, a grassroots-based, multimedia production collective located in Whitesburg, Kentucky. Appalshop operates a public radio station and produces documentary films for classroom and community use, musical recordings of important regional talent that otherwise might go unnoticed, and traveling plays that portray positive images of the region and its traditions of dissent. Appalshop artists have made it a policy to work closely with scholars and educators to produce representations of the region that nourish positive identities and broaden political awareness.

Beyond the actual content of research and writing, Appalachian Studies conferences also provide a significant forum for discussing the region's current problems and possibilities. A recent meeting of the ASA included in excess of five hundred participants and a hundred presentations from both grassroots and academic organizations. Institutionalized conversations among activists and scholars provide an important social space for discussions about the region's future. In the same way that shelters for battered women provide a feminist presence in rural Appalachian communities, and community-based mental health centers provide a "meeting place, a public space, and a forum for discussion and decision-making regarding programs for the community,"[8] Appalachian Studies conferences provide a context for important political conversations. In the absence of regionwide organizations that once served to connect grassroots struggles, such as the now defunct Appalachian Alliance and the Council of the Southern Mountains, conferences play a crucial role.

For academics, especially, the Appalachian Studies conferences are a welcome alternative to the high-pressure and intensely specialized meetings of the various academic disciplines. They not only help to sustain scholars' commitment to study Appalachia—a topic often marginalized in the academic disciplines—but also encourage them to relate their professional interests and skills to political issues. The conferences permit broader interdisciplinary conversations than those of other academic associations and help to inform academics about concerns and developments at the grassroots. In addition to formal panels and sessions, informal gatherings of academics, activists, artists, and musicians at the conferences nurture interpersonal connections that help to overcome the insularity and myopia of academic work.

At the same time, however, the increasing academic respect that has been won for Appalachian Studies threatens to undermine some of what has been most unique and healthy about the Association. Most recent participants would agree, and many would regret, that the annual conferences are becoming increasingly academicized. While providing an important outlet for academic studies of Appalachia, recent conferences have begun to give less and less attention to grassroots struggles, and we believe activists have begun to feel less at home there and to find the conferences less relevant to their concerns. Success contributes to this problem, since the proliferation of sessions forces selective participation. With many competing sessions, it is now possible to attend only sessions devoted to one's speciality, whether poetry, social science, or politics. Other than dinner keynote speeches, there are few sessions that compel broad participation and focus attention on the common concerns that originally motivated the establishment of the Association.

From its inception, the ASA has been structured to bridge academic and community terrains. For example, annual meetings alternate between regional college campuses and public parks in the hope that nonacademic participants will be encouraged to attend. An annual Appalachian Youth Conference involving several hundred youths and parents occurs at the same time as the ASA conference and includes several sessions that are integrated with the ASA. Nominations for leadership roles in the ASA have been made to reflect the diversity in the region and the Association. The first African American president of the ASA has recently finished his term in office, and in 1991 members for the first time chose a public school teacher as president. They will hold an upcoming annual conference on the campus of one of the region's high schools.

Such efforts address problems of elitism and racism and show that the collaboration between regional citizens, activists, and academicians is valued by ASA members. But the tendencies toward academicization and compartmentalization will require continuing attention. Such tensions parallel those occurring in other movement-based groups such as Women's Studies that are similarly committed to broad-based struggles against exploitation, domination, and cultural denigration. For example, members of the Women of Color Caucus formally walked out of a recent meeting of the National Women's Studies Association because of institutionalized racism. Trisha Franzen and Lois Helmbold report: "The NWSA leadership acted as if the organization had already done its anti-racism work, and the trust that NWSA was committed to anti-racism was like a title granted for life, not something which could be re-examined."[9] The ASA, too, must consciously struggle to sustain itself as a forum for oppositional politics.

Not only will the ASA have to address the problems of academicization and the politics of gender, race, and class, but it will need to confront the possibilities and pitfalls engendered by the turn toward postmodernism. Just as Teresa Ebert asserts that "postmodernism has become an unavoidable issue for femnists—activists and theorists alike,"[10] we believe that postmodernism, primarily because of its stress on difference and diversity, is beginning to open up new possibilities for thinking and writing about Appalachia. At the same time, postmodernism complicates the politics of coalition-building within the ASA and the region.

What Is Postmodernism?

The meaning of "postmodernism" is hotly debated in the arts, literature, philosophy, and social sciences. Some writers view postmodernism as an entirely new era of history and a new form of society.[11] They picture a society marked by fragmentation and heterogeneity, where Star Wars and Disney World replace social reality and substitute for meaning. Others interpret postmodernism less grandly as the ideological expression of the "cultural logic" of mass-consumer capitalism.[12] Still others view postmodernism even more narrowly as simply an artistic or narrative style. We choose to think about postmodernism as a new sensibility that involves a heightened and healthy skepticism about truth claims. "Postmodernism," as the feminist scholar Michelle Barret puts it, "is a cultural climate as well as an intellectual position, a political reality as well as an academic fashion."[13] This way of understanding postmodernism has important implications for how people think and write about the world, including Appalachia.

The postmodern sensibility calls into question common-sense notions about thinking (reason) and how thoughts are expressed (representation). With Clifford Geertz, we take postmodernism to be a new "way of thinking about the way we think." This new sensibility entails "not just another redrawing of the cultural map . . . but an alteration of the principles of mapping."[14] In Appalachian Studies, such new mapping principles have important political implications for how we think about and represent Appalachian regional identities as well as for the relationship between scholars and grassroots activism.

The modern understanding of thinking—which postmodernism leaves behind—came into being most fully during the eighteenth-century Enlightenment. It took the objectivity of reason as an article of faith. Enlightenment philosophers assumed that human reason was the vehicle that would lead to progressive social change, the means through which people could throw off their chains. For example, when Thomas Jefferson and the other signers of the Declaration of Independence justified the American colonies' secession from Great Britain in terms of "truths" they held "to be self evident," they expressed the belief that reason's truths were readily apparent to all who could think for themselves—all those, that is, freed from the blinders of dogma and tradition.[15]

What we are calling "postmodernism" signals an end to this faith in reason and its effects. As the authors of *Brave New World* and *1984* depict, and as Hiroshima and Auschwitz symbolize, rationality has deeply penetrated most aspects of life in modern society, yet it has failed to secure life, liberty, and happiness. We are left in a position where rationality without reason permeates all aspects of social life, where schooling is informative but not enlightening, where work is sustaining but not humanizing, and agriculture is efficient but not sustainable.[16]

As early as the late nineteenth century, Friedrich Nietzsche, whose ideas were a precursor to postmodernism, challenged the "god's eye" view of truth that was taken for granted by the Enlightenment in general and science in particular, noting that it presupposes "an eye such as no living creature can imagine, an eye required to have no direction, to abrogate its active and interpretive powers—precisely those powers alone that make seeing, seeing something." Thus, according to Nietzsche, "all seeing is essentially perspective, and so is all knowing."[17] Since Nietzsche, the idea that truth is always and inevitably relative to one's cultural standpoint has been widely advanced.

We have come to understand, for instance, that the natural sciences do not operate with an objective god's eye. Scientific "facts" are not independently existing realities waiting "out there" to be discovered but rather are produced through the application of theories, assumptions, conventions, methods, procedures, and beliefs held by the scientific community.[18] In this view, science, no less than any other art or discipline, is understood to be a culturally conditioned way of acting upon the world, of seeing as well as not seeing. In large measure, "what we call postmodern philosophy today is precisely about questioning the fundamental authority of science."[19] Consequently, as science loses the aura of absolute certainty that once seemed to privilege it among other ways of knowing, the demarcations between science, the humanities, the arts, and other cultural belief systems become unsure. These fields, as Geertz notes, become "blurred genres."[20]

Besides making explicit the cultural givens and practices that make thinking possible, postmodernism also refutes the naive idea that meaning precedes representation. Rather than being transparent vessels that convey truths without influencing their content, representations help to shape what can be seen and thus accepted as true. As Hayden White observes, "in any account of reality"—whether its genre is science, history, or fiction—"narrativity is present." He adds that "every narrative, however seemingly full, is constructed on the basis of a set of events which might have been included but were left out."[21]

One example of the importance of narrativity is a recent representation of Appalachia by David Cattell-Gordon as "a [regionwide] culturally transmitted traumatic stress syndrome."[22] Heavily indebted to the views of Appalachia espoused by Caudill and Weller, this account of "the effects of [Appalachian] history" as social trauma "bred in the bones of the people of the region" is flawed because it constitutes Appalachians solely as "victims" and obscures the potentiality of diverse subjects' making history. In particular, oppositional movements and actions are excluded from the narrative, thereby minimizing the possibilities for agency and empowerment. Such an account leaves unquestioned paradigmatic views of Appalachia that have the effect of either marginalizing and excluding Appalachians as fully human beings or else treating them as a monolithic category. In contrast to Cattell-Gordon's clinical portrait, a postmodern sensibility would suggest that a more kaleidoscopic view of culture and history is essential for capturing the complexity of Appalachia's past and·potential.

Many writers are troubled by postmodernism's abandonment of the unitary vision of objective truth in favor of unapologetically partial viewpoints. Some interpret postmodernism as "cultural helplessness," claiming that "postmodernism is above all post-1960s. . . . It is post–Viet Nam, post–New Left, post-hippie, post-Watergate . . . [where] belief has become difficult."[23] Others are even more critical, claiming that the "corrosive skepticism and nihilism" of most postmodernist thinking "disables both theoretical inquiry and political practice."[24] We reject such harshly critical views of postmodernism. Like Geertz, we discern "a distinctly democratic temper" in postmodernism's "fluid, plural, uncentered, and ineradicably untidy" approach.[25] Thus, we see postmodernism as having the potential to point Appalachian Studies in some important new directions. In particular, we believe that a cautious use of postmodern insights can guide our efforts in making sure that Appalachian Studies continues to be one of the region's voices of dissent.

The Postmodern Challenge: Avoiding Universalism and Essentialism

Appalachian Studies and Women's Studies both emerged as prominent features of university life in the 1970s in response to democratic impulses at the grassroots level in the late 1960s. Both have struggled with how to critique widespread stereotypes, accommodate the plurality of experiences and perspectives among participants, and further the common goals of academics and activists in struggles for social justice. We believe that the feminists' extensive wrestling with postmodernism, its political implications for feminist practice, and its place in the academy has much to contribute to Appalachian Studies. Applications include not only how to incorporate an understanding of gender into our work on Appalachia, but also how to think about regional identities in new and less restrictive ways.

Increasingly, many feminists are beginning to represent the social world in a postmodern manner in order to avoid explanations that are universalistic. These feminists question the validity of any unitary ways of knowing that claim to understand and describe the complexity of social relations in a totalistic fashion. Such universalistic knowledge claims and truth assertions—"metanarratives"—are rejected as reductionistic and ahistorical. As Nancy Fraser and Linda Nicholson note, feminists are calling into question "the dominant [modernist] philosophical project of seeking objectivity in the guise of a god's eye view which transcends any situation or perspective."[26]

As power conversations or privileged discourses, metanarratives are the ideological manifestations of inequitable social relations. In the case of gender, they falsely universalize white male expressions and experiences and, at the same time, peripheralize the diverse experiences of women. Instead, many feminist scholars are taking a more kaleidoscopic point of view that does not collapse the multiplicity of women's experiences, preoccupations, and expressions into the universal woman. They debunk descriptions that lump women into a monolithic category by exploring not only commonalities but differences among women.[27]

Thus, as postmodernists, feminist scholars have grown deeply suspicious of any descriptions of women and men, minorities, or humanity in general—and here we should add regions and regional populations—that rely on a universal image, model, norm, or method. They challenge as ideological assertions that repress multiplicity and diversity. Feminists also advocate a "deconstructive strategy" that takes apart falsely unified conceptions such as "women"—or, in our case, "Appalachians"—in order to reveal the internal diversity and plurality that such representations mask.

These feminist scholars are calling for approaches that are non-universalistic, self-conscious about perspective and values, and open to the multiplicity and diversity of experiences. If applied to Appalachian Studies, this approach would challenge us to replace unitary notions of Appalachians and Appalachian identity with plural and complexly constructed conceptions of social identity. The paradigmatic Appalachian would thus be replaced by a conception that represents Appalachian regional identities—these being decidedly plural—as "one strand among others, attending also to class, race, ethnicity, age, and sexual orientation . . . in short . . . more like a tapestry composed of many threads of many hues than one woven in a single color."[28]

In addition to a critique of universalistic thinking that represses the diversity of experiences among Appalachian peoples, postmodern feminist scholars can also teach us to challenge essentialistic thinking about Appalachia. "Essentialism" is the tendency to treat historical and social constructions as "fixed, natural, and absolute."[29] Essentialistic thinking further tends to reduce complex relations to fixed, and often binary, oppositions that are hierarchically ordered. In Appalachian Studies, we are accustomed to thinking in terms of such oppositions as Appalachian/non-Appalachian, insider/outsider, scholars/activists, culture folk/action folk. In such cases, interrelatedness is reduced to sets of either/ors. Postmodernism challenges us to rethink these taken-for-granted categories and to ask instead how they are constituted in historically situated social relations.

Taken together, opposition to universalistic and essentialistic thinking provides Appalachian Studies with avenues to transform our knowledge base and inform our practice of regional politics. In the remainder of this chapter, we wish to highlight steps in this direction already evident in Appalachian Studies.

Postmodern Directions in Appalachian Studies

Several recent contributions to the Appalachian literature advance a postmodern sensibility. Herbert Reid, for instance, challenges the either/or of class versus culture in Appalachian Studies by suggesting how a "critical and viable concept of [Appalachian] regionalism" can be developed that does not obscure the continuities between regional and national cultural life as well as cultural and class differences within the region. Ron Lewis and Sally Maggard discount, respectively, the either/ors of class versus race and class versus gender in studies of the interplay of the lived experiences of gender, race, and class stratification in the Appalachian coalfields. John Gaventa, Barbara Smith, and Alex Willingham connect struggles for economic justice and alternative forms of economic development in Appalachia to similar grassroots struggles in other parts of the South and to national patterns of deindustrialization.[30]

Perhaps the earliest and, in many ways, still the most radically postmodern study of Appalachia is Henry Shapiro's *Appalachia on Our Mind*. Shapiro's intellectual history of the "idea of Appalachia" does much to deconstruct the "mythic system" that interprets Appalachia as "a coherent region with a uniform culture and homogenous population." Shapiro shows that the representation of the Appalachian population as "a distinct people with distinct and describable characteristics" owes much to a stereotyped tradition of writing about life in the southern mountains that originated in late nineteenth-century local color fiction as well as in missionaries' accounts depicting Appalachia as "a strange land and a peculiar people."[31]

The radical implications of Shapiro's work for Appalachian Studies are overlooked when his text is read simply as providing empirical support for an essentialistic and reductionistic understanding of Appalachia as a "colony." In such accounts, an essentialistic understanding of Appalachia as a traditional or poverty subculture is replaced by an equally essentialistic understanding of Appalachia as an exploited colony. But Shapiro does much more than simply document the imperialistic practices of missionaries and social workers in the region's past. By remaining skeptical about the existence of any essential Appalachian experience or unitary Appalachian identity, Shapiro calls attention to how mythical versions of Appalachia are produced every day in discursive representations of the region. Thus he highlights the fact that activists and scholars produce partial versions of reality every time they write about or act in the name of Appalachia. The obvious shortcoming of Shapiro's work, however, is that there is more to Appalachia than simply language about the region.[32] Thus, his work overlooks the nondiscursive realities in the region: real-life events such as death and injury in the mines; black lung and brown lung; economic exploitation, poverty, and unemployment; gender and racial oppression. The problem that Shapiro's study of representation raises is how to deconstruct universalizing and essentializing myths of Appalachia while sustaining viable forms of regional politics.

A partially successful effort in this direction combines Shapiro's stress on how Appalachia is represented in discourses with large narratives about changes in social organization. Rodger Cunningham's *Apples on the Flood* is a sophisticated and deeply probing application of the colonial model of Appalachia and an extended essay on the cultural and psychological consequences of peripheralization.[33] Its thesis is that the internalization of pejorative discourses and opinions about Appalachia by Appalachians results in their infantilization and the development of damaged selves. Such a "psychological heredity" would undoubtedly have important negative implications for contemporary Appalachians' ability to make their own history and organize themselves collectively to resist exploitation and oppression. Floating like apples on the tide of historical circumstances, today's Appalachians are tragically portrayed by Cunningham as damaged souls—in the final analysis, victims of the pernicious effects of modernity itself—who are overidentified with their oppressors and closed off from an authentic and self-centered existence.

In style—but not in substance—Cunningham's work partakes of the new postmodern sensibility we have been describing. The author deliberately blurs the genres of anthropology, history, psychology, folklore, sociology, and comparative literature to produce an ambiguous and challenging text that defies categorization as factual social history, social science, fiction, or autobiography. He calls attention to the power of representations by showing how they operate through internalization in the social psychology of colonialism, and he directs attention toward their operation in his own text by pointing out his own narrative strategies and the effects he hopes them to have upon his readers. But in marked contrast with postmodern writers who deliberately produce ambiguous, contradictory, and open-ended texts in order to "destabilize stable ways of looking at the world" and to include the reader as an active participant in constructing the various meanings a text may come to have,[34] Cunningham supplies fixed and final answers in his portrayal of a paradigmatic Appalachia. In doing so, he subverts his own wish for Appalachian peoples to be the authors of their own identities by succumbing to the temptation of writing a metanarrative from a god's eye perspective no less Olympian than that of Caudill and Weller, of whom he is critical.

Whereas Shapiro critically examines the pejorative discourses that constitute the "myth of Appalachia," Cunningham's exploration of the psychological consequences of the internalization of such discourses has the effect of universalizing and essentializing his understanding of the Scotch-Irish experience in a manner that reduces the complexity and open-endedness of Appalachian experiences to a static and bleakly pessimistic caricature: Li'l Abner with a severely neurotic personality.[35]

Just as women, blacks, and the Eastern European miners of West Virginia and eastern Kentucky are erased from Cunningham's narrative of Appalachian history, so too is the likelihood of resistance and dissent. And having presented a deterministic account of "the present mainly as a product of past forces" and admittedly told "only half the story," Cunningham's only way out lies in "the liberating power of true myth." Thus an author "repelled . . . by [Appalachian] social activists' tendency to dismiss, ignore, or pigeonhole cultural questions" in the early seventies dispatches activism to the "realm of imagination."[36]

We believe that the solution to Cunningham's dilemma—how to convey the interrelationship of politics and culture in Appalachia—lies in adopting a postmodern view of culture. In contrast to Cunningham's essentialistic understanding of culture as a singular "structure of meanings," we suggest the value of Jerome Bruner's conceptualization of culture as "a forum for negotiating and re-negotiating meaning." According to Bruner, "it is the forum aspect of culture that gives its participants a role in constantly making and remaking the culture—an active role as participants rather than as performing spectators who play out their canonical roles according to rule when the appropriate cues occur."[37] This non-essentialistic view of culture allows for multiplicity and diversity at the same time that it recognizes culture as providing ample resources for its participants to engage in the sort of "identity politics" modeled above by contemporary feminists.

Stephen Foster's recent study, *The Past Is Another Country*,[38] makes exemplary use of such a model of culture in an investigation of grassroots resistance in Appalachia that is premised on an appreciation of Appalachia's cultural diversity. Rather than presenting a fixed image of local culture as a set of collective traits, Foster documents the "politics of culture" in Ashe County, North Carolina—that is, the changing and strategic discourses of self- and community representation. From this perspective Foster remarks that the local culture "appears in this context as extraordinarily fluid and changeable; it operates as a placeholder, a representation that shifts, deviates, and often wobbles in an unstable and quixotic fashion, depending on the desires, options, constraints, and interventions operating at the crossroads of the present."[39]

In his analysis of the successful efforts of local citizens in 1975 to prevent the Appalachian Power Company from damming a portion of the New River to create a reservoir that would have displaced 287 families, Foster examines local resistance as a "politics of representation." In stark contrast to Cunningham's interpretation that the "mountaineer's notorious 'present-orientation'" is evidence of his "being cut off from the past," Foster highlights the practices whereby Ashe County citizens objectified a version of their culture and their past to planners and outside policymakers as a way of life worth preserving. Here, the "domination of imposed discourses of economic necessity and economic interest" by elites were countered by local folk festivals that served both to mobilize support to "save the river" and to objectify local culture. Ironically, however, by choosing to represent their threatened way of life in terms of stereotyped images, folk-culture artifacts, and music, grassroots activists opened the door to the commodification of a partial version of their culture and thus potentially to further elite domination. Foster returned to Ashe County nearly ten years later to find that the embrace of mythic forms of ethnic identity that had served to stop the dam project had also begun to change the rhetorical forms through which local people understood themselves, their history, and their community.

Foster's image of culture as a discursive forum rather than a configuration of traits or a unitary structure of meaning should alert us in Appalachian Studies to the variety of discourses that constitute social identity as well as to the diversity of subjects actively involved in making history in Appalachia. Further, his refusal to describe local culture the way it "really" is, in any fixed or final way—that is, his refusal to write a "metanarrative"—exemplifies the postmodern ethnographic ideal of "apprehend[ing] and inscrib[ing] 'others' in such a way as not to deny or diffuse their claims to subjecthood."[40] As such, his study provides not only important insights into problematic aspects of grassroots activism but also a model for how Appalachian scholars can learn to write about the region without succumbing to the temptation of speaking like the invisible, know-it-all "over-voice" that is a commonplace in television advertising and mass media broadcasting.

Conclusion

In challenging the notion that writers can attain a god's eye view of truth and represent reality in its totality, postmodernism has the potential to make all of us, activists and scholars, more humble and reflective about what we claim and assert. From the recognition that "truths" are always "truths for some particular person or group," it follows that our common-sense notions of what "Appalachia" is, or who "Appalachians" are, can always be opened up to include more diversity or, as postmodernists like to say, more "difference." Yet, as many feminists have been forced to admit, the recognition of difference and diversity is a political challenge. As Teresa Ebert notes, the recognition of differences among women "opens up the multiplicity of differences among (within) women, but in doing so it undermines the unity or collectivity of women and gender as categories on which an oppositional politics can be based."[41] The achievement of diversity and unity can only result from political effort.

The recognition of difference—indeed, the positive valorization of difference—that postmodern thinking encourages should help us to appreciate that what we have been doing in the Appalachian Studies movement and in the Appalachian Studies Association has been a positive yet fragile accomplishment. Still, if the Appalachian Studies movement is to fulfill its promise of "help[ing] to reconstruct a public sphere through which people can participate in democratizing the structures of political economy and everyday life,"[42] difference and diversity must be further embraced and accommodated. Mythical images of a homogeneous Appalachia must not be allowed to suppress the important class, race, ethnic, and gender differences that figure in the life of the region. Likewise, the organizational structures and processes of the ASA must be revised in ways that support such diversity.

Ours, as we have seen, is not the only scholarly association to face new organizational tensions that result from growth and success and raise concerns about how to remain connected to founding ideals—the grass-roots basis of our common identity and purpose. Many current tensions in the ASA mirror those in other movement-based organizations that are likewise committed to supporting democratic struggles. For instance, Lisa Hall has observed that the linkages between community- and academically based participants in women's studies and ethnic studies have weakened. "Academic feminism and ethnic studies as a whole," she says, "have not maintained the direct connections with the communities that helped to create them."[43]

Organizational reforms within the ASA itself may help to combat the trend toward academicization and contribute to the preservation and strengthening of ties between the Appalachian Studies movement and the grassroots. If ASA conferences are becoming too large and its sessions too specialized, then noncompetitive plenary sessions, arranged to include scholarly activists and activist scholars, can be used to front-stage important conversations that have regionwide implications. Ideally, annual conferences—now typically coordinated by local colleges—could be co-sponsored by local grassroots organizations that would conduct off-site sessions highlighting local issues and struggles and thus challenging the ASA to reaffirm its original goal of relating scholarship to regional needs and the concerns of Appalachian people. The steering committee that governs the association, increasingly peopled by academicians, can change its membership criteria to create formal slots for individuals representing grassroots organizations, while caucuses can be organized to reflect and encourage diversity within the general membership. We hope that such small but self-conscious efforts can help to keep alive an important form of cooperation in the region that has great potential to contribute further to Appalachian and American public life.

Notes

1. John Gaventa, "Inequality and the Appalachian Studies Industry," *Appalachian Journal* 5 (1978) : 322.
2. See Jack Weller, *Yesterday's People* (Lexington: University Press of Kentucky, 1965); and Harry M. Caudill, *Night Comes to the Cumberlands: A Biography of a Depressed Area* (Boston: Little, Brown/Atlantic Monthly, 1962). Rupert Vance summarized Weller's thesis in a foreword to *Yesterday's People* (p. iv): "Thus mountain isolation, which began as physical isolation enforced by rugged topography, became mental and cultural isolation, holding people in disadvantaged areas, resisting those changes that would bring them into contact with the outside world. The effect of conditions thus becomes a new cause of conditions, but *the cause is now an attitude, not a mountain. . . . To change the mountains is to change the mountain personality.*" Emphasis added.
3. Helen Lewis, "Fatalism or the Coal Industry?" *Mountain Life & Work*, December 1970.
4. For example, see Alan Banks, "Labor and the Development of Industrial Capitalism in Eastern Kentucky" (Ph.D. diss., McMaster University, 1980); Dwight B. Billings, "Religion as Opposition: A Gramscian Analysis," *American Journal of Sociology* 96 (1990) : 1–31; David Alan Corbin, *Life, Work, and Rebellion in the Coal Fields: The Southern West Virginia Miners, 1880–*

1922 (Urbana: University of Illinois Press, 1981); Ronald D. Eller, *Miners, Millhands, and Mountaineers: Industrialization of the Appalachian South, 1880–1930* (Knoxville: University of Tennessee Press, 1982); John Hevener, *Which Side Are You On?* (Urbana: University of Illinois Press, 1978).

5. Notably John Gaventa, *Power and Powerlessness: Quiescence and Rebellion in an Appalachian Valley* (Urbana: University of Illinois Press, 1980).

6. For example, Altina L. Waller, *Feud: Hatfields, McCoys, and Social Change in Appalachia, 1860–1900* (Chapel Hill: University of North Carolina Press, 1988).

7. The Appalachian Land Ownership Task Force was a coalition of scholars and activists in the region that managed to obtain funding for an impressive seven-volume participatory study of land ownership patterns in Appalachia. Members of the ALOTF produced *Landownership Patterns and Their Impacts on Appalachian Counties: A Survey of Eighty Counties*, which documents ownership patterns for both surface and mineral rights. A summary of the findings of the ALOTF study can be found in *Who Owns Appalachia? Landownership and Its Impact* (Lexington: University Press of Kentucky, 1983). Also see Pat Beaver, "Participatory Research on Land Ownership in Rural Appalachia," in Allen W. Batteau, ed., *Appalachia and America: Autonomy and Regional Dependence* (Lexington: University Press of Kentucky, 1983), 252–66.

    For more on the Appalachian Alliance, see Appalachian Alliance, "Appalachia 1978: A Protest From the Colony," pamphlet (1978); and Appalachian Alliance, "National Sacrifice Area," pamphlet (1979).

8. Richard Couto, "Appalachian Innovations in Health Care," in Batteau, *Appalachia and America*, 185. Also see Karen W. Tice, "A Case Study of Battered Women's Shelters in Appalachia," *Affilia* 5 (Fall 1990) : 83–100.

9. Trisha Frazen and Lois R. Helmbold, "What Is To Be Done?" *Women's Review of Books* 8 (February 1991) : 29.

10. Teresa Ebert, "Postmodernism's Infinite Variety," *Women's Review of Books* 8 (January 1991) : 24.

11. Jean Baudrillard, *Selected Writings*, ed. Mark Poster (Stanford, Calif.: Stanford University Press, 1988); Jean-Francois Lyotard, *The Postmodern Condition* (Minneapolis: University of Minneapolis Press, [1979] 1984).

12. For example, Fredric Jameson, "Postmodernism or the Cultural Logic of Late Capitalism," *New Left Review*, no. 146 (July–August 1984) : 53–92.

13. Quoted in Ebert, "Postmodernism's Infinite Variety," 24–25.

14. Clifford Geertz, *Local Knowledge* (New York: Basic Books, 1983), 20.

15. The model for such freethinking was empirical science. Simply observing the world as it really was—rather than passively accepting the way it was described by religious or political authorities—promised liberation from ignorance, superstition, and fear. And, until the past few decades, many people have shared the Enlightenment faith that when the eye of reason judged social institutions, it would guarantee a critical vision that would lead the march to Progress.

16. Along with the loss of faith in reason's ability to perfect society, we have also

become increasingly skeptical about reason's ability even to understand and represent social life. In particular, the simple, unmediated, unitary vision of reason has been called into question.

17. Quoted in W. T. Jones, *Kant and the Nineteenth Century* (New York: Harcourt Brace Jovanovich, 1975), 237.

18. Thomas S. Kuhn, *The Structure of Scientific Revolutions* (Chicago: University of Chicago Press, 1970).

19. Cornel West, "Interview," in Andrew Ross, ed., *Universal Abandon?* (Minneapolis: University of Minnesota Press, 1988), 272.

20. See Geertz, *Local Knowledge*, 19.

21. Hayden White, *The Content of the Form* (Baltimore: Johns Hopkins University Press, 1987), 14.

22. David Cattell-Gordon, "The Appalachian Inheritance: A Culturally Transmitted Traumatic Stress Syndrome?" *Journal of Progressive Human Service* 1 (1990) : 41–57. Also see Karen W. Tice and Dwight B. Billings, "Appalachian Culture and Resistance," *Journal of Progressive Human Services* 2 (1991) : 1–18.

23. See Todd Gitlin, "Hip Deep in Post-Modernism," *New York Times Book Review*, November 6, 1988, 35–36.

24. For example, Douglas Kellner, "Critical Theory and the Crisis of Social Theory," *Sociological Perspectives* 33 (Spring 1990) : 11–17.

25. Geertz, *Local Knowledge*, 21.

26. Nancy Fraser and Linda Nicholson, "Social Criticism Without Philosophy: An Encounter Between Feminism and Postmodernism," *Theory, Culture & Society* 5 (1988) : 391.

27. For example, the work of Carol Gilligan on women's moral development and Nancy Chodorow on mothering has been criticized for their failure to consider important differences between white women and women of color and the accommodations that slavery and domestic work have demanded of African-American women. See Fraser and Nicholson, "Social Criticism"; Sandra Morgan, *To See Ourselves, To See Our Sisters* (Memphis, Tenn.: Memphis State University Press/Center for Research on Women, 1986); and Carol Stack, "The Culture of Gender: Women and Men of Color," *Signs* 11(1986) : 321–24.

28. Fraser and Nicholson, "Social Criticism," 391.

29. Joan Scott, "Deconstructing Equality-Versus-Difference: Or, The Uses of Poststructuralist Theory for Feminism," *Feminist Studies* 14 (1988) : 33–50.

30. Herbert Reid, "Appalachian Studies: Class, Culture and Politics—II," *Appalachian Journal* 9 (1982) : 144; Ronald L. Lewis, *Black Coal Miners in America: Race, Class, and Community Conflict, 1780–1980* (Lexington: University Press of Kentucky, 1987); Sally Maggard, "Eastern Kentucky Women on Strike: A Study of Gender, Class and Political Action in the 1970s" (Ph.D. diss., University of Kentucky, 1988); and John Gaventa, Barbara E. Smith, and Alex Willingham, eds., *Communities in Economic Crisis: Appalachia and the South* (Philadelphia: Temple University Press, 1990). Also note that many of

these points are raised in a special issue of *Appalachian Journal* 9, entitled "Assessing Appalachian Studies" (Winter/Spring 1982).

31. Henry D. Shapiro, *Appalachia on Our Mind: The Southern Mountains and Mountaineers in the American Consciousness, 1870–1920* (Chapel Hill: University of North Carolina Press, 1978), 265.

32. See Herbert Reid, "Appalachian Policy, the Corporate State and American Values," *Policy Studies Journal* 9 (Special Issue no. 2, 1980–81) : 622–33.

33. Rodger Cunningham, *Apples on the Flood: The Southern Mountain Experience* (Knoxville: University of Tennessee Press, 1987).

34. Gurney Norman and Lance Olsen, "Frankenstein in Palestine or: Postmodernism in Appalachia," in *Pine Mountain Sand and Gravel*, ed. Jim Webb et al. (Whitesburg, Ky.: Appalshop Productions, 1988), 83.

35. By taking the Scotch-Irish as the predominant ethnic group to settle and influence the region, Cunningham suppresses much of the diversity that can be found throughout Appalachia, essentializing it as a Scotch-Irish enclave. For a different look at early settlement patterns, see John Solomon Otto, "The Migration of the Southern Plain Folk: An Interdisciplinary Synthesis," *Journal of Southern History* 51 (1985) : 183–200. For a look at the ethnic and racial diversity that came to characterize coal camp living, see Lewis, *Black Coal Miners in America*.

36. Cunningham, *Apples on the Flood*, xvii, 160, 162.

37. Jerome Bruner, *Actual Minds, Possible Worlds* (Cambridge: Harvard University Press, 1986), 94, 123.

38. Stephen William Foster, *The Past Is Another Country: Representation, Historical Consciousness, and Resistance in the Blue Ridge* (Berkeley, Los Angeles and London: University of California Press, 1988).

39. Ibid., 203.

40. Frances Mascia-Lees et al., "The Postmodernist Turn in Anthropology: Cautions from a Feminist Perspective," *Signs* 15 (1989) : 12.

41. Ebert, "Postmodernism's Infinite Variety," 24.

42. Reid, "Appalachian Studies," 141.

43. Lisa Hall, "Trapped in the Ivory Tower?" *Women's Review of Books* 11 (May 1991) : 25.

15

Politics, Expressive Form, and Historical Knowledge in a Blue Ridge Resistance Movement

Stephen William Foster

By the end of the nineteenth century, political turmoil, urbanization, a revolution in aesthetics, changing economic and labor relations, and new techniques of transport and communication brought about what is now called modernity.[1] In the process, imperialists and corporate administrators reshuffled territories and redefined cultures as disposable resources, as commodities that could be bought and sold.[2] This diagnosis pertains to Appalachia as well as to what is known as the Third World. Disagreement, disruption, and disintegration seem to hold sway. A particularly virulent and unhappy version of modernity has been imposed. Increasingly, Appalachians have become and have seen themselves as victims of invasive development. They cannot regard their regional identity and autonomy as geographic or cultural givens.[3] These conditions have, in turn, challenged Appalachians to undertake cultural innovation and political resistance.

As it pertains to Appalachia, the storybook fantasy of close-knit, harmonious rural communities was laid to rest by social critics, journalists, and local writers who exposed the grim and tragic underside of the region's history. Little was done to improve the lives of the region's people. Outsiders saw Appalachia as a region "ripe for development" (one also thinks of the Amazon), but "development" had become a dramatic euphemism for exploitation. The wealth generated by "developing" the region went elsewhere to build the glittering towers that represent civilization's soaring advance. While the Kentucky coalfields provide the "ideal type" of the region's exploitation, other parts of Appalachia, which come closer to fulfilling the promise of bucolic agrarian life, have also had to face the developers, outside agents who promise affluence and civilization at an unspecified cost. Ashe County, North Carolina, where I lived for a year of ethnographic research, is a case in point. The countryside of the Blue Ridge was to me idyllic; the county had not previously been studied by an anthropologist; and there was no urban population. As in Kentucky, the politics of culture touched directly upon the local citizenry's prospects for pursuing their chosen way of life.

Ashe, the state's most northwestern county, borders Tennessee on the west and Virginia on the north. It is still a largely agricultural region, dotted with small farms and rural communities. The north and south forks of the New River flow through a maze of hills and hollows to join in the north of Ashe County. The river then runs through Virginia and West Virginia to become part of the Ohio River. The New River dispute, over whether or not a significant portion of the county's land would be flooded for a vast hydroelectric generating facility, became the occasion for local residents to formulate a version of regional identity that had explicit political and pragmatic motivations. During the fourteen-year struggle over the possible construction of dams on the river, regionalism was articulated in terms of economic interests, with obvious implications for land use and resource management. The dispute became an arena in which personal worth, independence, local autonomy, economic survival, and cultural identity were seriously contested. For the residents of Ashe County, the New River became a symbol of change, representing a complex of meanings that were explicated and refashioned in the course of the struggle.[4]

Arguments against the project assumed the unity of people and land as the basis of historical continuity, social survival, and political power. Once identity became "spatialized" in this fashion, inscribed in the geography of the county itself, regionalism became a burning issue for county residents. They were compelled to assert a regional identity and distinctive culture, assertions that were in part based on the American values of freedom and self-sufficiency. This chapter discusses regionalism as it emerged in this political context, specifically in reference to a dramatic performance presented during a political rally intended to promote county solidarity and resistance to the hydroelectric project. In examining this local performance, the strategic use of an expressive form in articulating and promoting regional identity can be seen as a cultural resource that local residents successfully utilized in their struggle with the national economy and the modern world system. This expressive form was a narrative composed of elements of rhetoric and representation deeply resonant in the hearts and minds of the local citizenry.[5]

In 1962 the Appalachian Power Company announced a plan for the Blue Ridge Power Project that would include damming the New River.[6] Initially, most of the land to be affected by the project was in Virginia. It was only with the revision and expansion of the plan in 1966 that people in Ashe County began to organize their protests. This new plan called for flooding 42,000 acres, 8,400 of which were in Ashe County (about

3 percent of the county's total area and some of its best farmland). Public hearings were held and environmental studies conducted. People living along the river in Ashe County began to say that because no power generated by the proposed facility would be used locally, their farms were being sacrificed to solve another area's need for electricity. Regional identity was thus placed on the political agenda.

The plan called for the construction of two dams on the New River across the state line from Ashe County in Grayson County, Virginia. Water would be released by the upper dam to generate power during peak-use periods. During off-periods, water would be pumped from the lower reservoir back into the upper reservoir in readiness for the next high-use period. Because power would have to be used to lift the water back into the upper reservoir, the overall system would consume more power than it produced. The facility would have a life span of only twenty-five to thirty years before silting would make it inoperable. Short-term fluctuations of water levels would be considerable. Unattractive mud flats would result, posing formidable problems for Appalachian Power's recreational development plans for the areas around the reservoirs.

The Federal Power Commission held public hearings on the project from 1966 to 1970. During the hearings, residents from Ashe County and neighboring Alleghany County contended that the dams would cause irreparable environmental damage. Despite these objections, the Federal Power Commission licensed the project in July 1974. Construction was postponed, however, pending the outcome of law suits that had previously been brought against the project. Two years earlier, North Carolina's governor had asked the U.S. Department of Interior to grant the New River status as a National Wild and Scenic River. This action would block the project, since federal law prohibits constructing dams along designated Scenic Rivers. North Carolina asked the U.S. Court of Appeals to reopen hearings even after the project was licensed, arguing that the Federal Power Commission had not taken account of decreased energy demands or the required environmental impact statements, and had failed to consider the Wild and Scenic River alternative.

Not all Ashe County people were in sympathy with the resistance to the project. Some pointed out the economic advantages of the dams, from new employment opportunities to the "development" of the county through increased tourism and recreation. Others argued that to block construction of the project would be to promote backwardness and to prevent progress. They predicted that the county's population would continue its "normal decline," industry would not be attracted to the area, employment opportunities would be limited, stagnation and malaise would continue, and the advantages of modernity would pass them by. They looked to business, real estate, and industrial interests outside the region to provide relief from what they regarded as the area's backwater insularity. Although these views were a minority opinion, they suggested the possibility that outside interests might ally with local residents dissatisfied with the status quo. As it turned out, the arguments for development were overridden and overwhelmed by the protests against constructing the dams. Despite divided opinion within the county, a strong community sentiment emerged to resist the Blue Ridge Project.

By January 1976 letters from local residents, environmentalists, and sympathetic "Tar Heels" were pouring into the offices of congressmen and the Interior Department, protesting the project. The letters waxed eloquent on the natural beauty and historical importance of the river, the advantages of the traditional economy, and the virtues of indigenous styles of life. An editorial in the *Detroit News* commented that "the FPC [Federal Power Commission] says the [power] plant's reservoirs would make dandy recreation areas. Yes, and Paris could demolish the Louvre to build a bowling alley."[7] The dispute had become national in scope. It was appropriated as a vote-getting issue in the 1976 presidential primaries in North Carolina, and major newspapers across the country carried stories on the controversy's latest developments. American Electric Power, which owned the Appalachian Power Company, told its stockholders that more than two hundred newspapers had printed editorials against the project. Presidential hopefuls Jimmy Carter, Henry Jackson, and Ronald Reagan went on record against it.

Opposition continued to grow. During the summer of 1976, the U.S. House and Senate both considered bills to invalidate the project's license. In August, Congress overwhelmingly passed a bill designating 26.5 miles of the New River in Ashe County a National Wild and Scenic River. This measure superseded the outstanding court proceedings and effectively blocked construction. President Gerald Ford signed the bill into law two weeks later.[8]

Major elements of the local rhetoric of resistance had been given voice at the New River Festival, held on the river banks on July 16, 1975. One member of the organizing committee said it was to be "a day for fun and not politicking." Yet the political implications of the festival were obvious. Estimates of the turnout varied, but reporters claimed that thousands of people from as far away as California attended. The site for the festival was a farm in the bottom lands that had been worked by the same family for more than two hundred years, a site chosen specifically to highlight the significance of the event and of the dispute as well. Speakers who addressed the crowd pointed out that if the dams were built, this land would be under one hundred feet of water. Local craftsmen displayed and sold their wood carvings, leather goods, jewelry, quilts, and other wares. They did a brisk business. Many local people contributed food and other necessities. Expenses were covered by a donation bucket that kept overflowing. An information booth provided materials on the history and geology of the New River and on the development of the dispute itself.

The festival was a multimedia event. Entertainment was presented in a natural amphitheater formed by a curve in the river. Bluegrass and country music predominated. Six original songs about the New River were premiered. The performances had an undisguised propagandistic tone. Participants had come together for this political ritual to reinforce their opposition to the Blue Ridge Project and to broaden their base of support. The event provided a forum for transmitting grassroots opposition to a larger public. Speeches given by state and federal officials, including congressmen from North Carolina and West Virginia, were excerpted for television newscasts. The success of the festival was widely reported in newspapers and by North Carolina television stations.

The festival was a microcosm of the dispute as a whole. The participants came from diverse geographic and social backgrounds. Together, they experienced a reaffirmation of local culture through protest songs, the modeling of the event on the family reunion, and the performance of a pageant of local history, discussed below.[9] Informal interaction also broadened the range and depth of meanings available to them for interpreting the issues. As an occasion for elaborating the culture of resistance that had grown over the long course of the dispute, the festival heightened solidarity, expanded the social contacts through which political support could be conducted, permitted the formation and strengthening of personal alliances and networks, and encouraged individuals to participate in further protests against the project. Subsequently, protest increased to a veritable deluge. The "marketing techniques" used at the festival propelled dissent into a wider arena and provided a rhetorical model for the participants while helping to shift the dispute from the local to the national level.[10] The resistance movement caught the attention of "the media" and interest groups outside the region. It became a *cause célèbre,* its rising momentum reported on a daily basis.

Local historian and genealogist Eleanor Reeves wrote an "epic" narrative to illustrate the grand sweep of local history from colonial times to the present.[11] As she read her story at the festival, each of its episodes was dramatized by actors in authentic, colorful costumes. The scenes on stage were punctuated by musical interludes and dances appropriate to each epoch. The story portrayed the changes that had come to Ashe County over time and emphasized social progress. Impediments were consistently seen as challenges turned to profit, attesting to the resilience and stamina of Ashe County's citizenry throughout its history. Mrs. Reeves's narrative comprised a medley of fragmentary, arbitrarily selected events, molded into a myth of origin and a model of regional identity within a progressive history of social development. The narrative explains the successful unfolding of local history in terms of the character of the inhabitants: a God-fearing, self-reliant people braving the wilderness. The flow of the New River itself represents the continuity of local identity and denotes the human landscape that nurtured it.

As the pageant begins, the New River is discovered in 1740 by European explorers. Soon after, the first white settlers arrive. The Cherokee, Shawnee, and Creek Indians are at war in the vicinity (the possibility that such warfare might have been induced by the settlers' presence is not considered). In 1773 James Baker becomes the first "white man" to obtain legal title to land in what would become Ashe County after the American Revolution. This event is the anchor point for later claims to land in the area. Local identity is secured by means of the historical narrative that begins with this event. The American Revolution legitimates the Europeans' claim to the region. Throughout the history narrated during the performance, local, regional, and national identity are all understood in reference to the political changes brought about by American independence and nationhood.

The early settlers begin to routinize community life, evidenced by the first marriage in the county and the founding of the county's first churches. In 1800, the county is legally incorporated. By 1860, slavery becomes an issue for its citizens. During this period, the county is divided into three parts because it is too large to administer from a single county seat. The town of Jefferson, the original county seat, remained the administrative center after the partition left Ashe County the 427 square miles that make up its area today.

It is not until the end of the nineteenth century that a system of public education is instituted. The narrative takes note of the decade of the Gay Nineties, "which brings about a more progressive way of life. . . . There is more time for leisure and pleasure." In 1914, the Norfolk and Western Railroad comes to the county. World War I takes its toll of local young men. Then come the Roaring Twenties: "The Charleston and the Big Apple tickled the feet of the young at heart." The Great Depression introduces new difficulties, although agriculture protects the people from its worst consequences, the Works Progress Administration helps to employ the county's residents, and the road system is improved significantly. World War II finally lifts the Depression once and for all. "Again, many of Ashe County's most promising young men lost their lives and many others carry marks of varying degrees, received in that tragic conflict." The presentation closes with a quotation from a present-day county notable: "Ashe County is a corridor of unspoiled beauty. The New River was here when the only access to the outside world was by an old turnpike that followed the streams and wound around the hills rather than over them. The New River is our heritage. We want it left to flow gently on its way."

Mrs. Reeves's narrative is elegiac in tone and intent, and its dramatization was a centerpiece for the New River Festival. As political ritual, it was played to a receptive audience. As cultural rhetoric, it presented the issues of economic autonomy, security, and survival in the guise of history, an expressive form that appropriated the appeal of longstanding orientations and values. History expressed identity and celebrated the abilities of Ashe County people to set up an enduring community in spite of many difficulties. During the Revolution, the world wars, and the Great Depression, the citizens "do their part" to contribute to the nation's historical destiny. The narrative secures the development of local practices within history as a national undertaking.

The narrative stylizes history so as to place local claims of legitimacy beyond question. As a symbolic system, history is understood to disclose directly "who we are." It is viewed as undebatable cultural knowledge. Thus, local history teaches county residents *and* outsiders about the sources and attributes of local identity. It parallels the nation's history and assumes that "somehow we must be able to share each other's past in order to be knowingly in each other's present."[12] This assumption implies that sharing the present must involve a negotiated, possibly harmonious coexistence, rather than one in which local people are subordinated and exploited. In this way, local cultural distinctiveness is placed in the context of common historical roots and shared cultural assumptions. The performance at the festival was a public ritual in which local versions of historical and cultural knowledge were injected into the discourse of the dispute as carried on through confrontations, arguments, claims, and legal proceedings. It brought together local people's commitment to the meaning of these representations with their commitment to resisting the Blue Ridge Project. This amalgamation of deeply rooted cultural elements and the passions ignited by the immediate political circumstances is what gave Mrs. Reeves's narrative its persuasiveness and its power in expressing regional identity.

Initially, the discourse of the dispute was expressed in terms aimed at convincing outside administrators and politicians of the merits of the resistance; survey research, statistical data, economic indicators, and ecological analysis were the prevailing modes of argument.[13] During congressional hearings and in litigation, the arguments for and against the Blue Ridge Project were thus scientifically grounded, scientifically presented, and scientifically evaluated. Arguments against the project were initially based mainly on its potential environmental damage rather than on its potential social impact or human cost. But "rational argumentation" was only part of the battle. These understandings also had to be made to appeal broadly; persuasion had to be multifaceted; arguments had to touch people deeply, to speak to their emotions, to touch off their rage and their self-righteousness. They had to activate deeply ingrained cultural values and even respond to people's aesthetic sense. They had to connect with local ideas of "the good, the true, and the beautiful." They had to galvanize solidarity among local citizens and their supporters in the resistance. The "scientific" arguments undertaken during years of politicking were crucial in preparation for the "showdown." But at the New River Festival, they were complemented by aesthetic elements and arguments "from the heart." The performance's rhetorical ploys made the festival and the historical pageant particularly effective as political ritual, because, ultimately, resistance had to become visceral, from the gut.

In response to the threat that the Blue Ridge Project posed to Ashe County residents, a rhetoric was developed that contested this intervention from the outside.[14] Local rhetoric questioned imposed practices and representations, and made a claim of local autonomy. In this context, resistance assumed the necessity of claiming a distinctive regional identity. In turn, regionalism demanded the maintenance of locally and historically situated patterns of land management, economic adaptation, and self-determination, as described in the narrative history. During the dispute, regional identity was expressed in terms of the distinctiveness of local culture.

Resistance thus involved modifying or rephrasing local knowledge in order to demand power in the decision-making process, which was imposed from the outside. As a system of symbols, history certified the continuity of the people's relation to their land and territory, and the value of their way of life. Local culture was redefined as quintessentially "American," and therefore inviolate on those grounds as well as on grounds of uniqueness—a claim that was, in turn, justified in terms of self-determination. Resistance could only succeed by appealing to mainstream ideas and values. It created new self-understandings, which were expressed in terms of the region's historical tradition.

Arguments against the project, by turns rational and rhetorical, made truth claims in domains ranging from values such as self-sufficiency, through the ecological integrity of the land base, to the aesthetic appeal of a "unique" geography and scenic landscape. In addition, resistance defined and proposed a pathway for social and cultural change. Given history as locally understood, it proposed to direct and manage change in order to control an influx of population, patterns of land and resource management, forms of economic adaptation, labor utilization, and the distribution of wealth. It claimed the existence of a culture, however fragile and tenuous, designed specifically to keep outside domination in check and to counter the erosion of local values. Local expressive forms posed not only an argument, but a comprehensive world view as well.

Analyzing local resistance movements can itself be a form of resistance. It can reveal how domination is perpetuated by the dominant group's cooptation of local values and tradition. In Ashe County, cooptation was made more difficult when local resistance appealed to the legitimacy and distinctiveness of their tradition. In addition, citizens actively promoted regionalism in reference to values and symbols of the dominant group itself, as represented by legislators, industrialists, and government administrators. As in the discourse of the dispute more generally, Mrs. Reeves's version of local history claimed regional identity on the basis of commonly held values and a common national history, *rather than* on the basis of cultural distinctiveness alone. Her narrative intimately connects local experience with historicized national identity and national culture. Resistance succeeds, in this case, by appropriating aspects of the dominant culture, a strategy that blocked appropriation by the dominant group and promoted the dissemination of the rhetoric of the resistance through "the media," newspapers, and television.

One of the lessons of this resistance movement is that expressive forms derived from local tradition can serve as a decisive resource in catalyzing and promoting regional identity. The local citizenry became more reflective about their own values and traditions because the dispute forced them to; the meaning of tradition was being eroded, and so local citizens were compelled to explicate it. As corporate interests pressured for change, local residents could no longer take their own identity for granted. Culture became fluid, was up for grabs, and was variously claimed and contested.[15] It was employed as a vehicle of knowledge and as a means of demanding power. This instability of representation and culture opened up the possibility of inventing alternative expressive forms and then of stabilizing their meaning through political rituals such as the New River Festival *long enough* to achieve political advantage.[16]

As in the dramatization of Mrs. Reeves's narrative, such expressive forms often attempt to define a geographic and historical space through traditional representations. Territory, region, and regional identity, as locally understood, are defined and redefined not only in reference to material concerns such as resource management and economic survival, but also in reference to more global and more deeply psychological elements such as history, aesthetics, national destinies, and the value of an entire way of life. Through these means, resistance attempts to make local practices *less* problematic and to make the encroaching systems of knowledge, power, and practice *more* problematic. Resistance must be meticulous in its scrutiny and in its criticism of the rhetoric and the expressive forms associated with the encroaching system. The dominated group must then refashion local expressive forms in relation to imposed ones, as Mrs. Reeves did so eloquently in her historical narrative. Thus, regional identity cannot be formulated in a vacuum, as separate from encompassing political, geographic, or social realities. It must be defined in relation to an external, often imposed system of values *and* in relation to a larger whole, a nation, a continent, or the world system. Regionalism is a "part-whole" proposition; a region must be a "region within."[17]

The rhetoric of the dispute was processed through a variety of institutions inside and outside the county. It infiltrated the county's livestock and agricultural markets, where farmers discussed and worried together about their economic survival and self-sufficiency. It informed real estate speculation and entered informal conversations in town, at the courthouse, after church, and at school. Local musicians were another group with networks inside and outside the county, and with links to "the media," recording companies, and radio stations. These links permitted alliance building in yet another arena and promoted the wider dissemination of arguments against the project. As I have shown, the rhetoric also appealed to national conservation and environmental groups. This wide array of institutional focuses induced and synergized support and harmonized self-interest with collective well-being.

The alliances of local interests and institutions with voluntary organizations and media networks outside the county developed in the context of the county's relative affluence. There were indigenous leaders who knew how to use the legal system and the newspapers and television, and who had experience in government agencies and other organizations at the national level. The county's citizens had social and economic resources, communication and political skills, and the time to exercise them. The resistance thus drew on the county's economic viability and the talents of those of its citizens who had knowledge of outside institutions, university backgrounds, and urban contacts. These social factors were favorable conditions for the development and comprehension of, and a commitment to, the new expressive forms that made up the rhetoric of resistance.

Although timing, a variety of social and political circumstances, and a complex of psychological preconditions must come together to produce a positive outcome, the detailed fashioning and subtle refinement of expressive forms also have a major role in the creation of regional identity and resistance. Resisting the Blue Ridge Project and the social, cultural, and

economic changes that it would have produced demanded careful attention both to local tradition and to the dominant system, so that expressive
forms could be used to advantage in a competitive, political marketplace.
As is clear from Mrs. Reeves's narrative, the emerging expressive forms
had to be made meaningful and compelling for both local people *and*
outsiders. Struggle necessarily involves appropriating elements of rhetoric
and representation, but this appropriation must be highly selective and
critical. Nonlocal expressive forms and knowledge are thereby exploited
and preempted in order to "normalize" or to keep at bay the disruptions
and exploitations imposed by colonial and imperialist interests.

Acknowledgments

Ethnographic research was made possible by grants from the National Science
Foundation (no. SOC 13976) and the National Institutes of Health (no. MH
05422-01). I want to thank Jane Foster and Steve Fisher for their comments on
earlier drafts of this chapter.

Notes

1. For a carefully nuanced discussion of modernity and its relevance for
   anthropology, see James Faubion, "Possible Modernities," *Cultural Anthropology* 3 (1988) : 365–78.
2. David Harvey, *The Condition of Postmodernity* (Cambridge, Mass.: Basil
   Blackwell, 1989), 264.
3. The existence of Appalachia as a separate region may never have been *anything but* a cultural construction induced by interventions from "the outside."
   For a discussion of this point, see David E. Whisnant, *All That Is Native
   and Fine: The Politics of Culture in an American Region* (Chapel Hill: University of North Carolina Press, 1983). A similar argument is proposed in
   Stephen William Foster, *The Past Is Another Country: Representation, Historical Consciousness, and Resistance in the Blue Ridge* (Berkeley, Los Angeles,
   and London: University of California Press, 1988). More recently, Allen W.
   Batteau, in *The Invention of Appalachia* (Tuscon: University of Arizona Press,
   1990), elaborates the same theme, but errs in not acknowledging the previous work. Batteau states the case succinctly in his opening paragraph (p. 1):
   "Appalachia is a creature of the urban imagination. The folk culture, the depressed area, the romantic wilderness, the Appalachia of fiction, journalism,
   and public policy, have for more than a century been created, forgotten, and
   rediscovered, primarily by the economic opportunism, political creativity,
   or passing fancy of urban elites. The contemporary appearance of Appalachia, whether in movies about a coal miner's daughter or in the use of

rural themes in merchandizing, draws on the imagery and motivations that a generation ago transfixed an affluent society and sent legions of poverty warriors into the hills." For a broader interpretation of the importance of such constructions for the Appalachian region, see Harvey, *The Condition of Postmodernity*, 303: "The assertion of any place-bound identity has to rest at some point on the motivational power of tradition. . . . The irony is that tradition is now often preserved by being commodified and marketed as such. . . . At best, historical tradition is reorganized as a museum culture, not necessarily of high modernist art, but of local history, of local production, of how things once upon a time were made, sold, consumed, and integrated into a long-lost and often romanticized daily life. . . . Through the presentation of a partially illusory past it becomes possible to signify something of local identity and perhaps to do it profitably."

4. For an in-depth analysis of this dispute, see Foster, *The Past Is Another Country*. I conducted ethnographic field work for this study in Ashe County in 1975–76 and in 1987.

5. My approach to rhetoric in this paper and in earlier publications derives from the work of Edmund Burke, *A Rhetoric of Motives* (Berkeley and Los Angeles: University of California Press, 1950); J. Christopher Crocker, "The Social Functions of Rhetorical Forms," in *The Social Use of Metaphor*, ed. J. David Sapir and J. Christopher Crocker (Philadelphia: University of Pennsylvania Press, 1977); and Renato Rosaldo, "The Rhetoric of Control: Ilongots Viewed as Natural Bandits and Wild Indians," in *The Reversible World*, ed. Barbara A. Babcock (Ithaca, N.Y.: Cornell University Press, 1978). As Burke suggests, rhetoric is "*par excellence* the region of the Scramble, of insult and injury, bickering, squabbling . . . cloaked malice and subsidized lie." Along the same lines, Kathleen Stewart, in "On the Politics of Cultural Theory: A Case for 'Contaminated' Cultural Critique," *Social Research* 58 (1991) : 399, argues that the task of interpretation is "to understand the [rhetorical] operations by which . . . [regional] identities are ascribed, or contested, or even unintentionally produced as side-effects."

6. This history of the dispute derives from my field research and from documentary sources. Much of it was common "knowledge" among Ashe County residents and others at the time. Exhaustive references would falsify the dynamic of the discourse of the dispute as it unfolded in the course of its history. I have therefore not given detailed references for all information covered in this summary.

7. George F. Will, "A Utility Threatens a Carolina Valley," *Detroit News*, January 26, 1976.

8. The Appalachian Power Company subsequently attempted to build a similar hydroelectric facility in rural Virginia, but that project also had to be dropped after local protests. For a discussion of this "denouement," see Foster, *The Past Is Another Country*, 207–8.

9. Stewart, "On the Politics of Cultural Theory," 405, understands these expressive forms as a "performative, epistemological critique." They have the effect of "poetic intensifications" that "construct a [liminal] interpretive

space where, as they say in West Virginia, 'things are not what they seem' and 'anything could happen'" (p. 407). This understanding of expressive form applies to the festival as a whole as well as to the pageant in particular.

10. As county librarian Clarice Weaver told me in 1991, referring to the developers of the Blue Ridge Project, "a few farmers held them off until they could bring in the big guns."

11. The complete text of this narrative can be found in Stephen William Foster, "Identity as Symbolic Production" (Ph.D. diss., Princeton University, 1977), 314–21.

12. Johannes Fabian, *Time and the Other: How Anthropology Makes Its Object* (New York: Columbia University Press, 1983), 92.

13. As a dominated group, Ashe County citizens had to become experts in and to undertake such "practices of rationality." For an explanation of this necessity, see Peter Stallybrass and Allon White, *The Politics and Poetics of Transgression* (Ithaca, N.Y.: Cornell University Press, 1986), 43: "It is indeed one of the most powerful ruses of the dominant to pretend that critique can only exist in the language of 'reason', 'pure knowledge' and 'seriousness'."

14. This section is a revised version of Stephen William Foster, "Resistance and Representation," remarks presented at the Graduate Seminar in Social Geography, University of California, Berkeley, October 1988. For portrayals of culture as constituted through political processes, see Rick Fantasia, *Cultures of Solidarity: Consciousness, Action and Contemporary American Workers* (Berkeley and Los Angeles: University of California Press, 1988); and Foster, *The Past Is Another Country*. A discussion of a comparable local struggle and culturally based, local rhetoric among the Hopi of northern Arizona was presented in Stephen William Foster, "Rhetoric and the Politics of Culture," paper presented at the 23rd Annual Meetings, Kroeber Anthropological Society, Berkeley, Calif., April 1979.

15. For a more complete version of this argument, see Stephen William Foster, "Symbolism and the Problematics of Postmodern Representation," in *Victor Turner and the Construction of Cultural Criticism: Between Literature and Anthropology*, ed. Kathleen M. Ashley (Bloomington: Indiana University Press, 1990), 117–37.

16. For an excellent analysis of a contemporary American political ritual with deep historical roots, see Ronald L. Grimes, *Symbol and Conquest: Public Ritual and Drama in Santa Fe, New Mexico* (Ithaca, N.Y.: Cornell University Press, 1976).

17. Another aspect of this problem is mentioned in n. 3 above.

16

Conclusion

New Populist Theory and the Study of Dissent in Appalachia

Stephen L. Fisher

There has been a vigorous debate in community organizing circles during the past decade over what organizational instruments and strategies are best suited for building progressive citizen groups and political movements. A diverse coalition of intellectuals, politicians, and community activists, frequently labeled the "new populists" or "neo-populists," has posed a direct challenge to traditional Marxist notions of how radical movements originate and flourish. Drawing upon the work of a new generation of social and labor historians, the neo-populists insist that people are moved to action not by abstract principles of class consciousness, but by drawing upon and defending their own particular traditions, folkways, and culture.

Much in this debate pertains to the study and conduct of citizen resistance in Appalachia. The populist themes of tradition, shared cultural memory and values, religion, and family appear to be more relevant than notions of class solidarity in explaining the nature of local citizen revolts over such issues as strip mining, the broad form deed, the disappearance of small farms, the flooding of people's homes, and the pollution of the region's rivers, creeks, and groundwater systems. Yet, as their critics make clear, there remain a number of problems and unanswered questions in the new populists' analysis. The chapters in this volume offer an opportunity to examine and evaluate the strengths and weaknesses of neo-populist theory and to explore its usefulness as a tool for understanding dissent in Appalachia.

The New Populist Argument

The writings of such scholars and activists as Harry Boyte, Sara Evans, Lawrence Goodwin, Jean Bethke Elshtain, and Christopher Lasch set forth the basic tenets of the new populism.[1] These authors disagree on many important questions but share common themes about present-day populism.

For the new populists, democracy is the key issue in contemporary political and social life. They maintain that we live today in a profoundly undemocratic society and that every one of the country's basic institutions "is antidemocratic in spirit, design, and operation." However, they do not define democracy in institutional terms. Rather, they view it as a process of popular rule, a situation in which power is exercised by a democratically organized people.[2]

Accordingly, the new populists criticize those forces they believe are undermining democracy. These include modernization (and modernism), which, by uprooting people, leads to depoliticization and conformity; the modern state that remains unaccountable to most of its citizens; the logic of the marketplace, which has led to large-unit production that has become increasingly hierarchical over time; the concentration of wealth and power in the hands of a very few people who control the nation's major corporations; the increasing centralization of knowledge in the hands of experts, technicians, and professionals who have the power to make key decisions about our lives; and the large-scale bureaucracies of unions and political parties, which see their members more as clients than as active participants. The main enemies are bigness and centralization—the highly unified, modernizing, growth-oriented tendencies in American society that are undermining democracy and the possibility of democratic experiences.[3]

These anti-democratic forces leave people cynical, apathetic, and powerless. Because we lack the political space to nurture democratic skills, we have lost many of them and do not know how to regain them. Thus, for the new populists, the immediate task before us is that of empowerment—transforming social relationships, developing democratic consciousness and skills, enhancing people's control over their everyday lives. This requires building a political culture where democratic politics, especially immediate, direct, face-to-face participation, can occur.[4]

The neo-populists offer a conception of community as the main locus of democracy. Although their notion of community often encompasses a spatial dimension—a "neighborhood"—the new populists most frequently speak of community as depending on a complex set of social relationships that overlap and reinforce each other. Thus, Craig Calhoun describes community as a "greater 'closeness' of relations" than is true for society as a whole, a closeness that involves "face-to-face contact, commonality of purpose, familiarity, and dependability."[5] Communities are what give people the interests for which they will risk their lives.[6]

It is in communities that one finds what Sara Evans and Harry Boyte call "free social spaces," the "settings between private lives and large-scale institutions where ordinary citizens can act with dignity, independence, and vision."[7] Free spaces are voluntary associations ranging from churches and synagogues to citizen organizations, service and self-help groups, union locals, consumer cooperatives, and neighborhood and ethnic groups. In these spaces, grounded in the fabric of daily life, people can learn democratic values and leadership skills, obtain alternative sources of information about the world, form a coherent pattern of group identity and a vision of the common good, and act on their values and beliefs. In sum, free spaces can supply critical experiences in democratic sociability and became the foundation for mass-based social movements.[8]

Neo-populism suggests that traditional values and institutions can be a part of a progressive political outlook. Free spaces, as autonomous institutions deeply rooted in the experiences and values of people in local communities, can produce a vocabulary of democratic action that is rich in cultural meaning and historical memory. It is a language of inheritance drawn from the traditional values of family, religion, and democracy. The argument is not that people's traditions are inherently radical; on the contrary, they are most frequently a conservative force. But these traditions, when under attack, can provide the commitments and categories out of which radical protest will emerge.[9]

For many Appalachian scholars and activists, much in the neo-populist analysis rings true. The chapters in this volume describe the devastating impact of modernization, trickle-down economics, an unresponsive government, and concentrated corporate ownership and power on people's lives, jobs, and communities in Appalachia. Shaped by the values and activities of missionaries, social workers, and government and corporate planners and developers, modernization invaded the region in destructive ways, undermining cooperative life and work in families and communities while leaving people dependent upon a national economy and subject to outside corporate forces.[10] Several chapters document the alarming human costs of more recent governmental and corporate policies that are changing the nature and magnitude of the region's economic crisis.[11]

Resistance in the mountains to these undemocratic forces has centered more often around the concept of "community" than the centralized workplace of the mine, mill, or factory. During the past three decades, the residents of Ashe County, Clear Creek, Marrowbone Creek, Yellow Creek, and numerous other localities have fought to save their land, to preserve their way of life.[12] Important regional and statewide resistance efforts—the anti–strip mining movement, the black lung movement, Kentuckians For

The Commonwealth (KFTC), Save Our Cumberland Mountains (SOCM), the Community Farm Alliance (CFA)—have been community-based. The chapters by Richard Couto, Jim Sessions and Fran Ansley, Ben Judkins, and Mary Anglin demonstrate the importance of community relationships and support systems in struggles for social and economic justice in the coal, textile, and mica industries.[13]

Free spaces have been at the heart of these community and labor struggles.[14] Sherry Cable describes in Chapter 4 how the coal industry promoted competition among miners and undermined free spaces. Recent corporate and governmental actions and policies have had similar effects. In reaction, some Appalachians have sought refuge in their families and religion.[15] Helen Lewis, Sue Kobak, and Linda Johnson have described the various ways in which Appalachians have relied on their family systems to preserve traditional mountain culture against outside efforts to change it.[16] David Corbin documents how miners in the early mine wars drew upon religious values to establish common bonds and justify their struggles. Similarly, Maxine Waller and her colleagues explain how a Bible study group has performed similar functions for citizens in Ivanhoe, Virginia.[17] The many citizen groups described in this volume provide public spaces in communities throughout Appalachia where residents learn democratic skills and gain a sense of their own strength and independence. During the Pittston strike, Camp Solidarity became a meeting place where striking miners and their supporters could share common memories and experiences, recount the day's events, and build bonds of solidarity. The Appalachian Studies Association meetings operate as a social space for oppositional discourse. The Highlander Center continues to serve as a free space where citizens across the region can meet to share ideas and information.

Historical memory and a reliance on and defense of traditional values—a strong commitment to land and family, an emphasis on self-rule and social equality, and patriotism—have fueled many of the resistance efforts examined in this book. Outrage over the destruction of land that had been passed down through families for generations led women in Knott County to block the strip mine bulldozers. Traditional rural values of egalitarianism and fairness fueled anger over a tannery's contamination of Yellow Creek. Stephen Foster explains how a pageant of local history at the New River Festival selectively portrayed community values and traditions so as to increase opposition to a dam project that would have destroyed many residents' homes and livelihoods. The Carawans illustrate how people's cultural heritage, especially their music, provides a valuable resource for dissent. The chapters by Richard Couto and by Jim Sessions and Fran Ansley stress the central role of historical memory in shaping and strengthening the miners' resolve during the Pittston strike. Indeed, the fact that so many of the protests in Appalachia have been a result of defensive behavior—action to prevent the destruction of a way of life and a set of values that could be labeled traditional or conservative—has led Helen Lewis to refer to Appalachian activists as "reactionary radicals."[18]

Thus, the new populists' attempt to Americanize radicalism by connecting protest to traditions, roots, and values based on popular institutions is especially relevant to the study of dissent in Appalachia. Moreover, their argument provides ammunition for critics of efforts to use Marxist analysis to explain protest in the region.

The neo-populists admit that Marxist scholars offer important insights about the introduction and spread of capitalism and the accompanying catastrophic dislocation of the lives of ordinary people. Capitalism destroyed preexisting institutions and practices in the process of making all elements of the social order marketable commodities, and it continues today to tear apart stable communities, traditions, and loyalties. Marxist thought certainly has much to contribute in an analysis of the origin and nature of economic exploitation in Appalachia.

Neo-populists part with Marxist analysis over the significance of this destruction. Many traditional Marxists view the dislocation of rooted, communal institutions and values as a tragic but necessary precondition of progress and progressive action. Marx and Engels equated tradition with the dead hand of the past, saw rural areas as the backwaters of culture, and considered ethnic, kinship, religious, and other traditional relations as major obstacles to individual emancipation. There must be, said Marx, a "radical rupture" with the past. Humans must shed their past institutions and cultural identities as a precondition for developing the collective awareness that is the essence of class consciousness. In other words, to be free is to be uprooted. Today, some on the left continue to hold a negative view of communal and traditional institutions, believing them to be primarily mechanisms for transmitting and upholding mainstream values.[19]

The new populists charge that Marxists, by seeing revolutionary consciousness as abstract universalism or rootless cosmopolitanism, have assimilated the underlying principles of the social order they claim to criticize—that is, they assume that people are and must be that to which capitalism reduces them.[20] Moreover, the left's indifference to voluntary associations explains why class-oriented organizing efforts have rarely been successful in Appalachia or the United States. To the extent that such efforts have gained popularity, they have usually been linked with populist slogans or movements. Furthermore, the left's obsession in the past with the "class struggle" has led it to focus on large-scale settings, such as industrial factories, and to misperceive the contemporary forms of activism that are occurring in local communities throughout this nation.

In sum, many observers of Appalachian events and conditions would agree that the populist notions of "free space" and "community" are more useful concepts than the Marxist theory of class for understanding the nature of radical insurgency. The radicals in the Appalachian mountains, they insist, have been those with roots, with something to lose— not those who have lost "all but their chains."[21]

Critique of the New Populist Argument

There is much that is attractive and important in new populist theory for Appalachian scholars and activists. But new populism is not without its critics, who raise important questions about its assumptions, implications, and viability.

While neo-populist intellectuals are keenly aware of the crisis in the central categories of Marxism, they often fail to appreciate the confusion in their own. Their references to "community," "popular democracy," and "free spaces" are largely devoid of concrete structural definitions.[22]

This is particularly true of their pivotal term, "community."[23] When asked to explain who makes up the community, the new populists reply "the people." But "the people" as an analytical category is as imprecise and artificial as leftist sectarian slogans (like "proletariat") that the new populists criticize.[24] Too frequently, the cultural homogeneity, progressive nature, and good will of "the people" are taken for granted in new populist writing. This conveniently ignores the ethnic, racial, gender, class, and cultural differences that so often divide "the people."

Community in our history entails exclusion as well as inclusion. Tradition and local values include racism, sexism, homophobia, and isolationism. It should not be surprising, then, that African Americans and feminists view the new populism with suspicion. Cornel West reminds us that racism is deeply imbedded in the culture of local communities and that racial progress has resulted not so much from the good will of local citizens as from policies imposed from the outside by the federal courts and government.[25]

Feminists express similar reservations. Elizabeth Minnich cautions that the old values of community, church, and family were sexist and homophobic and trivialized and omitted women.[26] Yet much of the new populist theory contains scarcely any mention of patriarchy and little explicit recognition of the need to struggle against male domination within families and community institutions.

The neo-populist response to these concerns takes several forms, depending upon the situation.[27] As Don Manning-Miller explains in Chapter 3, many organizers for personal and strategic reasons will try to submerge or evade issues related to the racism of their constituencies.[28] In other instances organizers will simply add African Americans and women to their agenda. But, even though the interests of African Americans and women often overlap with the interests of other powerless people, there are specifically African American and feminist concerns that differ from each other and from the concerns of powerless white males in Appalachia and the United States. As populist-oriented groups prioritize their demands, African Americans and feminists find their specific interests sacrificed. Thus, neo-populist groups might take up those "minority" concerns (such as education, housing, or health care) that can be easily integrated into a pragmatic organizing strategy, while downplaying or ignoring affirmative action, abortion, comparable worth, or racial and sexual violence.[29] In addition, African Americans or women are frequently asked or encouraged to assume well-publicized new and important tasks during a particular struggle and then, after the battle is over, are expected to fade back into old patterns and roles. For example, wives of coal miners played crucial frontline roles in union victories at Brookside and Pittston, but afterward experienced pressure from husbands and the union to return to traditional gender roles.[30]

In sum, the new populists, to borrow from Alan Banks, Dwight Billings, and Karen Tice's discussion of postmodernism in Chapter 14, tend to universalize white male middle-class experiences and, in so doing, peripheralize the diverse experiences of women and African Americans. The goal, say critics, should not be to equate equality with sameness by simply adding African Americans and women to the new populist agenda. Rather, equality as a goal involves recognition of differences, and this requires a rethinking and re-forming by the present-day populists of their most basic thoughts, goals, and ways of acting from the perspectives of women, African Americans, and other groups.[31]

Critics also suggest that the new populists' notion of community romanticizes traditional community institutions of the past while ignoring the ways in which these institutions have been undermined and transformed. The growth of the consumer society has encouraged citizens to think mainly of their own self-interest, and the reorganization of neighborhood life and social spaces by modern capitalism has dramatically reduced the number of traditional public meeting places. In addition, as the chapters by Richard Couto, Joe Szakos, and Hal Hamilton and Ellen Ryan make quite clear, more and more of the important decisions that affect our lives are made by distant corporations and state and national political figures, not in local city halls. Thus our very experiences of "community" have changed over time. We can no longer assume, as do some of the new populists, the existence of community and community institutions. The issue facing local citizens today is not so much the recapture and defense of traditional institutions as the renewal and reconstitution of communities.[32]

Many involved in research on Appalachia are open to this criticism, for much of the literature on Appalachian life romanticizes traditional notions of community while ignoring the ways in which communities have been transformed. But several of the chapters in this book illustrate how important it is to be aware of these changes. Sherry Cable and Guy and Candie Carawan describe the absence of community relationships at Yellow Creek and on Marrowbone Creek and examine the conscious efforts necessary to re-create them. Stephen Foster explains how the citizens of Ashe County were forced to rethink and reshape their notion of community life and how that process ultimately led them to change the ways in which they understood themselves, their history, and their community.

The new populists' concept of "democracy" is as vague as their notion of "community." When talking about democracy, populists frequently use words and phrases such as "empowerment," "decentralization," "localism," and "face-to-face relationships." The new populists assume that, if given the opportunity, a majority of "the people" will make decisions that are progressive and fair-minded. But empowerment is not a magical process that suddenly wipes away human bigotry, greed, organizational problems, and social and class conflicts.[33] The neo-populists respond that we must distinguish progressive from regressive behavior, but they seldom offer satisfactory criteria for doing so.

This problem would be less disturbing if the new populists had a clear notion of a political process that made empowerment a positive experience in the community at large. But they have failed to spell out how in a populist democracy "governmental decisions should be made, services should be delivered, participation formalized, bureaucracy transcended."[34]

There are also unanswered questions concerning the idea of "free social spaces." Michael Kazin points out that the availability or absence of free spaces can explain only a little about the origins and growth of a movement. Changes in ideology and material conditions, he insists, are more important.[35] The contributors to this book describe the significance of such variables as economic recessions and depressions, changes in corporate management, structure and ideology, favorable court decisions, the creation of particular governmental programs, and the presence or absence of role models in creating free spaces or in turning conservative free spaces into forums for democratic political behavior. To cite just one example, Sherry Cable notes the importance of the rise of a national environmental movement, the creation of the Environmental Protection Agency, and local school consolidation in creating the conditions for collective dissent in Yellow Creek. Moreover, not all oppositional behavior has radical implications; for instance, Dwight Billings explains how churches in Appalachia and the South, drawing from identical religious traditions, have served both to undermine and to justify opposition.[36] The issue, then, is not so much the existence of free spaces as how they are used and the conditions under which they become forces for democratic change. Most new populist analyses do not adequately address these concerns.[37]

The new populists sidestep several key strategic and ideological issues because of their emphasis on gaining local power, developing local institutions, and improving local economies. Localism offers a number of advantages, but few significant problems can be solved today at the local level. Local resources have been depleted and local economies gutted by national and global market forces and the actions of multinational corporations, forces that must be confronted at the national and international level. Moreover, it has been mainly national action that has compelled local communities to rethink racism and sexism. But the new populists' glorification of militant localism blinds them to the positive functions of the state. As many of the chapters in this volume make clear, government per se is not the enemy. Chris Weiss, for example, shows in Chapter 8 how certain policies of the Carter administration provided a window of opportunity for the creation of three women's employment organizations. The issue is not just more government or less government, but for whom government works and how it works. Organizers must make clear the connections that exist between local work and national and international politics if local citizens are to understand the importance of national and international forces as determinants of what happens locally and to see themselves as actors at the national level. But new populist groups frequently fail to develop such links.[38]

Three chapters drive home the importance of these links. Beth Bingman explains how the failure of activists to understand these connections led to the decline of the anti–strip mining movement. Stephen Foster describes how crucial was the effort to tie local traditions to those of the dominant system in rallying support to stop the flooding of parts of Ashe County. Richard Couto relates how an understanding of changes in the coal industry and government policy led to the mineworkers' union to adopt new and innovative strategies during the Massey and Pittston strikes.

The new populists lack a transformative approach to power relations in American society. While critical of elements of the economic system, the present-day populists see big and unaccountable power rather than capitalism as the fundamental problem. Neo-populists accept the mainstream pursuit of economic growth as a necessary condition for a higher standard of living. Yet this growth supposedly requires the productivity and efficiency of big government, big business, and big labor, which neo-populists oppose. Their critics suggest that, if forced to choose, most new populists "would choose a higher standard of living with bigness and the concomitant maldistribution of wealth over a lower standard . . . of living with the decentralization they cherish."[39] Indeed, the new populists' lack of focus on equality of condition as a central theme is particularly disturbing to many on the left.[40] As Cornel West puts it, the populists want "modern liberal capitalist democracy without impersonal forms of bureaucracy, centralized modes of economic and political power, and alienating kinds of cultural practices."[41]

The new populists, say their critics, fail to realize that respect for tradition and attention to community are inadequate starting points for re-creating democratic politics in this society. Without consciously seeking to create a new economic balance of power, a new politics, and new power bases, the populists end up accepting, almost by default, the institutions and ideological imperatives of the bureaucratic, corporate state. As a result, when they try to pressure existing institutions, they end up doing so in terms those institutions have defined.[42] Thus, the struggle to eliminate strip mining is reduced to haggling over reclamation standards, and the battle over black lung becomes a debate over who will interpret X-rays and determine eligibility standards.

Without attention to the larger questions of power in society, the new populists offer community groups little guidance in preparing for the political, legal, and cultural forces that established powers will bring against them. This results in a politics of gradualism—a strategy of adaptation and retrenchment—and leads to citizen action that is, for the most part, defensive and reactive. Further, it does not create the conditions necessary for coalition work with potential allies—feminists, environmentalists, peace activists, people of color.[43] Many local revolts throughout Appalachia and the United States turn out to be "flashes of independent anger" rather than sustained efforts at effective movement building precisely because they lack an analysis of power and society beyond the local level.[44]

In sum, the new populists' critics insist that a strategy to rehabilitate traditional ideas and culture without simultaneously challenging the underlying institutions and logic of the system is bound to fail. Fundamental change requires a conception of politics, economy, and society that goes beyond what the dominant culture is prepared to accommodate.

But the new populist vision is result-oriented, rejecting long-term goals for that which is currently available. It is narrow, abandoning a vision of a societywide political sphere in favor of localized conflict. And it is backward-looking, relying too heavily on the past as a definition of the future.[45]

Toward a New Critical Discourse and Practice

The neo-populist debate raises a number of questions relevant to the study of dissent in Appalachia. To what extent can local struggles, often bound by provincialism, successfully challenge the dominant centers of power? What criteria enable us to distinguish between those dimensions of traditional institutions such as the church and the family that are capable of promoting a new democratic politics, and cultural values that support racism, sexism, and homophobia? What are the political forms and class content of cultural transformation?

These are difficult and complex questions, but ones those interested in fundamental economic and political change in Appalachia must debate openly and directly. We must begin with the recognition that although the new populists and Marxists offer important insights, neither, alone, provides an adequate theoretical framework for activism.[46] What is needed is a critical discourse and practice "rooted in an awareness of popular traditions and resistance, but not blind to the wider contours of power within national and international capital." This requires a knowledge of both a "people's" history and a history of capitalism.[47] It means pursuing a dialectical approach that blends new ideas with traditional values and language. It involves the creation of resistance organizations that take culture and community seriously as spaces for political action while encouraging their members to discover the ways in which their grievances are a result of "structural processes occurring at an economic, geographic, and political level far beyond the particular locale where the grievance is experienced."[48] It requires creating an alternative radicalism that chooses to complicate rather than simplify by incorporating themes from the many movements and traditions present in Appalachia and the United States.[49]

Fortunately, activists and scholars in Appalachia are currently making important contributions to this discourse. They increasingly recognize that a cultural emphasis is not antagonistic to a class approach. The neo-populists tend to dismiss the concept of class, but the task is to develop it further, to think about it differently. Although classes are shaped by economic concerns, they are cultural configurations.[50] Indeed, the United States is one of the few places where class and culture are thought of separately. Lived experience is different—our lives are a messy amalgam of identities out of which social relations are conducted.[51] The new populists are right when they insist that class is not the sole explanation of social relations, that class relations may be far more important in the experiences of some than others, and that a common form of class struggle springs from a defense of traditional values and institutions.[52] But class issues are often implicit in the ways that race, gender, family, and community issues present themselves, and quite often a kind of class intuition or memory fuels populist revolts.[53] The difficult but crucial task is not to decide between class and culture, but to discover how class, race, and gender conflicts express themselves today in cultural and political formations.[54]

In Appalachian research, some of the most important work in this regard is being done by Mary Anglin and Sally Maggard. Utilizing different approaches and studying resistance in different locales and industries, both Anglin and Maggard probe the ways in which gender, kinship, and social class interact to specify women's political experience, action, and consciousness. Their work indicates that neither class nor gender alone is a sufficient tool for understanding political action—that, in fact, it makes no sense to talk about the one without the other. Moreover, they demonstrate convincingly how and why political action must be situated in a web of work, family, and community needs and histories.[55] Other significant contributions include Michael Yarrow's investigation of the ways in which Appalachian coal miners' gender consciousness affects their class consciousness; Altina Waller's analysis of the Hatfield-McCoy feud as part of a larger conflict between local culture and an emerging industrial order; Richard Couto's discussion of community-based approaches to environmental risks; and Dwight Billings' use of Antonio Gramsci's approach to religion and social class militancy to explain activism and quiescence among textile workers and coal miners.[56] Other relevant works are discussed by Alan Banks, Dwight Billings, and Karen Tice in Chapter 14.

In addition, many of the articles in this volume offer important insights on these questions. Sherry Cable examines the interaction of class and gender issues in Yellow Creek. Richard Couto and Jim Sessions and Fran Ansley describe the different ways in which class, kinship, religion, and community were interwoven and expressed in the Pittston strike. Ben Judkins explains how the shared class experience of workers in three industries created a "community" not bound by geographic terrain. Stephen Foster describes how local cultural traditions are selective and fluid in nature, why it is necessary to understand the relationship of these traditions to the national, dominant culture, and the dynamic process involved in shaping these traditions to serve as a resource in political struggles against the dominant culture. The Carawans make clear that cultural expression does not always arise spontaneously in struggles to challenge oppression or inequality. The seeds for such expression exist, but these seeds must be deliberately cultivated and nourished by organizers and institutions that recognize the value of cultural forms to resistance efforts.

There exist, then, significant intellectual efforts in Appalachia that grapple with some of the key issues raised in the new populist debate. There are also important efforts occurring in the community organizing sphere. In the past, citizen resistance in the Appalachian mountains often involved narrow, single-issue, reactive campaigns. These groups drew from traditional values, were community-based, and offered free spaces where participants acquired the information and some of the democratic skills they needed to fight the strip miners, dam builders, or polluters who were threatening their homes and livelihoods. They won occasional victories, and their accomplishments should be applauded and admired. Most often, however, these groups were without a larger transformative social and political vision and usually disappeared quickly from the scene.

In contrast, over the past two decades the region has witnessed several multi-issue, membership-run organizations that cover a wide geographic area, have won significant victories, and have demonstrated long-term staying power. The chapters on SOCM, KFTC, and CFA describe an organizing approach that is flexible, pragmatic, and grounded in the past and present of members' lives. But unlike the narrow single-issue organizing of the past, these groups' primary concern is to empower their members for the long haul—to provide a schooling in politics, to offer what Hal Hamilton and Ellen Ryan call in Chapter 7 a "living university for leaders."[57] A self-conscious leadership training process is designed to develop democratic skills and build a sense of ownership and community. As Connie White, a past SOCM president, puts it in Chapter 5, "We don't just care about winning issues; we care more about helping people get stronger. In the long run, that is how you win issues and make real changes."

These organizations provide free spaces where "people's history" can be connected to a systematic critique of the political economy; where participants can begin to see the connection between their concerns and those of other exploited people; where members can come to confront issues of racism and sexism; and where people can start to envision new alternatives to the world in which they live. Such changes in people's ways of viewing their world do not come easy. They require a strong commitment on the part of organizers and leaders to anti-racist and anti-sexist strategies, to programs of economic education, to systematic planning and evaluation, and to coalition building. As noted in the Introduction and in Don Manning-Miller's chapter, Appalachian groups have not always been successful in these areas. But the commitment is there, as witnessed by

SOCM's recent work on the issue of temporary workers and its joint retreat with JONAH, a predominantly black community organizing group in west Tennessee, by CFA's efforts to forge links with urban low-income groups and to educate its members about national and global farm issues, and by KFTC's recruitment of low-income and minority members and deliberate long-range planning. The best evidence of the success and potential of these grassroots organizations comes from the members themselves. Their voices, as recorded in this volume, are testimony to how their lives have been transformed.

There is no easy path; there are no neat resolutions. The critical discourse and practice called for above require courage, commitment, struggle, and patience, and at times it is difficult to envision that they are even possible.[58] But occasionally an event occurs which helps us focus, which provides us with a glimpse of what could be. The UMWA's occupation of the Moss 3 coal preparation plant during the Pittston strike was one such occasion. The resistance leading up to the takeover was fueled by family, community, and union loyalties that had instilled in generation after generation a deeply felt class awareness and anger. Camp Solidarity, the Binns-Counts Community Center, and weekly rallies provided free spaces where striking miners, relatives, and supporters from all over the country shared life stories and experiences that reinforced bonds of community and class solidarity. Old labor and gospel hymns intermixed with new anti-Pittston songs rang out along the picket lines. American flags and yellow ribbons became symbols of resistance to uncaring corporate and governmental leaders and structures. The miners and their supporters drew upon their religious beliefs to strengthen their resolve and justify their dissent. Strike leaders worked hard to educate the miners about the issues of the strike, to forge links with other social movements both nationally and abroad, and to involve African Americans and women in a wide variety of strike activities. Mistakes were made, and much remains unresolved. But as we read Jim Sessions and Fran Ansley's moving account of how these factors were played out during the occupation, we are made, as Ansley says, to "*feel* the possibilities that reside in us, in the people around us, and in the groups of which we are or can be a part."

Notes

1. Sara M. Evans and Harry C. Boyte, *Free Spaces: The Sources of Democratic Change in America* (New York: Harper & Row, 1986); Lawrence Goodwyn, "Organizing Democracy: The Limits of Theory and Practice," *democracy* 1

(January 1981) : 41–60; Jean Bethke Elshtain, "Feminism, Family and Community," *Dissent* 29 (1982) : 442–49; and Christopher Lasch, *The True and Only Heaven: Progress and Its Critics* (New York: Norton, 1991).

2. Sheldon Wolin, "Why Democracy?" *democracy* 1 (January 1981) : 3; see also David Plotke, "Democracy, Modernization, 'democracy,'" *Socialist Review* 14 (March–April 1984) : 31.

3. Plotke, "Democracy," 32; and George Shulman, "The Pastoral Idyll of 'democracy,'" *democracy* 3 (Fall 1984) : 43.

4. Evans and Boyte, *Free Spaces*, 17–20, 191–94.

5. Craig J. Calhoun, "Community: Toward a Variable Conceptualization for Comparative Research," *Social History* 5 (January 1980) : 111; and Evans and Boyte, *Free Spaces*, 187.

6. Craig J. Calhoun, "The Radicalism of Tradition: Community Strength or Venerable Disguise and Borrowed Language?" *American Journal of Sociology* 88 (1983) : 898.

7. Evans and Boyte, *Free Spaces*, 17.

8. Ibid., 17–20; Harry C. Boyte, "Populism and Free Spaces," in *The New Populism: The Politics of Empowerment*, ed. Harry C. Boyte and Frank Riessman (Philadelphia: Temple University Press, 1986), 309–11; and James C. Scott, *Domination and the Arts of Resistance: Hidden Transcripts* (New Haven: Yale University Press, 1990), 120–24.

9. Harry C. Boyte, "Beyond Politics as Usual," in Boyte and Riessman, *The New Populism*, 8; Calhoun, "The Radicalism of Tradition," 900; and David Thelen, "Memory and American History," *Journal of American History* 75 (1989) : 1117–29.

10. For additional information on this historical process, see Ronald D. Eller, *Miners, Millhands, and Mountaineers: Industrialization of the Appalachian South, 1880–1930* (Knoxville: University of Tennessee Press, 1982); Henry Shapiro, *Appalachia on Our Mind: The Southern Mountains and Mountaineers in the American Consciousness, 1870–1920* (Chapel Hill: University of North Carolina Press, 1978); David E. Whisnant, *Modernizing the Mountaineer: People, Power and Planning in Appalachia* (Boone, N.C.: Appalachian Consortium Press, 1981); and David E. Whisnant, *All That Is Native and Fine: The Politics of Culture in an American Region* (Chapel Hill: University of North Carolina Press, 1983).

11. See also John Gaventa, Barbara E. Smith, and Alex Willingham, eds., *Communities in Economic Crisis: Appalachia and the South* (Philadelphia: Temple University Press, 1990); and Commission on Religion in Appalachia, *Economic Transformation: The Appalachian Challenge* (Knoxville, Tenn.: CORA, 1986).

12. *Mountain Life & Work* and *The Appalachian Reader* are the best general sources of information on the wide variety of past and present resistance efforts in Appalachia. For information on Appalachian citizen groups not discussed in these chapters, see "Dissent in Appalachia: A Bibliography" below.

13. See also David A. Corbin, *Life, Work, and Rebellion in the Coal Fields: The*

Southern West Virginia Miners, 1880–1922 (Urbana: University of Illinois Press, 1981); and Jacquelyn Dowd Hall et al., *Like a Family: The Making of a Southern Cotton Mill World* (Chapel Hill: University of North Carolina Press, 1987).

14. It is important to note, as James Scott reminds us, that many of the everyday resistance activities that occur in these free spaces may not be easily discernible. Most forms of struggle stop short of outright collective defiance and assume the forms of gossip, footdragging, noncompliance, rumors, and so on. Scott describes these activities as part of the "hidden transcript" of resistance and labels such forms of struggle as "infrapolitics": see *Domination and the Arts of Resistance*, 183–201. For a discussion of how this infrapolitics has worked in parts of Appalachia, see Rhoda H. Halperin, *The Livelihood of Kin: Making Ends Meet "the Kentucky Way"* (Austin: University of Texas Press, 1990); and Helen M. Lewis, "Backwoods Rebels: Resistance in the Appalachian Mountains," in *Conflict and Peacemaking in Appalachia*, ed. Coalition for Appalachian Ministry (Amesville, Ohio: CAM, 1987), 16–26. See also Chapter 4 by Sherry Cable and Chapter 13 by Mary Anglin in this volume.

15. It is difficult to overemphasize the importance of family as a free space when other social spaces are not available. As Bell Hooks points out, family life is at times the only sustained support system for exploited and oppressed peoples. She acknowledges that sexist oppression often perverts and distorts the positive function of the family and argues that we must rid family life of its abusive dimensions without devaluing it. Bell Hooks, *Feminist Theory: From Margin to Center* (Boston: South End Press, 1984), 37.

16. Helen M. Lewis, Sue E. Kobak, and Linda Johnson, "Family, Religion, and Colonialism in Central Appalachia, or Bury My Rifle at Big Stone Gap," in *Colonialism in Modern America: The Appalachian Case*, ed. Helen M. Lewis, Linda Johnson, and Donald Askins (Boone, N.C.: Appalachian Consortium Press, 1978), 131–36; see also Sari L. Tudiver, "Political Economy and Culture in Central Appalachia, 1790–1977" (Ph.D. diss., University of Michigan, 1984), 392–400.

17. Corbin, *Life, Work, and Rebellion in the Coal Fields*, 146–75; and Maxine Waller et al., " 'It Has to Come from the People': Responding to Plant Closings in Ivanhoe, Virginia," in Gaventa, Smith, and Willingham, *Communities in Economic Crisis*, 17–28.

18. Lewis, "Backwoods Rebels," 22.

19. See the discussion in Harry C. Boyte, "Populism and the Left," *democracy* 1 (April 1981) : 58; Boyte, "Beyond Politics as Usual," 5–6; Harry C. Boyte, *The Backyard Revolution: Understanding the New Citizen Movement* (Philadelphia: Temple University Press, 1980), 178–80; and Evans and Boyte, *Free Spaces*, 182–87. The new populists tend to oversimplify Marxist discussions of traditional values and institutions and to ignore the wide diversity of opinions among those who call themselves Marxist. Thus, it is important to note that many Marxists do not accept the critique of traditional relations presented here.

20. For a discussion of the new populist critique of the left, see Lasch, *The True and Only Heaven*; Goodwyn, "Organizing Democracy"; Lawrence Goodwyn, "The Cooperative Commonwealth and Other Abstractions: In Search of a Democratic Premise," *Marxist Perspectives* 10 (Summer 1980) : 8–42; Boyte, "Populism and the Left," 53–66; Harry Boyte, *Commonwealth: A Return to Citizen Politics* (New York: Free Press, 1989), 35–45; Calhoun, "The Radicalism of Tradition," 886–914; and Jerry Watts, "The Socialist as Ostrich: The Unwillingness of the Left to Confront Modernity," *Social Research* 50 (Spring 1983) : 3–56.

21. Evans and Boyte, *Free Spaces*, 115.

22. Carl Boggs, "The New Populism and the Limits of Structural Reforms," *Theory and Society* 12 (1983) : 351; and Jeff Lustig, "Community and Social Class," *democracy* 1 (April 1981) : 109. The inability to define pivotal concepts should come as no surprise to Appalachian scholars, since many of the key concepts in Appalachian Studies, including the notion of Appalachia itself, remain vague and ill-defined.

23. A term like "community" is not unambiguous, and it can assume different meanings and locales depending upon the perspectives and strategies of those making the appeal. In urban areas, "community" relationships most frequently take place in neighborhoods, but, as a number of the chapters in this volume make clear, in rural Appalachia they often occur in the context of a county. For the most part, the new populists end up defining a community largely by its struggles. However, such a definition frequently creates "uncertain boundaries, uncertain citizens, and dismayed outsiders and bystanders": Michael Ansara and S. M. Miller, "Democratic Populism," in Boyte and Riessman, *The New Populism*, 150; see also Joseph M. Kling and Prudence S. Posner, "Class and Community in an Era of Urban Transformation," in *Dilemmas of Activism: Class, Community, and the Politics of Local Mobilization*, ed. Joseph M. Kling and Prudence S. Posner (Philadelphia: Temple University Press, 1990), 29–33. For an effort to identify the various dimensions of community, see Harry C. Boyte, *Community Is Possible: Repairing America's Roots* (New York: Harper & Row, 1984); and Boyte, *Commonwealth*.

24. See Boyte's response to these charges in *Commonwealth*, 30–33.

25. Cornel West, "Populism: A Black Socialist Critique," in Boyte and Riessman, *The New Populism*, 208.

26. Elizabeth K. Minnich, "Toward a Feminist Populism," in Boyte and Riessman, *The New Populism*, 194.

27. This discussion is not meant to imply that many new populist organizers and intellectuals are not deeply concerned about these issues. Indeed, they increasingly acknowledge that racism, sexism, and homophobia are deeply imbedded in community traditions, and some admit that new populist groups are often unable or unwilling to directly confront these issues. See, for example, Boyte, *Commonwealth*, 67, 93, 127–28.

28. Don Manning-Miller focuses on racism in Chapter 3, but much of his analy-

sis of how and why organizers avoid confronting racism no doubt also applies to sexism and homophobia.

29. Boggs, "The New Populism," 358; Boyte, *Commonwealth*, 127–28.

30. Jim Sessions and Fran Ansley describe in Chapter 10 the key role women played in the Pittston strike. For a discussion of how the women fared after the strike, see Marat Moore, "Women's Stories from the Pittston Strike," *Now and Then* 7 (Fall 1990) : 6–12, 32–35. For a discussion of women and the Brookside strike, see Sally Ward Maggard, "Gender Contested: Women's Participation in the Brookside Coal Strike," in *Women and Social Protest*, ed. Guida West and Rhoda Lois Blumberg (New York: Oxford University Press, 1990), 75–98.

31. Boggs, "The New Populism," 358; Margaret Cerullo, "Autonomy and the Limits of Organization: A Socialist-Feminist Response to Harry Boyte," *Socialist Review*, no. 43 (February 1979) : 95; Minnich, "Toward a Feminist Populism," 195–97; and West, "Populism," 209. See also Joan Scott, "Deconstructing Equality-Versus-Difference: Or, The Uses of Poststructuralist Theory for Feminism," *Feminist Studies* 14 (Spring 1988) : 33–50. For a discussion of the ways in which Appalachian Studies has universalized the white male experience, see Sally Ward Maggard, "Class and Gender: New Theoretical Priorities in Appalachian Studies," in *The Impact of Institutions in Appalachia: Proceedings of the Eight Annual Appalachian Studies Conference*, ed. Jim Lloyd and Anne G. Campbell (Boone, N.C.: Appalachian Consortium Press, 1986), 100–113; and William H. Turner and Edward J. Cabbell, eds., *Blacks in Appalachia* (Lexington: University Press of Kentucky, 1985).

32. Harry Boyte and Sara Evans have been critical of the tendency to romanticize traditional notions of community. See Evans and Boyte, *Free Spaces*, 85–88; Harry C. Boyte and Sara Evans, "Strategies in Search of America: Cultural Radicalism, Populism, and Democratic Culture," *Socialist Review* 14 (May–August 1984) : 190–95, 201–2; and Harry C. Boyte, "Politics as Education," *Social Policy* 20 (Spring 1990) : 35–42. See also Gar Alperovitz, "The Coming Break in Liberal Consciousness," *Christianity and Crisis* 46 (March 3, 1986) : 62.

33. Ansara and Miller, "Democratic Populism," 150–51.

34. Ibid.

35. Michael Kazin, "Grass-Roots History," *Nation* 242 (May 17, 1986) : 704; see also Robert Fisher and Joseph M. Kling, "Leading the People: Two Approaches to the Role of Ideology in Community Organizing," in Kling and Posner, *Dilemmas of Activism*, 74–77; and James Green, "Populism, Socialism and the Promise of Democracy," *Radical History Review*, no. 21 (Fall 1980) : 31–32.

36. Dwight B. Billings, "Religion as Opposition: A Gramscian Analysis," *American Journal of Sociology* 96 (1990) : 1–31.

37. Some of the new populists recognize this problem. See Evans and Boyte, *Free Spaces*, 15; and Boyte, *Commonwealth*, 30–33.

38. Ansara and Miller, "Democratic Populism," 145–54; Robert N. Bellah,

"Populism and Individualism," in Boyte and Riessman, *The New Populism*, 103; Prudence S. Posner, "Introduction," in Kling and Posner, *Dilemmas of Activism*, 14–17; and Frank Riessman, "The New Populism and the Empowerment Ethos," in Boyte and Riessman, *The New Populism*, 54.

39. West, "Populism," 209; see also Michael Kazin, "Populism: The Perilous Promise," *Socialist Review* 16 (September–October 1986) : 104.
40. See for example Green, "Populism," 32–37.
41. West, "Populism," 208.
42. Boggs, "The New Populism," 355–60; and Lustig, "Community and Social Class," 103–6.
43. Boggs, "The New Populism," 357–58.
44. Jim Green, "Culture, Politics and Workers' Response to Industrialization in the U.S.," *Radical America* 16 (January–February 1982) : 114. A number of contributors to this volume characterize most attempts at social change in Appalachia as piecemeal, temporary, and without a long-term vision. See, for example, the chapters by Bill Allen, Mary Beth Bingman, John M. Glen, and Joe Szakos.
45. Boggs, "The New Populism," 353–55; Plotke, "Democracy," 38; and Shulman, "Pastoral Idyll," 53.
46. Posner, "Introduction," 5.
47. Barry Goldberg, "A New Look at Labor History," *Social Policy* 12 (Winter 1982) : 61. For an example of this type of history, see Helen M. Lewis and Suzanna O'Donnell, eds., *Ivanhoe, Virginia: Remembering Our Past, Building Our Future* (Ivanhoe, Va.: Ivanhoe Civic League, 1990).
48. Posner, "Introduction," 5.
49. Green, "Culture," 117; Plotke, "Democracy," 50; and Shulman, "Pastoral Idyll," 53–54. See also Chapter 14, by Alan Banks, Dwight Billings, and Karen Tice, in this volume.
50. E. P. Thompson, *The Making of the English Working Class* (New York: Vintage Books, 1966).
51. James C. Scott, *Weapons of the Weak: Everyday Forms of Resistance* (New Haven: Yale University Press, 1985), 45.
52. Ibid.
53. Ibid.; and Boyte, *Commonwealth*, 31.
54. Lustig, "Community and Social Class," 109–11.
55. See Anglin's essay in this volume (Chapter 13) and her Ph.D. dissertation, " 'A Lost and Dying World': Women's Labor in the Mica Industry of Southern Appalachia" (New School for Social Research, 1990). See also Maggard, "Gender Contested," and her Ph.D. dissertation, "Eastern Kentucky Women on Strike: A Study of Gender, Class, and Political Action in the 1970s" (University of Kentucky, 1988).
56. Michael Yarrow, "The Gender-Specific Class Consciousness of Appalachian Coal Miners: Structure and Change," in *Bringing Class Back In: Historical and Contemporary Perspectives*, ed. Scott G. McNall, Rhonda F. Levine, and Rick Fantasia (Boulder, Colo.: Westview, 1991), 285–310; Michael Yar-

row, "Capitalism, Patriarchy and 'Men's Work': The System of Control of Production in Coal Mining," in Lloyd and Campbell, *The Impact of Institutions in Appalachia*, 29–47; Altina L. Waller, *Feud: Hatfields, McCoys, and Social Change in Appalachia, 1860–1900* (Chapel Hill: University of North Carolina Press, 1988); Richard A. Couto, "Failing Health and New Prescriptions: Community-Based Approaches to Environmental Risks," in *Current Health Policy Issues and Alternatives: An Applied Social Science Perspective*, ed. Carole E. Hill (Athens: University of Georgia Press, 1986): 53–70; Billings, "Religion as Opposition."

57. See Harry Boyte's *Commonwealth* for a discussion and critique of how this "schooling in politics" has worked in various projects of the Industrial Areas Foundation, the church-based network founded by the late Saul Alinsky.

58. Prudence Posner makes this point in her introduction to the collection of essays she and Joseph Kling edited. The debate over the new populism is at the heart of *Dilemmas of Activism*, and its contributors offer penetrating critiques and valuable case studies that go beyond or build on the arguments offered here. This is an important source for those interested in this debate.

BIBLIOGRAPHY, DIRECTORY OF ORGANIZATIONS, LIST OF CONTRIBUTORS

Dissent in Appalachia:
A Bibliography

Stephen L. Fisher

The Appalachian Region

This section includes a few of the most important works on the Appalachian region. The books by Batteau (1990), Cunningham, Shapiro, and Whisnant (1983) discuss and critique various aspects of the development of the concept of Appalachia. Eller offers the best history of the Appalachian coalfields, and Raitz and Ulack have written an important geography of the region. Pudup's dissertation undermines a number of the prevailing myths concerning preindustrial Appalachia, while Waller's groundbreaking work on the Hatfield-McCoy feud describes the social and economic tensions that accompanied industrialization in the mountains. The Appalachian Land Ownership Task Force's study and Fisher's collection (1979) provide an overview of land ownership and taxation patterns and issues in Appalachia.

In 1962 Harry Caudill's *Night Comes to the Cumberlands* introduced the nation to Appalachia's economic plight. The Catholic bishops' letter delivered a similar message in 1975, and works by the Commission on Religion in Appalachia, DeLeon, Gaventa, Smith, and Willingham, and the Southeast Women's Employment Coalition document current economic conditions and problems, and offer possible solutions. Whisnant (1981) describes the failure of government efforts to address the region's social and economic problems. Couto's work provides important demographic data, and Wells's dissertation is a comprehensive critique of the Appalachian political economy.

Farr's bibliography, Turner and Cabbell's anthology, and Hudson's book are jumping off points for the study of women, blacks, and Native Americans in Appalachia. Studies by Coles and by Obermiller and Philliber describe issues and problems faced by Appalachian migrants, and Obermiller's bibliography lists other important sources on urban Appalachians. The collections by Batteau (1983), Ergood and Kuhre, and Lewis, Johnson, and Askins include essays on a wide variety of Appalachian issues and concerns. For additional sources on Appalachia, see the bibliographies by Fisher and Ross.

Appalachian Land Ownership Task Force. *Who Owns Appalachia? Landownership and Its Impact.* Lexington: University Press of Kentucky, 1983.

Batteau, Allen W. *The Invention of Appalachia.* Tucson: University of Arizona Press, 1990.

————, ed. *Appalachia and America: Autonomy and Regional Dependence.* Lexington: University Press of Kentucky, 1983.

Catholic Bishops of Appalachia. *This Land Is Home to Me: A Pastoral Letter on Powerlessness in Appalachia.* Whitesburg, Ky.: Catholic Committee of Appalachia, 1975.

Caudill, Harry M. *Night Comes to the Cumberlands: A Biography of a Depressed Area.* Boston: Little, Brown/Atlantic Monthly, 1962.

Coles, Robert. *Migrants, Sharecroppers, and Mountaineers.* Vol. 2 of *Children of Crisis.* Boston: Little, Brown/Atlantic Monthly, 1971.

Commission on Religion in Appalachia. *Economic Transformation: The Appalachian Challenge.* Knoxville, Tenn.: CORA, 1986.

Couto, Richard A. *Appalachia: An American Tomorrow—A Report to the Commission on Religion in Appalachia on Trends and Issues in the Appalachian Region.* Knoxville, Tenn.: Commission on Religion in Appalachia, 1984.

Cunningham, Rodger. *Apples on the Flood: The Southern Mountain Experience.* Knoxville: University of Tennessee Press, 1987.

DeLeon, Paul, ed. *Appalachia's Changing Economy: A Reader.* New Market, Tenn.: Economics Education Project, Highlander Center, 1986.

Eller, Ronald D. *Miners, Millhands, and Mountaineers: Industrialization of the Appalachian South, 1880–1930.* Knoxville: University of Tennessee Press, 1982.

Ergood, Bruce, and Bruce E. Kuhre, eds. *Appalachia: Social Context Past and Present.* 3rd ed. Dubuque, Iowa: Kendall/Hunt, 1991.

Farr, Sidney S. *Appalachian Women: An Annotated Bibliography.* Lexington: University Press of Kentucky, 1981.

Fisher, Steve. "A Selective Bibliography for Appalachian Studies, Revised, Summer 1990." In *Appalachia: Social Context Past and Present,* ed. Bruce Ergood and Bruce E. Kuhre, 375–416. 3rd ed. Dubuque, Iowa: Kendall/Hunt, 1991.

————, ed. *A Landless People in a Rural Region: A Reader on Land Ownership and Property Taxation in Appalachia.* New Market, Tenn.: Highlander Center, 1979.

Gaventa, John, Barbara E. Smith, and Alex Willingham, eds. *Communities in Economic Crisis: Appalachia and the South.* Philadelphia: Temple University Press, 1990.

Hudson, Charles M. *The Southeastern Indians.* Knoxville: University of Tennessee Press, 1976.

Lewis, Helen M., Linda Johnson, and Donald Askins, eds. *Colonialism in Modern America: The Appalachian Case.* Boone, N.C.: Appalachian Consortium Press, 1978.

Obermiller, Phillip J. *An Annotated Bibliography on Urban Appalachians.* Cincinnati, Ohio: Urban Appalachian Council, 1984.

Obermiller, Phillip J., and William W. Philliber, eds. *Too Few Tomorrows: Urban Appalachians in the 1980s.* Boone, N.C.: Appalachian Consortium Press, 1987.

Pudup, Mary Beth. "Land Before Coal: Class and Regional Development in Southeast Kentucky." Ph.D. diss., University of California, Berkeley, 1987.

Raitz, Karl B., and Richard Ulack. *Appalachia—A Regional Geography: Land, People, and Development.* Boulder, Colo.: Westview, 1984.

Ross, Charlotte T., ed. *Bibliography of Southern Appalachia.* Boone, N.C.: Appalachian Consortium Press, 1976.

Shapiro, Henry D. *Appalachia on Our Mind: The Southern Mountains and Mountaineers in the American Consciousness, 1870–1920.* Chapel Hill: University of North Carolina Press, 1978.

Southeast Women's Employment Coalition. *Women of the Rural South: Economic Status and Prospects.* Lexington, Ky.: SWEC, 1986.

Turner, William H., and Edward J. Cabbell, eds. *Blacks in Appalachia.* Lexington: University Press of Kentucky, 1985.

Waller, Altina L. *Feud: Hatfields, McCoys, and Social Change in Appalachia, 1860–1900.* Chapel Hill: University of North Carolina Press, 1988.

Wells, John C., Jr. "Poverty Amidst Riches: Why People Are Poor in Appalachia." Ph.D. diss., Rutgers University, 1977.

Whisnant, David E. *All That Is Native and Fine: The Politics of Culture in an American Region.* Chapel Hill: University of North Carolina Press, 1983.

———. *Modernizing the Mountaineer: People, Power, and Planning in Appalachia.* Boone, N.C.: Appalachian Consortium Press, 1981.

Dissent and Strategies of Change in Appalachia

This section includes books and articles that outline particular strategies for change and discuss issues of class, gender, culture, and regional identity.

Works by Anglin, Billings and Goldman, Hall, Maggard, the Southern Mountain Research Collective, Stewart (1990), Sari Tudiver, and Yarrow offer important insights into the ways in which class and/or gender conflicts are expressed today in cultural and political formations and struggles in Appalachia. Stephen Foster, Halperin, Lewis (1987), Lewis, Kobak, and Johnson, Plaut, Stewart (1991), and Whisnant (1970, 1981, 1991) focus on cultural strategies of resistance and change. By comparing Wales and Appalachia, Clavel, Day, and Lewis (1983, 1986) draw important conclusions about the relationship of region, class, and community. Markusen uses a number of Appalachian examples to illustrate her argument that territorial differentiation and conflicts have emerged as major determinants in the spatial transformation of American regions. Whisnant (1980) discusses the political values and pitfalls of regional identity in Appalachian resistance efforts.

The collection edited by McGowan and the essays by Blaustein and Gaventa examine and debate the role of Appalachian Studies in fostering change.

Various economic development strategies and examples are discussed in works by Arnold, Bookser-Feister and Wise, Gaventa, Smith, and Willingham, Kobak and McCormack, Neil Tudiver, and Weiss. Particularly important are the workbooks by Lewis and Gaventa and by Luttrell, which describe community-based economic education experiments. Fisher, Gaventa and Horton, and Liden offer rationales and strategies for land reform in the region.

In addition to the above, there exist a number of works that debate the reasons for quiescence and resistance in Appalachia and/or offer a wide variety of strategies for change. Some of the more important of these works are annotated below.

Anglin, Mary K. "'A Lost and Dying World': Women's Labor in the Mica Industry of Southern Appalachia." Ph.D. diss., New School for Social Research, 1990.

Appalachian Alliance. *Appalachia in the Eighties: A Time for Action*. New Market, Tenn.: Appalachian Alliance, 1982. Offers a critique of and solutions for a number of the problems facing Appalachians and calls for coalitions of opposition, advocacy, and the creation of alternatives.

Arnold, E. Carroll. "Appalachian Cooperatives: Economies of the Third Kind." *Appalachia* 11 (December 1977–January 1978) : 20–27.

Billings, Dwight B. "Religion as Opposition: A Gramscian Analysis." *American Journal of Sociology* 96 (1990) : 1–31. Uses Antonio Gramsci's approach to religion and social class militancy to explain activism and quiescience among textile workers and coal miners.

Billings, Dwight B., and Robert Goldman. "Religion and Class Consciousness in the Kanawha County School Textbook Controversy." In *Appalachia and America: Autonomy and Regional Dependence*, ed. Allen W. Batteau, 68–85. Lexington: University Press of Kentucky, 1983.

Blaustein, Richard. "Regionalism and Revitalization: Towards a Comparative Perspective on Appalachian Studies." In *Remembrance, Reunion, and Revival—Celebrating a Decade of Appalachian Studies: Proceedings of the 10th Annual Appalachian Studies Conference*, ed. Helen Roseberry, 14–20. Boone, N.C.: Appalachian Consortium Press, 1988.

Bookser-Feister, John, and Leah Wise, eds. "Everybody's Business: A People's Guide to Economic Development." *Southern Exposure* 14 (September–December 1986).

Clavel, Pierre. *Opposition Planning in Wales and Appalachia*. Philadelphia: Temple University Press, 1983.

Daley, Nelda, and Sue Ella Kobak. "The Paradox of the 'Familiar Outsider.'" *Appalachian Journal* 17 (Spring 1990) : 248–60. Important and insightful discussion of the impact of a new type of reformer who has lately appeared in Appalachia.

Day, Graham. "The Reconstruction of Wales and Appalachia: Development and Regional Identity." In *Contemporary Wales: An Annual Review of Economic and Social Research*, vol. 1, 73–89. Cardiff: University of Wales Press, 1987.

Fisher, Steve. "Land Reform and Appalachia: Lessons from the Third World." *Appalachian Journal* 10 (1983) : 122–40.

———. "National Economic Renewal Programs and Their Implications for Appalachia and the South." In *Communities in Economic Crisis: Appalachia and the South*, ed. John Gaventa, Barbara E. Smith, and Alex Willingham, 263–78. Philadelphia: Temple University Press, 1990. Critiques three "models" for reforming the national economy (Reaganomics, Industrial Policy, and progressive proposals) and suggests ways in which activists in Appalachia can play a role in developing a realistic strategy for achieving fundamental economic change.

—————. "The Nicaraguan Revolution and the U.S. Response: Lessons for Appalachia." *Appalachian Journal* 14 (1986) : 22–37. Describes how and why peace and solidarity groups and local citizen organizations should join forces.

Fisher, Steve, and Jim Foster. "Models for Furthering Revolutionary Praxis in Appalachia." *Appalachian Journal* 6 (1979) : 170–94. Argues that radical change is possible in Appalachia through integrating theory and practice ("praxis"). Examines a number of Appalachian resistance efforts, some serving as potential models for praxis, and others illustrating the results of a lack of praxis.

Foster, Jim, Steve Robinson, and Steve Fisher. "Class, Political Consciousness, and Destructive Power: A Strategy for Change in Appalachia." *Appalachian Journal* 5 (1978) : 290–311. Argues that concepts of "class," "consciousness," and "destructive power" can help us better understand the nature of oppression in Appalachia. Proposes revolutionary praxis as a strategy for fundamental change.

Foster, Stephen William. *The Past Is Another Country: Representation, Historical Consciousness, and Resistance in the Blue Ridge*. Berkeley, Los Angeles, and London: University of California Press, 1988.

Gaventa, John. "Inequality and the Appalachian Studies Industry." *Appalachian Journal* 5 (1978) : 322–29.

—————. *Power and Powerlessness: Quiescence and Rebellion in an Appalachian Valley*. Urbana: University of Illinois Press, 1980. Important study of the historical development and contemporary workings of power relationships in Clear Fork Valley. Conceptualizes power as having three dimensions, develops a model that explains why quiescence exists in an exploited community, and explores the conditions under which resistance begins to emerge.

Gaventa, John, and Bill Horton. "Land Ownership and Land Reform in Appalachia." In *Land Reform, American Style*, ed. Charles C. Geisler and Frank J. Popper, 233–44. Totowa, N.J.: Rowman & Allanheld, 1984.

Gaventa, John, Barbara E. Smith, and Alex Willingham, eds. *Communities in Economic Crisis: Appalachia and the South*. Philadelphia: Temple University Press, 1990.

Hall, Jacquelyn Dowd. "Disorderly Women: Gender and Labor Militancy in the Appalachian South." *Journal of American History* 73 (1986) : 354–82.

Halperin, Rhoda H. *The Livelihood of Kin: Making Ends Meet "the Kentucky Way."* Austin: University of Texas Press, 1990.

Kahn, Si. "New Strategies for Appalachia." *New South* 25 (Summer 1970) : 57–64. Critiques traditional approaches to change that have failed in the region and suggests specific actions that could be taken at the state and local levels.

Kobak, Sue Ella, and Nina McCormack, with assistance from Nancy Robinson.

Workshop on Developing Feasibility Studies for Community-Based Business Ventures. New Market, Tenn.: Economics Education Project, Highlander Center, 1988.

Lewis, Helen M. "Backwoods Rebels: Resistance in the Appalachian Mountains." In *Conflict and Peacemaking in Appalachia,* ed. Coalition for Appalachian Ministry, 16–26. Amesville, Ohio: CAM, 1987.

————. "Industrialization, Class and Regional Consciousness in Two Peripheral Regions: Wales and Appalachia." In *Reshaping the Image of Appalachia,* ed. Loyal Jones, 54–71. Berea, Ky.: Berea College Appalachian Center, 1986.

————. "Wales and Appalachia: Coal Mining, Culture, and Conflict." *Appalachian Journal* 10 (1983) : 350–57.

Lewis, Helen M., and John Gaventa. *The Jellico Handbook: A Teacher's Guide to Community-Based Economics.* New Market, Tenn.: Economics Education Project, Highlander Center, 1988.

Lewis, Helen M., Sue E. Kobak, and Linda Johnson. "Family, Religion, and Colonialism in Central Appalachia, or Bury My Rifle at Big Stone Gap." In *Colonialism in Modern America: The Appalachian Case,* ed. Helen M. Lewis, Linda Johnson, and Donald Askins, 113–39. Boone, N.C.: Appalachian Consortium Press, 1978.

Liden, David. "Pulling the Pillars: Energy Development and Land Reform in Appalachia." In *Land Reform, American Style,* ed. Charles C. Geisler and Frank J. Popper, 101–16. Totowa, N.J.: Rowman & Allanheld, 1984.

Luttrell, Wendy. *Claiming What Is Ours: An Economics Experience Workbook.* New Market, Tenn.: Economics Education Project, Highlander Center, 1988.

McGowan, Thomas, ed. "Assessing Appalachian Studies." *Appalachian Journal* 9 (Winter–Spring 1982).

Maggard, Sally Ward. "Class and Gender: New Theoretical Priorities in Appalachian Studies." In *The Impact of Institutions in Appalachia: Proceedings of the Eighth Annual Appalachian Studies Conference,* ed. Jim Lloyd and Anne G. Campbell, 114–27. Boone, N.C.: Appalachian Consortium Press, 1986.

————. "Eastern Kentucky Women on Strike: A Study of Gender, Class, and Political Action in the 1970s." Ph.D. diss., University of Kentucky, 1988.

————. "Gender Contested: Women's Participation in the Brookside Coal Strike." In *Women and Social Protest,* ed. Guida West and Rhoda Blumberg, 75–98. New York: Oxford University Press, 1990.

Markusen, Ann R. *Regions: The Economics and Politics of Territory.* Totowa, N.J.: Rowman & Littlefield, 1987.

Merrifield, Juliet. *Putting the Scientists in Their Place: Participatory Research in Environmental and Occupational Health.* New Market, Tenn.: Highlander Center, 1989. Reviews issues of control over the production and use of scientific knowledge and describes ways in which Appalachian groups fighting toxic chemicals in the environment and workplace have worked to develop a "new" science that is responsive to people's needs.

O'Connell, Barry. "Whose Land and Music Shall Ours Be? Reflections on the History of Protest in the Southern Mountains." *Appalachian Journal* 12 (1984) : 18–30. Insightful discussion of the role of music in political struggle.

Offers comparisons between Appalachia and El Salvador and Appalachia and the civil rights movement.

Peoples Appalachia 3 (Summer 1974). Special issue: "New Federalist Papers." Articles by members of the Peoples Appalachian Research Collective focusing on a decentralist form of struggle—community unions, worker control, and so on.

Pignone, Mary M. "Development and Theology in Central Appalachia." *Saint Luke's Journal of Theology* 22 (March 1979) : 87–102. Divides Appalachian resistance groups into three categories: groups working in cooperation with the present system, groups making demands on the system, and groups that exist as alternatives to the current system.

Plaut, Thomas. "Conflict, Confrontation, and Social Change in the Regional Setting." In *Appalachia and America: Autonomy and Regional Dependence*, ed. Allen W. Batteau, 267–84. Lexington: University Press of Kentucky, 1983.

Powers, Evelyn B. "Revolution in Appalachia." *Appalachian Journal* 5 (1978) : 246–55. Uses social movement theory to discuss resistance in Appalachia.

Reid, Herbert G. "Appalachian Policy, Social Values, and Ideology Critique." In *Policy Analysis: Perspectives, Concepts and Methods*, ed. William N. Dunn, 203–22. Greenwich, Conn.: JAI Press, 1986. Describes how Appalachia's "modernization" has never lacked a politics of resistance and alternative development.

Simon, Richard, and Roger Lesser. "A Working Community Commonwealth: A Radical Development Strategy for the Mountains." *Peoples Appalachia* 3 (Spring 1973) : 9–15. Proposes research, educational, and organizing strategies for achieving socialist institutions in Appalachia.

Southern Mountain Research Collective, ed. "Essays in Political Economy: Toward a Class Analysis of Appalachia." *Appalachian Journal* 11 (Autumn–Winter 1983–84).

Stewart, Kathleen C. "Backtalking the Wilderness: 'Appalachian' En-genderings." In *Uncertain Terms: Negotiating Gender in American Culture*, ed. Faye Ginsburg and Anna L. Tsing, 43–56. Boston: Beacon Press, 1990.

———. "On the Politics of Cultural Theory: A Case for 'Contaminated' Cultural Critique." *Social Research* 58 (1991) : 395–412.

Tice, Karen W., and Dwight B. Billings. "Appalachian Culture and Resistance." *Journal of Progressive Human Services* 2 (1991) : 1–18. Provides a valuable overview of oppositional movements and actions in the region.

Tudiver, Neil. "Why Aid Doesn't Help: Organizing for Community Economic Development in Central Appalachia." Ph.D. diss., University of Michigan, 1973.

Tudiver, Sari L. "Political Economy and Culture in Central Appalachia, 1790–1977." Ph.D. diss., University of Michigan, 1984.

Weiss, Chris. "Organizing Women for Local Economic Development." In *Communities in Economic Crisis: Appalachia and the South*, ed. John Gaventa, Barbara E. Smith, and Alex Willingham, 61–70. Philadelphia: Temple University Press, 1990.

Whisnant, David E. "Developments in the Appalachian Identity Movement: All Is Process." *Appalachian Journal* 8 (1980) : 41–47.

———. "Farther Along: The Next Phase of Cultural Work in the South." *Southern Changes* 13 (May 1991) : 1–10.

———. "Finding New Models for Appalachian Development." *New South* 25 (Fall 1970) : 70–77.

———. "The Folk Hero in Appalachian Struggle History." *New South* 28 (Fall 1973) : 30–47. Describes the importance of the discovery, cataloguing, and evaluation of folk heroes to the success of resistance efforts, and identifies regional heroes worthy of emulation.

———. *Modernizing the Mountaineer: People, Power, and Planning in Appalachia.* Boone, N.C.: Appalachian Consortium Press, 1981.

Yarrow, Michael. "The Gender-Specific Class Consciousness of Appalachian Coal Miners: Structure and Change." In *Bringing Class Back In: Historical and Contemporary Perspectives*, ed. Scott G. McNall, Rhonda F. Levine, and Rick Fantasia, 285–310. Boulder, Colo.: Westview, 1991.

———. "How Good Strong Union Men Line It Out: Explorations of the Structure and Dynamics of Coal Miners' Class Consciousness." Ph.D. diss., Rutgers University, 1982.

Labor Issues and Struggles

Although focusing on the history of the United Mine Workers of America (UMWA) since 1960, this section also lists several works on organizing efforts by textile workers, in addition to books and articles by Ray Marshall, Miller, Roydhouse, *Southern Exposure*, Wells, and Wise and Booker-Feister that offer overviews of worker conditions and union struggles in Appalachia and the South. Information on specific labor struggles in Appalachia can be found in issues of *Mountain Life & Work* and *The Appalachian Reader* (see the discussion of these two magazines in the next section of this bibliography, "Community Organizing in Appalachia").

The early history of the coal industry and the UMWA is well documented (Munn) and will not be covered in detail here. Those seeking information on union activities before 1960 should see the histories by Finley, Fox, Harris, Long, and Taplin, and Dubofsky and Van Tine's biography of John L. Lewis. The works by Fox and Long include useful bibliographies. Corbin's book on the southern West Virginia miners is an outstanding social history of this early period. Lewis and Trotter have written important histories of black coal miners. Wilkinson's bibliography, Moore's interviews (1990), "Women and the UMWA," the film *Coal-mining Women*, and the article by Yurchenco offer a starting point for understanding women coal miners' issues and concerns and the role women have played in union activities. (See also the works on the Coal Employment Project listed under "Community Organizing in Appalachia." McAteer (1985) has compiled a miner's manual on health and safety.

Seltzer's *Fire in the Hole* provides a good overview of events in the 1960s and 1970s. Very little attention has been paid to the roving picket movement of the early 1960s, but the film *Roving Pickets* and Black's article are a good beginning. Smith's *Digging Our Own Graves* is a very important and insightful work on the black lung movement. For additional information on this movement, which helped spark the union reform campaigns of the late 1960s and early 1970s, see the works by Denman and Judkins. For coverage of the Miners for Democracy and the democratization of the union, see Brunstetter, Gaventa, Hopkins, Hume, Jenson, Nyden, and Takamiya. Works by Bethell, Brett and Goldberg, Clark, Green (1978), Dan Marshall, Perry, Simon, and Ury describe the wildcat strikes, the long 1977–78 strike, and other events that occurred during Arnold Miller's presidency. For information on the 1974 Brookside strike, see the document produced by the Citizens' Public Inquiry Into the Brookside Strike, the book by Woolley and Reid, works by Maggard (1988, 1990) listed in the previous section of this bibliography, and the film *Harlan County, USA*. Couto writes about the 1976–77 Stearns strike. Mills (1986), Moore (1987), and the film *Mine War on Blackberry Creek*, examine the Massey strike of the mid-1980s. Green (1990), Hollyday, Mills (1990), Moore (1990b), the film *Out of Darkness*, Saltz, and Yates discuss the 1989–90 Pittston strike. See Couto's chapter in this volume for further sources on Massey and Pittston. The *United Mine Workers Journal* offers up-to-date coverage of union activities and issues.

Hall and her colleagues and Tullos have written insightful social histories of southern textile workers, and both books include comprehensive bibliographies of the most important works on this topic. Current conditions and labor relations in the textile industry are discussed by Leiter, Schulman, and Zingraff and by Truchil. The latter work provides a helpful bibliography on textile sources. Conway, Judkins, and Judkins and Dredge describe the history of the brown lung movement, while articles by McConville and by Mullins and Luebke assess the impact of efforts to unionize J. P. Stevens. Beardsley, Byerly, Frankel, and Fredrickson examine the history of black and women workers in the southern textile industry. McAteer (1986) has written a guide to health and safety issues for textile workers.

Beardsley, Edward H. *A History of Neglect: Health Care for Blacks and Mill Workers in the Twentieth-Century South.* Knoxville: University of Tennessee Press, 1987.

Bethell, Thomas N. "The UMW: Now More Than Ever." *Washington Monthly*, March 1978, 12–23.

Black, Kate. "The Roving Picket Movement and the Appalachian Committee for Full Employment, 1959–1965: A Narrative." In *Transformation of Life and Labor in Appalachia: Journal of the Appalachian Studies Association*, vol. 2, ed. Ronald L. Lewis, 110–27. Johnson City, Tenn.: Center for Appalachian Studies and Services, East Tennessee State University, 1990.

Brett, Jeanne M., and Stephen B. Goldberg. "Wildcat Strikes in Bituminous Coal Mining." *Industrial and Labor Relations Review* 32 (1979) : 465–83.

Brunstetter, Maude P. "Desperate Enterprise: A Case Study of the Democratization of the United Mine Workers in the 1970's." Ph.D. diss., Columbia University, 1981.

Byerly, Victoria. *Hard Times Cotton Mill Girls: Personal Histories of Womanhood and Poverty in the South.* Ithaca, N.Y.: ILR Press, 1986.

Citizens' Public Inquiry Into the Brookside Strike. *Proceedings of the Citizens' Public Inquiry Into the Brookside Strike, March 11 and 12, 1974, Harlan County, Kentucky.* Evarts, Ky.: Citizens' Public Inquiry, 1974.

Clark, Paul F. *The Miners' Fight for Democracy: Arnold Miller and the Reform of the United Mine Workers.* Ithaca, N.Y.: New York State School of Industrial and Labor Relations, Cornell University, 1981.

Coalmining Women. A film directed by Elizabeth Barret. Distributed by Appalshop, 1982.

Conway, Mimi. *Rise Gonna Rise: A Portrait of Southern Textile Workers.* Garden City, N.Y.: Anchor/Doubleday, 1979.

Corbin, David Alan. *Life, Work, and Rebellion in the Coal Fields: The Southern West Virginia Miners, 1880–1922.* Urbana: University of Illinois Press, 1981.

Couto, Richard A. *Redemptive Resistance: Church-Based Intervention in the Pursuit of Justice.* Whitesburg, Ky.: Catholic Committee of Appalachia, 1981.

Denman, William. "The Black Lung Movement: A Study in Contemporary Agitation." Ph.D. diss., Ohio University, 1974.

Dubofsky, Melvyn, and Warren Van Tine. *John L. Lewis: A Biography.* New York: Quadrangle/New York Times, 1977.

Finley, Joseph E. *The Corrupt Kingdom: The Rise and Fall of the United Mine Workers.* New York: Simon & Schuster, 1972.

Fox, Maier B. *United We Stand: The United Mine Workers of America, 1890–1990.* Washington, D.C.: United Mine Workers of America, 1990.

Frankel, Linda J. "Southern Textile Women: Generations of Survival and Struggle." In *My Troubles Are Going to Have Trouble with Me: Everyday Trials and Triumphs of Women Workers,* ed. Karen B. Sachs and Dorothy Remy, 39–60. New Brunswick, N.J.: Rutgers University Press, 1984.

Fredrickson, Mary. "Four Decades of Change: Black Workers in Southern Textiles, 1941–1981." *Radical America* 16 (November–December 1982): 27–44.

Gaventa, John. *Power and Powerlessness: Quiescence and Rebellion in an Appalachian Valley.* Urbana: University of Illinois Press, 1980.

Green, Jim. "Camp Solidarity: The United Mine Workers, the Pittston Strike and the New 'People's Movement.'" In *Building Bridges: The Emerging Grassroots Coalition of Labor and Community,* ed. Jeremy Brecher and Tim Costello, 15–24. New York: Monthly Review Press, 1990.

———. "Holding the Line: Miners' Militancy and the Strike of 1978." *Radical America* 12 (May–June 1978) : 3–27.

Hall, Jacquelyn Dowd, James Leloudis, Robert Korstad, Mary Murphy, Lu Ann Jones, and Christopher B. Daley. *Like a Family: The Making of a Southern Cotton Mill World.* Chapel Hill: University of North Carolina Press, 1987.

Harlan County, USA. A film directed by Barbara Kopple. Distributed by Columbia Pictures, 1980.

Harris, V. B. *Kanawha's Black Gold and the Miners' Rebellion.* Ann Arbor, Mich.: Brown-Brumfield, 1987.

Hollyday, Joyce. "Amazing Grace." *Sojourners* 18 (July 1989): 12–22.

Hopkins, George William. "The Miners for Democracy: Insurgency in the United Mine Workers of America, 1970–1972." Ph.D. diss., University of North Carolina, Chapel Hill, 1976.

Hume, Brit. *Death and the Mines: Rebellion and Murder in the United Mine Workers.* New York: Grossman, 1971.

Jenson, Richard J. "Rebellion in the United Mine Workers: The Miners for Democracy, 1970–1972." Ph.D. diss., Indiana University, 1974.

Judkins, Bennett M. *We Offer Ourselves as Evidence: Toward Workers' Control of Occupational Health.* New York: Greenwood Press, 1986.

Judkins, Bennett M., and Bart Dredge. "The Brown Lung Association and Grass-Roots Organizing." In *Hanging by a Thread: Social Change in Southern Textiles,* ed. Jeffrey Leiter, Michael D. Schulman, and Rhonda Zingraff, 121–36. Ithaca, N.Y.: ILR Press, 1991.

Leiter, Jeffrey, Michael D. Schulman, and Rhonda Zingraff, eds. *Hanging by a Thread: Social Change in Southern Textiles.* Ithaca, N.Y.: ILR Press, 1991.

Lewis, Ronald L. *Black Coal Miners in America: Race, Class, and Community Conflict, 1780–1980.* Lexington: University Press of Kentucky, 1987.

Long, Priscilla. *Where the Sun Never Shines: A History of America's Bloody Coal Industry.* New York: Paragon House, 1989.

McAteer, J. Davitt. *Miner's Manual: A Complete Guide to Health and Safety Protection on the Job.* 3rd ed. Washington, D.C.: Center for Law and Social Policy, 1985.

———. *Textile Health and Safety Manual: A Complete Guide to Health and Safety Protection on the Job.* Washington, D.C.: Occupational Safety and Health Law Center, 1986.

McConville, Ed. "A Step Forward, Two Steps Back: J. P. Stevens Contract." *Nation* 232 (March 21, 1981) : 330–32.

Marshall, Dan. "The Miners and the UMW: Crisis in the Reform Process." *Socialist Review,* no. 40–41 (July–October 1978) : 65–115.

Marshall, Ray. "Southern Unions: History and Prospects." In *Perspectives on the American South,* vol. 3, ed. James C. Cobb and Charles R. Wilson, 163–78. New York: Gordon & Breach, 1985.

Miller, Marc S., ed. *Working Lives: The Southern Exposure History of Labor in the South.* New York: Pantheon, 1980.

Mills, Nicolaus. "Solidarity in Virginia: The Mine Workers Remake History." *Dissent* 37 (1990) : 237–42.

———. "War in Tug River Valley: A Long and Bitter Miners' Strike." *Dissent* 33 (1986): 45–52.

Mine War on Blackberry Creek. A film directed by Anne Johnson. Distributed by Appalshop, 1986.

Moore, Marat. "Cleaning Out the Courthouse: Rank-and-File Political Victory in Mingo County, W.Va." *United Mine Workers Journal* 98 (February 1987): 11–15.

———. "Hard Labor: Voices of Women from the Appalachian Coalfields." *Yale Journal of Law and Feminism* 2 (1990a) : 199–239.

———. "Women's Stories from the Pittston Strike." *Now and Then* 7 (Fall 1990b) : 6–12, 32–35.

Mullins, Terry, and Paul Luebke. "Symbolic Victory and Political Reality in the Southern Textile Industry: The Meaning of the J. P. Stevens Settlement for Southern Labor Relations." *Journal of Labor Research* 3 (Winter 1982): 81–88.

Munn, Robert F. *The Coal Industry in America: A Bibliography and Guide to Studies.* Morgantown: West Virginia University Library, 1977.

Nyden, Paul J. "Miners for Democracy: Struggle in the Coal Fields." Ph.D. diss., Columbia University, 1974.

Out of Darkness: The United Mine Workers Story. A film directed by Barbara Kopple and Bill Davis. Distributed by the Labor History and Cultural Foundation, 1990.

Perry, Charles R. *Collective Bargaining and the Decline of the United Mine Workers.* Philadelphia: Industrial Research Unit, Wharton School, University of Pennsylvania, 1984.

Roving Pickets. A film directed by Anne Johnson. Distributed by Appalshop, 1991.

Roydhouse, Marion W. "'Big Enough to Tell Weeds from the Beans': The Impact of Industry on Women in the Twentieth-Century South." In *The South Is Another Land: Essays on Women in the Twentieth-Century South,* ed. Bruce Clayton and John A. Salmond, 85–106. Westport, Conn.: Greenwood, 1987.

Saltz, David M. "Working People Have a Voice: How UMWA Members Sent a Coal Miner to the Virginia Statehouse." *United Mine Workers Journal* 101 (February 1990): 5–7.

Seltzer, Curtis. *Fire in the Hole: Miners and Managers in the American Coal Industry.* Lexington: University Press of Kentucky, 1985.

Simon, Richard M. "Hard Times for Organized Labor in Appalachia." *Review of Radical Economics* 15 (Fall 1983): 21–34.

Smith, Barbara E. *Digging Our Own Graves: Coal Miners and the Struggle Over Black Lung Disease.* Philadelphia: Temple University Press, 1987.

Southern Exposure 9 (Winter 1981). Special issue: "Working Women: A Handbook of Resources, Rights, and Remedies."

Takamiya, Makoto. *Union Organization and Militancy: Conclusions from a Study of the United Mine Workers of America, 1940–1974.* Meisenheim am Glan: Anton Haig, 1978.

Taplin, Ian M. "Miners, Coal Operators, and the State: An Examination of Strikes and Work Relations in the U.S. Coal Industry." Ph.D. diss., Brown University, 1986.

Trotter, Joe W., Jr. *Coal, Class, and Color: Blacks in Southern West Virginia, 1915–32.* Urbana: University of Illinois Press, 1990.

Truchil, Barry E. *Capital-Labor Relations in the U.S. Textile Industry.* New York: Praeger, 1988.

Tullos, Allen. *Habits of Industry: White Culture and the Transformation of the Carolina Piedmont.* Chapel Hill: University of North Carolina Press, 1989.

United Mine Workers Journal. Washington, D.C. (monthly).

Ury, William L. "Talk Out or Walk Out: The Role and Control of Conflict in a Kentucky Coal Mine." Ph.D. diss., Harvard University, 1982.

Wells, John C. "Organized Labor in Central Appalachia." In *The Land and the Economy of Appalachia: Proceedings from the 1986 Conference on Appalachia*, ed. Appalachian Center, University of Kentucky, 123–29. Lexington: Appalachian Center, 1987.

Wilkinson, Carroll W. "A Critical Guide to the Literature of Women Coal Miners." *Labor Studies Journal* 10 (Spring 1985) : 25–45.

Wise, Leah, and John Bookser-Feister. *Betrayal of Trust: Stories of Working North Carolinians*. Durham, N.C.: Southerners for Economic Justice, 1989.

"Women and the UMWA: From Mother Jones to Brookside." *United Mine Workers Journal* 87 (March 1976) : 10–27.

Woolley, Bryan, and Ford Reid. *We Be Here When the Morning Comes*. Lexington: University of Kentucky Press, 1975.

Yates, Michael D. "From the Coal Wars to the Pittston Strike." *Monthly Review* 42 (June 1990): 25–39.

Yurchenco, Henrietta. "Trouble in the Mines: A History in Song and Story by Women of Appalachia." *American Music* 9 (1991): 209–24.

Community Organizing in Appalachia

This section focuses on local community organizing in Appalachia since 1960 and includes sources on particular resistance efforts and grassroots groups and institutions, as well as research guides.

For years *Mountain Life & Work*, published by the Council of the Southern Mountains, was the chief source of information on grassroots organizing in the region. It ceased publication in 1988, but *The Appalachian Reader*, which is not affiliated with any organization, began publication the same year and today serves as the most important and up-to-date source of information on local citizen organizing in Appalachia. Specific articles and news briefs from these two magazines are not included in this bibliography, but anyone interested in learning more about particular groups or about the history of community organizing in Appalachia should consult these publications. Another important source of information consists of newsletters from the citizens' groups themselves. The Directory of Organizations at the end of this volume lists the newsletters for the organizations discussed in this volume.

No one has written a comprehensive history of the battle against strip mining; bits and pieces about this struggle can be found in works by Baber, Branscome (1973), Branscome and Holloway, Carawan and Carawan, Caudill, Council of the Southern Mountains, Dunbar, Finnissey, Hoffman, Landy, and Squillace. The Appalachian Volunteers, especially in eastern Kentucky, played an active role in anti–strip mining activities and were harassed by coal operators and government officials. See the works by Braden, Good, Jackson, and Whisnant (1981).

Works on Save Our Cumberland Mountains (SOCM) and Kentuckians For The Commonwealth (KFTC) often include information on their anti–strip mining activities. Despite its long and successful history, little has been written on SOCM

(Howard, McCarthy). There is more information available on KFTC: "Forum," *On Our Own Land*, Joe Szakos, Kristin Szakos (1986, 1990), Szakos and Szakos, and Zuercher. The creative efforts of the citizens of Ivanhoe, Virginia, to save their community are discussed in articles by Lewis, Waller, and Waller et al. The community-based histories (Lewis and O'Donnell) put together by the residents of Ivanhoe are particularly fine examples of the important role of participatory research and oral history in community organizing.

Many organizing campaigns in the region have risen in response to efforts by federal agencies and private dam builders to flood or take people's land. The successful struggle to block the Appalachian Power Company's bid to build the largest pump storage dam in the nation on the New River and later at Brumley Gap, Virginia, is described by Austin, Blanton, Foster, Schoenbaum, and Whisnant (1973). Opposition to the dam-building policies of the Tennessee Valley Authority is discussed by Caldwell, Hayes, and MacWhirter, by Wheeler and McDonald, and by Whisnant (1981).

Citizen battles against the land policies of the U.S. Forest Service and the National Park Service are chronicled by Dunn, Fine, Frome, and Mastran and Lowerre. Other land-related battles are recounted in works by Jones and by Schweri and Van Willigen. Beaver describes how the Appalachian Land Ownership Task Force organized local citizens to investigate who owns the land and minerals in their counties. Cirillo and Garland discuss efforts to establish a land trust in Clairfield, Tennessee, and Hardt makes the case for a Central Appalachian Land Bank.

Organizing among Appalachian migrants is described in works by Carawan and Carawan, Gitlin and Hollander, Sullivan and Miller, and Tucker. Couto (1975, 1989), McDonald, Peddle, and the film *Mud Creek Clinic* examine organizing around health care, while organizing around housing is discussed by Baker, Branscome (1980), and articles in *Southern Exposure*. Battles for better schools are discussed by Martin, in the film *I'm What This Is All About*, and by White and Merrifield. Groups are fighting on a number of fronts to preserve their environment and to protect their drinking water. Couto (1986), Cable and Degutis, Cable and Walsh, Staub, and the film *Yellow Creek* describe the efforts of the Yellow Creek Concerned Citizens. For information on other environmental struggles, see the film *Chemical Valley*, "Forum," Bob Hall, Henson, Hodges and Hodges, Howell, *Katuah Journal*, Jubak, Norris-Hall, Reutter, Selfridge et al., and Zimet.

Organizations formed by women to fight for better economic opportunities are discussed by Couto et al. and the Rural Community Education Cooperative (Mountain Women's Exchange); Betty Jean Hall and Thrasher (Coal Employment Project); and Lippin (Southeast Women's Employment Coalition). Tice describes the nature and work of battered women's shelters in Appalachia.

Much has been written recently on the Highlander Research and Education Center and its founder, Myles Horton. While the Highlander Center's own collection of writings, Woodside's interview with John Gaventa, the special issue of *Social Policy*, and the film *You Got to Move* contain some material on Highlander's "Appalachian" period, John Glen's chapter in this volume is the first effort to deal systematically with Highlander's Appalachian work. For information on Horton and Highlander's educational philosophy and early history, see the works by Adams, Glen (1988b), Aimee Horton, Myles Horton, Horton and Freire, and Moyers.

The important contributions of Appalshop's cultural work are discussed by Aufderheide and by Shelby and Shelby, while Foxfire's innovative educational and cultural work is described by Puckett and Wigginton. Glen (1988a) and Whisnant (1974, 1981) evaluate the social, cultural, and political work of the Council of the Southern Mountains.

Little has been written on the two major efforts to organize a regionwide movement. See Whisnant (1981) on the Congress for Appalachian Development and Clavel on the Appalachian Alliance.

This section also includes a number of research, organizing, and information guides and handbooks. See Appalachian Community Fund; Batt; Horton, Liden, and Weis; Si Kahn; Liden; Merrifield; *Mountain Life & Work* (1983); and Schlesinger, Gaventa, and Merrifield.

Works describing other resistance groups and activities are annotated below.

Adams, Frank, with Myles Horton. *Unearthing Seeds of Fire: The Idea of Highlander*. Winston-Salem, N.C.: John F. Blair, 1975.

Appalachian Community Fund. *A Guide to Funders in Central Appalachia and the Tennessee Valley*. Knoxville, Tenn.: ACF, 1988.

The Appalachian Reader: An Independent Citizens Quarterly (1988–present).

Arnow, Pat. "Upsetting the Apple Cart in Eastern Kentucky: Appalred Attorneys John Rosenberg and Tony Oppegard." *Now and Then* 8 (Summer 1991): 18–20, 36–37. Describes the nature and success of legal services in eastern Kentucky.

Aufderheide, Pat. "Talk of the Mountain: An Appalachian Arts Center Comes of Age." *Progressive* 54 (April 1990) : 34–36.

Austin, Richard C. "The Battle for Brumley Gap." *Sierra* 69 (January–February 1984) : 120–24.

Baber, Bob H. "Blue Knob: Gone but Not Forgotten." *Appalachian Journal* 17 (1990) : 156–74.

Baker, Deborah M. "Flood Without Relief: The Story of the Tug Valley Disaster." *Southern Exposure* 6 (Spring 1978) : 20–27.

Batt, Laura. *Coal Industry Research Guide*. Lexington: East Kentucky Chapter, National Lawyers Guild, 1980.

Beaver, Patricia D. "Participatory Research on Land Ownership in Appalachia." In *Appalachia and America: Autonomy and Regional Dependence*, ed. Allen W. Batteau, 252–66. Lexington: University Press of Kentucky, 1983.

Blanton, Bill. "Not by a Dam Site: Brumley Gap, Virginia—How One Community Fought Back." *Southern Exposure* 7 (Winter 1979) : 98–106.

Braden, Anne. "American Inquisition, Part II: The McSurely Case and Repression in the 1960s." *Southern Exposure* 11 (September–October 1983) : 20–27.

Branscome, James. "Paradise Lost." *Southern Exposure* 1 (Summer–Fall 1973) : 29–41.

———. "People's Houses: Appalachia—East Kentucky Housing Development Corporation." *Southern Exposure* 8 (Spring 1980) : 44–47.

Branscome, James, and James Y. Holloway. "Non-Violence and Violence in Appalachia." *Katallagete* 5 (Winter 1974) : 32–42.

Cable, Sherry, and Beth Degutis. "The Transformation of Community Consciousness: The Effects of Citizens' Organizations on Host Communities." *International Journal of Mass Emergencies and Disasters* (November 1991) : 383–99.

Cable, Sherry, and Edward Walsh. "The Emergence of Environmental Protest: Yellow Creek and Three Mile Island Compared." In *Communities at Risk: Collective Responses to Technological Hazards*, ed. Stephen R. Couch and J. Stephen Kroll-Smith, 113–32. New York: Peter Lang, 1991.

Caldwell, Lynton, Lynton R. Hayes, and Isabel M. MacWhirter. *Citizens and the Environment: Case Studies in Popular Action*. Bloomington: Indiana University Press, 1976.

Carawan, Guy, and Candie Carawan. *Voices from the Mountains*. Urbana: University of Illinois Press, 1982. Uses songs, photographs, and personal statements to tell the history of resistance to strip mining, unsafe mines, poverty, forced migration, and other exploitative conditions. A valuable source.

Carter, Michael V. "The Rural Church, Can It Be an Arena for Change? An Example from Appalachia." *Human Services in the Rural Environment* 11 (Winter 1988) : 31–33. Describes the work of the Commission on Religion in Appalachia.

Caudill, Harry M. *My Land Is Dying*. New York: Dutton, 1973.

Chemical Valley. A film directed by Anne Johnson and Mimi Pickering. Distributed by Appalshop, 1991.

Cirillo, Marie. "Service Development by and for Citizens." In *Appalachia Looks at Its Future: Proceedings of a Regional Forum Conducted at East Tennessee State University, Johnson City, Tenn., 11–13 June 1975*, ed. J. Paxton Marshall, 50–64. Blacksburg, Va.: Cooperative Extension Service, Virginia Polytechnic Institute and State University, 1977.

Clavel, Pierre. *Opposition Planning in Wales and Appalachia*. Philadelphia: Temple University Press, 1983. Provides information on a number of resistance groups.

Council of the Southern Mountains. *People Speak Out on Strip Mining*. Berea, Ky.: CSM, 1972.

———. *We Will Stop the Bulldozers*. Berea, Ky.: CSM, 1972.

Couto, Richard A. "Failing Health and New Prescriptions: Community-Based Approaches to Environmental Risks." In *Current Health Policy Issues and Alternatives: An Applied Social Science Perspective*, ed. Carole E. Hill, 53–70. Athens: University of Georgia Press, 1986.

———. "The Political Economy of Appalachian Health." In *Health in Appalachia:*

Proceedings from the 1988 Conference on Appalachia, ed. Appalachian Center, University of Kentucky, 5–16. Lexington: Appalachian Center, 1989.

————. *Poverty, Politics, and Health Care: An Appalachian Experience*. New York: Praeger, 1975.

Couto, Richard, Pat Sharkey, Paul Elwood, and Laura Green. "Relevant Education: Sharing Life's Glories." *Southern Exposure* 14 (September–December 1986) : 60–61.

Crittenden, Beth. "West Virginia Elders Make a Difference." *Southern Exposure* 13 (March–June 1985) : 52–56. Gives examples of senior citizens' advocacy at the grassroots level in West Virginia.

Dunbar, Tony. *Our Land Too*. New York: Pantheon, 1971.

Dunn, Durwood. *Cades Cove: The Life and Death of a Southern Appalachian Community, 1818–1937*. Knoxville: University of Tennessee Press, 1988.

Fine, Elizabeth C. "Resisting the Hegemony of Development: The Struggle of Nellie's Cave Community." In *Environmental Voices: Cultural, Social, Physical, and Natural. Journal of the Appalachian Studies Association* 4, ed. Garry Barker, 69–78. Johnson City, Tenn.: Center for Appalachian Studies and Services, East Tennessee State University, 1992.

Finnissey, John C., Jr. "The Politics of Protest: People and Strip Mining in Western Maryland." Ph.D. diss., Temple University, 1987.

"Forum on Appalachian Citizen Action to Preserve the Environment: Kentuckians For The Commonwealth, West Virginia Highlands Conservancy, Oak Ridge Environmental Peace Alliance." In *Environment in Appalachia: Proceedings from the 1989 Conference on Appalachia*, ed. Jane W. Bagby, 91–98. Lexington: Appalachian Center, University of Kentucky, 1990.

Foster, Stephen William. *The Past Is Another Country: Representation, Historical Consciousness, and Resistance in the Blue Ridge*. Berkeley, Los Angeles, and London: University of California Press, 1988.

Frome, Michael. *Conscience of a Conservationist: Selected Essays*. Knoxville: University of Tennessee Press, 1989.

————. *Promised Land: Adventures and Encounters in Wild America*. New York: Morrow, 1985.

Garland, Anne W. "Tell It on the Mountain: Marie Cirillo Helps People in Appalachia Take Charge of Their Lives." *Progressive* 52 (July 1988) : 22–25.

Gitlin, Todd, and Nanci Hollander. *Uptown: Poor Whites in Chicago*. New York: Harper & Row, 1970.

Glen, John. "The Council of the Southern Mountains and the War on Poverty." *Now and Then* 5 (Fall 1988a) : 4–12.

————. *Highlander: No Ordinary School, 1932–1962*. Lexington: University Press of Kentucky, 1988b.

Good, Paul. "Kentucky's Coal Beds of Sedition." *Nation* 205 (September 4, 1967) : 166–69.

Hall, Betty Jean. "Women Miners Can Dig It, Too!" In *Communities in Economic Crisis: Appalachia and the South*, ed. John Gaventa, Barbara E. Smith, and Alex Willingham, 53–60. Philadelphia: Temple University Press, 1990.

Hall, Bob, ed. *Environmental Politics: Lessons from the Grass Roots*. Durham, N.C.: Institute for Southern Studies, 1988.

Hardt, Jerry. *The Feasibility and Design of a Central Appalachian Land Bank*. Berea, Ky.: Human/Economic Appalachian Development Corporation, 1979.

Henson, Mike. "Fighting Back Against Toxics in Appalachia." *Guardian*, April 25, 1990, 7.

Highlander Center. *Highlander Research and Education Center: An Approach to Education Presented Through a Collection of Writings*. New Market, Tenn.: Highlander Center, 1989.

Hodges, Jill, and Steve Hodges. *Upstream Battle: The Pigeon River*. Hartford, Tenn.: Americans for a Clean Environment, 1990.

Hoffman, Edwin D. *Fighting Mountaineers: The Struggle for Justice in the Appalachians*. Boston: Houghton Mifflin, 1979. Describes in very general terms seven episodes of resistance, including the fight against strip mining and the union struggle at the Levi Strauss factory in northeast Georgia from 1966 to 1975.

Horton, Aimee I. *The Highlander Folk School: A History of Its Major Programs, 1932–1961*. Brooklyn, N.Y.: Carlson, 1989.

Horton, Bill, Dave Liden, and Tracey Weis. *Who Owns It: Researching Land and Mineral Ownership in Your Community*. Prepared for the Appalachian Alliance. Prestonsburg, Ky.: Mountain Printing Co., 1985.

Horton, Myles, with Judith Kohl and Herbert Kohl. *The Long Haul: An Autobiography*. New York: Doubleday, 1990.

Horton, Myles, and Paulo Freire. *We Make the Road by Walking: Conversations on Education and Social Change*, ed. Brenda Bell, John Gaventa, and John Peters. Philadelphia: Temple University Press, 1990.

Howard, Thomas F. K. "Moving Mountains." *In These Times*, July 16–26, 1980.

Howell, Benita J. "Mediating Environmental Policy Conflicts in Appalachian Communities." In *Environment in Appalachia: Proceedings from the 1989 Conference on Appalachia*, ed. Jane W. Bagby, 103–9. Lexington: Appalachian Center, University of Kentucky, 1990.

I'm What This Is All About. A film directed by Anne Johnson and Mimi Pickering. Distributed by Appalshop, 1985.

Jackson, Bruce. "In the Valley of the Shadows: Kentucky." *Transaction* 8 (June 1971) : 28–38.

Jones, Lindsay, ed. *Citizen Participation in Rural Land Use Planning in the Tennessee Valley*. Nashville: Agricultural Marketing Project, 1979.

Jubak, Jim. "West Virginia's Water Watchers." *Environmental Action* 23 (July–August 1981) : 16–19.

Kahn, Kathy. *Hillbilly Women*. New York: Doubleday, 1973. Women activists tell their own stories.

Kahn, Si. *Organizing: A Guide for Grassroots Leaders*. New York: McGraw-Hill, 1982.

Katuah Journal. A bioregional journal of the southern Appalachians that provides information on the activities of local environmental groups.

Landy, Marc K. *The Politics of Environmental Reform: Controlling Kentucky Strip Mining.* Washington, D.C.: Resources for the Future, 1976.

Lewis, Helen M. "Maxine Waller: The Making of a Community Organizer." *Now and Then* 7 (Spring 1990) : 12–14.

Lewis, Helen M., and Suzanna O'Donnell, eds. *Ivanhoe, Virginia: Remembering Our Past, Building Our Future.* Ivanhoe, Va.: Ivanhoe Civic League, 1990.

————. *Telling Our Stories—Sharing Our Lives.* Ivanhoe, Va.: Ivanhoe Civic League, 1990.

Liden, David. *Rights: Yours and Theirs—A Citizens' Guide to Oil and Gas Development and Leasing in Appalachia.* New Market, Tenn.: Appalachian Alliance, 1983.

Lippin, Tobi. "Southeast Women's Employment Coalition." *Southern Exposure* 9 (Winter 1981) : 52.

Long, Kate. "Progressive Network/Progressive Gains." *Southern Exposure* 12 (January–February 1984) : 60–67. A look at the birth of a progressive coalition in West Virginia and its effect on that state's Democratic Party.

McCarthy, Colman. *Disturbers of the Peace.* Boston: Houghton Mifflin, 1973.

McDonald, Kevin. "Outreach and Outrage: The Student Health Coalition." *Southern Exposure* 6 (Summer 1978) : 18–23.

Martin, Linda. "The Politics of School Reform in the Eighties." In *Education in Appalachia: Proceedings from the 1987 Conference on Appalachia,* ed. Appalachian Center, University of Kentucky, 59–63. Lexington: Appalachian Center, 1988.

Mastran, Shelly S., and Nan Lowerre. *Mountaineers and Rangers: A History of Federal Forest Management in the Southern Appalachians, 1900–81.* Washington, D.C.: Government Printing Office, 1983.

Merrifield, Juliet. *We're Tired of Being Guinea Pigs! A Handbook for Citizens on Environmental Health.* New Market, Tenn.: Highlander Center, 1980.

Moran, Jane. "Is Everyone Paying Their Fair Share? An Analysis of Taxpayers' Actions to Equalize Taxes." *West Virginia Law Review* 85 (1982–83) : 209–37. Historical overview of West Virginia taxpayers' actions for fair taxes.

Mountain Life & Work.

Mountain Life & Work 59 (June 1983). Special issue: "Nonviolent Organizing in Eastern Kentucky."

Moyers, Bill. "The Adventures of a Radical Hillbilly: An Interview with Myles Horton." *Appalachian Journal* 9 (1982) : 248–85.

Mud Creek Clinic. A film directed by Anne Johnson. Distributed by Appalshop, 1986.

Neely, Jack. "Grassroots Power: Tennesseans Fight for Social Justice." *Southern Exposure* 13 (March–June 1985) : 40–45. Describes the activities of the Tennessee Valley Energy Coalition (TVEC) and Solutions to Issues of Concern to Knoxvillians (SICK).

Nigro, Carol A., and Ann M. Ventura. "Making a Career of Community Involvement: An Interview with Edna Compton." *Appalachia* 21 (Summer 1988) : 25–29. Discusses the activities of the Dungannon (Virginia) Development Commission.

Norris-Hall, Lachelle. *Pollution Industries in the South and Appalachia: Economy, Environment, and Politics.* New Market, Tenn.: Highlander Center, 1990.

Now and Then 7 (Fall 1990). Special issue: "Activism in Appalachia." Includes articles on Highlander and a number of book reviews.

On Our Own Land. A film directed by Anne Johnson. Distributed by Appalshop, 1988.

Overton, Jim. "Taking on TVA: Tennessee Valley Ratepayers Protest Soaring Electric Utility Charges." *Southern Exposure* 11 (January–February 1983) : 22–28. Case study of the Tennessee Valley Energy Coalition.

———, ed. "Tower of Babel: A Special Report on the Nuclear Industry." *Southern Exposure* 7 (Winter 1979) : 25–120. Describes citizen challenges to the nuclear and utility industries.

Peddle, Dorothy H. "To Do What's Right: Interviews with Eula Hall and Mike Sheets." *Southern Exposure* 11 (March–April 1983) : 39–43.

Peoples Appalachia 1:1–3:2 (March 1970–Summer 1974). Discusses a wide variety of resistance efforts; published by the Peoples Appalachian Research Collective.

Perry, Huey. *"They'll Cut Off Your Project": A Mingo County Chronicle.* New York: Praeger, 1972. Personal account of the local Office of Economic Opportunity's clash with the political machine in Mingo County, W.Va.

The Plow (October 1975–August 1979). Covered the activities of citizen groups in southwestern Virginia.

Puckett, John L. *Foxfire Reconsidered: A Twenty-Year Experiment in Progressive Education.* Urbana: University of Illinois Press, 1989.

Reutter, Mark. "The Raider and the Coal Town." *Southern Exposure* 19 (Summer 1991) : 48–55.

Rural Community Education Cooperative, Mountain Women's Exchange. *Claiming Our Economic History: Jellico, Tennessee.* Jellico, Tenn.: RCEC, 1987.

Schlesinger, Tom, John Gaventa, and Juliet Merrifield. *How to Research Your Local Military Contractor.* New Market, Tenn.: Highlander Center, 1983.

Schoenbaum, Thomas J. *The New River Controversy.* Winston-Salem, N.C.: John F. Blair, 1979.

Schweri, William F., II, and John Van Willigen. *Organized Resistance to an Imposed Environmental Change: A Reservoir in Eastern Kentucky.* Research Report no. 10. Lexington: Water Resources Research Institute, University of Kentucky, 1978.

Selfridge, Linda, John Gaventa, Juliet Merrifield, and Rob Currie. *Water: "You Have to Drink It with a Fork."* New Market, Tenn.: Highlander Center, 1985. Provides information on several struggles to secure safe drinking water.

Shackelford, Laurel, and Bill Weinberg. *Our Appalachia: An Oral History.* New York: Hill & Wang, 1977. Local residents describe their involvement in resistance efforts.

Shelby, Anne, and Graham Shelby. "Speaking for Themselves." *Southern Exposure* 19 (Summer 1991) : 60–63.

Social Policy 21 (Winter 1991). Special Issue: "Building Movements, Educating Citizens: Myles Horton and the Highlander Folk School."

Southern Exposure 8 (Spring 1980). Special Issue: "Building South."

Squillace, Mark. *The Stripmining Handbook: A Coalfield Citizens' Guide to Using the Law to Fight Back Against the Ravages of Strip Mining and Underground Mining.* Washington, D.C.: Environmental Policy Institute and Friends of the Earth, 1990.

Staub, Michael. " 'We'll Never Quit It!' Yellow Creek Concerned Citizens Combat Creekbed Catastrophe." *Southern Exposure* 11 (January–February 1983) : 43–52.

Sullivan, Maureen, and Danny Miller. "Cincinnati's Urban Appalachian Council and Appalachian Identity." *Harvard Educational Review* 60 (1990) : 106–24.

Szakos, Joe. "They're Not All Sitting Back and Taking It: Fighting for Change in Eastern Kentucky." In *The Land and Economy of Appalachia: Proceedings from the 1986 Conference on Appalachia,* ed. Appalachian Center, University of Kentucky, 91–96. Lexington: Appalachian Center, 1987.

Szakos, Kristin L. "People Power: Working for the Future in the East Kentucky Coalfields." In *Communities in Economic Crisis: Appalachia and the South,* ed. John Gaventa, Barbara E. Smith, and Alex Willingham, 29–37. Philadelphia: Temple University Press, 1990.

———. "Schools and Taxes: Making Industry Pay Its Way." *Southern Exposure* 14 (September–December 1986) : 24–27.

Szakos, Kristin L., and Joe Szakos. " 'The Older I Get the Closer I Get to the Ground': An Interview with Everett Akers." *Southern Exposure* 13 (March–June 1985) : 68–71.

Thrasher, Sue. "Coal Employment Project." *Southern Exposure* 9 (Winter 1981) : 47–50.

Tice, Karen W. "A Case Study of Battered Women's Shelters in Appalachia." *Affilia* 5 (Fall 1990) : 83–100.

Tucker, Bruce. "An Interview with Michael Maloney." *Appalachian Journal* 17 (1989) : 34–48.

Turner, William H., and Edward J. Cabbell, eds. *Blacks in Appalachia.* Lexington: University Press of Kentucky, 1985. Essays describing resistance efforts by blacks in Appalachia.

Waller, Maxine. "Local Organizing: Ivanhoe, Virginia." *Social Policy* 21 (Winter 1991) : 62–67.

Waller, Maxine, Helen M. Lewis, Clare McBrien, and Carroll L. Wessinger. " 'It Has to Come from the People': Responding to Plant Closings in Ivanhoe, Virginia." In *Communities in Economic Crisis: Appalachia and the South,* ed. John Gaventa, Barbara E. Smith, and Alex Willingham, 17–28. Philadelphia: Temple University Press, 1990.

Wheeler, William B., and Michael J. McDonald. *TVA and the Tellico Dam, 1936–1979: A Bureaucratic Crisis in Post-Industrial America.* Knoxville: University of Tennessee Press, 1986.

Whisnant, David E. "A Case Study in Appalachian Development." *New South* 28 (Spring 1973) : 34–43.

———. "Controversy in God's Grand Division: The Council of the Southern

Mountains." *Appalachian Journal* 2 (1974) : 7–45. See responses to this article in *Appalachian Journal* 2 (1975) : 171–91.

——. *Modernizing the Mountaineer: People, Power, and Planning in Appalachia.* Boone, N.C.: Appalachian Consortium Press, 1981.

White, Connie, and Juliet Merrifield. *A Foot in the Door: Rural Communities Involved in Educational Change.* New Market, Tenn.: Highlander Center, 1990.

Wigginton, Eliot. *Sometimes a Shining Moment: The Foxfire Experience.* Garden City, N.Y.: Anchor Press/Doubleday, 1985.

Woodside, Jane H. "Creating the Path as You Go: John Gaventa and Highlander." *Now and Then* 7 (Fall 1990) : 15–21.

Yellow Creek, Kentucky. A film directed by Anne Johnson. Distributed by Appalshop, 1984.

You Got to Move. A film directed by Lucy Massie Phenix. Distributed by First Run Features, 1985. Focuses on the Highlander Center and includes segments on citizen resistance efforts in Bumpas Cove, Tennessee, and Cranks Creek, Kentucky.

Zimet, Kristin C. "Making Peace with Earth." *Appalachian Peace Education Center News* (Abingdon, Va.), no. 42 (September–October 1989).

Zuercher, Melanie, ed. *Making History: The First Ten Years of KFTC.* Prestonsburg, Ky.: Kentuckians For The Commonwealth, 1991.

Directory of Organizations

Appalachian Community Fund, 517 Union Avenue, Suite 206, Knoxville, TN 37902; 615/523–5783. Newsletter: *Appalachian Actions*.

Appalachian Journal, Center for Appalachian Studies, Appalachian State University, Boone, NC 28608. Subscriptions: $18 per year.

The Appalachian Reader: An Independent Citizens Quarterly, P.O. Box 217, Banner, KY 41603. Subscriptions: $10 per year.

Appalachian Studies Association, Center for Appalachian Studies and Services, P.O. Box 70556, East Tennessee State University, Johnson City, TN 37614; 615/929–5348. Newsletter: *Appalink*.

Appalshop, 306 Madison Street, Whitesburg, KY 41858; 606/633–0108. Newsletter: *Appalshop Notes*.

Brown Lung Association, 202 Oak Street, Woodville Heights, Greenville, SC 29611; 813/269–8048.

Chicago Area Black Lung Association, 4409 N. Broadway, Chicago, IL 60640; 312/271–7377. Newsletter: *The Black Lung Newsletter*.

Coal Employment Project, 17 Emory Place, Knoxville, TN 37917; 615/637–7905. Newsletter: *Coal Mining Women's Support Team News*.

Commission on Religion in Appalachia, P.O. Box 10867, Knoxville, TN 37919; 615/584–6133. Newsletter: *CORAspondent*.

Community Farm Alliance, 200 Short Street, No. 10, Berea, KY 40403; 606/986–7400. Newsletter: *CFA NEWS*.

Foxfire Project, P.O. Box B, Rabun Gap, GA 30568; 404/746–5828. Publishes *Foxfire*.

Highlander Research and Education Center, 1959 Highlander Way, New Market, TN 37820; 615/933–3443. Newsletter: *Highlander Reports*.

Ivanhoe Civic League, P.O. Box 201, Ivanhoe, VA 24350; 703/699–1383. Newsletter: *Ivanhoe Newsletter*.

JONAH, 416 E. Lafayette Street, Room 217, Jackson, TN 38301; 901/427–1630. Newsletter: *The Jonah Story*.

Katuah Journal, P.O. Box 638, Leicester, NC 28748. Subscriptions: $10 per year.

Kentuckians For The Commonwealth, P.O. Box 864, Prestonsburg, KY 41653; 606/886–0043. Newsletter: *balancing the scales.*

Mountain Women's Exchange, P.O. Box 204, Jellico, TN 37762; 615/784–8780. Newsletter: *Mountain Women's Exchange Newsletter.*

Now and Then: The Appalachian Magazine, Center for Appalachian Studies and Services, East Tennessee State University, Johnson City, TN 37614. Subscriptions: $9 per year.

Save Our Cumberland Mountains, P.O. Box 479, Lake City, TN 37769; 615/426–9455. Newsletter: *SOCM Sentinel.*

Southern Empowerment Project, 323 Ellis Avenue, Maryville, TN 37801; 615/984–6500. Newsletter: *Southern Empowerment Project News.*

Southern Exposure: A Journal of Politics & Culture, P.O. Box 531, Durham, NC 27702. Subscriptions: $24 per year.

United Mine Workers of America, 900 15th Street, NW, Washington, DC 20005; 202/842–7200. Publication: *United Mine Workers Journal.*

Western North Carolina Alliance, P.O. Box 18087, Asheville, NC 28814; 704/258–8737. Newsletter: *Accent.*

White Lung Association, 1601 St. Paul Street, Baltimore, MD 21202; 301/727–6029. Newsletter: *Asbestos Watch.*

Women and Employment, 601 Delaware Avenue, Charleston, WV 25302; 304/345–1298. Newsletter: *Women and Employment News.*

Yellow Creek Concerned Citizens, c/o Larry Wilson, Rt. 2, Box AA 68, Middlesboro, KY 40965; 606/248–8213.

List of Contributors

Bill Allen is a senior attorney with Rural Legal Services of Tennessee in Oak Ridge, Tennessee. He is a native of Anderson County and has been active in Save Our Cumberland Mountains since 1974.

Mary K. Anglin is a postdoctoral fellow in the Medical Anthropology Program at the University of California, San Francisco. She is currently engaged in research on breast cancer, focusing on issues of informed choice, access to care, and cancer activism. She is on leave from Lenoir-Rhyne College, where she is assistant professor of sociology and director of the Institute for Women's Studies, but she has not forgotten the mountains.

Fran Ansley teaches at the University of Tennessee College of Law. She and her husband, Jim Sessions, live with Elisha and Lee in Knox County, Tennessee.

Alan Banks is a professor of sociology at Eastern Kentucky University in Richmond, Kentucky.

Dwight Billings is a professor of sociology at the University of Kentucky.

Mary Beth Bingman has been involved in Appalachian organizations for many years. She currently is working in adult education as a teacher, a student, and a staff member at the Center for Literacy Studies at the University of Tennessee, Knoxville.

Sherry Cable is assistant professor of sociology at the University of Tennessee, Knoxville.

Guy and Candie Carawan have used songs and culture to develop educational programs throughout the South for thirty years. They have documented songs of the civil rights movement, African American heritage in the coastal islands of South Carolina, and Appalachian culture—particularly in times of resistance—in books, albums, and video recordings. They are based at the Highlander Center in Tennessee.

Richard A. Couto is professor of leadership studies at the Jepson School of the University of Richmond. He is the author of *Ain't Gonna Let Nobody Turn Me Round: The Pursuit of Racial Justice in the Rural South* and several reports on social and economic trends in Appalachia.

Stephen L. Fisher is Hawthorne Professor of Political Science at Emory & Henry College.

Stephen William Foster is an anthropologist, independent scholar, and nursing administrator in the Department of Psychiatry at San Francisco General Hospital. His interest in the Appalachian region began with discussions with his sister, who was a political organizer in Harlan County, Kentucky.

John M. Glen, associate professor of history at Ball State University in Muncie, Indiana, is author of *Highlander: No Ordinary School, 1932–1962,* winner of the University Press of Kentucky's 1986 Appalachian Award for the best book-length study of the region. He is writing a history of the War on Poverty in Appalachia.

Hal Hamilton is director of the Community Farm Alliance, a membership organization with county chapters across rural Kentucky. Before becoming a dairy farmer, he completed all requirements except a dissertation for a doctorate in American Studies from the State University of New York at Buffalo.

Bennett M. Judkins, professor of sociology at Meredith College, is the author of *We Offer Ourselves as Evidence: Toward Workers'. Control of Occupational Health,* a comparative history of the black lung and brown lung movements. He was born in a small textile town in Virginia, where many of his kin worked in the mill and his mother served as the company nurse. She later became an occupational health nurse with the United Mine Workers of America in the coalfields of Virginia and Tennessee.

Don Manning-Miller has been an activist and organizer, primarily in Mississippi, since the mid-1960s. He has been director of the Mississippi Hunger Coalition and an activist board member of the Delta Ministry of the National Council of Churches and of the Southern Conference Educational Fund. He is currently coordinator of the Eastern Kentucky Child Care Coalition in Berea, Kentucky.

Ellen Ryan is co-director of the Minnesota Rural Organizing Project. She has been a community organizer and a trainer of community organizers since 1976. Her experience is both urban and rural, in New England, the Upper South, and the Midwest.

Jim Sessions coordinates the Commission on Religion in Appalachia. He and his wife, Fran Ansley, live with Elisha and Lee in Knox County, Tennessee.

Joe Szakos has been the staff coordinator of Kentuckians For The Commonwealth since 1982. He previously worked as a field organizer for the Appalachian Alliance, newspaper reporter, coordinator of flood recovery and low-income housing programs, research assistant, home manager for a psychiatric halfway house, foundry worker, and truck driver. He has a master's degree from the University of

Chicago School of Social Service Administration. He and his wife, Kristin Layng Szakos, have two daughters, Anna and Maria.

Karen Tice, formerly director of women's studies and assistant professor of social work at Western Kentucky University, is completing a doctorate at the University of Kentucky.

Chris Weiss is senior program associate with the Economic Development Program of the Ms. Foundation for Women. She also operates Rural Strategies, providing consulting services to nonprofit organizations on rural economic development and women and economic development. In addition, she is a recipient of a three-year fellowship from the Kellogg International Leadership Program. She operates from an office in Charleston, West Virginia, where she has lived since 1972.